California

ADVENTURES IN TIME AND PLACE

James A. Banks

Barry K. Beyer

Gloria Contreras

Jean Craven

Gloria Ladson-Billings

Mary A. McFarland

Walter C. Parker

NATIONAL GEOGRAPHIC SOCIETY

ADOPTED IN 1911, OUR STATE'S FLAG SHOWS THE CALIFORNIA GRIZZLY BEAR, A SINGLE RED STAR, AND ONE RED STRIPE. IT HONORS THE BEAR FLAG REVOLT OF 1846, WHEN SETTLERS FROM THE UNITED STATES DECLARED CALIFORNIA FREE FROM MEXICO. THE GRIZZLY BEAR IS A SYMBOL OF STRENGTH. THE RED STAR AND STRIPE REFER TO THE STARS AND STRIPES OF THE UNITED STATES FLAG.

THE PRINCETON REVIEW

McGraw-Hill School Division

New York   Farmington

PROGRAM AUTHORS

Dr. James A. Banks
Professor of Education and
   Director of the Center for
   Multicultural Education
University of Washington
Seattle, Washington

Dr. Barry K. Beyer
Professor Emeritus, Graduate
   School of Education
George Mason University
Fairfax, Virginia

Dr. Gloria Contreras
Professor of Education
University of North Texas
Denton, Texas

Jean Craven
District Coordinator of
   Curriculum Development
Albuquerque Public Schools
Albuquerque, New Mexico

Dr. Gloria Ladson-Billings
Professor of Education
University of Wisconsin
Madison, Wisconsin

Dr. Mary A. McFarland
Instructional Coordinator of
   Social Studies, K–12, and
   Director of Staff Development
Parkway School District
Chesterfield, Missouri

Dr. Walter C. Parker
Professor and Program Chair for
   Social Studies Education
University of Washington
Seattle, Washington

NATIONAL
GEOGRAPHIC
SOCIETY
Washington, D.C.

CONSULTANTS FOR
TEST PREPARATION

THE
PRINCETON
REVIEW   The Princeton Review is not affiliated with Princeton University or ETS.

HISTORIANS/SCHOLARS

Dr. Carlos E. Cortés
Professor Emeritus of History
University of California
Riverside, California

Dr. John Bodnar
Professor of History
Indiana University
Bloomington, Indiana

Dr. Sheilah Clark-Ekong
Professor, Department of Anthropology
University of Missouri, St. Louis
St. Louis, Missouri

Dr. Darlene Clark Hine
John A. Hannah Professor of History
Michigan State University
East Lansing, Michigan

Council on Islamic Education
Fountain Valley, California

Dr. John L. Esposito
Professor of Religion and
   International Affairs
Georgetown University
Washington, D.C.

Dr. Gary Mason
Department of Geography
Michigan State University
East Lansing, Michigan

Dr. Juan Mora-Torres
Professor of Latin American History
University of Texas at San Antonio
San Antonio, Texas

Dr. Valerie Ooka Pang
Professor, School of Teacher Education
San Diego State University
San Diego, California

Dr. James J. Rawls
Department of History
Diablo Valley College
Pleasant Hill, California

Dr. Curtis C. Roseman
Professor of Geography
University of Southern California
Los Angeles, California

Dr. Joseph Rosenbloom
Professor, Classics Department
Washington University
St. Louis, Missouri

Dr. Robert Seltzer
Professor of Jewish History
Hunter College
City University of New York
New York, New York

Dr. Robert M. Senkewicz
Professor of History
Santa Clara University
Santa Clara, California

Dr. Peter Stearns
Dean, College of Humanities and
   Social Studies
Carnegie Mellon University
Pittsburgh, Pennsylvania

Dr. Clifford E. Trafzer
Professor of Ethnic Studies
University of California
Riverside, California

CALIFORNIA PROGRAM CONSULTANTS

Diane Bowers
Former Assistant Director of
   Education for the Yurok Tribe
Klamath, California

Dr. Karen Nakai
Lecturer of History-Social Science
Department of Education
University of California
Irvine, California

Shelly Osborne
Teacher/Literacy Mentor
Franklin School
Alameda, California

Lyn Reese
Director, Women in History Project
Berkeley, California

Evelyn Staton
Librarian
San Francisco School District
Member, Multiethnic Literature Forum
   for San Francisco
San Francisco, California

CONSULTING AUTHORS

Dr. James Flood
Professor of Teacher Education,
   Reading and Language Development
San Diego State University
San Diego, California

Dr. Diane Lapp
Professor of Teacher Education,
   Reading and Language Development
San Diego State University
San Diego, California

GRADE-LEVEL CONSULTANTS

Estela Castro–Corrales
Fourth Grade Teacher
Nestor Elementary School
San Diego, California

Howard Hume
Fourth Grade Teacher
Nicholas Elementary School
Sacramento, California

Laura Kusaba
Fourth Grade Teacher
Kettering Elementary School
Long Beach, California

Jerrie Martin
Fourth Grade Teacher
74th Street Elementary School
Los Angeles, California

Kyle Wong
Fourth Grade Teacher
Chabot Elementary School
Oakland, California

CONTRIBUTING WRITERS

Patricia Longoria
Torrance, California

Dr. James J. Rawls
Sonoma, California

Linda Scher
Raleigh, North Carolina

Acknowledgments

The publisher gratefully acknowledges permission to reprint the following copyrighted material:

From *Historical Memoirs of California* by Fray Francisco Palou ©1926 by The University of California Press. From *Never Turn Back* by James Rawls ©1993 by Dialogue Systems. From *California, A History* by Andrew Rolle ©1987 by Harlan Davidson, Inc. From *Junipero Serra* by Don DeNevi & Noel Francis Moholy ©1985 by Don DeNevi & Noel Francis Moholy. From *California Coast* by Donald Cutter ©1985 by the University of Oklahoma Press. From *Mission Santa Barbara* by Maynard Geiger ©1965 by the Franciscan Fathers of California. From "Not Quite Paradise" from "California History," Published by the California Historical Society ©1996. From *The History of Santa Cruz* by Edward Sanford Harrison ©1892 by the Pacific Press Publishing Company. From "Gender Status..." from the "American Indian Culture and Research Journal" Vol. 18 ©1994. From *Three Memoirs of Mexican California* by Carlos Hijar, Eulalia Perez, Agustin Escobar ©1988 by the Friends of the Bancroft Library, University of California, Berkeley. From *The Conflict Between The California Indian and White Civilization* by Sherburne Cook ©1976 by The Regents of the University of California. From "Toypurina the Witch and the Indian Uprising at San Gabriel" by Thomas Temple 11 from The Masterkey ©1958. From *California Dreaming* by Jim Rawls ©1995 by James J. Rawls & Leonard S. Nelson. From *A Different Mirror* by Ronald Takaki ©1993 by Ronald Takaki. From *Journey to Gold Mountain* by Ronald Takaki ©1994 by Chelsea House Publishing. From *Grapes of Wrath* by John Steinbeck ©1992 by Penguin Books. From *Missions of the Monterey Bay Area* by Emily Abbink ©1996 by Lerner Publications Company. From *California, An Interpretive History* by James Rawls & Walton Bean ©1993 by McGraw-Hill, Inc. From *The American Mosaic* by Joan Morrison & Charlotte Zabusky ©1980 by Joan Morrison & Charlotte Zabusky. From *Syllabus for the History of California* by James J. Rawls ©1993 by McGraw-Hill,

Inc. From *Rosie the Riveter* by Penny Colman ©1969 by John J. Loeb Company: Fred Ahlert Music Corp. From *Farewell to Manzanar* by Jeanne Houston & James Houston ©1973 by James D. Houston. From *The Kaiser Story* ©1968 by Kaiser Industries Corp. From *California Women: A History* by Joan Jensen & Gloria Ricci Lothrop ©1987 by Boyd & Fraser Publishing Company. From *New Directions in California History: a Book of Readings* edited by James J. Rawls ©1988 by McGraw-Hill. From *Frontier to Suburb*, The Story of the San Mateo Peninsula ©1982 by Star Publishing Company. From *Latin America* by John Francis Bannon, Robert Miller, Peter Dunne ©1977 by Benziger Bruce & Glencoe Inc. From *L. A Freeway, An Appreciative Essay* ©1981 by the Regents of the University of California. From *The California Dream* by Dennis Hale & Jonathan Eisen ©1968 by Dennis Hale & Jonathan Eisen. From *Indians, Franciscans, and Spanish Colonization* ©1995 by The University of New Mexico Press. From *An Indian Account of the Decline and Collapse of Mexico's Hegemony over the Missioned Indians of California* by Edward Castillo©1989 American Indian Quarterly. From *California Heritage* by John & Laree Caughey ©1971 by John & Laree Caughey. From *Indians of California* by James J. Rawls ©1984 by the University of Oklahoma Press. From *Westward Expansion* by Rae Allen Billington ©1960 by the Macmillan Company. From *History of Rancho de Los Meganos and John Marsh* by Karen Hurwitz ©1972 by Karen Hurwitz. From "Battle of San Pasquale" from *A Doctor Comes To California* by G.W. Ames, Jr. ©1943 by the California Historical Society. From "Speech to the Californios, 1846" from *Telling Identities* by Rosaura Sanchez ©1988 by the Friends of the Bancroft Library. From *Telling Identities* by Rosaura Sanchez ©1995 by the Regents of the University of Minnesota. From *The World Rushed In* by J.S. Holliday
(continued on page R41)

McGraw-Hill School Division

A Division of The McGraw·Hill Companies

McGraw-Hill School Division
Two Penn Plaza
New York, New York 10121

Printed in the United States of America

ISBN 0-02-148824-X

10 11 12 027/046 06 05 04

CONTENTS

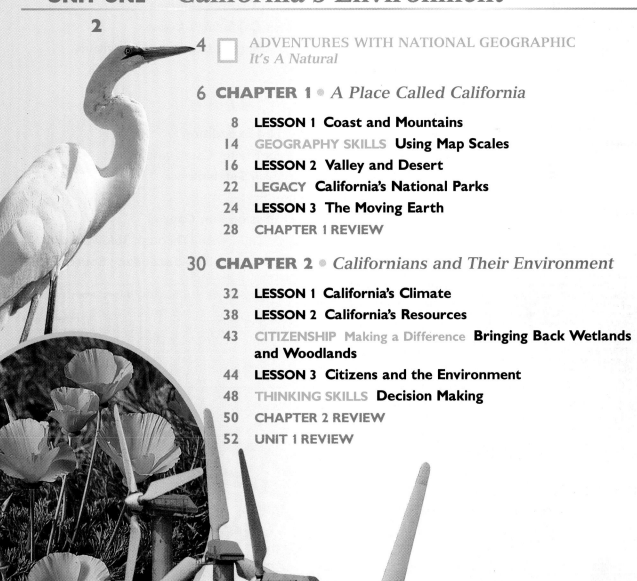

iii

UNIT THREE   *New Flags Above California*
130

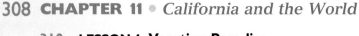

REFERENCE SECTION

STANDARDIZED TEST SUPPORT

FEATURES

SKILLS LESSONS

CITIZENSHIP

MANY VOICES

CHARTS, GRAPHS, & DIAGRAMS

CALIFORNIA'S TOP 5 IMPORTS AND EXPORTS

	IMPORTS	EXPORTS
1	Electrical machinery, sound and TV equipment	Electronics and electrical equipment
2	Boilers, machinery and parts	Industrial machinery and computer equipment
3	Road vehicles and parts	Transportation equipment
4	Optics, photo, medical and surgical instruments	Scientific and medical instruments
5	Toys, games, and sports equipment	Food (raw and processed)

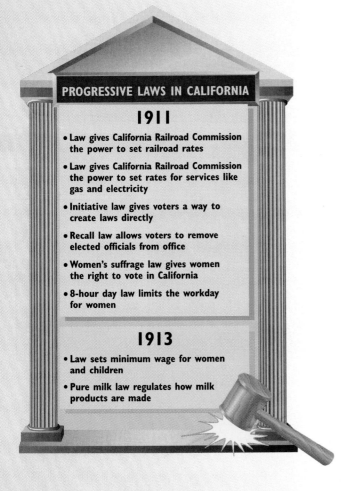

PROGRESSIVE LAWS IN CALIFORNIA

1911

- Law gives California Railroad Commission the power to set railroad rates
- Law gives California Railroad Commission the power to set rates for services like gas and electricity
- Initiative law gives voters a way to create laws directly
- Recall law allows voters to remove elected officials from office
- Women's suffrage law gives women the right to vote in California
- 8-hour day law limits the workday for women

1913

- Law sets minimum wage for women and children
- Pure milk law regulates how milk products are made

TIME LINES

1848
COLOMA
Men working for Johann Marshall discover gold

1849
MONTEREY
José Antonio Carrillo speaks at the constitutional convention

1851
RICH BAR
Dame Shirley writes letters about life in gold-mining camps

1855
SAN BERNARDINO
Biddy Mason wins her freedom

1872
LAVA BEDS NATIONAL MONUMENT
Kintpuash leads the Modoc in the Modoc War

MAPS

YOUR TEXTBOOK at a glance

Your book is called *California: Adventures in Time and Place*. It has twelve chapters and a reference section. Each chapter has two or more lessons. There are also many special features for you to study and enjoy.

NATIONAL GEOGRAPHIC

Five Themes of Geography

Place
What makes San Francisco a special city?

Region
What are some of California's regions?

▲ **Special pages bring you ideas and Adventures in geography from National Geographic.**

LESSON 1

THE FIRST CALIFORNIANS

READ ALOUD
"In the beginning, there was no Earth or sky or anything or anybody; only a dense darkness in space. This darkness seemed alive." So begins a story told by Cahuilla (kuh WEE uh) people of Southern California. It tells about a time before anyone lived in our state.

THE BIG PICTURE

Imagine traveling through what is now California 250 years ago. Along the way you meet many groups of people. Each group has its own language. People live in small villages. Their food comes from plants and animals found nearby. They wear clothing they made and live in houses they built themselves. Each group has a way of worshiping the God or gods its members believe in, or a religion.

How do we learn about this time long ago? One way is through oral history, the stories people pass down by telling them. Another way is through archaeology (ahr kee AHL uh jee). Archaeology is the study of old tools, old houses, and other things people leave behind. We call these things artifacts.

These 6,000-year-old artifacts were found near Santa Barbara. Tony Silva drew Coyote and Silver Fox (facing page).

Focus Activity

READ TO LEARN
Who were the first Californians?

VOCABULARY
religion
archaeology
artifact
ancestor
diversity

PLACES
Clear Lake
Mojave Desert

60

---

very good port." He decided to land. For six days he explored, gathering fresh water and food. He also met the local Kumeyaay people.

Sailing farther north, the ships passed near Tongva lands around present-day Los Angeles. As he looked out from his ship, Cabrillo noticed the air was thick with smoke. It was late fall, after the yearly seed harvest, and the Tongva people were burning off their land to make it ready for planting. Cabrillo called the place Bahía de los Fumos, "Bay of Smoke."

DID YOU KNOW?
How did California get its name?

No one knows for certain who gave California its name, but we do know where the name first appeared. A Spanish fantasy novel written in 1510 called *Las Sergas de Esplandián* (The Adventures of Esplandián) told of an island called California. It was said to be "very close . . . Paradise" and ruled by Queen Calafia, who was "more beautiful than all the rest." Spanish explorers named California after this imaginary island.

Using Software
You would not be able to do much on your computer without software. Software is a program, or set of instructions, that tells the computer what to do. Software lets you use your computer to write letters or school papers, add numbers, draw pictures, or play games.

There are about 6,500 software companies in California. More than half of them are in Silicon Valley. One type of software is known as multimedia (mul tih mee dee uh). Multimedia software mixes sounds, words, pictures, and movies. You can learn about geography or make up your own movies using multimedia software. In one part of San Francisco, there are so many multimedia software companies that it is nicknamed Multimedia Gulch. (A gulch is a narrow valley.)

Links to MATHEMATICS
Think Digital
Do you know what "0100000!" means! To a computer, these numbers stand for the letter A. Computers read a code that uses only binary numbers. Binary numbers are made up of two choices: 0 or 1. Each 0 or 1 is one "bit" of information. A string of eight bits—such as 01000001—is called a byte. There are one million bytes in a megabyte. A personal computer may store thousands of megabytes of information.

No matter what we want a computer to remember, the computer stores it as binary numbers. Such computers are "digital" because they use numbers, or digits, to stand for any kind of information.

Going On-line
The Internet is the newest advance in computers. You read in Chapter 9 that the Internet is a computer network. It connects computers all over the world. If you have an Internet connection, you can "talk" on your computer to just about any other computer in the world that also has an [connection.]

◀ **Some lessons have features called Links or Did You Know?— activities to try and interesting information to share.**

xiv

Look for a variety of lessons and features. **Infographics** inform you with pictures and maps. You will build **Skills**, learn about **Legacies** that connect us to the past, and meet people who show what **Citizenship** is. ▶

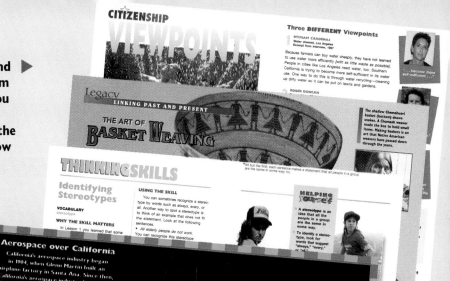

CITIZENSHIP
VIEWPOINTS

Three DIFFERENT Viewpoints

MYRIAM CARDENAS
Water chemist, Los Angeles
Excerpt from interview, 1997

Because farmers can buy water cheaply, they have not learned to use water more efficiently [with as little waste as possible]. People in cities like Los Angeles need water, too. Southern California is trying to become more self-sufficient in its water use. One way to do this is through water recycling—cleaning up dirty water so it can be put on lawns and gardens.

ROGER DUNCAN

...become more
self-sufficient...

The shallow Chemehuevi basket (bottom shows snakes. A Chumash weaver made the box to hold small items. Making baskets is an art that Native American weavers have passed down through the years.

Legacy
LINKING PAST AND PRESENT
THE ART OF
BASKET WEAVING

THINKING SKILLS

Identifying Stereotypes

VOCABULARY
stereotype

WHY THE SKILL MATTERS
In Lesson 1 you learned that some

USING THE SKILL
You can sometimes recognize a stereotype by words such as always, every, or all. Another way to spot a stereotype is to think of an example that does not fit the statement. Look at the following sentences.
• All elderly people do not work. You can recognize this stereotype

*All but the first; each sentence makes a statement that all people in a group are the same in some way.

HELPING YOURSELF
• A stereotype is an idea that all the people in a group are the same in some way.
To identify a stereotype, look for words that suggest "always," "every," or "all."

Infographic Aerospace over California

California's aerospace industry began in 1904, when Glenn Martin built an airplane factory in Santa Ana. Since then, California's aerospace industry has grown. What contributions to aerospace transportation has California made?

APOLLO 11
In July 1969 astronauts

X-29A
A plane with wings that go forward? That's what the X-29A, first flown in 1984, had. Forward-angled wings can make it easier for a plane to make tight twists and turns

COMING TO CALIFORNIA

Archaeologists believe that the first people in North America came from Asia about 40,000 years ago. Some came to what is now California.

In the 1930s an archaeologist made an exciting discovery. Chester Post found carved tools near Clear Lake, in the Coast Ranges. Archaeologists have also found stone knives, scrapers, and drills in the Mojave Desert. These tools were tested to find out their age. According to the tests, people have been living in California for at least 12,000 years.

A Creation Story

Native Americans have different beliefs about how their ancestors (AN ses turz) came to California. Ancestors are people in your family who lived long before you.

Achumawi (ah choo MAH way) people have a creation story. It tells how two gods they believed in created Earth, people, and animals. What did they use?

MANY VOICES
LITERATURE

Excerpt from
Achumawi creation story, compiled by
Edward Winslow Gifford and
Gwendolyn Harris Block.

While Coyote slept Silver Fox combed his hair and saved the combings. . . . Silver Fox rolled them in his hands, stretched them out, and flattened them between his hands. Then he . . . spread them out until they covered all the surface of the water. This became the earth. . . .

Coyote woke and looked up. He saw the trees and heard crickets. "Where are we," he asked; "What place is this we have come to?"

"I don't know," Silver Fox replied. . . . "Here is solid ground. I am going ashore, and am going to live here."

So they landed and built a house and lived in it.

After a time they thought about making people. They made little sticks of service-berry, and thrust them all about in the ceiling of the house. By and by all became people of different sorts, with the names of birds, animals, and fishes.

serviceberry:
a shrub with white flowers and red or purple fruit

281

F-117
The F-117 "stealth" fighter has a secret coating that makes it "invisible" to devices that detect planes from great distances.

COLUMBIA
Columbia was the first space shuttle. It was launched in 1981. Much of the shuttle was built in Palmdale.

On July 4, 1997, the Mars Pathfinder landed on the planet Mars. It released a small rover called Sojourner, shown here. Sojourner explored Mars for three months, sending information back to scientists in Pasadena.

291

The end of your book has a **Reference Section** with many types of information. Use it to look up words, people, and places. ▼

Gazetteer
Manila • Palo Alto

M
Manila (ma nil'a) The capital of the Philippines. (m. 82, t. 92)

N
Napa (nap'a) A city in Northern California; 38°N, 122°W (t. 329)

Helvetia (hu hel vē'sha) One of the first settlements in the Sacramento Valley, by Johann Sutter from Switzerland. (t. 153)

Spain (nū spān) The Spanish colony in North America, made up of all or parts of the U.S., now called Mexico, Central America, and United States. (m. 85, t. 85)

America (nôrth a mer'i ka) A continent in the Northern and Western hemispheres. (m. G4, t. G4)

ern Hemisphere (nôr'tharn hem'i sfir) The half of Earth north of the equator. (m. G3, t. G5)

nd (ōk'land) A city on the east side of San Francisco Bay; a major West Coast shipping and railroad terminus; 37°N, 122°W (2, t. 343)

n Trail (ôr'i gon trāl) A wagon trail the pioneer party followed west from Missouri. (54, t. 154)

Valley (o'anz val'ē) A high mountain valley 200 miles northeast of Los Angeles. (156, t. 252)

Coast region (pa sif'ik kōst rē'jan) One of four regions of California. (m. 9, t. 9)

Ocean (pa sif'ik ō'shan) An ocean that borders western North and South America and eastern Asia. (m. G4, t. G4)

Springs (pām springs) A city in the desert region of California; 34°N, 117°W (21, t. 20)

Alto (pal'ō al'tō) A town in Santa Clara County, near San Jose, where Stanford University is located; 37°N, 122°W (t. 326)

ANIMALS AND PLANTS OF CALIFORNIA

▲ Lessons begin with a **Read Aloud** selection and **The Big Picture.** Study with the **Read to Learn** question and a list of words, people, and places. Enjoy **Many Voices**—writings from many sources.

61

R33

NATIONAL GEOGRAPHIC

Five Themes of Geography

Place
What makes San Francisco a special city?

Region
What are some of California's regions?

Location
How do people know exactly where things are?

Movement
How do many people in California travel from one place to another?

Human-Environment Interaction
What challenges does California's landscape present?

GEOGRAPHY SKILLS

PART 1
Using Globes

VOCABULARY

ocean   hemisphere
continent   equator

What does a globe show?

- A globe is a small copy of Earth. Like Earth, a globe is a round object, or sphere.

- Globes show the parts of Earth that are land and the parts that are water. Earth's largest bodies of water are called oceans. There are four oceans— the Atlantic, Arctic, Indian, and Pacific oceans. Look at the globe shown here. What color is used to show oceans?

- Globes also show the seven large bodies of land called continents. The continents are Africa, Antarctica, Asia, Australia, Europe, North America, and South America. Find North America and South America on the globe below. Which oceans are shown bordering these continents?

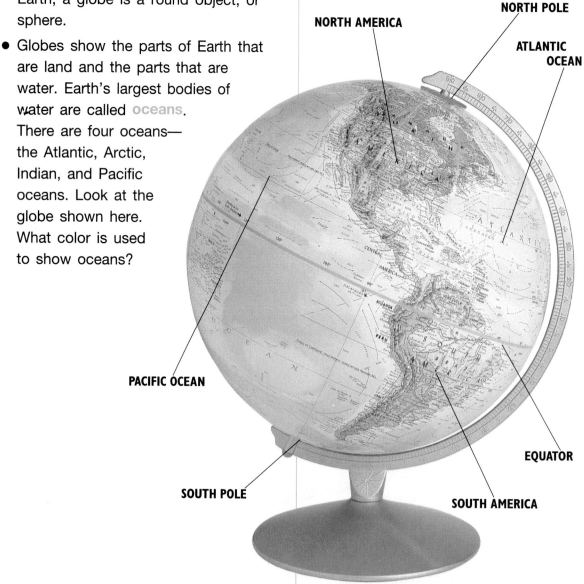

NORTH AMERICA

NORTH POLE

ATLANTIC OCEAN

PACIFIC OCEAN

SOUTH POLE

EQUATOR

SOUTH AMERICA

What are the four hemispheres?

- Look again at the globe on the previous page. Can you see the whole globe? You can see only half of a globe or sphere at any one time. A word for half a sphere is hemisphere. The word *hemi* means "half."

- Earth is divided into the Northern Hemisphere and Southern Hemisphere by the equator. The equator is an imaginary line that lies halfway between the North Pole and the South Pole. Look at these maps. What continents are located on the equator?

- Earth can also be divided into two other hemispheres. What are the names of these hemispheres? In which hemispheres do you live?

More Practice

There are more maps in this book that show the equator. For example, see pages 96, 333, and R10–R11.

THE HEMISPHERES

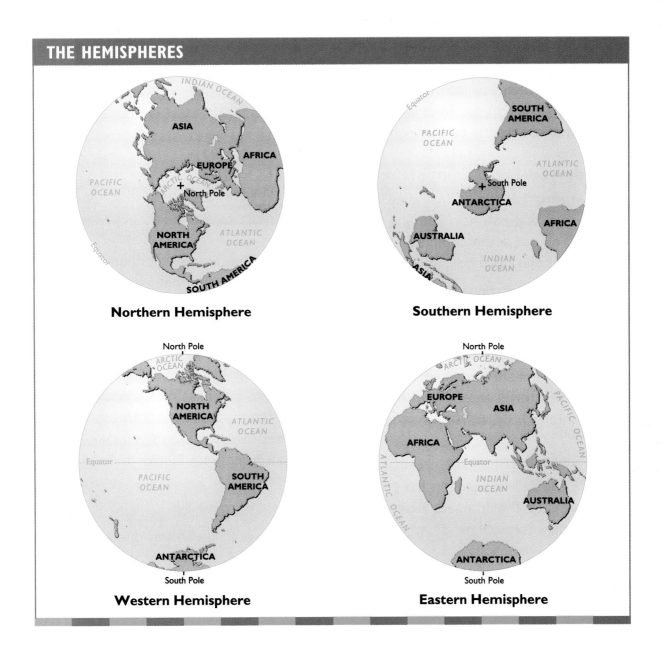

Northern Hemisphere

Southern Hemisphere

Western Hemisphere

Eastern Hemisphere

PART 2

Using Maps

VOCABULARY

cardinal direction
compass rose
intermediate direction
symbol
map key
scale
locator

What are cardinal directions?

- North, south, east, and west are the main directions, or cardinal directions.

- If you face the North Pole, you are facing north. When you face north, south is directly behind you. West is to your left. What direction is to your right?

How do you use a compass rose?

- A compass rose is a small drawing on a map that can help you find directions. You will see a compass rose on most maps in this book.

- The cardinal directions are sometimes written as **N**, **S**, **E**, and **W**. Find the compass rose on the map to the right. In which direction is Stockton from Sacramento? In which direction would you travel to get from Fresno to Monterey?

What are intermediate directions?

- Notice the spikes between the cardinal directions on the compass rose. These show the intermediate directions, or in-between directions.

- The intermediate directions are northeast, southeast, southwest, and north-

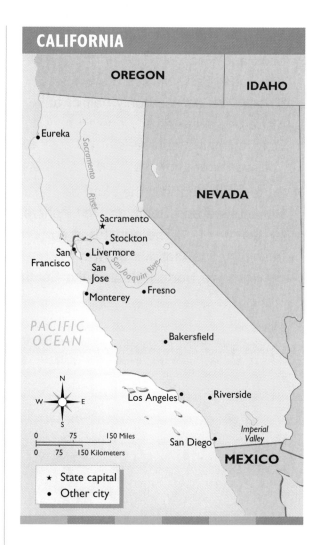

CALIFORNIA

State capital
Other city

west. The direction northeast is often written as **NE**. What letters are used for the other intermediate directions? Which intermediate direction lies between south and east? Which one is between north and west?

- Use the compass rose again. In which direction is San Jose from Los Angeles? Which direction would you take if you were going from Eureka to San Diego?

More Practice

You can practice finding directions with a compass rose on most maps in this book. For examples, see pages 113, 190, and 220.

Why do maps have titles?

- When using a map, first look at the map title. The title names the area the map shows. It may also tell you the kind of information shown on the map. Look at the maps below. What is the title of each?

Why do maps include symbols?

- A symbol is something that stands for something else.

- On a map common symbols include dots, lines, triangles, and colors. Many maps use the color blue to stand for water, for example. What do dots sometimes stand for?

- Maps often use symbols that are small drawings of the things they stand for. A drawing of a tree, for example, might stand for a forest. What could an airplane stand for?

How can you find out what map symbols stand for?

- Often the same symbol stands for different things on different maps. For this reason, many maps include a map key. A map key gives the meaning of each symbol used on the map.

- When you look at a map, you should always study the map key. Look at the maps on this page. What symbol marks places of interest on the map of Sacramento? What does the same symbol stand for on the map of California ports? How many ports do you see on the map?

More Practice

There are many maps with symbols and map keys in this book. For examples, see pages 163, 220, and 365.

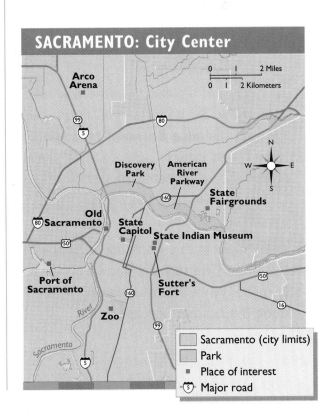

CALIFORNIA'S PORTS

Map key:
- Other city
- Major port

Eureka, Sacramento River, NEVADA, Richmond, Sacramento, Stockton, San Francisco, Oakland, San Jose, Monterey, Fresno, CALIFORNIA, San Joaquin River, PACIFIC OCEAN, Bakersfield, AZ, Los Angeles, Long Beach, San Diego

0   75   150 Miles
0   75   150 Kilometers

SACRAMENTO: City Center

0   1   2 Miles
0   1   2 Kilometers

Arco Arena, Discovery Park, American River Parkway, Old Sacramento, State Capitol, State Fairgrounds, State Indian Museum, Port of Sacramento, Sutter's Fort, Zoo, Sacramento River

Map key:
- Sacramento (city limits)
- Park
- Place of interest
- Major road

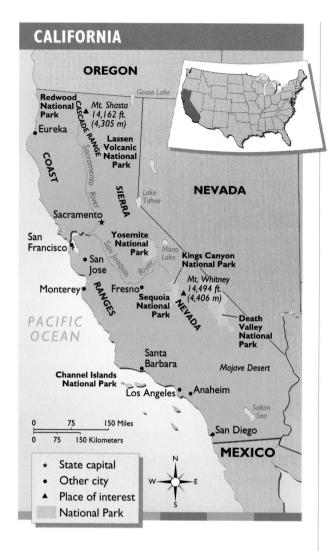

CALIFORNIA

* You can also make a scale strip like the one shown below. Place the edge of a strip of paper under the scale lines on the map to the left. Mark the distances in miles. Slide your strip over, and continue to mark miles until your strip is long enough to measure the whole map.

* Use your scale strip to measure the distance between Eureka and Sacramento. Place the edge of the strip under the two cities. Line the zero up under Eureka. What is the distance between Eureka and Sacramento in miles?

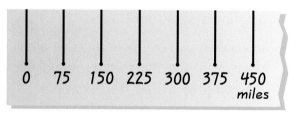

What do locators show?

* A locator is a small map set onto the main map. It shows where the area of the main map is located. Where is the locator on the map to the left?

* Most of the locators in this book show either the United States or the world. The area shown by the main map is highlighted in red on the locator. Look at the map on the left. What area does the locator show?

What is a map scale?

* All maps are smaller than the real area they show. So how can you figure out the real distance between places? Most maps include a scale. The scale shows the relationship between distances shown on a map and the real distances.

* The scales in this book are drawn with two lines. The top line shows distance in miles. What unit of measurement does the bottom line use?

How do you use a map scale?

* You can use a ruler to measure distances on a map.

More Practice

You can find scales and locators on many maps in this book. For examples of scales, see pages 11, 172, and 370. For examples of locators, see pages 14, 85, and 179.

PART 3

Different Kinds of Maps

VOCABULARY
political map
physical map
landform map
transportation map
historical map

What is a political map?

- A political map shows information such as cities, capital cities, states, and countries. What symbol is used to show state capitals on the map below?

- Political maps use lines to show borders. The states or countries are also often shown in different colors. Look at the map below. What color is used to show California?

More Practice

There are other political maps in this book. For examples, see pages R10 and R12.

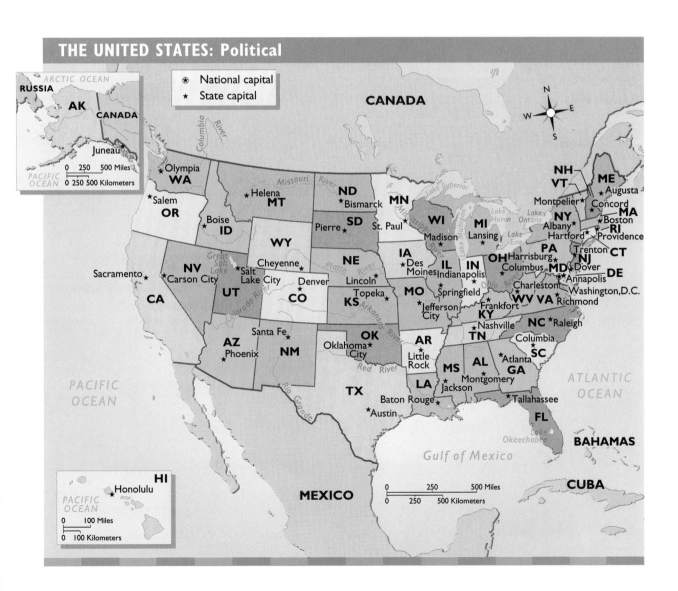

THE UNITED STATES: Political

⊛ National capital
★ State capital

What are physical maps?

- Maps that show the natural features of Earth are called physical maps. There are different kinds of physical maps in this book.

- One kind of physical map shows landforms, or the shapes that make up Earth's surface. These maps are called landform maps. Mountains, hills, and plains are all examples of landforms. Landform maps also show bodies of water such as lakes, rivers, and oceans.

- Look at the map of the United States. What kinds of landforms are found in the United States? What large bodies of water are shown?

What is a transportation map?

- A transportation map is a kind of map that shows how you can travel from one place to another.

- Some transportation maps show roads for traveling by car, by bike, or on foot. Others may show bus, train, ship, or airplane routes. What kinds of routes are shown on the map to the right? What bridge is shown?

More Practice

For other physical maps, see pages 11, R14, and R18. For other transportation maps, see pages 370 and 373.

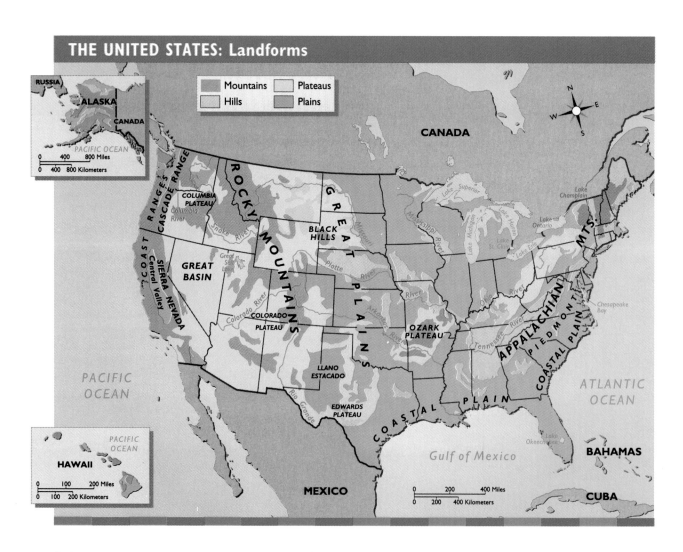

THE UNITED STATES: Landforms

Mountains | Plateaus
Hills | Plains

RUSSIA
ALASKA
CANADA
PACIFIC OCEAN
0 400 800 Miles
0 400 800 Kilometers

CANADA

COAST RANGES
CASCADE RANGE
COLUMBIA PLATEAU
Columbia River
ROCKY MOUNTAINS
Snake River
GREAT BASIN
SIERRA NEVADA
Central Valley
Great Salt Lake
Colorado River
COLORADO PLATEAU
BLACK HILLS
GREAT PLAINS
Platte River
Missouri River
Arkansas River
OZARK PLATEAU
LLANO ESTACADO
EDWARDS PLATEAU
Rio Grande
Lake Superior
Lake Michigan
Lake Huron
Lake St. Clair
Lake Erie
Lake Ontario
Lake Champlain
Ohio River
Tennessee River
APPALACHIAN MTS.
PIEDMONT
COASTAL PLAIN
Chesapeake Bay

PACIFIC OCEAN

COASTAL PLAIN
Lake Okeechobee
ATLANTIC OCEAN

Gulf of Mexico
BAHAMAS

HAWAII
PACIFIC OCEAN
0 100 200 Miles
0 100 200 Kilometers

MEXICO
0 200 400 Miles
0 200 400 Kilometers
CUBA

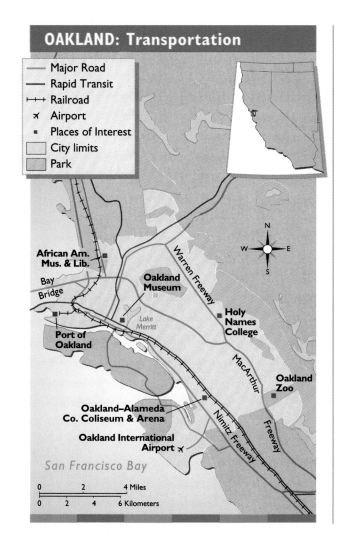

OAKLAND: Transportation

Map key:
—— Major Road
—— Rapid Transit
+—+ Railroad
✈ Airport
▪ Places of Interest
☐ City limits
☐ Park

African Am. Mus. & Lib.
Bay Bridge
Port of Oakland
Warren Freeway
Oakland Museum
Lake Merritt
Holy Names College
MacArthur Freeway
Oakland Zoo
Nimitz Freeway
Oakland–Alameda Co. Coliseum & Arena
Oakland International Airport ✈
San Francisco Bay

0   2   4 Miles
0   2   4   6 Kilometers

What is an historical map?

- An **historical map** is a map that shows information about past events and where they occurred.

- When you look at an historical map, first study the map title. What does the title tell you about the historical map below?

- Historical maps often show dates in the title or on the map. Study the map below. What time period does it show?

- Next look at the map key. The map key tells you what the symbols stand for on the map. What is the symbol for a settlement? Which of the United States shown on the map had Spanish missions? How many Spanish settlements did California have?

More Practice

There are other historical maps in this book. For examples, see pages 85, 106, and 172.

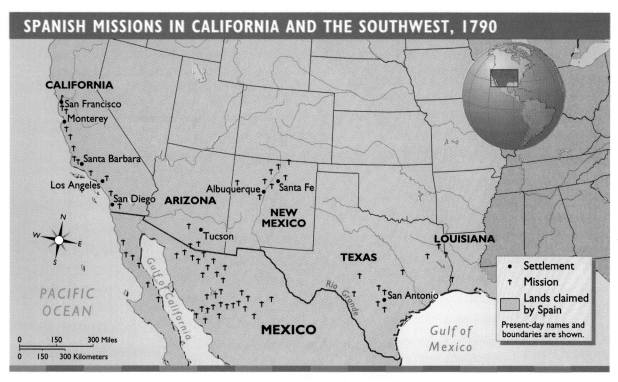

SPANISH MISSIONS IN CALIFORNIA AND THE SOUTHWEST, 1790

CALIFORNIA
San Francisco
Monterey
Santa Barbara
Los Angeles
San Diego
ARIZONA
Tucson
Albuquerque
Santa Fe
NEW MEXICO
LOUISIANA
TEXAS
San Antonio
Rio Grande
PACIFIC OCEAN
Gulf of California
MEXICO
Gulf of Mexico

Map key:
• Settlement
✝ Mission
☐ Lands claimed by Spain
Present-day names and boundaries are shown.

0   150   300 Miles
0   150   300 Kilometers

G11

OIL WELL IN THE SAN
JOAQUIN VALLEY (ABOVE)
YOSEMITE NATIONAL
PARK (BELOW)

WELL
137-26

BALD EAGLE

2

California's Environment

"Each region has its own personality."

Geologist Julie Donnelly-Nolan
See page 9.

WHY DOES IT MATTER?

Our state has the best of everything. Wide rivers and rushing mountain streams run through it. Inside of its borders you can find deserts, ocean beaches, and towering forests. It has high, snow-topped mountains and gently rolling hills. Our state is also rich in resources, from rare minerals such as gold to some of the best farmland in the world.

Read on. Unit 1 will introduce you to the geography, climate, and resources that make California a very special place to live.

WALNUTS (LEFT)
CALIFORNIA POPPIES
AND STARFISH (ABOVE)

3

Adventures with
NATIONAL GEOGRAPHIC

It's A Natural

Redwood trees—the world's tallest living things—grow along the northern reaches of our state's Pacific Coast. Sea otters and other marine life thrive in Monterey Bay. Along our state's eastern border, the spectacular vistas of Yosemite National Park rise among the rugged Sierra Nevada. To the south stretch deserts, home to hardy palms and giant yuccas. So pick a place, any place, and get out and enjoy our state's abundant natural beauty!

GEO JOURNAL

What is your favorite outdoor area in California?

A Place Called California

THINKING ABOUT
GEOGRAPHY AND CULTURE

You know that California is on the western edge of the
United States. California is so big that we break it into
four regions of its own. What makes each region of
our state special? Why do earthquakes happen here?
Find out as you read Chapter 1.

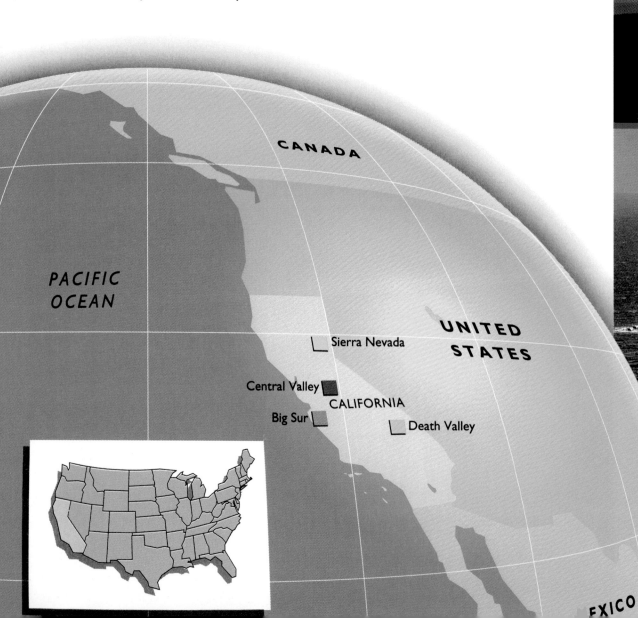

CANADA

PACIFIC
OCEAN

UNITED
STATES

Sierra Nevada

Central Valley

CALIFORNIA

Big Sur

Death Valley

MEXICO

**Mountains
SIERRA NEVADA**

The snow in the mighty Sierra Nevada melts to form many of California's rivers.

**Sand Dunes
DEATH VALLEY**

Despite their harsh conditions, California's deserts are home to many plants and animals.

**Highway 1
BIG SUR**

On its western edge, California meets the Pacific Ocean, forming a coastline that is more than 840 miles long.

**Farm
NEAR MODESTO**

California's Central Valley is one of the main agricultural regions in the world.

7

COAST AND MOUNTAINS

READ ALOUD

From 1860 to 1864, William Brewer studied plants and rocks all over California. He climbed mountains. He saw the "calm, blue, and beautiful" ocean. "I have counted up my traveling in the state," he said. "It amounts to . . . 15,105 miles. Surely a long trail!"

THE BIG PICTURE

Imagine following William Brewer's "long trail" today. Some things might be very different, but the landforms would be the same. Landforms are the shapes that make up Earth's surface. Mountains and hills are examples of landforms.

You would learn a lot about geography (jee AHG ruh fee). Geography is the study of Earth and the things that are on it. Geographers study the landforms, people, animals, and plants on Earth.

Geographers also study where things are located. California is on the western edge of North America. It is next to the Pacific Ocean. Three states and one country share a border with California. A border is a line people agree on to separate one place from another. Look at the map to the right. Which state borders California to the north? What country lies to the south of California?

Focus Activity

READ TO LEARN
How do California's location and natural features make it special?

VOCABULARY
landform
geography
border
region
coast
bay
harbor
plain
urban
source

PEOPLE
John Muir

PLACES
Pacific Coast region
Coast Ranges
Mountain region
Sierra Nevada
Mount Whitney

The Pacific Coast Highway runs along much of California's beautiful coastline.

FOUR CALIFORNIAS

It is hard to find one word to describe a place as big as California. Is it flat? Is it mountainous? Is it wet or dry? In fact, California is all of these things. The state is like a big puzzle made up of four very different pieces. One piece has many mountains, another has lots of flat land. Another piece is wet, and yet another is very dry.

These puzzle pieces have a name. Geographers call each piece a region (REE jun). A region is an area with common features that set it apart from other areas.

Regions help us know about a place. We can describe California by thinking about it in regions. In this chapter you will learn about four regions of California. These regions are called Pacific Coast, Mountain, Central Valley, and Desert. "Each region has its own personality," says Julie Donnelly-Nolan.

Donnelly-Nolan is a geologist. A geologist studies rocks to find out how Earth's surface was formed. She says that "each region tells us different things about how California formed." You will learn much more about California's land as you read this chapter.

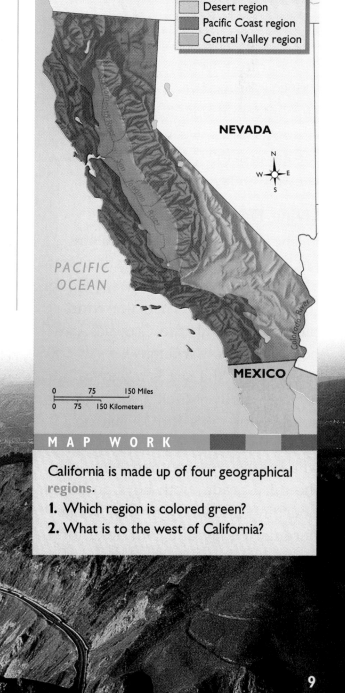

CALIFORNIA'S FOUR REGIONS

- Mountain region
- Desert region
- Pacific Coast region
- Central Valley region

OREGON

NEVADA

PACIFIC OCEAN

MEXICO

0   75   150 Miles
0   75   150 Kilometers

M A P   W O R K

California is made up of four geographical regions.

1. Which region is colored green?
2. What is to the west of California?

ALONG THE PACIFIC COAST

As you know, to the west of California lies the Pacific Ocean. The land that lies along an ocean is known as a coast. We call the coastal area of California the Pacific Coast region.

Living Near the Sea

The Crews family lives in the Pacific Coast region, in Santa Cruz. The family's house is only six blocks from the beach. When the wind blows just right, the Crewses can hear sea lions barking.

Living by the sea is a way of life for the family. Mitch Crews is in sixth grade. "It's fun to just go down there and lie on the beach," Mitch says. His brother, Neil, is in the third grade. Both boys go boogie boarding and bodysurfing. Their parents, Peggy and Phil, take long walks and camp on the beach.

Learning from the Ocean

On a school field trip, Neil went to look at tide pools. When the tide goes out, little pools of water are left behind. There Neil saw sea urchins, sea stars, and tiny crabs.

Neil has also seen kelp "forests." Kelp, a kind of seaweed, grows in thick patches in the bay near his house. A bay is a part of the ocean that extends into the land. "In the kelp forests, the fish eat seaweed, and the sea otters get clams," explains Neil.

Neil's father is a scientist who studies an animal called the sea sponge. He hopes to learn how to use it to treat diseases, such as cancer.

The Coast Changes

Santa Cruz has a harbor. A harbor is a sheltered place along the coast where ships can dock. Many other cities, such as San Francisco and Los Angeles, have big harbors with space for lots of boats. Along most of the Pacific Coast, however, the land is rocky or plunges right into the ocean. No ships can dock safely there.

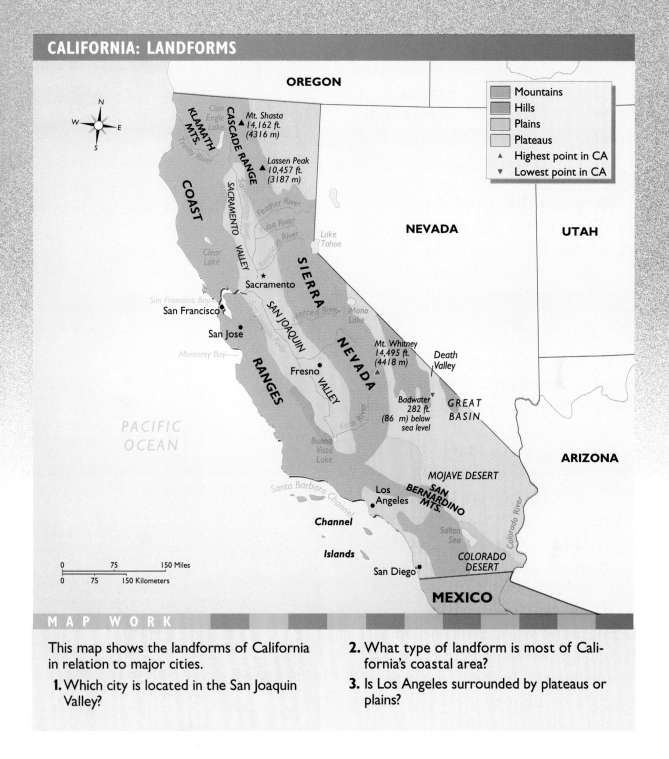

Mountains
Hills
Plains
Plateaus
▲ Highest point in CA
▼ Lowest point in CA

OREGON

KLAMATH MTS.
Clair Engle Lake
Trinity River
CASCADE RANGE
Mt. Shasta 14,162 ft. (4316 m)
Lassen Peak 10,457 ft. (3187 m)
Sacramento River
Feather River
Yuba River
American River
COAST
SACRAMENTO VALLEY
Clear Lake
Lake Tahoe
NEVADA
UTAH
★ Sacramento
San Francisco Bay
San Francisco
San Jose
Monterey Bay
Merced River
SIERRA
SAN JOAQUIN
Mono Lake
RANGES
VALLEY
Fresno
NEVADA
Mt. Whitney 14,495 ft. (4418 m) ▲
Death Valley
PACIFIC OCEAN
Kern River
Badwater 282 ft. (86 m) below sea level ▼
GREAT BASIN
Buena Vista Lake
ARIZONA
Santa Barbara Channel
MOJAVE DESERT
SAN BERNARDINO MTS.
Los Angeles
Colorado River
Channel
Salton Sea
Islands
COLORADO DESERT
San Diego
MEXICO

0   75   150 Miles
0   75   150 Kilometers

This map shows the landforms of California in relation to major cities.

1. Which city is located in the San Joaquin Valley?

2. What type of landform is most of California's coastal area?

3. Is Los Angeles surrounded by plateaus or plains?

Along much of the Pacific Coast, there are low, rolling mountains. These are the Coast Ranges. A mountain range is a chain of mountains. Find the Coast Ranges on the landform map. Around Los Angeles the land is mostly flat. These flat areas are called plains.

Almost three out of every four Californians live in the Pacific Coast region. Most live in large urban areas like San Jose or San Diego. *Urban* means "of a city." Museums, stores, tall buildings, and busy streets make urban areas fun places to live in or to visit.

11

IN THE HIGH PEAKS

Look at the landforms map again. Can you find other mountains in California? Close to the border with Nevada is the Mountain region.

Muir's Mountains

More than 200 years ago, a Spanish traveler saw a range of mountains. He named them Sierra Nevada, or "snowy mountains." You can find Mount Whitney on the landforms map. It is the tallest mountain in the United States outside Alaska. How high is it? Lake Tahoe is famous for its deep, blue waters. What other mountain range is in this region?

Another traveler, John Muir (MYOOR), fell in love with the Sierra Nevada. When he was 11 years old, his family moved from the country of Scotland to Wisconsin. There he dreamed of going on a great adventure. In 1868, when he was almost 30, Muir went to California.

For many years, Muir visited the mountains. He climbed to the top of Mount Shasta during a snowstorm. He held on tight to slippery rocks to look into a tall waterfall.

Muir wrote about the Sierra Nevada. He hoped to tell people how special the Mountain region is. He founded the Sierra Club. The Sierra Club works to protect wild land all over our country for the future. In 1890 part of the Sierra Nevada became a park. It is called Yosemite National Park.

As Muir knew, the mountains are the source, or starting point, of many of California's rivers. In the winter, snow falls on the high mountains. The snow melts and flows downhill.

Read what Muir wrote about the Sierra Nevada. How do you think he felt about these streams?

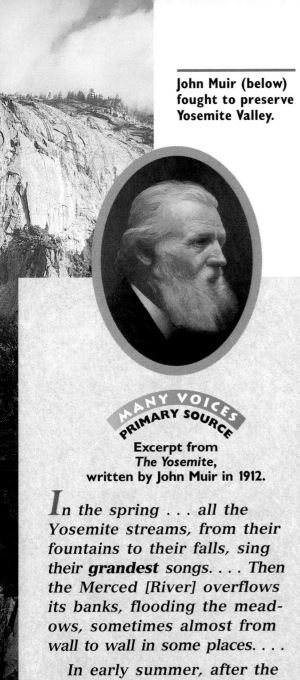

John Muir (below) fought to preserve Yosemite Valley.

Excerpt from
The Yosemite,
written by John Muir in 1912.

*In the spring . . . all the Yosemite streams, from their fountains to their falls, sing their **grandest** songs. . . . Then the Merced [River] overflows its banks, flooding the meadows, sometimes almost from wall to wall in some places. . . .*

*In early summer, after the flood season, the Yosemite streams are . . . deep and full. . . . The weather is cloudless and everything is at its brightest—lake, river, garden and forest with all their life. Most of the plants are in full flower. The blessed **ouzels** have built their mossy **huts** and are now singing their best songs with the streams.*

grandest: fanciest
ouzels: birds
huts: nests

WHY IT MATTERS

The tall mountains and long coast give California great beauty. For many years, they made it hard to get to California. The rocky, foggy coast made it dangerous for ships. It was hard to cross the Sierra Nevada.

In the next lesson you will learn about California's other two regions, the Central Valley region and the Desert region.

✓ Reviewing Facts and Ideas

MAIN IDEAS

- California is located in the western United States.
- California can be divided into the Pacific Coast, Mountain, Central Valley, and Desert regions.
- The Pacific Coast region lies along the coast. The Mountain region contains the Cascade Range and the Sierra Nevada.

THINK ABOUT IT

1. Where is California located?

2. How does studying a particular region help you learn about a large state like California?

3. **FOCUS** What are some natural features of the Pacific Coast and Mountain regions?

4. **THINKING SKILL** *Compare and contrast* the Pacific Coast and Mountain regions.

5. **GEOGRAPHY** Find the area in which you live on the map on page 11. On what landform do you live?

GEOGRAPHY SKILLS

Using Map Scales

VOCABULARY

scale

WHY THE SKILL MATTERS

Would you like to visit Yosemite National Park in the Mountain region? If so, you could look at the maps on these pages to plan your trip. Map A on this page shows the park and the surrounding area. Map B shows a closer view of the park.

These maps are the same size on the page. But Map A shows a larger area than Map B. How can maps be the same size and show different areas? The answer is scale.

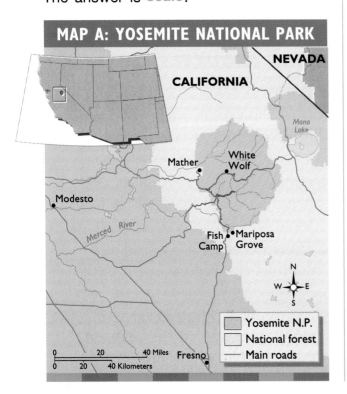

MAP A: YOSEMITE NATIONAL PARK

NEVADA

CALIFORNIA

Mono Lake

Mather

White Wolf

Modesto

Merced River

Fish Camp • Mariposa Grove

N
W · E
S

Fresno

0   20   40 Miles
0   20   40 Kilometers

Yosemite N.P.
National forest
Main roads

Scale is the measurement a map uses to indicate the real size of a place on Earth. Every map has a scale, because no map is the same size as the area it shows. The scale of Map A is different from that of Map B. By reading a map scale, you can figure out how far apart places really are. This will help you to plan travel time.

Why are maps drawn to different scales? A map that shows a larger area probably cannot show very much detail about that area. If a map shows only a very small area, it can include much more detail. On Map B, for instance, you can see mountain peaks, rivers, and even waterfalls.

USING THE SKILL

It is easy to find out a map's scale. Look for a double line that looks like a ruler. On Map A the scale is at the bottom of the map. The top line shows how many miles on Earth are shown by 1 inch on the map. The bottom line shows how many kilometers on Earth are shown by 1 centimeter. As you can see, 1 inch stands for 40 miles on Map A.

On the trip you are planning to the park, you might want to know how far Fresno is from the town of Fish Camp. Look at Map A. There is an easy way to use the scale on the map to figure out how far apart these two places are. You can use the map scale to make a scale strip.

First get a piece of paper with a straight edge. Put the paper below the map scale. For every mark on the scale, make a mark right below it on your piece of paper. Then move your piece of paper so that your last mark lines up with the first mark on the scale. Make more marks, and label them with the correct number of miles. Your scale strip should look like this:

Now put the scale strip between Fresno and Fish Camp. Make sure the zero is lined up at Fresno. Then read the number beneath Fish Camp. You can see that the distance is about 55 miles, or about 90 kilometers. How far is Modesto from Mather? What is this distance in inches on the map? In centimeters?

TRYING THE SKILL

Compare the map scales on Map A and Map B. On which map does 1 inch stand for a greater distance? What does this tell you about each map? Use the Helping Yourself box for hints.

Using your scale strip, measure the distance between the Mariposa Grove and the Yosemite Museum. What is the distance in miles? What is the distance in kilometers?

Which map would be better for planning your stay in the park? If you answered Map B, you are right. It shows many of the park's natural features you may want to see.

REVIEWING THE SKILL

1. What is a scale on a map?

2. Why is it helpful to use a scale strip?

3. How many miles across is the park? How many inches does it measure on Map A? On Map B?

4. Which map would help you find your way home from the park? Explain your answer.

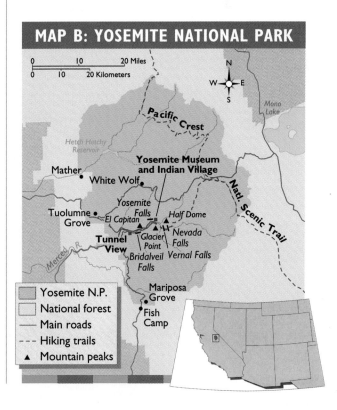

MAP B: YOSEMITE NATIONAL PARK

VALLEY AND DESERT

READ ALOUD

The Chemehuevi (chem e WAY vee) Native Americans live in a very dry region of California. To some people this region seems like a difficult place to live. "[But] to us," said one Chemehuevi, "it is [like] a supermarket."

Focus Activity

READ TO LEARN
What natural features make California's Central Valley and Desert regions special?

VOCABULARY
valley
tributary
delta
wetland
fertile
agriculture
culture
rural
desert

PLACES
Desert region
Central Valley region
Sacramento River
San Francisco Bay
San Joaquin River
Palm Springs
Joshua Tree National Park

THE BIG PICTURE

The Chemehuevi live in the dry Desert region. The Desert region is a place of extremes. It gets very little rain. In the summertime the temperature can climb to 120 degrees Fahrenheit (or 120°F) in the daytime, only to drop to 60°F at night. But plants, animals, and people, too, can manage to thrive in the Desert region.

The Central Valley region is California's major farming area. The northern part of the Central Valley gets more rain than the southern part. But the Central Valley's rich soil grows many types of crops.

16

BETWEEN THE MOUNTAINS

CENTRAL VALLEY REGION

As you have read, the Coast Ranges run along the coast. East of them lies the Sierra Nevada. In between lies the long Central Valley region. A valley is an area between mountain ranges. Valleys may be flat, V-shaped, or U-shaped.

The Central Valley is 450 miles long and only about 50 miles wide. This one region is nearly three times the size of Massachusetts!

Two Rivers

Many rivers flow through the Central Valley. They flow down from the mountains, bringing sand, gravel, and rich dirt into the valley.

The Sacramento River starts in the Klamath Mountains and flows 382 miles into San Francisco Bay. Along the way, smaller rivers flow into it. These are its tributaries (TRIHB yuh ter eez). The Feather River is one tributary.

The San Joaquin (wah KEEN) River starts in the Sierra Nevada. It meets the Sacramento River near San Francisco Bay. When the two rivers enter the bay, they leave behind much of the soil and sand they were carrying. The soil and sand form land called a delta.

The delta area is known as a wetland. Wetlands are lands that are wet much of the time. Swamps and marshes are two kinds of wetlands. Animals love wetlands. Wetlands are home to fish, ducks, and geese. Bald eagles once lived in the delta area. Wetlands also help prevent floods by soaking up extra water.

The Central Valley used to have many more wetlands. Over many years, people have drained the wetlands' water to create farmland. Today only 450 square miles of the original 6,000 square miles are left.

The wetlands near Los Banos are the home to white egrets such as this.

The Bains family (left) owns a farm (below) in the Central Valley region.

RICHES OF THE VALLEY

If you want to visit a farm, the Central Valley is the place to go. This region has more than half of California's farms. Flat land makes it easy to plant fields. The valley's soil is very fertile, or good for growing crops. Water from the Central Valley rivers helps crops grow. Fields and orchards stretch for miles and miles.

When you eat a peach, it probably came from California. California farmers raise four out of every five peaches grown in the United States. In fact, California farms grow more than half of all the fruits, vegetables, and nuts eaten in the whole United States! "If it's for breakfast, lunch, or dinner," says one proud Californian, "it was probably grown right here in California."

"Agriculture is the single most important thing in the valley," notes a farmer there, Jasswinder Bains. Agriculture (AG rih kul chur) is the business of growing crops and raising animals.

A Valley of Farmers

Jasswinder Bains and his family own a farm near Yuba City, north of Sacramento. They grow peaches, plums, and walnuts.

Bains's parents came to California from India in 1949. They settled in a place where they knew other Indian farmers. Bains was six years old when he started doing small chores on the farm. "When we started, we didn't have much," he explains. "We struggled and we worked hard."

Most of the farms in California are owned by families like the Bainses. On a family farm, everyone helps out. Jasswinder Bains's brothers help him run the farm. "We're always busy," he says. From July until September, the family picks its crops. Before the rains start in November, the brothers race to get the fields cleaned up and watered for the next season.

Farming is hard work. "The hardest part to accept sometimes is Mother Nature," Bains explains. If it rains in the summer, a whole crop can be destroyed. Too long a period of dry weather is just as bad! In winter floods can hurt the trees and damage the farm buildings.

Valley Culture

California is the leading agricultural state in the country. Farming is part of the culture, or way of life, of the Central Valley. Work, play, and family life are all a part of culture. In the Central Valley much of the culture has to do with farming.

Like the Bains family, many farm families stay near to each other to help out on their farms. Close to harvest time, many farmers go to county fairs to show off their crops and animals. Cowboy hats and boots are popular at Central Valley rodeos.

The Central Valley has a rural, or country, way of life. But there are big cities, too. Sacramento, our state's capital, is in the Central Valley. It hosts the state fair. Maybe you would like to go and watch pig races and the rodeo. Bakersfield, Stockton, Modesto, and Fresno are some of the valley's other big cities.

Farm machines (left and below) make it easier to harvest crops like walnuts (right).

LIVING IN THE DESERT

Most of California's Desert region is also rural. This dry region of the state gets less than 5 inches of rain a year. It can get as hot as 120 degrees in the summer!

Three Deserts

The Desert region, in southeastern California, has three deserts— the Colorado Desert, the Mojave (moh HAH vee) Desert, and the Great Basin. A desert is an area that gets less than 10 inches of rain in an average year. Together the three deserts are the size of Ohio.

Most towns in the Desert region are fairly small, though Lancaster is home to nearly 100,000 people. Tracy Liegler lives in one such small town, Snow Creek Village, near Palm Springs.

Liegler likes taking walks in the desert. There are many wonderful things to see. Thick cactus trees, for example, store water in their trunks. That way they can survive for a long time without rain.

Many desert creatures come out only at night. "It's wonderful to go out during a full moon," says Liegler. She sees bats and hears owls. She hears coyotes howl.

People who live in the desert often stay indoors on hot summer days. In winter people are very active outside.

Liegler takes students on camping trips to the Mojave Desert. There they visit Joshua Tree National Park. Joshua trees have spiky green leaves at their tips. Birds make their homes in the trees.

Yucca plants (below) bloom in the Mojave Desert, also home to the collared lizard (far right).

The deserts inspire many people who live in or visit them. Diane Siebert wrote a poem about the Mojave Desert. How does the desert change as the seasons change?

MANY VOICES
LITERATURE

Excerpt from *Mojave*, written by Diane Siebert in 1988.

I dream of spring, when I can wear
The **blossoms** of the **prickly pear**,
Along with flowers, wild and bright,
And butterflies in joyful flight.
My summer face is cracked and dry . . .
Until the coming of a storm
When thunderclouds above me form . . .
But soon the blazing sun breaks through . . .
Till autumn breezes, cool and sweet,
Caress my face, now brown and burned,
To tell me autumn has returned.

blossoms: flowers
prickly pear: type of cactus
caress: stroke

WHY IT MATTERS

Would it be fun to see Joshua trees or visit a peach orchard? How about sailing in Monterey Bay or hiking in the Sierra Nevada? You can do all of these things in the four regions of California. Their very different features have made California a popular place to live and visit.

✓ Reviewing Facts and Ideas

MAIN IDEAS

- The Central Valley is between the Coast Ranges and Sierra Nevada.
- Agriculture is very important in the Central Valley region.
- The Desert region is home to many special plants and animals.

THINK ABOUT IT

1. What are wetlands? Why are they found in the Central Valley?

2. How do people and animals live in the Desert region?

3. **FOCUS** What natural features make the Central Valley and Desert regions different?

4. **THINK** *Decide* which of the regions of California you would like to visit. How did you make your decision?

5. **GEOGRAPHY** What are the major cities in the Central Valley and Desert regions?

California's National Parks

Look at your things at home. Is there anything there you would like to keep for a long time? It might be a drawing you made or a baseball glove. It probably reminds you of something or someone special.

Now look ahead to the future. Would you like to give this special thing to your children or grandchildren? If you do, it will be a legacy. A legacy is something we get from the past that we want to pass on to the future.

The wild areas of California are a legacy. As you have read, California has rocky coasts, towering trees, and harsh deserts. Many areas have been changed by people. Some of the tall redwoods have been cut down. The wetlands are smaller. That is why we save what we have left of these treasures. They are a beautiful and important legacy for all Americans.

At Redwood National Park (far left), the trees tower over visitors. Cholla cactus plants dot the Joshua Tree National Park (left).

The Point Reyes Lighthouse overlooks the Pacific Ocean (above). Steam rises at Lassen Volcanic National Park (left).

THE MOVING EARTH

READ ALOUD

Early one morning in January 1994, the earth in Los Angeles began to shake. "It woke me up," said Monica Carillo. "It [was] almost like there was thunder underneath the floor, popping it up and down. I quickly got out of bed and checked to see that my family was okay."

Focus Activity

READ TO LEARN
How do earthquakes affect Californians?

VOCABULARY
earthquake
plate tectonics
fault
Richter scale
government

PLACES
San Andreas Fault

THE BIG PICTURE

Such shaking of the earth is called an earthquake. You have probably heard of earthquakes. Three California geologists helped us understand why they happen. Richard Doell, Allan Cox, and Brent Dalrymple helped develop the idea of plate tectonics. This idea tells us that Earth's surface is made up of huge plates about 60 miles thick. These plates are always grinding slowly against each other. Sometimes they slip or slide quickly against one another. We feel this slipping as an earthquake.

Two of Earth's plates meet in California at the San Andreas Fault. A fault is a crack in the ground caused by the moving plates. The movement of these plates sometimes causes earthquakes in our state.

The 1906 earthquake destroyed many homes in San Francisco.

The Call-Chronicle-Examiner
SAN FRANCISCO, THURSDAY, APRIL 19, 1906.

**EARTHQUAKE AND FIRE:
SAN FRANCISCO IN RUINS**

24

THE GREAT QUAKE

It was just after five o'clock on the morning of April 18, 1906. Most of San Francisco's 400,000 people were still asleep. Then the earthquake hit. For 60 scary seconds, Earth shook under the city. "My bed was going up and down in all four directions at once," said one man.

The city's people rushed into the streets in their nightclothes. Buildings fell down. Streets were torn apart. Emma Burke saw "bricks and broken glass everywhere!" But the worst was still to come.

The Fire

During the quake, people's woodstoves fell over and started fires. There was little water to fight the fires because the earthquake had broken water pipes. In three days much of San Francisco burned. About 250,000 people were left without homes.

San Franciscans promised to build again. People set up shops along sidewalks. Small houses rose quickly. Three years later, new buildings filled the city.

MAJOR EARTHQUAKES IN CALIFORNIA

Richter Scale Value (y-axis: 0–9)

Year (x-axis): 1906 San Francisco, 1971 San Fernando, 1983 Coalinga, 1984 Morgan Hill, 1989 Loma Prieta, 1994 Northridge

GRAPH WORK

California is a land of earthquakes.
Which earthquakes shown on the graph were of the same strength?

25

AN EARTHQUAKE IN CALIFORNIA

Most of the big earthquakes in California happen along the San Andreas fault. What causes an earthquake?

SAN ANDREAS FAULT

San Francisco

4. Most of the time the two plates are locked together. But when they slip, they cause an earthquake.

1. The Pacific plate and the North American plate rub up against each other.

3. The North American plate moves South.

Los Angeles

2. The Pacific plate moves North.

NORTH AMERICAN PLATE

PACIFIC PLATE

PEOPLE AND EARTHQUAKES

Every region of our country must deal with natural hazards, or dangers. In California we have to deal with earthquakes. More earthquakes happen in our state than in any other state.

Many scientists have studied earthquakes in California. They want to find out why earthquakes happen. Look at the diagram to see some of what they have learned.

Facing the Danger

Scientists also want to find out how we can stay safe when an earthquake happens. One tool that geologists use is the Richter (RIHK tur) scale. The Richter scale measures how strong an earthquake is.

Geologists have learned that some buildings stand up to an earthquake better than others. They have also learned that buildings built on rock are safer than those built on muddy or sandy soil. Using this knowledge,

26

most cities today build their schools, large buildings, bridges, and homes stronger.

The town of San Leandro is near San Francisco. It has thousands of older homes. Many are too weak to hold up in a strong earthquake. So the city's government came up with a plan. A government is the laws and people that run a place. The government decided to show people how to make their houses safer.

Stephan Kiefer works for the town's government. He teaches people how to bolt, or fasten, their home to its base. "It's not that difficult, and the gains in safety are incredible." For about $300 to several thousand dollars, families can save their homes from being ruined.

WHY IT MATTERS

California is not the only place that has many earthquakes. Japan, Mexico, Peru, and the islands of

Indonesia also have many earthquakes. These countries are along the edge of the Pacific Ocean. They are part of a region of earthquakes and volcanoes known as the Ring of Fire. Plate tectonics links California and its neighbors along the Pacific Ocean.

✓✓ **Reviewing Facts and Ideas**

MAIN IDEAS

- Earthquakes are caused by the movements of plates on Earth's surface.
- An earthquake and fire in 1906 damaged San Francisco.
- Californians have made their large buildings, bridges, and homes stronger in order to prepare for earthquakes.

THINK ABOUT IT

1. How did the earthquake of 1906 damage San Francisco?

2. Why does California have so many earthquakes?

3. **FOCUS** How do earthquakes affect people in California?

4. **THINKING SKILL** *Predict* how a large earthquake would change life in your town.

5. **WRITE** Write a list of things to improve safety in an earthquake.

CHAPTER 1 REVIEW

THINKING ABOUT VOCABULARY

Number a sheet of paper from 1 to 5. Next to each number write the letter of the definition that best matches the word.

1. region
   a. The shapes that make up Earth's surface
   b. The land that lies along an ocean
   c. An area with common features that set it apart from other areas
   d. A line that separates one place from another

2. Richter scale
   a. A measure of the distance between different places
   b. A measure of how fertile soil is
   c. A measure of the height of a mountain
   d. A measure of how strong an earthquake is

3. geography
   a. The study of the people who live on Earth
   b. The study of Earth and the things on it
   c. The study of the ocean
   d. The study of plants and animals

4. culture
   a. A way of doing business
   b. A way of life
   c. An area between mountain ranges
   d. A country way of life

5. fault
   a. A crack in the ground caused by moving plates
   b. A sheltered place along the coast
   c. A flat area
   d. Soil that is good for growing crops

THINKING ABOUT FACTS

1. What are California's four regions?
2. Which region has over one-half of California's people?
3. What landforms are the source of many rivers?
4. What are three natural features found in the Pacific Coast region?
5. Name the three deserts in California's Desert region.
6. Name two types of wetlands.
7. Why is the Central Valley such a good place to farm?
8. Buildings constructed on what sort of ground are safer during an earthquake?
9. Why do earthquakes happen?
10. What city was nearly destroyed by an earthquake in 1906?

THINK AND WRITE

WRITING A COMPARISON

Write a paragraph that describes the differences and similarities between the Central Valley and Desert regions. Include information about the types of things you would see in each region.

WRITING A DESCRIPTION

Suppose you are taking a hike in the Mountain region of California. Write a paragraph describing what you might see.

WRITING AN INTERVIEW

Suppose you are a reporter preparing for an interview with a person who experienced an earthquake. Write three questions you might ask, along with possible answers.

APPLYING GEOGRAPHY SKILLS

USING MAP SCALES

Refer to the map on this page to answer the following questions.

1. What is a scale strip used for?

2. What is the distance between San Francisco and San Jose? What is the distance between Los Angeles and San Francisco?

3. Approximately how many miles is it from Eureka to Santa Barbara?

4. Which city is closer to Fresno— Sacramento or Bakersfield? Which city is farther from San Bernardino— Los Angeles or San Diego?

5. Why is it useful to have maps drawn to different scales?

CALIFORNIA

Summing Up the Chapter

Use the following main–idea chart to organize information from the chapter. Fill in the blank spaces with information from the chapter. When you have filled in the chart, use it to write a paragraph that answers the question "How do California's special features affect what people do and how they live?"

Pacific Coast/Mountain

LOCATION:

DESCRIPTION:

IMPORTANCE:

Central Valley/Desert

LOCATION:

DESCRIPTION:

IMPORTANCE:

Earthquakes

LOCATION:

DESCRIPTION:

IMPORTANCE:

Californians and Their Environment

THINKING ABOUT GEOGRAPHY AND CITIZENSHIP

You have read about California's different types of land. In Chapter 2 you will learn about the different kinds of weather in our state. You will also learn about the people of California and how we use and protect Earth.

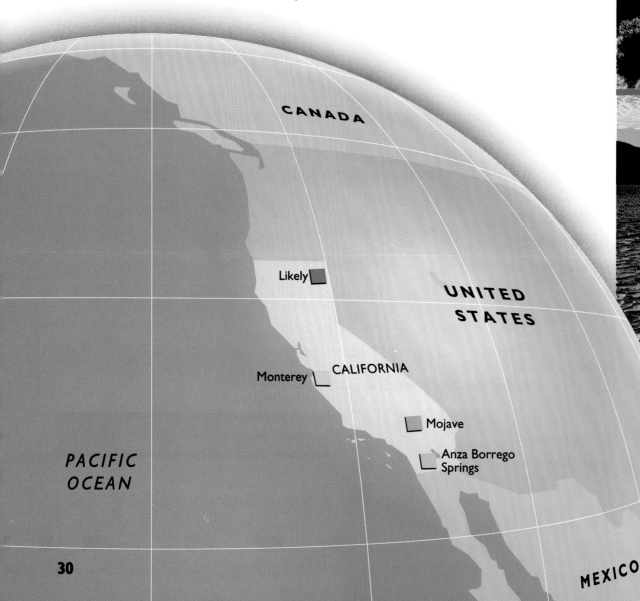

CANADA

UNITED STATES

Likely

CALIFORNIA

Monterey

Mojave

Anza Borrego Springs

PACIFIC OCEAN

MEXICO

**Fisherman's Wharf
MONTEREY**

Fish are a major resource in Monterey and other places along California's coast.

**Lemon Farm
ANZA BORREGO SPRINGS**

California's warm climate is good for growing lemons and other fruits.

**Dry Lake Bed
DEATH VALLEY**

With only 2 inches of rain a year, the land in Death Valley dries and cracks.

**Cattle Ranch
LIKELY**

Beef and dairy cows are an important part of California agriculture.

31

CALIFORNIA'S CLIMATE

Focus Activity

READ TO LEARN
Why are there different climates in California?

VOCABULARY
climate
temperature
precipitation
rain shadow
environment

PLACES
Death Valley
Boca

READ ALOUD

When it's summer in one part of California, it feels like winter in another part. One hot August day, it got up to 113°F in Death Valley. But in the Sierra Nevada town of Boca, an August day might have felt awfully chilly at a low 36°F!

THE BIG PICTURE

California's weather comes in hot, cold, and everything in between. Weather describes the air outdoors at a certain time and place. The weather can be hot or cold, wet or dry, and windy or calm.

The weather affects us every day. You probably think of the weather when you get dressed in the morning. If it is rainy, you might bring a jacket or umbrella. Hot weather calls for shorts and T-shirts.

All places have a pattern of weather over many years. This pattern is a climate. Climate describes what the weather will usually be like at a certain time of year. Knowing about the climate of a place will help you make plans. Would you want to spend your summer vacation in Death Valley?

California has many different climates. In this lesson you will find out why that is.

HOT AND COLD

Can you imagine being in Death Valley on its hottest day? If so, you would probably go to the nearest shady spot to wonder about the temperature (TEM pur uh chur). Temperature is a measure of how hot or cold the air is.

Roberta Gonzales thinks about temperature every day. She is a weather reporter for a television station in the San Francisco Bay Area. She studies information from weather satellites and other instruments to predict the weather.

Gonzales has given weather reports from elementary schools around the Bay Area. At each school students helped her gather information. They measured temperature and other weather facts.

Many things affect temperature, explains Gonzales. One thing is how far away a place is from the equator. Places near the equator are very hot. The farther a place is from the equator, the lower its temperatures generally will be. California lies about halfway between the equator and the North Pole, which is very cold. Therefore much of California has mild temperatures.

Elevation also affects temperature. Places at high elevations have cooler temperatures than places at low elevations. That is why Boca, high in the Sierra Nevada, is so much cooler than Death Valley.

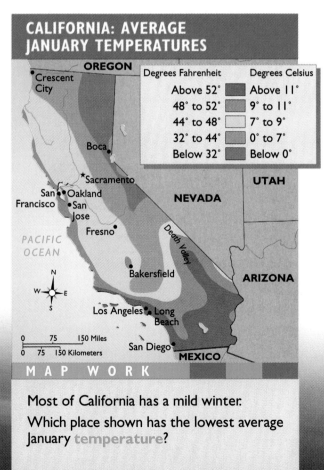

CALIFORNIA: AVERAGE JANUARY TEMPERATURES

Degrees Fahrenheit	Degrees Celsius
Above 52°	Above 11°
48° to 52°	9° to 11°
44° to 48°	7° to 9°
32° to 44°	0° to 7°
Below 32°	Below 0°

MAP WORK

Most of California has a mild winter.

Which place shown has the lowest average January temperature?

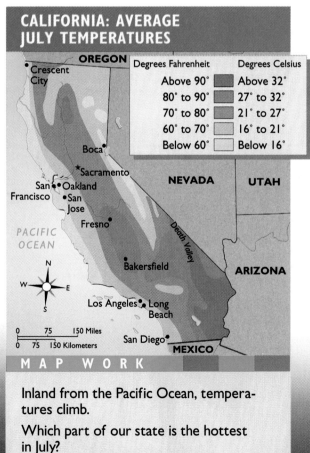

CALIFORNIA: AVERAGE JULY TEMPERATURES

Degrees Fahrenheit	Degrees Celsius
Above 90°	Above 32°
80° to 90°	27° to 32°
70° to 80°	21° to 27°
60° to 70°	16° to 21°
Below 60°	Below 16°

MAP WORK

Inland from the Pacific Ocean, temperatures climb.

Which part of our state is the hottest in July?

WET AND DRY

In Chapter 1 you read about two very different regions: the Pacific Coast and the Desert. What makes the coast rainy and the desert dry?

Falling Water

Third-grade students at Hollister School in Goleta run their own weather station. They use things such as plastic pop bottles to make tools for measuring weather facts. One such tool, a rain gauge (shown in the photo above), measures precipitation (prih sihp ih TAY shun). Precipitation is the moisture, or water, in the air that falls to the ground. It can fall as rain, snow, sleet, or hail. The students have learned that places get different amounts of precipitation in different seasons. The students have also learned that location affects how much precipitation a place gets.

Some places near the coast, for example, tend to get more precipitation. There the wind blows moist ocean air onto the land.

Roberta Gonzales explains that landforms such as the San Bernardino Mountains can also affect how much precipitation a place gets.

Storms blow off the ocean. It takes a while for a storm to lift

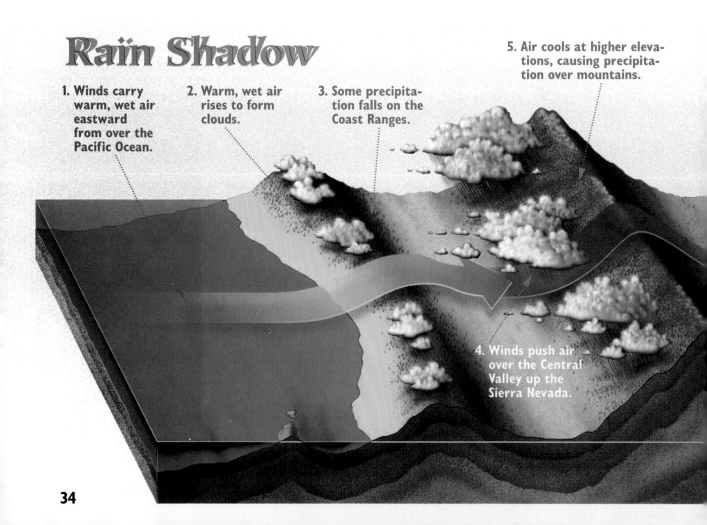

Rain Shadow

1. Winds carry warm, wet air eastward from over the Pacific Ocean.

2. Warm, wet air rises to form clouds.

3. Some precipitation falls on the Coast Ranges.

4. Winds push air over the Central Valley up the Sierra Nevada.

5. Air cools at higher elevations, causing precipitation over mountains.

up over the mountains. Some-times the storm bumps up against the mountains, and then you get heavy rains.

The Rain Shadow

As you read in Chapter 1, the Desert region gets very little precipitation. That is because high mountains block the wet air from reaching the desert.

What happens to the wet air? Look at the diagram below. It shows that when the moist air moves toward the mountains, it begins to rise. Do you remember that temperatures are colder at higher elevations? As the moist air rises, the cooling moisture forms clouds. As the clouds rise and get cooler still, the moisture in them becomes tiny drops of water or ice. These drops fall out of the clouds as precipitation.

When the clouds reach the top of the mountains, they have lost most of their moisture. The other side of the mountains, away from the ocean, gets much less precipitation. The land on this dry side of the mountains is in the rain shadow.

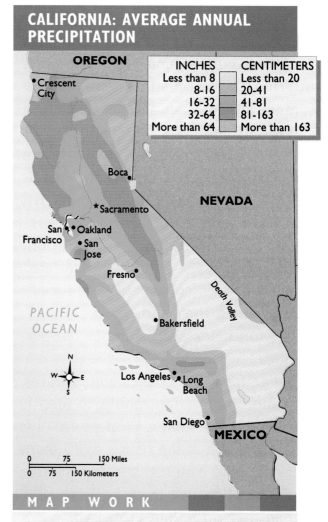

CALIFORNIA: AVERAGE ANNUAL PRECIPITATION

INCHES	CENTIMETERS
Less than 8	Less than 20
8-16	20-41
16-32	41-81
32-64	81-163
More than 64	More than 163

MAP WORK

Most of California's precipitation falls in the northern half of the state.

What city on the map receives the most precipitation?

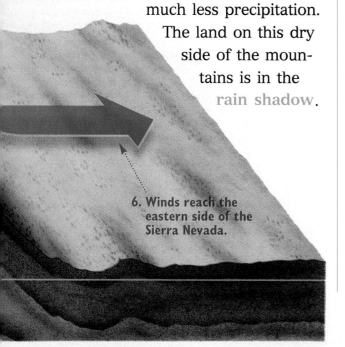

6. Winds reach the eastern side of the Sierra Nevada.

On one family vacation Gonzales saw how rain shadow affects weather. She and her family drove from the desert to the coast. East of the San Bernardino Mountains, they "saw only a sprinkle or two. But when we went over the mountains toward the coast, heavy rains were falling," Gonzales reports.

Look at the map on this page. Why, do you think, has Bakersfield a drier climate than Los Angeles?

THE COASTAL CLIMATE

Have you ever gone swimming on a hot day and found your teeth chattering? Water changes temperature more slowly than air. So when it is hot outside, the ocean is still cool. In cool weather the ocean stays warmer.

This fact explains why the Pacific Coast region has a mild climate. The ocean keeps temperatures on nearby land from becoming too hot or too cold. In the summer warm air moving over cold water produces fog, which the wind blows inland. The fog helps keep summer temperatures mild.

Far from the coast, temperatures change more from month to month. Summers are hotter. Winters are often cooler. Look at the temperature maps on page 33. You can see that the temperatures change more in Sacramento than they do in San Francisco.

The ocean also affects precipitation. Most of California's precipitation falls in the winter. Summers are much drier. That is because heavy, cool air over the ocean keeps most storms away in the summer. Gonzales calls this type of air a high-pressure air mass.

The climate in the Pacific Coast region is similar to that around the Mediterranean Sea in Europe and northern Africa. It is known as a Mediterranean climate. You can find the Mediterranean Sea on the map on page R11.

Climate and the Environment

The different climates of California create many environments. Environment is the surroundings in which people, plants, and animals live. Different kinds of plants and animals live in different environments.

As you read in Chapter 1, many plants and animals thrive in the hot, dry desert environment. The creosote

bush, for example, has a greasy film over its leaves. This helps its leaves hold more water. The Mediterranean climate is just right for growing grapes in the Napa Valley.

On the northern coast, lots of rain and mild temperatures create thick forests. Redwood trees grow very tall in this environment.

WHY IT MATTERS

California's many different climates and environments make the state a rich place to live in and visit. In the winter many people take a break from the rain on the coast. They go to Palm Springs and other parts of the sunny desert. In the summer they can escape the heat of the valleys and deserts. They can visit the cool coast or mountains.

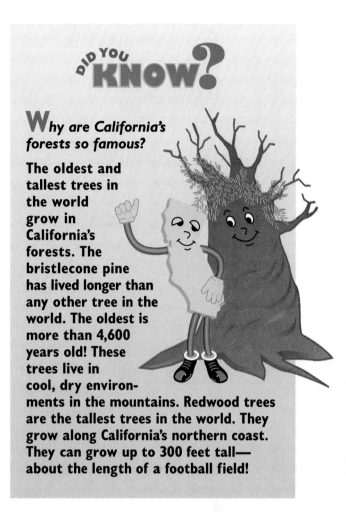

DID YOU KNOW?

Why are California's forests so famous?

The oldest and tallest trees in the world grow in California's forests. The bristlecone pine has lived longer than any other tree in the world. The oldest is more than 4,600 years old! These trees live in cool, dry environments in the mountains. Redwood trees are the tallest trees in the world. They grow along California's northern coast. They can grow up to 300 feet tall—about the length of a football field!

✓ Reviewing Facts and Ideas

MAIN IDEAS

- Climate is the pattern of weather in a place over time.
- At higher elevations the temperature is generally cooler.
- The ocean gives the Pacific Coast region a mild climate.
- Climate and landforms shape the environment of a place.

THINK ABOUT IT

1. What is climate?
2. How does the ocean affect California's climate?
3. **FOCUS** Why are the climates of California's regions different?
4. **THINKING SKILL** _Compare and contrast_ the climates of the Pacific Coast and Mountain regions.
5. **WRITE** Write a travel brochure describing why California's climate makes our state a nice place to visit.

California is home to animals like (left to right) the coyote, the scaled quail, and the black bear. The golden poppy (left) is California's state flower.

CALIFORNIA'S RESOURCES

READ ALOUD

In just one year, more than 2 billion feet of wood was cut in California's forests. That's enough wood to build a walkway winding 17 times around the equator. Fish caught in state waters could have fed every American almost a pound of fish each year. Oil drillers took out enough oil to run most of the cars in California for one year.

THE BIG PICTURE

Trees, fish, and oil are just some of our state's natural resources. A natural resource is something found in the environment that people can use.

Look around the environment you live in. What natural resources do you use every day? You use water when you take a bath or shower. When you write a note, you might use paper and a pencil made from trees. The air you breathe is a natural resource you cannot live without.

When we use these resources, we often change the environment in which we live. For example, we build walls across rivers to store water. We cut down forests for wood. We build roads across the land.

Californians are lucky to have a huge number of natural resources. In what ways do we use them?

Focus Activity

READ TO LEARN
How do Californians use the resources of our state?

VOCABULARY
natural resource
renewable resource
fertilizer
economy
nonrenewable resource
mineral
petroleum
fuel
human resource
population

PLACES
Santa Barbara

RESOURCES UNDER YOUR FEET

One of the most important natural resources is right under your feet! It is the land. We build houses, apartment buildings, and schools on the land. Trees and other plants grow in the land. Farmers use the soil that covers our land to grow the food we eat.

A Wealth of Soil

In Chapter 1 you read about the fertile soil of the Central Valley. You read about how important that soil is to Jasswinder Bains and other farmers. "We're connected to the land because it feeds us," Bains says. "If I hurt the land, I would hurt myself."

Because we can use it over and over again, soil is a renewable resource. A renewable resource is a natural resource that can be renewed, or replaced.

Soil can wear out, however, if crops are grown in it for too many years. That is why Bains adds fertilizers to the soil. Fertilizers give plants the "food" they need. Some are chemicals made by people. Other fertilizers are natural products such as animal waste.

California's soil gives us more than our food. By selling crops, farmers also make money. The crops that are grown in California contribute to our economy. The economy is the way that a country or other place uses or makes natural resources, goods, and services. In 1994 farming the soil added $24 billion to the state's economy. That's some resource!

Soil and water are important natural resources.

39

RENEWING RESOURCES

Water, like soil, is a renewable resource. It is renewed, for example, when rain falls. But water can run low if people use it faster than it is renewed. You will learn more about the value of water in this book.

California has resources that can run out. These are nonrenewable resources. Nonrenewable resources cannot be replaced. Once they run out, they are gone.

The Riches of the Earth

Minerals are one kind of nonrenewable resource. Minerals are metals and rocks found in the earth. We use minerals to make things we use every day. Cement, sand, and gravel, for example, come from minerals. We use them to make highways, buildings, and sidewalks. Gold is another mineral. Later in this book, you will learn more about gold's role in California's history.

Petroleum (pih TROH lee um) is one of the most important nonrenewable resources. Petroleum is a heavy liquid that formed underground from the remains of dead plants. You might know it as oil. "It's something that everybody uses," says Mei Chang. Chang's job is to find and remove petroleum from deep underground.

Petroleum is a fuel. A fuel is something that is burned to make energy. Petroleum makes the energy that runs cars and buses. It is burned in power plants to give us electricity. Natural gas is another fuel found under the earth. Your home might have a gas stove. It burns natural gas to cook your food.

Renewable Energy

We can also get energy, or power, from renewable resources. Wind is one renewable resource. It can be turned into energy using machines called turbines. The wind spins the blades of the turbine. This makes electricity. California has many turbines. Along the Altamont Pass near Livermore there are so many turbines, you might think it is a turbine forest!

Turbines in the Altamont Pass turn wind into electricity.

40

ℹnfographic

California's Resources

As you have read, California is rich in natural resources. How do some of California's natural resources contribute to our state's economy?

Oil / gas
Crops
Minerals
Cattle
Fishing
Forests

WHAT A GAS!
California is the 10th leading producer of natural gas in the United States. Big power plants use it to produce electricity. In many homes it is also used to power water heaters and stoves.

LIGHT UP YOUR LIFE
California is the only state in the country that mines tungsten. Tungsten is used to make the thin filament, or glowing part, of a light bulb.

GOOD TO GROW
People use the trees in forests to make paper and build homes. Animals like the spotted owl live in forests. People are trying to save animals by cutting fewer trees.

HOME SWEET HOME

ISLANDS OF OIL
California is fourth in the country in petroleum production. Much of it is taken from under the seafloor by specially built oil-drilling platforms.

GOOD AS GOLD
In 1995 California mined about 65,000 pounds of gold, second only to Nevada. That weight is equal to about 1,000 fourth graders!

SOMETHING FISHY
California is one of the most important fishing states. In 1995 our state's fishers caught $158 million worth of fish. Santa Barbara was our state's top fishing port.

HUMAN RESOURCES

None of our natural resources would be useful without human resources. Human resources are the knowledge, skills, and energy of people. Fishers, for example, must know how to catch fish. Petroleum workers must know where to drill for petroleum.

California is rich in human resources. Our state has the biggest population of any state in the United States. Population is the number of people who live in a place. Nearly 32 million people live in California! They come from all over the world. People make up California's most important resource.

WHY IT MATTERS

For thousands of years, people have used California's natural resources. The earliest people found food and shelter from the ocean, forests, and wetlands. The discovery of gold in 1848 brought a huge rush of people here to look for this resource. As you learn about California's history, think how resources have played a role in people's lives and decisions.

✓ Reviewing Facts and Ideas

MAIN IDEAS

- Natural resources are things found in the environment that people can use.
- Some resources can be renewed, while others may run out.
- Human resources are needed to make natural resources useful.

THINK ABOUT IT

1. Give an example of a renewable and a nonrenewable resource.
2. What is population?
3. **FOCUS** How do Californians use our state's resources?
4. **THINKING SKILL** How are soil and water *alike*? How are they *different*?
5. **GEOGRAPHY** Look at the map on page 41. Where is most of California's petroleum found?

Fisher in Richmond shows off his crab catch.

Bringing Back Wetlands and Woodlands

GALT—Ashlea Hargrove goes to Fairsite Elementary School in Galt. Every spring and fall, she and hundreds of her schoolmates help to restore a valuable resource—the land.

In the 1860s farmers drained the natural wetlands along the Consumnes River near Galt to grow crops and graze cattle. The animals that were living in the wetlands died or went away.

In many winters, however, heavy rains made the Consumnes River flood. Then the land around it filled with water. That was bad news for the farmers, whose crops were ruined by the floods. Over time, many farmers decided it would be better to sell their land. They helped create the 62-square-mile Consumnes River Preserve. "It's a unique place," says fourth-grade teacher John Durand, who got the Fairsite students involved in the preserve. "It protects woodlands and wetlands that are disappearing in California."

Each spring, Ashlea and other students plant tules (TOO leez), a plant like a cattail or bulrush. The tules provide a place for wetland birds to nest in winter or hide from predators. In the fall the students and other volunteers gather acorns and plant them. They hope to grow a new forest of valley oaks from scratch. The tules and the oaks will one day provide food and shelter for many types of animals.

Ashlea knows how important it is to preserve California's natural environment. "After all," she says, "if you want plants and animals to be on this Earth, you have to take care of them and give them a good home."

" . . . you have to take care of them . . ."

Ashlea Hargrove

Focus Activity

READ TO LEARN
Why do we protect our resources?

VOCABULARY
pollution
smog
citizen
conservation
recycle

PLACES
Quincy
El Segundo

CITIZENS AND THE ENVIRONMENT

READ ALOUD

"We feel like millionaires," say Andy and Katie Lipkis. "Instead of dollars earned, millions of trees are planted," they explain. Andy founded the group TreePeople in 1973, when he was 18. TreePeople members teach people to plant trees. They have helped plant millions of trees in Los Angeles.

THE BIG PICTURE

As you have read, trees are just one of the many resources in California. The book you are reading is made from trees. In 1993 Americans used 100 billion pounds of paper—all from trees.

It once seemed that our resources would never run out. But today we know that is not true. Non-renewable resources like petroleum can run out. Our air and water can become polluted. Pollution is anything that makes air, water, or soil dirty or unsafe to use. The garbage we throw away can pollute the land. Smoke and fog can mix to form smog, a kind of air pollution.

As you have read, resources give California its wealth and its beauty. Resources help people work, learn, and play. The people of California make tough choices every day as they try to use the resources without using them up.

PROTECTING THE ENVIRONMENT

In Chapter 1 you read about how a town's government helped people prepare for earthquakes. Governments also help save resources. But many times it is citizens who solve a problem. A citizen is a person who is born in a country or who has earned the right to become a member of that country.

Saving Trees and Jobs

For years citizens have tried to save the forests of the Sierra Nevada. They asked the government to stop people from cutting trees in the national forests—forests owned by the citizens of our country.

Many people in Sierra Nevada towns like Quincy are loggers. They make their living by logging, or cutting down, trees. "We want to stay in business for a long, long time," says Tom Nelson. Nelson works for a lumber company. Michael B. Jackson is a lawyer and an environmentalist. Environmentalists try to protect environments and the creatures that live in

them. Jackson wanted to save the forests. He also believed it was important for loggers to have jobs. "These people are my neighbors," he said.

These citizens had a hard problem to solve. How could they save the loggers' jobs and trees at the same time?

Nelson, Jackson, and others began meeting in the Quincy town library in 1992. In 1995 they agreed to a plan. Only a certain number of trees would be cut down each year. "I don't know anywhere in the United States [where] an entire county has gotten environmentalists and people interested in jobs to agree," said County Supervisor Bill Coates. He helped make the plan. The "Quincy Library Plan" may be used in other states to allow logging in national forests.

People in Quincy (below) worked to save trees and jobs. Reusing newspapers (above) saves trees.

CONSERVING OUR RESOURCES

Using natural resources without wasting them is called conservation (kahn sur VAY shun). If we use conservation, we can make resources last for the future.

Tough Choices

Conservation is not always easy. It can involve some tough choices. You read, for example, how the citizens of Quincy had to work hard to save jobs while saving trees.

Citizens have looked for ways to conserve fuel. You have read that wind energy can be used in order to save petroleum or natural gas. What can you do to save fuel? Have you ever walked or taken a bus instead of driving somewhere? If so, you have conserved fuel.

Another way to conserve resources is to recycle. This means using something again instead of throwing it away.

In El Segundo, a group of students called the Tree Musketeers started the city's first recycling center in 1990. Many people in El Segundo did not want to recycle. They thought it would be too hard to do. But the Tree Musketeers showed how recycling would help use fewer trees, less water, and less energy.

Recycling soda cans (below) helps to keep Earth healthy.

ALUMINUM BEVERAGE CANS

No other metal containers PLEASE!

Read the following newspaper article written by 12-year-old Tree Musketeer Tanya White. What should we do before we recycle?

Excerpt from "Recycling Is Only One of the Five 'R's," written by Tanya White in 1990.

*R*educe *the amount of trash. . . . Switch to cloth towels and napkins rather than paper; use* **reusable** *containers rather than plastic bags and wrap; take your own bags to the grocery store; take a mug to work and put trash in the can, without a bag.*

Reuse everything you can. . . . Mend and repair rather than **discard** *and replace. Can someone else use it? . . .*

Recycle when the back side of the paper has been used, when you have all the mayonnaise jars your kitchen will ever need. . . .

Think before you toss.

_____
reusable: able to be used more than once
discard: throw away

WHY IT MATTERS

More and more people come to California every day. This means we use up natural resources faster. Citizens must work together to use resources wisely. It is up to Californians to identify and solve problems in our environment so that we can enjoy our resources without using them up.

✓ Reviewing Facts and Ideas

MAIN IDEAS

- Conservation means using resources without wasting them.
- Citizens may have different perspectives on how best to use the environment.
- Recycling is one key way to conserve resources.

THINK ABOUT IT

1. What is conservation?
2. In what ways have citizens tried to conserve resources in California?
3. **FOCUS** Why is it necessary to conserve resources?
4. **THINKING SKILL** *Predict* what would happen if California ran out of water or another resource.
5. **WRITE** Write a list of things you would do to conserve an important resource, such as water, trees, or fuel.

THINKING SKILLS

Decision Making

VOCABULARY
decision

WHY THE SKILL MATTERS

Decision making is a skill people use every day. A decision is a choice about what to do. Making a decision is the same as making a choice. You have to select the best one from a number of choices.

Decisions may be simple, like deciding what clothes to wear. But they can also be very difficult, like deciding how to conserve resources. Knowing how to make the right decision will help you succeed at what you want to do.

USING THE SKILL

To make a good decision, you have to know what your goal is. The goal of the citizens in Quincy was to do what was best for their community.

After you state your goal, identify all the possible choices you can make. We call these possible choices alternatives.

Next, predict the results of each alternative. Then you can choose the alternative that is most likely to help you reach your goal. Now read about an example of decision making in action.

In Rapid City citizens care about conservation. They want to help save nonrenewable resources by conserving fuel. That is their main goal.

To make a decision, the citizens first identify all their alternatives, then predict the results of each. One alternative is to create bike lanes in the streets to encourage people to bike to work and school instead of driving. What would be the results of this alternative? People would use no fuel, and they would save money. In bad weather, however, riding bicycles could be dangerous.

Another alternative is to start a program so that people can share rides together. This would not take very much

money. It would use less fuel. People who share rides would have to agree on when and where they want to go.

Some citizens suggested building a light-rail system. Small trains would run on tracks in the city. This alternative would save a great deal of fuel. But it would take a long time and be very expensive to build the tracks.

The town could also buy more buses and start more bus routes. Buses would make it easier for people to get around. But the city would have to spend more money to buy and run the buses.

Each of these alternatives would conserve fuel. The citizens discussed the alternatives. After predicting the results of each choice, they decided that the alternative of buying more buses would best meet their goals.

TRYING THE SKILL

Suppose you are going to a friend's birthday party. How will you get there? Use the Helping Yourself box to help make your decision.

Your friend's home is a long walk from yours. You are bringing a gift in a large box, so riding your bicycle would be difficult. You could ride the bus, but then you must come home before dark. Your father offered to drive you when he gets home, but that may be after the party starts.

HELPING Yourself

- A **decision** is a choice about what to do.
- Identify the possible choices you have, and predict the likely results of each.
- Select the alternative that best helps you reach your goal.

Light-rail trains in San Diego (top) and Sacramento (above) reduce the number of cars.

What is your decision? Why is the alternative you chose the best alternative? What steps did you take to arrive at your decision?

REVIEWING THE SKILL

1. What is a decision?
2. Look at the section called Trying the Skill. What did you predict the possible results of your father driving you home would be?
3. How will predicting the results of choices help you make a good decision?
4. Why is making a decision an important skill for a citizen?

49

CHAPTER 2 REVIEW

THINKING ABOUT VOCABULARY

Number a sheet of paper from 1 to 10. Next to each number write the word from the list that best fits the description.

citizen   fuel

climate   pollution

conservation   precipitation

economy   recycle

environment   renewable resource

1. The way that a place uses or makes natural resources, goods, and services

2. The idea of using resources without wasting them

3. Something that is burned to make energy

4. A person who is born in a country or has the right to become a member of the country

5. A natural resource that can be used over and over again, or replaced

6. Anything that makes air, water, or soil dirty or unsafe to use

7. A pattern of weather over many years

8. Moisture or water that falls to the ground

9. The surroundings in which people, plants, and animals live

10. Using something again instead of throwing it away

THINKING ABOUT FACTS

1. What are two things that affect temperature?

2. Where does most of California's precipitation fall?

3. Why does the Desert region get so little rain?

4. How does the ocean affect the Pacific Coast region's climate?

5. What is the difference between a renewable and a nonrenewable resource?

6. Name three renewable resources.

7. Why is petroleum an important non-renewable resource?

8. Name three ways people can conserve resources.

9. Name three things that can become polluted.

10. How does recycling help the environment?

THINK AND WRITE

WRITING AN EXPLANATION

Write a paragraph explaining the process that creates rain shadows.

WRITING A PETITION

Think of a resource that you believe should be protected or conserved. Write a letter to your mayor or principal describing your resource and explaining why it should be preserved. Leave room for other students to sign it—if they agree with you.

WRITING A SUMMARY

Write a summary of "Renewing Resources" in Lesson 2. Describe the kinds of nonrenewable resources in California and how they are used.

APPLYING THINKING SKILLS

DECISION MAKING

Suppose you and your friends notice that people in your community are forgetting to recycle things they should. What do you do about it? Answer the following questions to practice your skill at making decisions.

1. What is your goal?
2. What are the choices you can make to reach your goal?
3. What do you think the results of each choice will be?
4. Which choice will you make?
5. Do you think you made a good decision? Why?

Summing Up the Chapter

Use the horizontal organizational chart below to organize information from the chapter. Copy the chart on a sheet of paper. Under each main topic write at least two more words or phrases from the chapter that are related to the topic. When you have completed the chart, use it to write a paragraph that answers the question "How do Californians make the most of our state's natural features?"

CLIMATE	RESOURCES	PROTECTING RESOURCES

UNIT 1 REVIEW

THINKING ABOUT VOCABULARY

Number a sheet of paper from 1 to 10. Next to each number write the word or phrase from the list that best completes the sentence.

conservation   landform
environment   mineral
fertile   natural resource
fuel   petroleum
government   valley

1. A _____ is a metal or rock found in the earth.

2. _____ is a heavy liquid that formed underground from dead plants.

3. _____ soil is good for growing crops.

4. A _____ is something found in the environment that people can use.

5. A shape that makes up Earth's surface is a _____.

6. An area between mountain ranges is a _____.

7. Something that is burned to make energy is a _____.

8. _____ is the idea of using resources without wasting them.

9. The _____ is the surroundings in which people, plants, and animals live.

10. A _____ is the laws and people that run a place.

THINK AND WRITE

WRITING A PARAGRAPH
Write a paragraph that describes the importance of natural resources to California.

WRITING A REPORT
Do some research in the library about the San Andreas Fault, and write a report on it.

WRITING A TRAVEL PAMPHLET
You have read about the many regions and natural features in California. Write a travel guide to one of the regions.

BUILDING SKILLS

1. **Map scales** Why might you want to have the same area mapped at different scales?

2. **Map scales** Look at the maps on pages 14 and 15. Find three details that are shown on Map B that are not on Map A.

3. **Map scales** If you were planning a trip by car in California, which map would you take?

4. **Decision making** What is the first thing you should do when you need to make a decision?

5. **Decision making** Why is it important to learn how to make decisions?

YESTERDAY, TODAY &
TOMORROW

You have read about the importance of resources to how we live and work. Suppose, in ten years' time, we use up a nonrenewable resource such as petroleum. What might we need to do?

READING ON YOUR OWN

These are some of the books you could find at the library to help you learn more.

MOJAVE
by Diane Siebert
The desert tells its own story, with pictures showing the landscape.

JOHN MUIR—WILDERNESS PROPHET
by Peter Anderson
The life story of California's environmental pioneer.

EARTHQUAKES
by Franklin M. Branley
What causes earthquakes and what you need to know to do when they happen.

UNIT REVIEW PROJECT

Making a California Geography Mobile

1. Think about the natural features and resources of California.
2. Work in a group. Have each group member choose one natural resource or feature.
3. Then cut a shape from a piece of construction paper. You might draw a circle, square, or star.
4. Draw on each shape a picture of the natural resource or feature you chose.
5. Then color each picture, and write a caption beneath it. The caption can include the region in which you would see the feature or resource.
6. Punch a hole in the top of each shape, and attach it to a piece of string.

7. Cut three rectangles of cardboard. Punch holes at the end, and tie the rectangles together to form a triangle.
8. Next, punch a hole at the top of each piece of cardboard. Attach a piece of string to each one, and tie the strings together at the top.
9. Finally, tape each natural resource picture to the cardboard.

GASPAR DE PORTOLÁ (LEFT)
TELESCOPE AND COMPASS (RIGHT)
SIGNATURE OF FATHER SERRA (BELOW)
MISSION SAN DIEGO DE ALCALÁ
(BOTTOM)

Settling California

"... a rich land and a mild climate are gifts ..."

from a book by Professor Edward Castillo
See page 72.

WHY DOES IT MATTER?

Who were the first people to live in our state? Why did they come here? What do we know about their ways of life? What other people made journeys to learn about California?

In Unit 1 you studied California's geography. Unit 2 begins our study of California's history. You will find out about the Native Americans who were the first people to live in the land we call California. You will also read about Spanish and English people who came to explore our state.

KIDS AT NATIVE AMERICAN
FESTIVAL (ABOVE)
CALIFORNIA NATIVE
AMERICAN BASKETS (RIGHT)

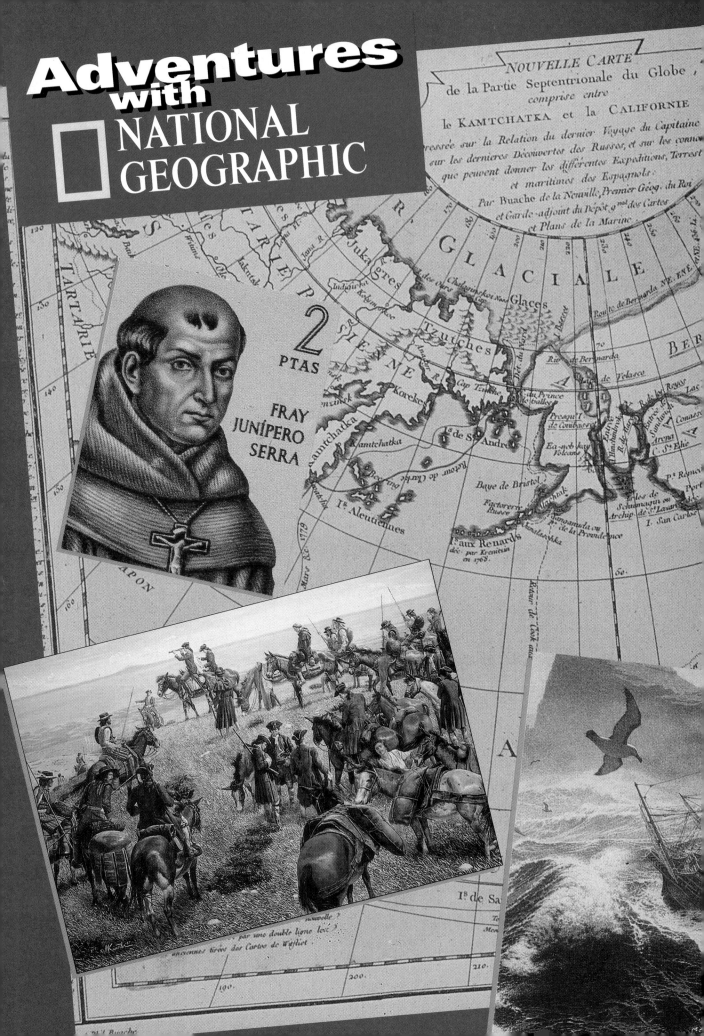

Adventures with NATIONAL GEOGRAPHIC

FRAY
JUNÍPERO
SERRA

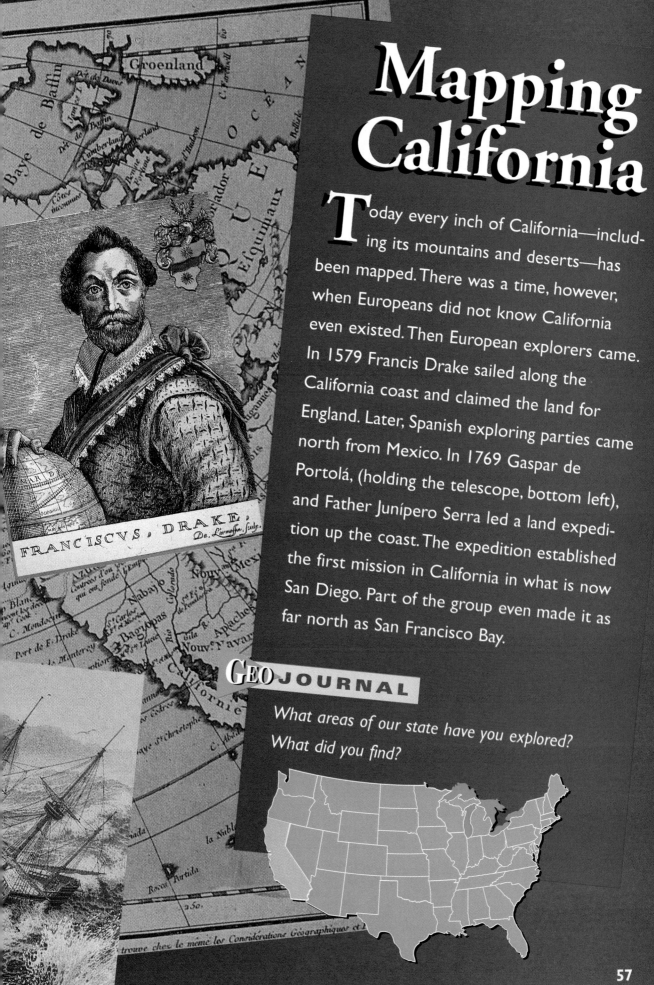

Mapping California

Today every inch of California—including its mountains and deserts—has been mapped. There was a time, however, when Europeans did not know California even existed. Then European explorers came. In 1579 Francis Drake sailed along the California coast and claimed the land for England. Later, Spanish exploring parties came north from Mexico. In 1769 Gaspar de Portolá, (holding the telescope, bottom left), and Father Junípero Serra led a land expedition up the coast. The expedition established the first mission in California in what is now San Diego. Part of the group even made it as far north as San Francisco Bay.

GEOJOURNAL

What areas of our state have you explored? What did you find?

CHAPTER 3

Native Americans of California

THINKING ABOUT HISTORY AND GEOGRAPHY

Who were the first people to live in California? In Chapter 3 you will find the answer to this and other questions. You will also read how California's first people developed different cultures in the different regions of our state. Read on to find out what California was like long ago.

40,000 YEARS AGO	12,000 YEARS AGO	1600s
ALASKA	**CLEAR LAKE**	**CENTRAL VALLEY**
People travel from Asia to North America	Hunters chip arrowheads from stone	Miwok people harvest acorns in groves of oak trees

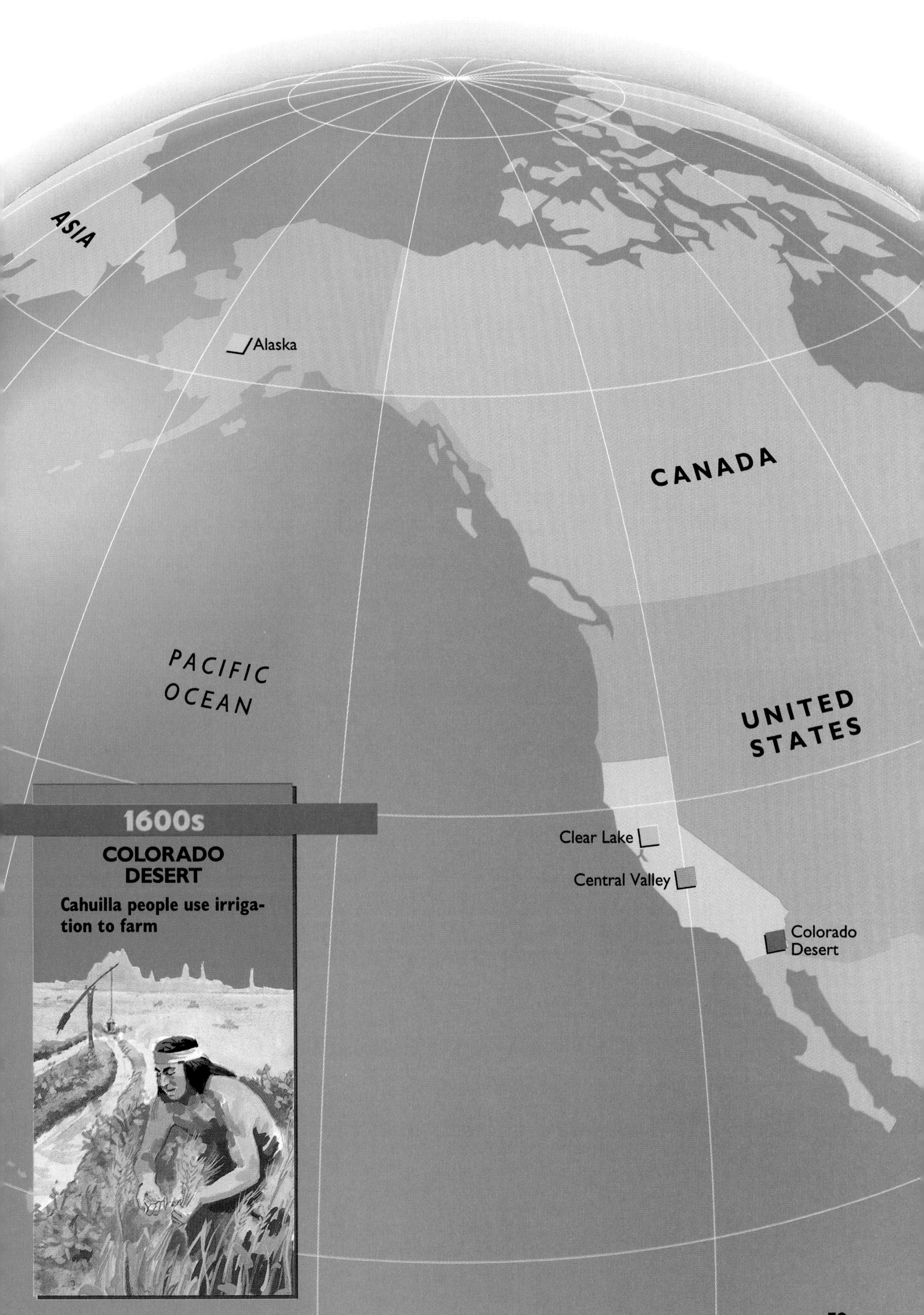

ASIA

/Alaska

CANADA

PACIFIC
OCEAN

UNITED
STATES

Clear Lake

Central Valley

Colorado
Desert

1600s

COLORADO DESERT

Cahuilla people use irrigation to farm

THE FIRST CALIFORNIANS

Focus Activity

READ TO LEARN
Who were the first Californians?

VOCABULARY
religion
archaeology
artifact
ancestor
diversity

PLACES
Clear Lake
Mojave Desert

READ ALOUD

"In the beginning, there was no Earth or sky or anything or anybody; only a dense darkness in space. This darkness seemed alive." So begins a story told by Cahuilla (kuh WEE uh) people of Southern California. It tells about a time before anyone lived in our state.

THE BIG PICTURE

Imagine traveling through what is now California 250 years ago. Along the way you meet many groups of people. Each group has its own language. People live in small villages. Their food comes from plants and animals found nearby. They wear clothing they made and live in houses they built themselves. Each group has a way of worshiping the God or gods its members believe in, or a religion.

How do we learn about this time long ago? One way is through oral history, the stories people pass down by telling them. Another way is through archaeology (ahr kee AHL uh jee). Archaeology is the study of old tools, old houses, and other things people leave behind. We call these things artifacts.

These 6,000-year-old artifacts were found near Santa Barbara. Tony Silva drew Coyote and Silver Fox (facing page).

Santa Barbara Museum of Natural History

60

COMING TO CALIFORNIA

Archaeologists believe that the first people in North America came from Asia about 40,000 years ago. Some came to what is now California.

In the 1930s an archaeologist made an exciting discovery. Chester Post found carved tools near Clear Lake, in the Coast Ranges. Archaeologists have also found stone knives, scrapers, and drills in the Mojave Desert. These tools were tested to find out their age. According to the tests, people have been living in California for at least 12,000 years.

A Creation Story

Native Americans have different beliefs about how their ancestors (AN ses turz) came to California. Ancestors are people in your family who lived long before you.

Achumawi (ah choo MAH way) people have a creation story. It tells how two gods they believed in created Earth, people, and animals. What did they use?

MANY VOICES LITERATURE

Excerpt from Achumawi creation story, compiled by Edward Winslow Gifford and Gwendolyn Harris Block.

While Coyote slept Silver Fox combed his hair and saved the combings. . . . Silver Fox rolled them in his hands, stretched them out, and flattened them between his hands. Then he . . . spread them out until they covered all the surface of the water. This became the earth. . . .

Coyote woke and looked up. He saw the trees and heard crickets. "Where are we," he asked; "What place is this we have come to?"

"I don't know," Silver Fox replied. . . . "Here is solid ground. I am going ashore, and am going to live here."

So they landed and built a house and lived in it.

*After a time they thought about making people. They made little sticks of **service-berry**, and thrust them all about in the ceiling of the house. By and by all became people of different sorts, with the names of birds, animals, and fishes.*

serviceberry: a shrub with white flowers and red or purple fruit

61

MANY CULTURES

The first North Americans were hunters. They hunted bison, ground sloths, and other big animals. They used tools flaked from stone or animal bones. They also gathered roots, berries, and other parts of plants for food. Archaeologists believe that people came to California from other places in North America. These first people are the ancestors of Native Americans.

Diversity

Each group learned how to live in the region its people settled in. People living along the coast, for example, became fishers. They learned to weave fishing nets and build boats.

People who lived in desert areas learned how to farm. California gained a great diversity, or many different kinds, of cultures. People followed many different ways of life. About 100 languages were spoken in California!

Geographers locate six "culture areas" in California. A culture area is a kind of region. All the groups in one culture area have cultures that are alike in some ways. Many of the languages in the Central Culture area,

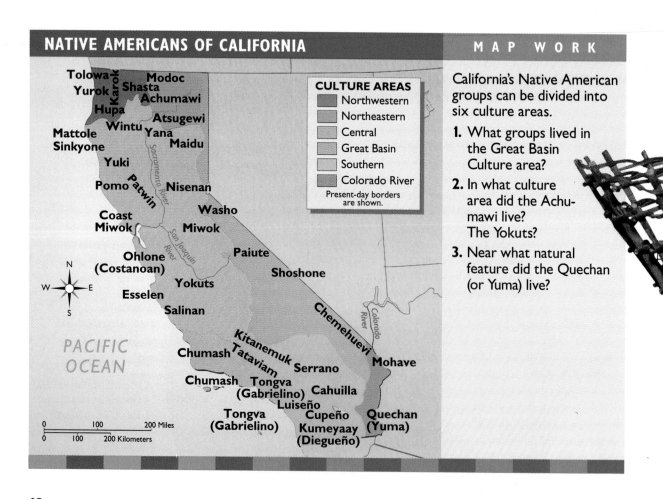

NATIVE AMERICANS OF CALIFORNIA

CULTURE AREAS
- Northwestern
- Northeastern
- Central
- Great Basin
- Southern
- Colorado River

Present-day borders are shown.

Tolowa, Yurok, Karok, Shasta, Modoc, Achumawi, Hupa, Atsugewi, Wintu, Yana, Mattole, Sinkyone, Maidu, Yuki, Pomo, Patwin, Nisenan, Coast Miwok, Washo, Miwok, Ohlone (Costanoan), Paiute, Shoshone, Esselen, Yokuts, Salinan, Chemehuevi, Chumash, Kitanemuk, Tataviam, Serrano, Mohave, Chumash, Tongva (Gabrielino), Cahuilla, Luiseño, Cupeño, Quechan (Yuma), Tongva (Gabrielino), Kumeyaay (Diegueño)

Sacramento River, San Joaquin River, Colorado River

PACIFIC OCEAN

0 — 100 — 200 Miles
0 — 100 — 200 Kilometers

MAP WORK

California's Native American groups can be divided into six culture areas.

1. What groups lived in the Great Basin Culture area?

2. In what culture area did the Achumawi live? The Yokuts?

3. Near what natural feature did the Quechan (or Yuma) live?

The Miwok necklace is made of abalone shells. Pomo people made the trap (below) to catch fish.

The Oakland Museum of California

for example, are alike. The groups in the Northwestern Culture area built homes of cedar or redwood boards. Identify the six culture areas on the map.

No one knows for sure how many people were living in California 250 years ago. Most archaeologists believe that California's population was at least 310,000. Others think it may have been as high as one million. Why did so many people make their homes here? As you read in Chapter 2, California has plenty of resources for food, clothing, and shelter.

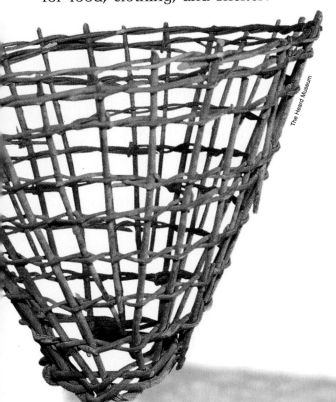

The Heard Museum

Why do we call people Native Americans? *Native* means "one of the first people to live in a land." Native Americans are also known as Indians.

WHY IT MATTERS

For thousands of years California has been home to a large and diverse population. California still has the largest and most diverse population of any state in our country today. Learning about the roots of California's diversity can help us better understand our state.

Reviewing Facts and Ideas

MAIN IDEAS

- Archaeologists think that people have lived in California for at least 12,000 years.
- Many Native Americans have different beliefs about how their ancestors came to live in California.
- Native Americans in California had a diversity of cultures.

THINK ABOUT IT

1. What is archaeology?

2. Why did Native Americans in California have such a diversity of cultures?

3. **FOCUS** Who were the first Californians?

4. **THINKING SKILL** Suppose you were one of the first people to settle in California. How would you *decide* where to live?

5. **WRITE** Write a short play about the first people coming to California.

Focus Activity

READ TO LEARN
How did Native Americans live in the Pacific Coast region?

VOCABULARY
tomol
asphalt
harvest
sweat house

PLACES
Santa Barbara Channel
Trinity River

LIFE IN THE PACIFIC COAST REGION

READ ALOUD

Each year thousands of salmon swim up the Trinity River to lay their eggs. The river flows through the land of the Hupa (HOO pah) people. The Hupa tell a story about an old woman who follows the salmon each year. They call her "Salmon's grandmother." She appears in the form of a flycatcher, a small gray-breasted bird.

THE BIG PICTURE

The Hupa were one of the groups in the Northwestern Culture area. The Yurok and Karok were neighbors of the Hupa. They, too, told stories about salmon. Their way of life was similar to that of the Hupa. Yet they spoke different languages. Each group thought of the others as you might think of people in another country. You might visit them and make friends. But you might think of them as a little different from yourself.

The Chumash belonged to the Southern Culture area. Their way of life was different from that of the Hupa. Yet both groups lived in what we think of as the Pacific Coast region of California. How did each group make use of the resources this region offered?

IN A CHUMASH VILLAGE

Imagine that you are a ten-year-old Chumash boy named Kuliwit (koo lih WEET). Your home is in a village along the coast of the ocean. You are up early today. In the morning sunlight you watch the waves curl and break with a roar along the sandy beach. Gulls fly low over the churning waves.

You and your friends climb out on a rocky point to gather mussels. You pry the blue shells loose from the rocks. One by one you drop them in a net bag tied to your waist. Your older brother and his friends are digging for clams in the wet sand. One young man is diving for abalone. These shellfish live on the sandy bottom. Your sister sits on the beach, learning to make a basket to carry the fish.

Suddenly a shout rings out. You look up and see several canoes heading for the shore. Your father, Konoyo (koh noh YOH), is in the first canoe. He waves as he passes by. His bearskin cape sparkles with spray. The canoes ride low in the water. They are heavy with piles of fish—skipjack and yellowfin tuna.

Building a Boat

The Chumash built a kind of canoe called a tomol (TOH mahl). A *tomol* was up to 30 feet long, yet so light that two people could carry it easily. Builders made *tomols* from thin boards of pine. Using bone tools, they punched rows of holes along the edges of the boards. Then they lashed the boards together with plant fibers. To keep out water, the *tomol*'s seams were filled with asphalt. Asphalt is a thick tar that can seep to Earth's surface. Basket weavers also used asphalt to line their baskets. That helped keep them from leaking. Today we use asphalt to pave our roads.

Santa Barbara Museum of Natural History

In 1914 Fernando Librado, a Chumash, showed these men how to build a tomol, like the one at left.

Santa Barbara Museum of Natural History

San Diego Historical Society

LIFE ON THE COAST

Like Kuliwit, most Chumash lived along the Santa Barbara Channel. This body of water lies between the coast and the Channel Islands. Other Chumash villages were farther inland.

Plentiful resources allowed the Chumash to live in villages of 2,000 people. Some villages had more than 100 homes. Most other Native American groups lived in villages smaller than that. Chumash houses were made of poles driven into the earth. The poles were tied together in the center. Over the poles were placed mats of woven grasses or other fibers.

Bringing in the Catch

Konoyo's fishing boat has landed! Everyone comes to the beach to help. You and other children unload the fish. Your mother, Lekte (lek TAY),

Most villages had a sweat house, where men and boys went before bathing.

Santa Barbara Museum of Natural History

begins gutting and scaling. Other women gather piles of wood to make fires. The cleaned fish are spread on racks to smoke. The smoking keeps the fish from spoiling. The men stretch their fishing nets on the beach. When the nets are dry, women will help them fix the torn nets.

The Chumash took their *tomols* to Santa Catalina Island to trade. They brought with them lumps of asphalt, bundles of clamshells, and otter furs. They traded these things to Tongva people for steatite (STEE uh tīt), a soft dark stone. From steatite the Chumash carved cooking pots, bowls, beads, and pipes.

CHUMASH

A Village at Play

Life for the Chumash was not all work. Villages had large areas for dancing and playing games. The hoop-and-pole game might have been your favorite. A small hoop was rolled along the ground. The players tried to throw a long pole through it while it rolled. It wasn't easy! During dances musicians played wooden flutes and bone whistles. They also used rattles made from sticks, turtle shells, or bunches of deer hooves.

Chumash Leaders

Each Chumash village or group of nearby villages had its own chief, called the *wot* (WOHT). The *wot* was most often a man, but some villages were ruled by women. The *wots* led their villages in peace and war.

The owners of *tomols* were also important people. A visitor to a Chumash village in 1775 wrote:

Among the men I saw a few with a little cape . . . reaching to the waist and made of bear skin, and by this mark . . . I learned that these were the owners and masters of the launches [boats].

Some parts of Chumash culture are a mystery to us now. We know very little about how the Chumash practiced their religion 250 years ago. Some answers may be in their paintings. Throughout Chumash lands people made colorful images on rocks. They used charcoal, minerals, animal oils, plant juices, and egg whites. Animal tails or stiff hairs from the soap plant were used as brushes.

The painters may have been religious leaders. No one knows for sure what the paintings mean. They may be pictures of spirits or ideas. Perhaps they are a form of writing. What do you see in the painting below?

Wall of Painted Cave, near San Marcos Pass in Santa Barbara, painted by Chumash artists probably between 200 and 500 years ago.

Santa Barbara Museum of Natural History

A WEALTHY PEOPLE

HUPA

Up the coast, in the northwest Coast Ranges, lived the Hupa. Most of their villages were nestled in the fertile valley of the Trinity River.

Each spring and fall the river filled with salmon. These fish swam upstream from the ocean to lay their eggs in small pools. Dotting the valley floor were giant oaks. Forests covered the nearby mountains.

Each fall came the acorn harvest. A harvest is a gathering of a crop or resource. Hupa women harvested the acorns from the oaks. With nets and spears Hupa men fished the salmon from the river. The salmon and acorn harvests nourished the Hupa throughout the year.

Contrasting Cultures

Hupa boats were very different from the light Chumash *tomols*. A Hupa boat was carved from a huge redwood log that had been hollowed out. Their boats could carry several thousand pounds. Like the Chumash, the Hupa used their boats to trade with their neighbors.

Hupa villages had between 50 and 200 people. Unlike the Chumash pole houses, Hupa homes were made of cedar planks. They were built partly below ground. They needed to be more sturdy because of the Northwest's cooler, rainy climate.

Each Hupa village had several sweat houses, known as *temescals* (te me SKAHLZ). Men and boys began each day in a sweat house. They sat around an open fire until they were sweating. Then they would rush out to bathe in the swift-flowing waters of the river.

The leading families in a Hupa village were those who had the most wealth. A wealthy family might have many white deerskins.

Hupa and other Northwestern Culture peoples built houses of wooden planks. Salmon were a big part of their diets.

Denver Art Museum

Hupa wore headdresses made of woodpecker scalps in ceremonies.

The Bancroft Library

These were prized by Northwestern Culture groups.

Hupa leaders did not have as much power as Chumash leaders. Conflicts among the Hupa were often settled peacefully. Fighting between groups was rare.

In the late summer or early fall, the Hupa held religious ceremonies. They held the White Deerskin Dance to renew Earth so that life would be good in the coming year. The Jump Dance was to ward off illness. Each lasted ten days and was held at a special place.

WHY IT MATTERS

The rich natural resources of California allowed Native Americans to live settled lives. In other parts of North America, people moved from place to place in search of food.

The people of the Pacific Coast region used their resources wisely. In the next lesson you will learn how the people of other regions lived.

✔️ Reviewing Facts and Ideas

MAIN IDEAS

- The Chumash and the Hupa lived in the Pacific Coast region.
- The Chumash built pine *tomols* and caught shellfish in the ocean.
- The Hupa used the forests of the Northwest for food and shelter and caught salmon in the rivers.

THINK ABOUT IT

1. How did Chumash boatbuilders make their *tomols*?

2. What were the two main foods in the Hupa diet?

3. **FOCUS** How did Native Americans live in the Pacific Coast region?

4. **THINKING SKILL** *Compare and contrast* the cultures of the Hupa and the Chumash.

5. **GEOGRAPHY** Look at the map on page 62. Why, do you think, is the climate in Hupa lands different from that in Chumash lands?

THE ART OF BASKET WEAVING

Native American basket weavers gathered in the early 1990s at a place called Ya-Ka-Ama, near Forestville in Sonoma County. They met to encourage one another and to share their knowledge. Jennifer Bates, a Miwok, was one of the weavers. She later wrote:

The gathering brought out tears and laughter, songs and dance, concerns and prayers. It brought all of us closer as a family of weavers.

After the meeting Bates helped organize the California Indian Basketweavers Association.

Some experts think that the baskets made by California Indians are the finest in the world. Like beautiful pottery, these baskets are works of art that are meant to be used as well as looked at.

Baskets from the past are a way for Native Americans to remember their heritage. The baskets they weave today are a legacy to future generations.

The shallow Chemehuevi basket (bottom) shows snakes. A Chumash weaver made the box to hold small items. Making baskets is an art that Native American weavers have passed down through the years.

San Diego Historical Society

The Heard Museum

Images of people were woven into the Yokuts basket (top) using darker materials. The Pomo basket decorated with feathers (left) was made as a gift.

San Diego Historical Society

LIFE IN THE DESERT AND IN THE VALLEY

Focus Activity

READ TO LEARN
How did Native Americans live in the deserts and in the Central Valley?

VOCABULARY
tule
irrigation
granary
shaman

PLACES
Central Valley
Mojave Desert
Colorado Desert

READ ALOUD

"The religious beliefs and traditions of the Indians of California teach that the blessings of a rich land and a mild climate are gifts from the Creator." Professor Edward Castillo wrote these words in the 1990s. His Cahuilla and Luiseño (loo ee SEN yoh) ancestors have lived in California for thousands of years.

THE BIG PICTURE

The Central Valley was a garden of incredible riches for the Miwok, Yokuts, and other Native Americans who lived there. Every fall the branches of oak trees hung heavy with acorns. Roaming the valley floor were herds of deer, elk, and antelope. Marshes were filled with otter, beaver, and tule (TOO lee). Tule is a kind of reed. It is so strong that people built houses and boats with it.

As you learned in Chapter 2, California has many desert areas. Life for the people who lived here was very different from life in the Central Valley. Yet the deserts gave the Cahuilla, the Mojave, and the Quechan all that they needed.

THE DESERT BLOOMS

Professor Castillo also wrote this about the resources of California's Native Americans:

CAHUILLA

Fish, deer, antelope, waterfowl, and wild seeds supplied all that the Indians needed for survival. . . . Only in the hot, dry deserts of southeastern California did they farm the land to feed themselves.

Desert Farmers

You might wonder, how could anyone farm in a desert? How do the crops get water? Quechan people in the eastern Mojave Desert planted crops along the banks of the Colorado River. They used water from the river to raise crops of corn, beans, and pumpkins.

The Cahuilla also practiced agriculture. Their homeland included the northern Colorado Desert. Where water was scarce, the Cahuilla used a kind of irrigation. Irrigation is the use of ditches or pipes to bring water to fields. The Cahuilla dug deep wells in the desert sand. By banking the sand around the wells, they created small lakes. They used the water to grow corn, squash, beans, and melons.

The Cahuilla used hundreds of other plants that grew in the desert. From honey mesquite (mes KEET), they gathered blossoms to make a refreshing drink. They ate the fruit and seeds of the prickly pear and the jumping cholla cactus. The leaves of the fan palm were used to roof Cahuilla homes. Today, Cahuilla Katherine Saubel teaches people how to use the plants of the desert.

The Huntington Library

A Cahuilla woman stores her acorn harvest. Some desert peoples traveled to oak groves in the hills each year for acorns.

Food from the Trees

1. Acorns are struck with rocks to open the shells, and the kernels are removed.

2. Kernels are winnowed, or tossed, to remove papery skins.

COAST MIWOK

MIWOK

HARVESTING THE OAKS

Imagine that you are a ten-year-old Miwok girl living in the Central Valley 250 years ago. It is autumn, and your village has gathered with others for the acorn harvest. This is your favorite time of year. You get to visit with all your friends from neighboring villages.

Today is the first day of the harvest. Your job is to climb high up an oak tree and knock the acorns loose. Holding tightly with your legs, you balance yourself on a huge limb. Overhead you hear the angry chattering of a gray squirrel. An acorn woodpecker cocks his head and watches suspiciously.

Slowly you reach out with a long pole and give a bunch of acorns a whack. The acorns rain down. Your mother and other women below begin gathering the acorns in large baskets. The harvest has begun.

Acorns as Food

In just a couple of weeks, your family will gather a year's supply of acorns. Where will you put all those acorns? In large granaries. A granary is a building used for storing food. The Miwok built granaries from poles laced with vines. Some were 12 feet high and 5 feet across. Thick sheets of bark placed on top kept out squirrels and woodpeckers.

From the acorns the Miwok made soup, mush, biscuits, and bread. Acorn mush is your favorite. Your mother puts ground acorn meal and water in a cooking basket. Then she puts hot rocks in to heat the water. She must stir very quickly or the rocks will burn the sides of the

3 Handfuls of kernels are pounded in a shallow rock basin to form a fine meal.

4 Meal is rinsed with water many times in a sandy basin to remove bitter tannin.

5 Washed meal is boiled in baskets to form mush or wrapped in leaves and baked in ovens to make bread.

basket! Fruit, herbs, or meat add flavor. Look at the flow chart above. Why was acorn meal rinsed with water?

Acorns played the role in the Miwok diet that wheat might play in yours. Our breads and cereals are made mostly from wheat. So are noodles and cakes. Like wheat, acorns have many vitamins.

Managing Resources

Along with acorns the Miwok gathered many plants, and they hunted a wide variety of animals. Most villagers burned parts of their land each August. The ash from the fires kept the soil fertile. This helped food plants, such as primrose and ripgut grass, to grow. Fires also removed brush, such as bushes and vines. This cleared land for deer and antelope to graze. An area of 1 square mile with thick brush can feed about 30 deer. A year after a fire, that area might feed 90 deer.

Today forest rangers still burn land to clear brush. These careful burns help prevent large, dangerous forest fires from starting.

Links to SCIENCE

From Acorns to Oaks

When you look at a mighty oak, it is hard to imagine that it began life as a single acorn.

After an acorn drops from a tree, it starts to grow as soon as the winter rains begin. The smooth hull, or shell, of the acorn falls apart. The acorn sends a tiny root downward. The root anchors the acorn in the soil. Then a shoot grows upward toward the sun. That shoot will grow into an oak sapling.

Try growing your own oak tree. Find a ripe acorn and put it in a small pot with some moist soil. See what comes up!

HEALERS

An important person in a Miwok village was a shaman (SHAH mun). Shamans were religious leaders. They were also healers. In most Native American communities, people believed that shamans had great powers. These might include handling fire, causing natural events such as rain, curing or causing diseases, or visiting spirit worlds.

The shamans of the Cahuilla were called *puvulam* (poo VOO lum). *Puvulam* were always men. The Cahuilla believed that *puvulam* could cure sickness. They also looked to the *puvulam* to bring rain to their desert lands. Hupa shamans were usually women. The Hupa believed that a shaman was able to remove pains from those who were ill.

A Shaman's Power

Not everyone in a community could become a shaman. This power was passed down in certain ways. In Miwok communities men could become shamans if one of their father's ancestors had been a shaman. The Hupa believed that shamans got their power from the spirits of their mothers.

Shamans had a job similar to that of doctors today. When people became ill or troubled, they went to a shaman for help. Shamans then gave them medicines made from plants. Cahuilla healers used more than 200 different types of plants. Today scientists are testing one of them, the prickly pear cactus. They hope it will be a cure for diseases.

National Museum of the American Indian

A Luiseño shaman prays for rain (above). The tubes in his hands were considered part of his power. Children learn to make bead ornaments at a Yurok camp (right).

NATIVE AMERICANS TODAY

California today has a larger population of Native Americans than any other state except Oklahoma. More than 240,000 live in California.

Most of these people live in cities such as Los Angeles and San Francisco. The languages they speak, the foods they eat, the houses they live in, and the work they do are like those of any Californians. Yet many Native Americans keep alive the traditions of their ancestors. Some go to gatherings like the basket weavers' meeting at Ya-Ka-Ama. Some learn their ancestors' languages. When Matt Vera first spoke Yowlumni, he said, "The sound . . . was like a beautiful song filling the air."

WHY IT MATTERS

The Native Americans of California did more than just harvest the rich resources that nature provided. By burning certain areas, they restored the soil and encouraged the growth of useful plants and animals. Knowing how Native Americans managed the environment has helped Californians conserve our resources.

✔️ Reviewing Facts and Ideas

MAIN IDEAS

- The Cahuilla people learned to farm in the desert.
- Acorns were a main source of food for the Miwok and other groups.
- Shamans were an important part of every Native American culture.
- Many Native Americans today are keeping alive the cultures of their ancestors.

THINK ABOUT IT

1. What crops did the Cahuilla grow?
2. What was the role of a shaman?
3. **FOCUS** How did Native Americans live in the deserts and in the Central Valley?
4. **THINKING SKILL** _Predict_ whether or not Native Americans will continue to keep alive the cultures of their ancestors. Explain the reasons for your prediction.
5. **WRITE** Write a story about an acorn harvest or about what it is like to farm in the Colorado Desert.

STUDY SKILLS

Writing Outlines

VOCABULARY

outline

WHY THE SKILL MATTERS

You have just read about some of the Native American cultures of California. What if you were asked to give a short presentation to the class? How would you prepare? You might use an outline. An outline is a plan for organizing written information about a subject.

USING THE SKILL

One of the many native groups that lived in the Northeastern Culture area was the Yahi. The Yahi were a small group of the Yana people. The following short article tells about a man who was a member of this group. Try taking notes in your own words as you read. Write down the main ideas of what you are reading. You should also jot down important facts that support your main ideas.

Place a Roman numeral beside each main idea and a capital letter beside each fact. Under each of your main ideas, group the facts that support it.

Study the outline to the right to see how it organizes information. According to the outline, the first main idea is "Ishi's early years." Three facts support this idea.

A Yahi man called Ishi was born in the mid-1800s. He grew up at a time when his people were being attacked by newcomers settling California. Ishi and a small band of his people hid from the settlers for more than 20 years. By the summer of 1911, Ishi was the only Yahi left alive. He decided to come out of hiding.

Two scientists at the University of California learned about Ishi. They brought him to San Francisco to live at the university's museum. Ishi taught the scientists many things about Yahi culture. He showed them how to use a fire drill and how to chip arrowheads. He built a Yahi house near the museum. After less than five years of living at the museum, Ishi died on March 25, 1916.

I. Ishi's early years
  A. grew up when Yahi were under attack
  B. hid for more than 20 years
  C. came out of hiding in 1911

II. Life in San Francisco
  A. lived at a museum
  B. taught scientists about Yahi culture
  C. died in 1916

TRYING THE SKILL

Read the article below about two other groups who lived in the Northeastern Culture area. Take notes as you read, then write an outline. Use the Helping Yourself box for hints. What are your main ideas? What facts support them? Do main ideas or facts get Roman numerals in your outline?

REVIEWING THE SKILL

1. How does writing outlines help you organize information? How could you use this information?

2. In your outline, are obsidian and pumice main ideas or supporting facts?

3. How did you decide which statements were main ideas and which were supporting facts?

4. How can taking notes and writing an outline help you learn more about the Native American cultures of California?

National Museum of the American Indian

Theodora Kroeber wrote a book about Ishi (above) called *Ishi: Last of His Tribe.*

The largest Native American groups in the Northeastern Culture area were the Achumawi and the Atsugewi (AHT soo gay wee). Every fall the Atsugewi held a festival called the *pakapi*, or "big time." The *pakapi* was a time of feasting and playing games. At the feast the Atsugewi ate acorn mush, meat, and sunflower seeds. The games included foot races, archery contests, weightlifting, and wrestling.

The Achumawi lived in the mountainous region along the Pit River. Two important resources in their land came from volcanoes. One was a black stone called obsidian. Obsidian is actually a kind of hard glass formed in the heat of the volcano. From it the Achumawi chipped arrow points, spear points, knives, and scrapers. They used another volcanic stone, pumice, to smooth the shafts of their arrows.

CHAPTER 3 REVIEW

THINKING ABOUT VOCABULARY

Number a sheet of paper from 1 to 10. Beside each number write the word from the list that best matches the definition.

ancestor   harvest
artifact   irrigation
asphalt   religion
diversity   shaman
granary   tule

1. A gathering of a crop or resource
2. A kind of reed that can be used to build houses and boats
3. A person in your family who lived a long time before you
4. A building used for storing food
5. A thick tar that seeps to Earth's surface
6. A way of worshiping the God or gods a group's members believe in
7. The use of ditches or pipes to bring water to fields
8. A religious leader and healer
9. Something people in the past left behind that helps us learn about them
10. Many different kinds

THINKING ABOUT FACTS

1. According to archaeologists, for how many years have people been living in California?
2. How many different "culture areas" are there in California?
3. What are two things for which the Chumash used asphalt?
4. What are two things the Chumash used their *tomols* to do?
5. What types of things did the Chumash trade with the Tongva?
6. Who were the leaders of the Hupa?
7. Why did the Hupa have special religious ceremonies?
8. What were three kinds of foods the Miwok made from acorns?
9. How did the Miwok keep their soil fertile?
10. What were three powers that Native Americans believed shamans had?

THINK AND WRITE ◄▬

WRITING A JOURNAL
Suppose you are a Miwok child. Write a journal entry describing a day during the acorn harvest.

WRITING AN EXPLANATION
Write a paragraph that explains why *tomols* were important to the Chumash.

WRITING AN INTERVIEW
Suppose you are a reporter preparing for an interview with an archaeologist. Write three questions you might ask the archaeologist, along with possible answers.

APPLYING STUDY SKILLS

WRITING OUTLINES

1. How can writing outlines help you organize information?

2. What are the steps in writing an outline?

3. Reread Lesson 2, pages 68–69, about the Hupa. Take notes as you read, and then write an outline.

4. How did you decide which pieces of information in your outline were main ideas and which were supporting facts?

5. How can taking notes and writing an outline help you learn more about a subject?

Summing Up the Chapter

Use this vertical organization chart to organize information from the chapter. Copy the chart on a sheet of paper, and fill in the blank spaces. Then use it to write a paragraph that answers the question "How did California's resources make it possible for groups to settle in permanent villages?"

FIRST CALIFORNIANS

Resources they had:

How they used these resources:

PACIFIC COAST GROUPS

Resources they had:

How they used these resources:

DESERT AND CENTRAL VALLEY GROUPS

Resources they had:

How they used these resources:

CHAPTER 4

Europeans Explore California

THINKING ABOUT HISTORY AND GEOGRAPHY

For thousands of years Native Americans were the only people to live in California. In the 1500s something happened that would change the lives of these people and others around the world. Europeans came in ships to the Western Hemisphere. Read Chapter 4 to find out about the first Europeans to visit California.

PHILIPPINES
Manila

1520–1521
TENOCHTITLÁN

Cortés defeats the Aztec emperor Moctezuma II

1542
SAN DIEGO BAY

Cabrillo explores the coast

1579
DRAKES BAY

Drake repairs his ship

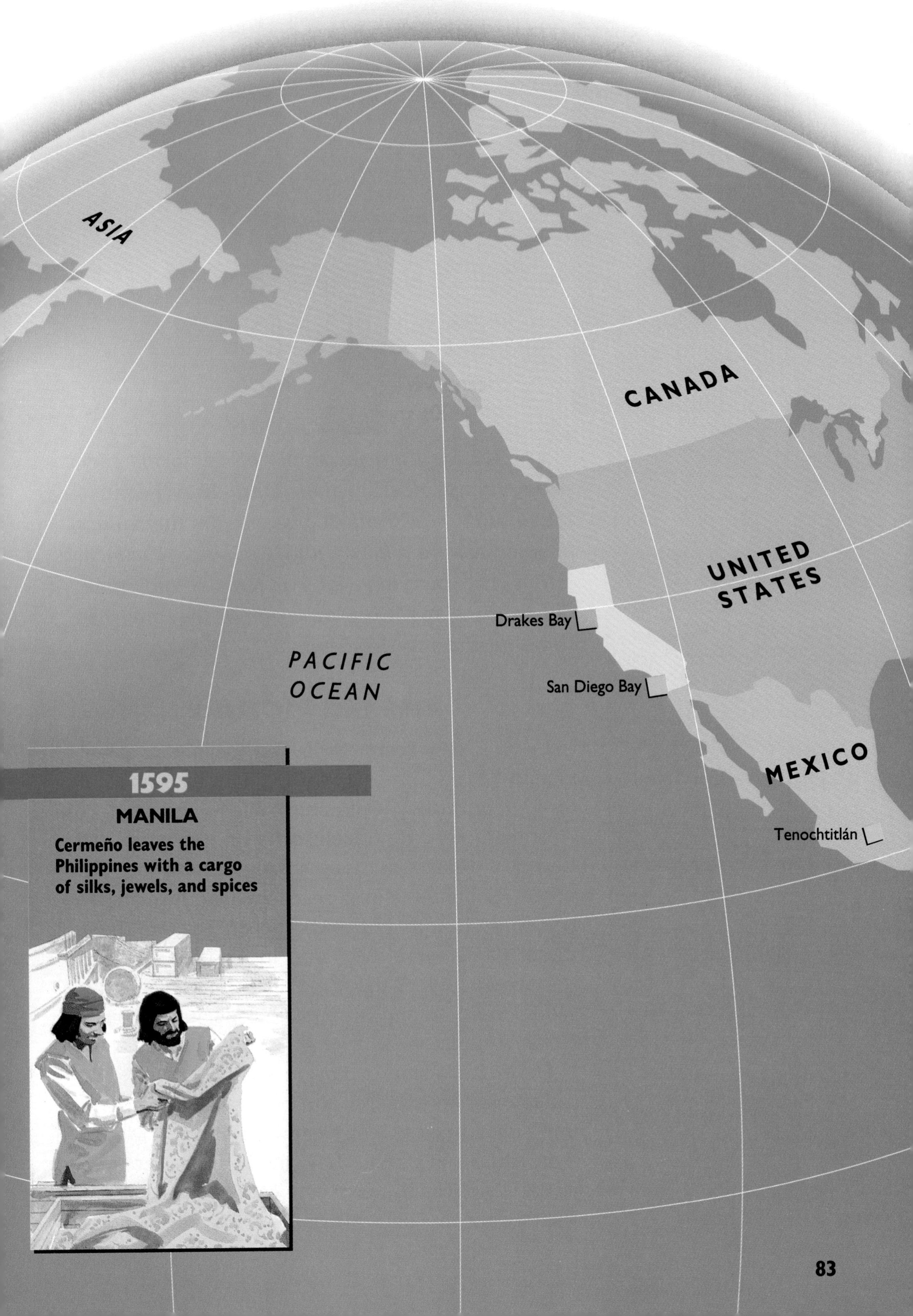

ASIA

CANADA

UNITED
STATES

Drakes Bay

San Diego Bay

MEXICO

Tenochtitlán

PACIFIC
OCEAN

1595

MANILA

Cermeño leaves the Philippines with a cargo of silks, jewels, and spices

THE SPANISH CLAIM CALIFORNIA

READ ALOUD

In 1542 the Tongva people of California saw strange ships nearing their land. They began "shouting . . . and making signs [for the sailors] to come ashore. Shortly [the Tongva] . . . launched a fine craft carrying eight or ten . . . and came out to the ships." The newcomers they met had come all the way from Spain.

THE BIG PICTURE

In 1492, fifty years earlier, an Italian sea captain named Christopher Columbus set out from Spain on a long journey. Columbus sailed west across the Atlantic Ocean. He hoped to find a new route from Europe to Asia. That way he could trade for Asian goods. Columbus never reached Asia. Instead, he landed on islands in the Caribbean Sea. He thought these islands were the Indies in Asia, so he called the people he met there Indians. Columbus and his sailors were among the first Europeans to visit North America.

Other European explorers soon followed Columbus. An explorer is a person who travels to unfamiliar places. Many came as conquistadors (kon KEES tah dorz). They planned to seize land in the Americas by force. In years to come, Spanish rulers claimed California as their own.

Focus Activity

READ TO LEARN
Who were the first Europeans to explore California?

VOCABULARY
conquistador
empire
colony
Strait of Anián
viceroy
expedition
slavery

PEOPLE
Christopher Columbus
Hernan Cortés
Moctezuma II
Juan Rodríguez Cabrillo
Bartolomé Ferrelo

PLACES
Tenochtitlán
New Spain
Point Mugu

NEW SPAIN

One of the explorers to follow Columbus was Hernan Cortés (kor TES). Like other Spanish conquistadors, Cortés was determined to conquer lands, find riches, and spread the Roman Catholic religion.

Cortés and Moctezuma II

In 1519 Cortés arrived in the land we now call Mexico. He set out to conquer the Aztec empire in central Mexico. An empire is a large area with different groups of people ruled by a single country or ruler. The Aztec empire was ruled by Moctezuma II (mahk tuh ZOO muh).

Cortés had only 500 soldiers. Along the way he joined some Indian enemies of the Aztec. When the Spanish arrived in Tenochtitlán (te noch tee TLAHN), the Aztec capital city, Cortés's soldiers captured Moctezuma. Later, during the fighting, the Aztec ruler was killed. The Spanish had to flee. Two years later, Cortés returned with more soldiers and weapons. Many Aztec grew sick and died from diseases carried by the Spanish. This time the Spanish captured Tenochtitlán and burned it to the ground.

The Spanish seized the Aztec empire of Moctezuma II (right) to mine its gold (above right).

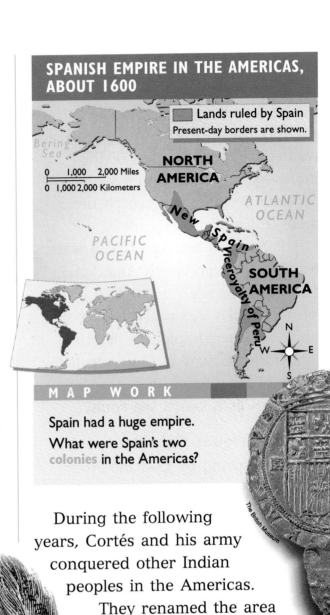

SPANISH EMPIRE IN THE AMERICAS, ABOUT 1600

Lands ruled by Spain
Present-day borders are shown.

Bering Sea

NORTH AMERICA

0   1,000   2,000 Miles
0   1,000 2,000 Kilometers

ATLANTIC OCEAN

PACIFIC OCEAN

New Spain

Viceroyalty of Peru

SOUTH AMERICA

N E S W

MAP WORK

Spain had a huge empire. What were Spain's two colonies in the Americas?

During the following years, Cortés and his army conquered other Indian peoples in the Americas. They renamed the area New Spain after their homeland. New Spain became the largest colony of the Spanish empire. A colony is a place that is ruled by another country. In many places conquistadors took the land and forced the Indians to work in the mines and fields that were once theirs. You can see part of the Spanish empire in the map above.

The British Museum

The Granger Collection

THE SEARCH FOR A SEA PASSAGE

The Spanish still hoped to find a sea route from Europe to Asia. They wanted to get the riches of the Indies—spices, beautiful silks, and precious jewels. That search brought them to California.

The Spanish believed that a waterway cut through North America. They called it the Strait of Anián (ah nee AHN). A strait is a narrow body of water. Explorers thought that the waterway might lie to the north of New Spain. We now know that there is no such sea route.

Juan Rodríguez Cabrillo

In the spring of 1542 the viceroy of New Spain gave Juan Rodríguez Cabrillo (kah BREE yoh), a conquistador and sea captain, an important job. A viceroy is a ruler picked by a king. The viceroy asked Cabrillo to make an expedition, or journey of exploration, along the coast of California. The viceroy hoped Cabrillo would find the Strait of Anián.

Cabrillo gathered a crew of about 250 soldiers and sailors.

About 24 of the crew were Africans and Indians held in slavery. Slavery is the practice of making one person the property of another. Some of the Africans were skilled in ship repair. They probably also worked as carpenters and sailmakers.

Cabrillo had only two small and poorly made ships, the *San Salvador* and the *Victoria*. The larger ship, the *San Salvador*, was just 100 feet long.

Heading North

Cabrillo set sail from Navidad, Mexico, on June 27, 1542. Travel was difficult because the sea and the wind along the coast both flowed from north to south, against the ships. For three months the tiny ships sailed slowly northward. The crew had to work long hours, and there was little to eat and drink.

On September 28 they entered what we now call San Diego Bay. Cabrillo was excited by the "closed and

The Cabrillo National Monument in San Diego has a statue of the explorer (far right). Most European explorers thought that California was an island off North America, as the English map from 1616 shows.

The Granger Collection

very good port." He decided to land. For six days he explored, gathering fresh water and food. He also met the local Kumeyaay people.

Sailing farther north, the ships passed near Tongva lands around present-day Los Angeles. As he looked out from his ship, Cabrillo noticed the air was thick with smoke. It was late fall, after the yearly seed harvest, and the Tongva people were burning off their land to make it ready for planting. Cabrillo called the place Bahía de los Fumos, "Bay of Smoke."

DID YOU KNOW?

How did California get its name?

No one knows for certain who gave California its name, but we do know where the name first appeared. A Spanish fantasy novel written in 1510 called *Las Sergas de Esplandián* (The Adventures of Esplandián) told of an island called California. It was said to be "very close to . . . Paradise" and ruled by Queen Calafía, who was "more beautiful than all the rest." Spanish explorers named California after this imaginary island.

Cabrillo and the Chumash

In mid-October the ships entered Chumash territory. Cabrillo wrote in his journal:

We saw an Indian town on the land next to the sea, with large houses built much like those of New Spain.

This was probably the village of Muwu, which means "beach" in Chumash. Today we call this place Point Mugu. Cabrillo was impressed by the "very good canoes, each of which held 12 or 13 Indians," that rowed out to meet his ships. So he called the place Pueblo de las Canoas, "Town of Canoes."

The Chumash gave Cabrillo some good news. They told him that far to the north, a great river flowed into the sea. Perhaps, Cabrillo thought, this was the Strait of Anián!

Cabrillo's crew sailed to the Channel Islands (above) to wait out winter storms.

DISAPPOINTMENT

By early November Cabrillo reached a point near present-day San Luis Obispo. A howling storm struck one night. The ships' sails ripped, and masts crashed to the decks. The crew prayed for their lives. Yet the storm delayed Cabrillo for only a few days. He continued to push his ships northward, reaching the mouth of what we now call the Russian River. Nowhere, however, could he find the Strait of Anián!

It was the middle of November. The winter weather made it too dangerous to continue. Greatly disappointed, Cabrillo ordered his damaged ships to turn south. They sailed to one of the islands in the Santa Barbara Channel to wait for better weather.

As the weeks dragged by, the Chumash on the island became impatient. They wanted the Spanish to leave. Perhaps the visitors had mistreated them. One of the sailors later said that "the Indians there never stopped fighting us." On Christmas Eve 1542, some of the sailors were attacked. Cabrillo went ashore to help his men. As he jumped from the boat, he slipped and fell on the hard, rocky ground. How serious was his injury?

MANY VOICES PRIMARY SOURCE

Excerpt from journal of Juan Rodríguez Cabrillo and Bartolomé Ferrelo, 1543.

While wintering at the island . . . on January 3, 1543, Juan Rodríguez, captain of these ships, departed this life from a fall . . . in which he broke an arm near the shoulder. He left as captain the chief pilot, Bartolomé Ferrelo. . . . At the time of his death he charged them [his crew] not to abandon the exploration of as much as possible of all that coast.

Ferrelo Takes Charge

The pilot Bartolomé Ferrelo became the leader of the expedition after Cabrillo's death. He ordered the crew to bury their lost commander on the island where he died. Ferrelo then called the island La Isla de Juan Rodríguez.

Ferrelo and the crew kept their promise to Cabrillo. In late February 1543, they left the Channel Islands and sailed northward once again. Historians are not sure how far north the expedition reached. It may have gotten as far as present-day Oregon.

We do know that the two ships became separated again in another terrible storm. This time both ships nearly sank. Giant waves crashed over the ships "as though over a rock." Several men died, and others became very ill. Once again the sailors prayed for their lives.

With the ships damaged and many of the supplies lost, Ferrelo decided to end the expedition. The ships arrived back in Navidad on April 14, 1543, nearly ten months after leaving. The journal says the crew was "sorrowful for having lost their commander."

The soldiers on Cabrillo's ships were armed with helmets and swords.

The Oakland Museum of California

The Seaver Center

WHY IT MATTERS

Cabrillo and Ferrelo failed to find the Strait of Anián. They did succeed in exploring lands that no Europeans had seen before. Soon large trading ships making their way from Asia to New Spain would sail into California's waters.

✔ Reviewing Facts and Ideas

MAIN IDEAS

- Europeans explored the Americas, searching for a sea route to Asia.
- Cortés defeated the Aztec and founded New Spain.
- Juan Cabrillo and Bartolomé Ferrelo led the first expedition of Europeans to explore California.

THINK ABOUT IT

1. Who were Cortés and Moctezuma II?

2. What was the main purpose of Cabrillo's expedition?

3. **FOCUS** Who were the first Europeans to explore California?

4. **THINKING SKILL** Why, do you think, did the Chumash people make the *decision* to tell Cabrillo that a great river lay far to the north?

5. **GEOGRAPHY** Look at the maps on pages 85 and 86. What are the similarities and differences between the two maps? Which do you suppose is more accurate?

89

National Geographic Image Collection

1500   1550   1579 1603   1650   1700

VOYAGES ON CALIFORNIA'S COAST

Focus Activity

READ TO LEARN
Why did Europeans explore California?

VOCABULARY
Northwest Passage
galleon

PEOPLE
Francis Drake
Sebastián Rodríguez
  Cermeño
Sebastián Vizcaíno

PLACES
Drakes Bay
Acapulco
Manila
Monterey Bay

READ ALOUD

In 1940 archaeologists digging in the ground near Point Reyes made an exciting discovery. They found Miwok beads over 350 years old! On closer examination the beads seemed unusual. They were made from bits of pottery that came all the way from China. How did Chinese pottery get to California? Who brought it?

THE BIG PICTURE

After Cabrillo, other explorers visited California. Spanish trading ships made a long journey across the Pacific to New Spain. An English sea captain named Francis Drake also explored California's coast. In 1577 the queen of England sent him to find a route to Asia through North America. What the Spanish called the Strait of Anián, the English called the Northwest Passage.

Still, Europeans knew little about California. Many years would pass before Europeans thought about living in California.

THE *GOLDEN HIND*

The queen gave Francis Drake another task. She ordered him "to annoy the King of Spain in his Indies." The queen meant Drake should attack Spanish ships and settlements and rob them.

Drake's ship, the *Golden Hind*, was at sea nearly two years. It was almost bursting with 60,000 pounds of stolen treasure. That is about the weight of 400 people. Drake knew that unless he found a place to land, his ship might sink!

Nova Albion

On June 17, 1579, Drake spotted "a convenient and fit harbor." He ordered the crew to land. The area's "white banks and cliffs" reminded him of England. So he called the land Nova Albion, or New England. Most historians believe the crew landed at Drakes Bay on the Point Reyes Peninsula. Drake stayed for six weeks. The crew unloaded the ship and fixed the leaks.

At first the Coast Miwok who lived nearby seemed scared of the strangers. Who were they? Where

National Portrait Gallery, London/Superstock

California Academy of Sciences

Archaeologists believe that this piece of a broken Chinese plate was dropped by Francis Drake (left) on Point Reyes Peninsula.

did they come from? After a time, however, the Miwok and the English started to trade. The Miwok held feasts for the crew and gave them food to take on board. A priest on the ship, Francis Fletcher, wrote that when the *Golden Hind* sailed away, the Miwok "ran to the tops of the hills to keep [it] in their sight as long as they could."

Drake left behind a plate of brass metal to claim the area for England. European explorers often claimed that the places they visited belonged to their country. They did not think it mattered that people already lived there.

Point Reyes Peninsula

SEARCH FOR A HARBOR

Drake's long journey made him a hero to the English. To the Spanish he was a thief and a pirate. With enemies like Drake on the ocean, how could the Spanish ships be safe?

Manila Galleons

Each year Spain sent one galleon between its colonies in New Spain and the Philippines. A galleon is a big, heavy ship for carrying cargo, or goods. You can see the route of the galleon below. It left from Acapulco and carried gold and silver from New Spain to Manila, the capital of the Philippines. It returned filled with silks, jewels, spices, and pottery from Asia. Look at the diagram to learn more about the galleons.

Westward winds and ocean currents sped the galleon from Acapulco to Manila in about three months. The return, however, took twice as long—half a year or more!

The return was also dangerous. The crew suffered from hunger, thirst, and scurvy. Scurvy is a sickness caused by a lack of vitamin C. It can make a sailor's teeth fall out or even kill him. The Spanish ships needed a place to find food, fresh water, and safety.

Cermeño Searches the Coast

Sebastián Rodríguez Cermeño (ser ME nyoh) was an experienced

Route of Manila Galleon

California

Pacific Ocean

Manila

Acapulco

N W E S

KEEL

and dependable ship captain. In 1595 the viceroy put Cermeño in charge of the Manila galleon. He was to sail from Manila to the California coast. There he would search for a safe harbor.

Cermeño left the Philippines on July 5, 1595. His ship, the *San Agustín*, was crowded with crates of cargo. Yet it reached the California coast in record time. Cermeño sighted land around Cape Mendocino in early November.

A storm soon struck. It nearly wrecked the *San Agustín*. But Cermeño was determined to explore California. On November 6, 1595,

92

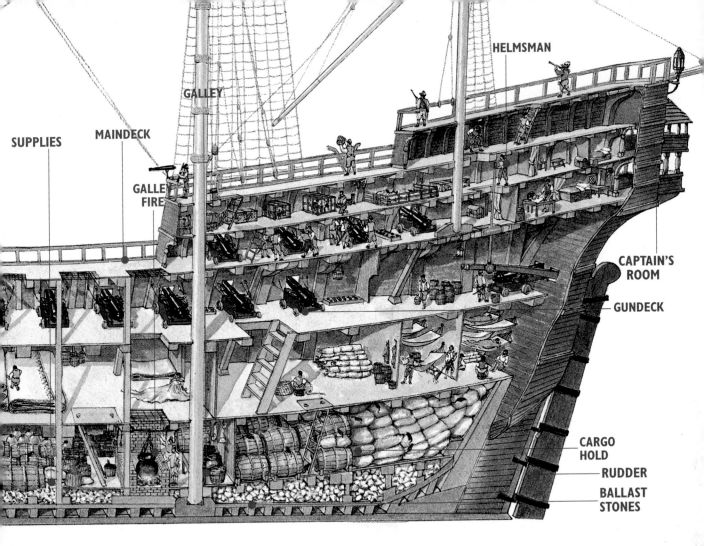

SUPPLIES

MAINDECK

GALLEY

GALLEY FIRE

HELMSMAN

CAPTAIN'S ROOM

GUNDECK

CARGO HOLD

RUDDER

BALLAST STONES

the ship anchored in a bay with white cliffs and sandy beaches. It was the same bay that Drake had visited 16 years earlier! Unlike Drake, however, Cermeño had arrived at the peak of the winter storm season.

Shipwreck

On November 30 a violent storm hit. The waves pounded the galleon against the shore. In a few hours the ship was in pieces. Its cargo washed ashore or sank. The Miwok beads you read about in the Read Aloud were probably made from pottery lost from the *San Agustín*.

One small open boat was not damaged. Cermeño's crew begged him to

return home quickly. But Cermeño refused. All 70 men had to squeeze on board the tiny boat. For food they had acorns given to them by the Coast Miwok.

Amazingly, Cermeño spent two more months searching for a harbor. He and the crew made maps of Monterey Bay and many other points along the coast.

In late January 1596, the small boat reached Navidad, New Spain. All the precious cargo was lost. A Spanish official wrote to the viceroy:

The vessel being so small it seems miraculous that [it] . . . reached this country with so many people on board.

Infographic

European Explorers in California

From 1542 to 1603, explorers from Spain and England made voyages along the California coast. When their journeys ended, they returned to their homes, leaving California to the Native Americans who lived there. Study the Infographic to learn more about these explorers' journeys.

TO MANILA 7,000 MILES

CAPE MENDOCINO

VIZCAÍNO

Expedition led by Francis Drake lands, June–July 1579.

POINT REYES

San Agustín destroyed, Nov. 30, 1595.

CABRILLO

DRAKE

MONTEREY BAY

Vizcaíno names Monterey Bay, Dec. 16, 1602.

CERMEÑO

POINT CONCEPTION

POINT MUGU

TO MEXICO CITY 1,450 MILES

TO ACAPULCO 1,650 MILES

TO NAVIDAD 1,350 MILES

Cabrillo dies, Jan. 3, 1543. Bartolomé Ferrelo takes command.

CHANNEL

ISLANDS

FERRELO

Cabrillo expedition meets Chumash people.

Cabrillo expedition lands in San Diego Bay, Sept. 28, 1542.

| JUAN CABRILLO (1542–1543) | FRANCIS DRAKE (1579) | SEBASTIÁN RODRÍGUEZ CERMEÑO (1595) | SEBASTIÁN VIZCAÍNO (1602–1603) |

N E S W

SEBASTIÁN VIZCAÍNO

In 1602 the viceroy sent another expedition to search California for a safe harbor. He picked Sebastián Vizcaíno (vees kah EE noh) to lead it. The viceroy promised Vizcaíno that if the expedition was a success, he would be made captain of the next Manila galleon. That could make Vizcaíno rich.

Vizcaíno was proud and boastful. When he visited places named by earlier explorers, he often gave them new names. For example, the place Cabrillo named Cabo Galera, Vizcaíno renamed Punta de Concepción. We call it Point Conception.

Vizcaíno bragged about what the expedition achieved. When he returned, he told the king of Spain that Monterey Bay was "all that can be [wanted] . . . for ships making the voyage [from] the Philippines [because it is safe] from all winds." Actually, winds from the ocean made the bay very dangerous, as you can see in the photo above. Why, do you think, did Vizcaíno not tell the truth?

After Vizcaíno's expedition, Spain lost interest in California for over 150 years. Because of fast ocean currents, the trip from California to Acapulco did not take long. It was not worth building a port in Monterey Bay. California remained a land of Native Americans. In the next chapter you will read how that changed when Spain sent settlers to California.

WHY IT MATTERS

Trade routes in the Pacific Ocean played an important role in California's past. They made Europeans interested in California's location. Today trade with countries across the Pacific is still an important part of our lives.

✔/// Reviewing Facts and Ideas

MAIN IDEAS

- Francis Drake landed in Coast Miwok territory in 1579.
- Manila galleons sailed between the Philippines and New Spain.
- Spanish explorers searched the California coast for a safe harbor for trading ships in the Pacific.

THINK ABOUT IT

1. What were the purposes of Drake's expedition?

2. What bay did Vizcaíno say would make a good harbor?

3. **FOCUS** Why did Europeans explore California?

4. **THINKING SKILL** Why did Cermeño *decide* to continue his voyage after the shipwreck?

5. **WRITE** Suppose you are a Miwok who met Francis Drake. Write an account of the meeting to share with people in a neighboring village.

GEOGRAPHY SKILLS

Using Latitude and Longitude

VOCABULARY

latitude
parallel
degree
longitude
prime meridian
meridian
global grid

WHY THE SKILL MATTERS

In the last lesson you read about how Cermeño's ship the *San Agustín* was destroyed in a winter storm. Suppose you are searching for some of the treasure that was lost when the ship broke apart. Your only clue is an old map. The writing on the map is faded, but you can just make out some lines that cross each other like a tic-tac-toe grid. Each line has a number on it.

You discover that these are imaginary lines invented long ago by mapmakers. The lines describe the location of particular places. They provide an "address" for every place on Earth.

Airline pilots use the same system to keep track of where they are. Up among the clouds a pilot must be sure of a plane's location at all times. Pilots also need an exact way to explain where they are going.

The faded lines on the map will help you find Cermeño's lost treasure. You will use these imaginary lines on maps in this book and in many other books.

USING LATITUDE

Let's study these imaginary lines. Look at the map on this page and place your finger on the equator. This is the starting point for measuring latitude. Latitude is a measure of how far north or south a place is from the equator.

Geographers also call lines of latitude parallels because they are parallel lines. Parallel lines always remain the same distance apart.

Each line of latitude has a number. You can see that the equator is labeled 0°, meaning zero degrees. Degrees are used to measure the distance on Earth's

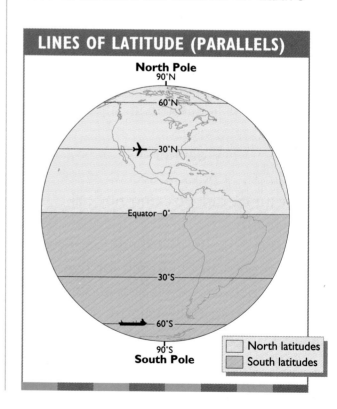

LINES OF LATITUDE (PARALLELS)

North Pole
90°N
60°N
30°N
Equator–0°
30°S
60°S
90°S
South Pole

North latitudes
South latitudes

surface. The symbol ° stands for degrees. Look again at the map. What is the latitude of the equator?

Now look at the lines of latitude north of the equator. Notice that these parallels are labeled N for "north." The North Pole has a latitude, too, which is 90°N. The parallels south of the equator are labeled S for "south." The latitude of the South Pole is 90°S.

Find the ship on the map. The ship is sailing west. It is located at 60°S. Now find the small airplane on the map. Along which parallel is it flying?

USING LONGITUDE

Now look at the map on this page. It shows lines of longitude. Like parallels, these are imaginary lines on a map or globe. But instead of measuring distance north or south, they measure distance east or west of the prime meridian. *Prime* means "first." Lines of longitude are also called meridians. The prime meridian is the first line, or starting place, for measuring lines of longitude. That's why the prime meridian is marked 0° on the map. Put your finger on the prime meridian. It runs through the western parts of Europe and Africa.

Look at the meridians to the west of the prime meridian. These lines are labeled W for "west." The lines to the east of the prime meridian are labeled E for "east." Longitude is measured up to 180° east of the prime meridian and up to 180° west of the prime meridian. Since 180°E and 180°W fall on the same line,

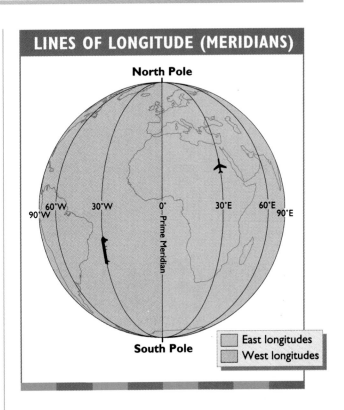

LINES OF LONGITUDE (MERIDIANS)

North Pole

90°W 60°W 30°W 0° Prime Meridian 30°E 60°E 90°E

South Pole

East longitudes
West longitudes

this line is marked neither E nor W. The line labeled 180° runs through the Pacific Ocean.

Unlike lines of latitude, meridians are not parallel to one another. Earth is round. Meridians divide Earth into pieces like the sections of an orange. Look at the map on this page again. As you can see, the meridians are far apart at the equator. They meet, however, at the North Pole and the South Pole.

Lines of longitude measure degrees east and west. Look at the ship on the map. It is sailing along the meridian known as 30°W. Now look at the airplane on the same map. It is flying over the continent of Africa. What meridian is it flying over? In which direction is the airplane traveling?

GEOGRAPHYSKILLS

GLOBAL GRID

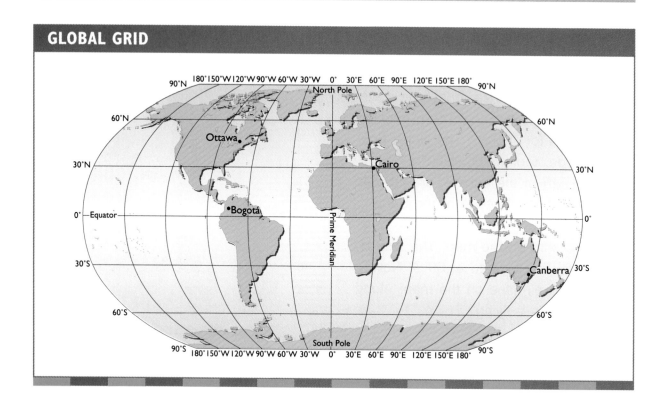

FINDING PLACES ON A MAP

In order to use latitude lines and longitude lines to find places, you must combine them on the same map. Look at the map of the world on this page. You can see that the lines of latitude and the lines of longitude cross to form a grid on the map. A grid is a set of crisscrossing lines.

The grid on this map is called a global grid because it covers the entire Earth. By using the global grid, you can locate the "address" of any place in the world. Look at the map again. Find Canberra, Australia, and Bogotá, Colombia. Which of these two cities is closer to the equator? How can you tell?

Now find Ottawa, Canada. Is this city east or west of the prime meridian? Find Cairo, Egypt. Is Cairo east or west of the prime meridian? Is Cairo north or south of the equator?

Look at the latitude and longitude map of California on the opposite page. Find Lake Tahoe. As you can see, it lies about halfway between 40°N latitude and 38°N. Its latitude is 39°N. You can also see that 120°W longitude runs right through the middle of the lake. So we say that the location or "address" of Lake Tahoe is about 39°N, 120°W.

When you locate a place on a map, you must always give the latitude first and the longitude second. You must also remember to give north or south for the latitude and east or west for the longitude. To describe a place that is not exactly at the point where two lines cross, you must use the closest lines.

TRYING THE SKILL

Try to find a city in California by its "address." This city is located at about 42°N, 124°W. What is the name of the city? Now describe the location of Los Angeles using latitude and longitude.

On your buried-treasure map are the following numbers: 38°N, 123°W. Do you understand what those

numbers mean? Where is your treasure buried? Start digging!

REVIEWING THE SKILL

Many maps include a grid of latitude and longitude. Use the California map on this page to answer these questions.

1. What are lines of latitude and longitude? How can they be helpful?

2. Give the approximate location of Sacramento using latitude and longitude.

3. Name two cities that share the same latitude. Name two cities that share the same longitude.

4. How did you find the answer to the last question?

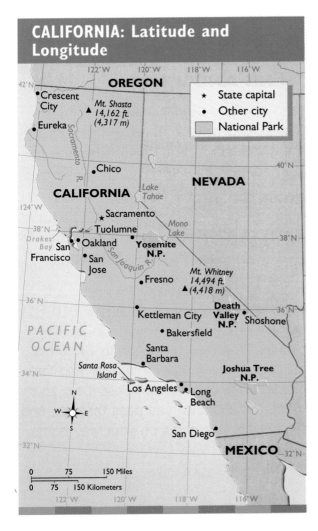

CALIFORNIA: Latitude and Longitude

CHAPTER 4 REVIEW

THINKING ABOUT VOCABULARY

Number a sheet of paper from 1 to 10. Next to each number write the word or term from the list that best completes the sentence.

colony   galleon
conquistador   latitude
degree   longitude
empire   prime meridian
expedition   slavery

1. An _____ is a journey of exploration.

2. A place that is ruled by another country is a _____.

3. The _____ is the starting place for measuring lines of longitude.

4. A _____ is a big ship that carries cargo or goods.

5. An _____ is a large area with different groups of people ruled by a single country or leader.

6. _____ is the practice of making one person the property of another.

7. _____ measures how far north or south a place is from the equator.

8. A _____ is someone who conquered lands by force.

9. _____ is the distance east or west of the prime meridian.

10. A _____ is used to measure distances on Earth's surface.

THINKING ABOUT FACTS

1. Why did some Indian groups join Cortés?

2. What helped Cortés defeat the Aztec?

3. Where did the Spanish believe the Strait of Anián was located? Why was it important for them to find it?

4. Why did Ferrelo end the expedition to find the Strait of Anián?

5. What did the English call the Strait of Anián?

6. What did Drake steal from the Spanish?

7. What kinds of items did the Spanish galleons bring back from the Philippines?

8. How did Drake claim Drakes Bay for England?

9. How did the Miwok show friendship to the English?

10. What did Cermeño make maps of?

THINK AND WRITE ◄═══▷

WRITING AN ADVERTISEMENT

Design and write a job advertisement for a sea captain in the 1500s. Describe the job and skills needed.

WRITING A JOURNAL

Suppose you are one of the sailors on the *San Agustín.* Write a journal entry describing what it is like on the ship.

WRITING AN EXPLANATION

Look at the world map on pages R10–R11 of this book. Imagine you are in another country. You must get back to California going only along lines of latitude and longitude. Write a paragraph describing your route, the countries you pass through, and the oceans you cross on your way home.

APPLYING GEOGRAPHY SKILLS

USING LONGITUDE AND LATITUDE

Answer the following questions about the map on this page to practice your skills with latitude and longitude.

1. What are lines of latitude and longitude?

2. What line of latitude is Los Angeles on?

3. What city is north of 38°N latitude and east of 122°W longitude?

4. What cities are located between 36°N and 38°N latitude? What cities are located between 120°W and 118°W longitude?

5. Why is it important to understand latitude and longitude?

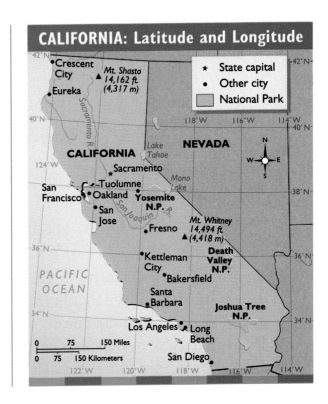

CALIFORNIA: Latitude and Longitude

Summing Up the Chapter

Use the following semantic map to organize information from the chapter. Copy the map on a sheet of paper. Then write at least one piece of information in each blank circle. When you have filled in the map, use it to write a paragraph that answers the question "What did explorers learn about California from their expeditions?"

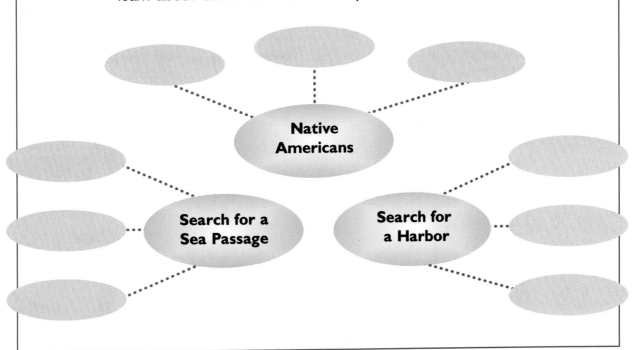

Native Americans

Search for a Sea Passage

Search for a Harbor

CHAPTER 5

Spanish California

THINKING ABOUT HISTORY AND GEOGRAPHY

Europeans first visited California in the 1500s. It was not until the 1700s, however, that Europeans began to settle here. What brought Europeans to California? What beliefs did these newcomers have? How did these beliefs differ from those of California's Native Americans? Read on to learn how the Europeans changed California forever.

1769

BAJA CALIFORNIA

Gaspar de Portolá leads the "Sacred Expedition"

1769

SAN DIEGO

Junípero Serra founds Mission San Diego in Kumeyaay land

1777

SAN JOSE

The first Spanish town is founded

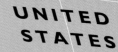

UNITED
STATES

San Jose

CALIFORNIA

Los Angeles

San Diego

Baja California

PACIFIC
OCEAN

1785

LOS ANGELES

Toypurina and Nicolas José lead a revolt at Mission San Gabriel

THE "SACRED EXPEDITION"

Focus Activity

READ TO LEARN
Why did the Spanish decide to settle in California?

VOCABULARY
mission
missionary
convert

PEOPLE
José de Gálvez
Junípero Serra
Gaspar de Portolá
Juan Crespí
José Ortega

PLACES
San Diego Bay
Monterey Bay
San Francisco Bay

READ ALOUD

"We left this port of San Diego, traveling by land . . . towards the north, to go in search of the much praised port of Monterey." A Spanish priest named Juan Crespí wrote these words in 1770. He had just returned from an expedition to find Monterey Bay.

THE BIG PICTURE

As you read in Chapter 4, the Spanish lost interest in California after the voyage of Vizcaíno. They did not try to settle it for another 167 years. Instead, they slowly spread their rule over northern Mexico, Baja (lower) California, and lands we now call Arizona, New Mexico, Texas, Louisiana, and Florida.

The key to their efforts was the building of missions. A mission is a religious settlement where Spanish priests, called padres (PAH drayz), taught Native Americans the Roman Catholic religion. Spanish leaders hoped to gain the loyalty of Native Americans by changing their way of life.

In 1765 a man named José de Gálvez, a special official of the Spanish king, arrived in New Spain. Gálvez made a decision that would change life in California forever.

THE SPANISH RETURN TO CALIFORNIA

José de Gálvez was a very ambitious man. He hoped to become important by founding new settlements for Spain. California seemed like the perfect place.

Gálvez told the Spanish king that settling California would bring new riches to the empire. He also reminded the king that Russian hunters and fishermen had visited the coast north of California. Unless Spain settled California, Russia or England might take it for their own. The king agreed with Gálvez. In 1768 Gálvez announced his plan to begin setting up missions in California.

This statue of Serra is at Mission San Gabriel. Gálvez is shown on a Spanish postage stamp.

Gálvez then turned to a padre named Father Junípero Serra (hoo NEE pe roh SE rah). Father Serra had come from Spain in 1749 to be a missionary. A missionary teaches religious beliefs to others who have different beliefs. By 1768 he led all the missions in Baja California.

Father Serra believed in his faith very strongly. He felt it was his duty as a missionary to convert Native Americans. To convert means to change a person's religious beliefs. Serra believed that if Native Americans became Roman Catholic, they would go to heaven after they died. He hoped to gather a "harvest of souls" among the Native Americans.

Gálvez asked Father Serra to start a new chain of missions in California. For Serra this would be a "Sacred Expedition." *Sacred* means "holy," or very religious. For Gálvez and other Spanish leaders, it was also a journey for riches and glory.

The Granger Collection

3 PTAS

JOSÉ DE GALVEZ

CORREOS
ESPAÑA
F. N. M. T.

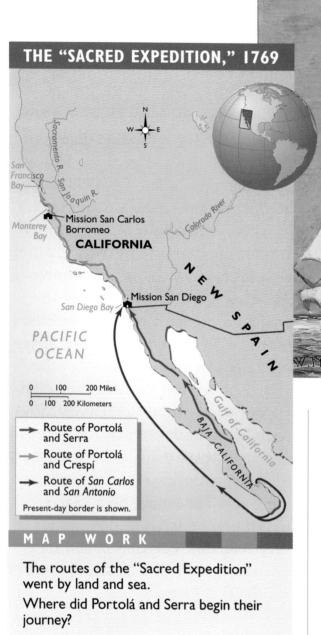

Mission San Carlos Borromeo
CALIFORNIA

Monterey Bay

San Francisco Bay

Sacramento R.
San Joaquin R.
Colorado River

NEW SPAIN

Mission San Diego
San Diego Bay

PACIFIC OCEAN

Gulf of California
BAJA CALIFORNIA

0   100   200 Miles
0   100   200 Kilometers

→ Route of Portolá and Serra
→ Route of Portolá and Crespí
→ Route of San Carlos and San Antonio

Present-day border is shown.

M A P   W O R K

The routes of the "Sacred Expedition" went by land and sea.

Where did Portolá and Serra begin their journey?

THE EXPEDITION SETS OUT

José de Gálvez planned the expedition well. He studied the maps and read the descriptions made by earlier explorers. He decided to locate the first settlement on the shores of San Diego Bay. The second settlement would be at Monterey Bay. There Gálvez expected to find the safe harbor that Vizcaíno had told of.

The expedition was divided into five parties, or groups. Two would travel by land and three by sea. The plan was to meet at San Diego. Trace the routes on the map at left.

Gálvez chose a captain in the Spanish army, Gaspar de Portolá (GAHS pahr DE por toh LAH), to lead the expedition. Nearly 300 missionaries, soldiers, sailors, carpenters, blacksmiths, mule drivers, and cooks were under Portolá's command.

Many of these people came from Spain. Catholic Indians from missions in New Spain also joined the expedition. Other members of the party, like the sailor Ignacio Ramírez and the doctor Pedro Prat, had African ancestors.

By Sea and by Land

The first small ship set sail from Baja California early in 1769. Shouts of *"Buen viaje!"*—"Have a

good trip!"—rang out as it sailed away from the port.

The first of the land parties left in March. Captain Portolá and Father Serra were in the last group to leave. They got underway in May.

Soon Serra met a group of Cochimí Indians. They exchanged gifts. Other meetings were not so friendly. At one point soldiers fired their guns to scare away an armed group of Native Americans that was following along the hilltops.

Hardships

As the expedition moved slowly northward, Serra began to suffer from an old leg wound. Portolá advised him to turn back. Serra refused. He wrote in his diary:

I trust that God will give me the strength to reach San Diego, as He has given me the strength to come so far. . . . Even though I [might] die on the way I shall not turn back.

A mule driver treated Serra's leg with a mixture of herbs. Soon Serra was able to walk again.

The expedition crossed harsh deserts in northern Mexico. Day after day the sun beat down. The soil was dry and rocky. The wind cut into the skin of men and animals. Food supplies ran low. Many members of the expedition became sick. Some died from scurvy. Others were starving. They did not know how to find food in this environment.

After six weeks of travel, the expedition neared San Diego. Some Kumeyaay people greeted the travelers with baskets of fresh fish.

When Father Serra saw San Diego Bay, he was filled with joy. When he saw two ships anchored in the bay, he wrote in his diary: "Thanks be to God."

Ships carried kits, like this one from the 1700s, to fix torn sails.

THE FIRST SPANISH SETTLEMENTS

Serra's joy soon turned to sadness. Only half of the crew remained. Nearly all of the Christian Indians had either died or left the expedition. One ship had been lost at sea. On the other two, many sailors had died from scurvy.

Portolá sent one of the ships, the *San Antonio*, back for new supplies. With about 60 men he then headed north to search for Monterey Bay. In a letter to a friend, he wrote:

I gathered the small portion of food which had not been spoiled in the ships and went on by land with that small company of persons, or rather skeletons, who had been spared by scurvy, hunger, and thirst.

Serra stayed in San Diego to care for the sick. There, on July 16, he founded Mission San Diego de Alcalá near a large Kumeyaay village. The San Diego River offered plenty of fresh water. Along the river grew trees for timber. The land was fertile.

good

The Journey Northward

Serra sent Father Juan Crespí (kres PEE) along with Portolá. Crespí kept a journal of the trip. Does his description of the Chumash villages along the Santa Barbara Channel remind you of what Cabrillo wrote 227 years before?

MANY VOICES
PRIMARY SOURCE

Excerpt from letter by Juan Crespí, February 6, 1770.

*This channel of Santa Barbara is very well settled, with towns composed of large huts roofed with thatch [reeds and branches] and with a very great number of peaceable and friendly Indians. . . . As we looked at [one town] from a distance it appeared that it might have a hundred houses, at least as many as that, and the number might amount to two hundred. We **conjectured** that this village alone might have about eight hundred souls.*

conjectured: guessed

Thomas Moran painted rocky Monterey Bay in 1912.

time he recognized it as the one Vizcaíno described. On June 3, 1770, Serra founded California's second mission, San Carlos Borromeo (bor roh ME oh), at the bay.

WHY IT MATTERS

The "Sacred Expedition" marked the beginning of European settlement in California. In the years to come, contact between people of different cultures would have huge effects on life in California.

✓ Reviewing Facts and Ideas

MAIN IDEAS

- José de Gálvez decided in 1768 that Spain should settle California.
- The "Sacred Expedition" faced many hardships.
- Junípero Serra founded missions at the bays of San Diego and Monterey.

THINK ABOUT IT

1. Who was José de Gálvez?
2. What did Junípero Serra believe was his duty as a missionary?
3. **FOCUS** Why did the Spanish decide to build settlements in California?
4. **THINKING SKILL** Make a *prediction* about how the coming of the Spanish would change life in California.
5. **GEOGRAPHY** Compare the map on page 106 to the Atlas map on page R10. What two countries today are on the lands crossed by the "Sacred Expedition" in the 1700s?

Where Is Monterey?

After many weeks Portolá reached Monterey Bay. The bay did not look at all like the fine harbor "sheltered from all winds" that Vizcaíno had described. So Portolá did not know that his party had reached its goal.

Heading farther north, however, one of Portolá's soldiers made an important discovery. From the top of a hill, near Pacifica, Sergeant José Ortega first saw San Francisco Bay. Crespí described it as "a very large and fine harbor," big enough to hold the warships of "all Europe." The party could not get around the bay. Portolá and his party went back to San Diego.

In March the *San Antonio* returned with supplies. Once again, Portolá went in search of Monterey Bay. This

THINKING SKILLS

Identifying Cause and Effect

VOCABULARY

cause

effect

WHY THE SKILL MATTERS

In the last lesson you learned that Junípero Serra was a very religious man. He believed it was his duty to convert Native Americans to Roman Catholicism. Because of this belief he led the expedition to build missions in California.

Serra's religious belief is a cause—something that makes something else happen. Leading the expedition is an effect of Serra's belief. An effect is what happens as a result of something else.

Understanding cause and effect allows you to connect facts in a meaningful way. It explains *why* things happen.

USING THE SKILL

José de Gálvez became Visitor-General in 1765. This was an important position in the government of New Spain. It gave Gálvez a lot of wealth and power. He wanted to make Spain's empire larger by building settlements in California.

Because of his ambition, Gálvez organized the "Sacred Expedition." He did everything he could to make it a success. He went to Baja California

to inspect the ships before they sailed. He even carried some of the supplies on board. As the ships left for San Diego, he sailed alongside in a small boat.

Gálvez's careful planning helped make the expedition a success. As a result, the king of Spain chose Gálvez to be Minister of the Indies, one of the most important jobs in the Spanish empire.

In this account of the "Sacred Expedition," Gálvez's ambition was the main *cause*. His ambition made the expedition happen. The expedition was an *effect*. It took place as a result of many things. Sometimes an effect has more than one cause.

Often an effect becomes a cause of something else in turn. If you think of the success of the "Sacred Expedition" as a cause, what was one of its effects?

TRYING THE SKILL

Read the two paragraphs below to find connections between causes and effects. Use the Helping Yourself box for hints.

"Native Americans joined the missions for different reasons. Some believed the missionaries had great religious power. Others joined because the missionaries offered them colored cloth and other gifts.

"Once the missions were well established, Native Americans joined for other

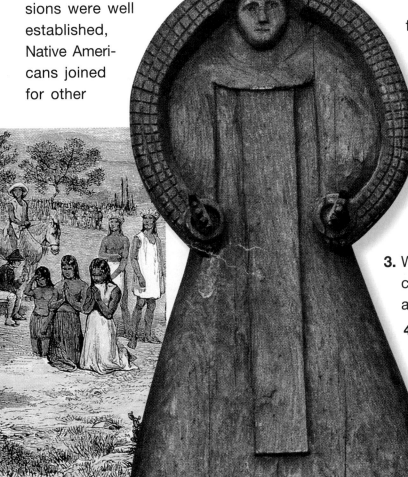

reasons. Many came to get food because their lands had been taken by the missions. Others came because they had no choice. Soldiers forced them from their homes and villages. Sometimes missionaries would convert young children and make them live at the mission. The parents then came to the mission to be with their children."

What were some causes of Native Americans joining the missions? Is the use of force a cause or an effect? Which fact might be seen as both a cause and an effect?

REVIEWING THE SKILL

1. What is a cause? What is an effect?

2. What can you do to identify connections between causes and effects?

3. Why is it useful to understand causes and effects when reading about the "Sacred Expedition"?

4. How might identifying cause and effect help you understand history?

Padres disapproved of the soldiers playing cards (far left). An Ohlone probably carved the statue (left) of St. Benedict.

111

1725   1750   **1776**   **1800**   1825

EARLY SPANISH SETTLEMENTS

Focus Activity

READ TO LEARN
What types of settlements did the Spanish have in California?

VOCABULARY
frontier
presidio
pueblo
alcalde
plaza

PEOPLE
Fermín Lasuén
Felipe de Neve
Francisco Reyes

PLACES
El Camino Real
San Jose
Los Angeles

READ ALOUD

Father Serra was glad to come to California, where he could reach his goal of converting Native Americans. "After desiring this for so many years," he wrote in his journal, he was thankful "for the favor of being among the [non-Christians] in their own land."

THE BIG PICTURE

Spanish missionaries, such as Serra, were not the only newcomers to North America in the 1700s. Settlers from England, France, and other countries also came. England, for example, had 13 colonies on the Atlantic Coast.

In 1776 the Spanish founded a mission near San Francisco Bay. Does that year ring a bell? On July 4, 1776, people from the 13 English colonies signed the Declaration of Independence. That statement said that the colonies were a separate country—the United States. We celebrate this date every year on Independence Day.

British Museum

112

A CHAIN OF MISSIONS

Father Serra founded nine missions. After Serra died in 1784, Father Fermín Lasuén (fer MEEN lahs WEN) added nine more.

Each mission was about a day's walk from the next. A dusty trail known as El Camino Real connected them. Each mission was located near Native American villages. There had to be a water supply and fertile soil. Look at the map. How many missions were there in all?

More than a thousand Native Americans lived and worked at the largest missions. Smaller ones had populations of a few hundred. Two priests ran each mission, with help from Spanish assistants.

Half a dozen soldiers also lived at each mission. Their job was to enforce the padres' rules. Breaking the rules often led to strong punishment such as beating and even death.

DID YOU KNOW?

What was California's first highway?

El Camino Real means "The Royal Road." The Spanish settlers named it in honor of the king of Spain. You can still walk on some parts of El Camino Real. Today Route 101 follows much of the path of California's first highway.

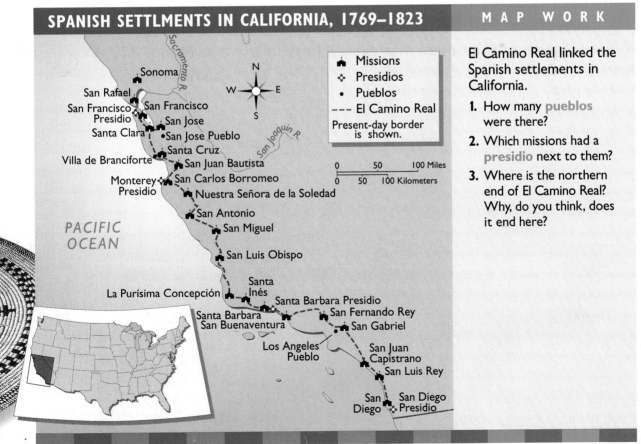

SPANISH SETTLMENTS IN CALIFORNIA, 1769–1823

Sacramento R.

Sonoma
San Rafael
San Francisco
San Francisco Presidio
San Jose
Santa Clara
San Jose Pueblo
Santa Cruz
Villa de Branciforte
San Juan Bautista
San Joaquin R.
Monterey Presidio
San Carlos Borromeo
Nuestra Señora de la Soledad
San Antonio
San Miguel
PACIFIC OCEAN
San Luis Obispo
Santa Inés
La Purísima Concepción
Santa Barbara Presidio
Santa Barbara
San Fernando Rey
San Buenaventura
San Gabriel
Los Angeles Pueblo
San Juan Capistrano
San Luis Rey
San Diego
San Diego Presidio

N
W E
S

- Missions
- Presidios
- Pueblos
- - - El Camino Real
Present-day border is shown.

0   50   100 Miles
0   50   100 Kilometers

MAP WORK

El Camino Real linked the Spanish settlements in California.

1. How many pueblos were there?

2. Which missions had a presidio next to them?

3. Where is the northern end of El Camino Real? Why, do you think, does it end here?

PRESIDIOS AND PUEBLOS

Other types of settlements helped protect the Spanish frontier. A frontier is the edge of an area that a group of people have settled.

Presidios for California

The Spanish also built presidios (pre SEE dee ohz). These were forts where soldiers lived. You can see them on the map on page 113. How many did they build?

The presidios guarded against enemy ships. They also guarded against attacks by Native Americans who were angry at the way the Spanish treated them. Each presidio had around 60 soldiers. The soldiers at the presidios were armed with swords, spears, and guns. They carried shields and wore thick deer-skin jackets.

The soldiers and the missionaries did not always get along well. The missionaries wanted to build more missions. The soldiers, however, were cautious. More missions meant more places for them to protect. Missionaries also complained that the soldiers were having a bad effect on the Native Americans. A padre named Father Estevan Tapis (es TE vahn TAHP ees) complained that the soldiers at the Santa Barbara Presidio were teaching the Native Americans to "become experts in playing cards."

California Pueblos

One of the biggest problems for the presidios was a lack of food. Governor Felipe de Neve (fe LEE pe DE NE ve) hoped to solve this problem by founding pueblos, or towns for farming. Neve offered people "cash, supplies, tools, animals, clothing [and] land" to settle in California. In return, the settlers agreed to give food to the presidios.

The first pueblo was founded at San Jose in 1777. Its settlers included 14 soldiers and their fami-

lies from the presidios of Monterey and San Francisco. Los Angeles, the second pueblo, was founded in 1781. It began with 44 men and women from New Spain. Over half had ancestors from Africa. Today Los Angeles is California's largest city, with nearly four million people.

A pueblo's most important official was its alcalde (ahl CAHL de). The alcalde was a mayor and a judge. Francisco Reyes, who had African and Spanish ancestors, was the first alcalde of Los Angeles.

Each pueblo was laid out around a plaza, or square park. The church, the council house, and the jail all faced the plaza. Some cities, such as Sonoma, still have plazas that were built by their Spanish settlers.

Life in the pueblos was often very hard at first. The settlers did not know much about farming. They were not able to send much food to the presidios. Over time, however, the tiny pueblos grew into the large cities you know today.

WHY IT MATTERS

Missions, presidios, and pueblos were the first Spanish settlements in California. Some of these settlements grew into the major cities of today. We still use their names in places like San Diego, Santa Barbara, and San Francisco.

Avila Adobe (above) was built in 1818 in Los Angeles. The city is shown at left in a late-1700s engraving.

Seaver Center

✔️ Reviewing Facts and Ideas

MAIN IDEAS

- Presidios were built to protect the missions.
- Pueblos, or towns, were built to provide food for the presidios.

THINK ABOUT IT

1. Who founded nine missions after Junípero Serra died?

2. What pueblo grew into California's largest city?

3. **FOCUS** How did the Spanish settle California?

4. **THINKING SKILL** What was the main *cause* of the founding of the California pueblos?

5. **WRITE** Imagine that you are a soldier at the Santa Barbara Presidio. Write a letter to a friend in Mexico City describing your life.

THE MISSION STYLE

Have you ever tried to "read" a building? If you know what to look for, a building can tell quite a story.

Mission buildings, for instance, tell us about Spanish California. They remind us that Native Americans made the bricks, cut the wooden beams, and baked the clay tiles for the roofs.

The missions also tell us about the missionaries who came from Spain. Roman arches and Moorish domes are two features the Spanish brought with them.

Many buildings in California today were built to look like missions. We call this the mission style. The mission style has become a part of what makes California special. The mission style reminds us of our state's unique heritage.

The dome of Mission San Carlos Borromeo (right) is similar to those built by Moors, a Muslim people, in Spain. The house in Santa Barbara (above), probably built around the 1920s, has a tile roof and white walls like those of many missions.

Many public buildings, like the Amtrak railroad station with a curved ceiling in San Diego (above), were built in the mission style.

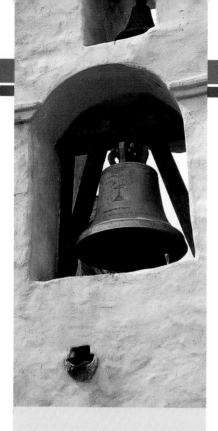

LIVING AT MISSION SAN GABRIEL

READ ALOUD

"[We] were governed somewhat in the military style," recalled an Ohlone named Lorenzo Asisara, who lived at Mission Santa Cruz. *"[We had] sergeants, corporals, and overseers who . . . reported to the padres any disobedience."*

THE BIG PICTURE

In this lesson you will learn about Mission San Gabriel, founded in Tongva lands in 1771. San Gabriel, like all the other missions, was a place where two worlds met. The missionaries believed that by changing the Native Americans, they were teaching them a better way to live. Some Native Americans accepted the strange new ways of the padres. Many others fought against being forced to give up their way of life.

Many Native Americans did not survive this meeting of cultures. Without knowing it, the Spanish brought diseases from Europe. These diseases were new to the Americas. That is why native people could not fight them off. People lived close together at the missions, so the diseases spread from person to person quickly. More than half of California's native population died this way. By 1814 the hospital at Mission San Gabriel was larger than the church.

Focus Activity

READ TO LEARN
What was life like for Native Americans at a mission?

VOCABULARY
llavera
adobe
revolt

PEOPLE
Bartolomea
Eulalia Pérez
Pablo Tac
Nicolas José
Toypurina

PLACES
Mission San Gabriel

COMING TO THE MISSION

Native Americans came to the missions for many different reasons. Tongva people first came to Mission San Gabriel, for instance, out of curiosity. They wanted to meet the new people who had come into their land. They enjoyed the gifts that the padres offered. Later, the missionaries forced people to come. Native Americans had learned things about the missions that made them afraid.

From a Tongva Village

One Tongva girl, Bartolomea, was only six years old when soldiers swept through her village of Comcrabit. We know her story because her husband, Hugo Reid, later wrote it down. Bartolomea told Reid that soldiers with guns captured everyone they could find and took them back to the mission. Reid described what happened:

Infants were then baptized [made Roman Catholics in a religious ceremony], as were also all children under eight years of age; the former were left with their mothers, but the latter kept apart from . . . their parents.

Not wanting to be kept from their children, the mothers agreed

to be baptized, too. "Finally the males gave way [to be with] wife and family."

Life at Mission San Gabriel was very different from what the Tongva had known. They had followed the changing seasons, free to go where they liked within their lands. Now they had to live under the rules and punishments of the padres. The ringing of the mission bell told them when to wake up, pray, eat, rest, and work. The jobs they did, the foods they ate, their clothing—everything was different.

People at San Gabriel spent much of their time in church (above). They found time to play games (left) they brought from their villages.

WORKING AT THE MISSION

Everyone had a job at the mission. One important job was that of llavera (yah VE rah). *Llavera* means "keeper of the keys." Eulalia Pérez was the *llavera* at Mission San Gabriel. She kept track of the mission's food and drink. She was also in charge of the *monjerio* (mohn her EE oh), a building where girls lived apart from their families. Each night she locked all the buildings, including the *monjerio*. Why, do you think, did she lock it?

MANY VOICES PRIMARY SOURCE

Excerpt from the memoir of Eulalia Pérez, recorded by Thomas Savage in 1877.

*A blind Indian named Andresillo stood at the door of the **nunnery** and called out each girl's name, telling her to come in. If any girl was missing at **admission** time, they looked for her the following day and brought her to the monjerio. Her mother, if she had one, was brought in and punished for having **detained** her, and the girl was locked up for having been careless in not coming in **punctually**.*

nunnery: *monjerio*
admission: coming in
detained: kept
punctually: on time

Meeting Needs at the Mission

People at the missions had to meet all their needs and those of the padres. Women made cloth from wool, prepared the meals, wove baskets, and made many other things that were needed. Girls learned to make candles and soap from tallow, a kind of animal fat. Men grew crops in the fields. They tended the mission's herds of sheep, cattle, and horses. Boys helped in the fields and kept animals from eating the crops.

As you can see in the Infographic, there were many buildings to be built. Most were built of adobe. Adobe is brick made from clay and straw that has been dried in the sun. The church was decorated with paintings or carvings.

There were few Spanish people in California. It was Native Americans who built the buildings and did most of the work of the missions. Without their efforts, there would have been no missions.

USC/Dept. of Special Collections

Leaving the Mission

Once Native Americans became a part of the mission, they were not allowed to return permanently to their villages. Many people ran away. Most often, soldiers on horseback went after them. One man said he ran away because "at the mission he was beaten a great deal." Another said simply that he "wanted to go back to his country."

infographic

Mission San Gabriel

Each mission was nearly self-sufficient. That means it took care of its own needs. Ships came from New Spain with supplies only once a year—or even less often. What kind of work did people at the mission do?

Living quarters

Tanning hides

Mule train

Making pottery

Weaving

Church

Building a *monjerio*

Bringing wheat from the fields

Harvesting olives

REVOLTS AGAINST THE PADRES

Native Americans had different feelings about the missions. Some, like Pablo Tac, were born at missions and thought of them as home. Tac lived at Mission San Luis Rey. He was thankful to the missionaries for teaching him the subjects taught in European schools.

Other Native Americans revolted against the Spanish. To revolt is to resist with violence. In November 1775 over 600 Kumeyaay people attacked Mission San Diego. They killed its padre and burned its buildings to the ground. It was eight months before the Spanish began to rebuild the mission.

Ten years later, Nicolas José and a Tongva woman shaman named Toypurina organized a revolt at Mission San Gabriel. They wanted to rid their land of people they thought of as invaders. "I hate the padres and all of you," Toypurina told the Spanish, "for trespassing [coming without permission] upon the land of my [ancestors]." The revolt failed.

A Spanish print (above) shows harsh treatment by the soldiers, which caused revolts.

WHY IT MATTERS

From the point of view of the missionaries, Father Serra's prayer for a "harvest of souls" seemed to have been answered. Eighty thousand people became Roman Catholics. Yet for many of California's Indians, the coming of the missions brought sadness.

Eva Pagaling, a Chumash, said recently that her people can still hear voices from the missions. "What they heard was the people in the missions, weeping and weeping."

✓ Reviewing Facts and Ideas

MAIN IDEAS

- At the missions Native Americans had a new way of life.
- Some people revolted against the harsh treatment at the missions.

THINK ABOUT IT

1. Who was Bartolomea?
2. What is a *monjerio*?
3. **FOCUS** What was life like for Native Americans at a mission?
4. **THINKING SKILL** What was an *effect* of the Europeans bringing new diseases to North America?
5. **GEOGRAPHY** Why were most of the missions built near the coast?

CITIZENSHIP
MAKING A DIFFERENCE

Through Tolowa Eyes

CRESCENT CITY—Loren Bommelyn's interest in Tolowa (TAH la wah) language and culture came naturally. He is a Tolowa Indian and grew up in the Tolowa community of Nelechundun (NE lee chun dun), just north of Crescent City. Bommelyn liked to talk with older men and women who knew the language well. He listened carefully at meetings and potluck suppers. Though his first language was English, he learned to speak Tolowa as well.

Few Native Americans in California speak the languages their ancestors spoke. Since the days of the missions, schools have discouraged them from learning these languages. Soon many families could no longer speak their native languages. Many of the 100 or more languages Californians once spoke have been lost.

Bommelyn wanted to make sure that young people had the chance to learn the languages of their ancestors. After he finished college, he trained to be a teacher. He became the first Tolowa-language teacher in the public schools.

Bommelyn says that it is not surprising that many Tolowa students don't know the language. "We are not a large group, and today there is no place where students can regularly hear people speaking Tolowa."

Jaytuk Steinruck took Bommelyn's class at Del Norte High School. "The class made me see things a little differently," he recalled. "I saw that the Tolowa language was complex. He told us where words came from and how they came about."

Besides learning Tolowa names of months, plants, foods, colors, and household objects, students learn about Tolowa literature and culture. Bommelyn says that many students take away something more important. "Studying our language helps us honor our culture. It helps us learn about how we as Tolowa people see the world. It helps us see the world through Tolowa eyes."

"Studying our language helps us honor our culture."

Loren Bommelyn

123

STUDY SKILLS

Using Primary and Secondary Sources

VOCABULARY

primary source
secondary source

WHY THE SKILL MATTERS

Suppose you wanted more information about a particular mission. You could get this information from two different kinds of sources.

One is a primary source. A primary source is information that comes from someone who saw or took part in what he or she is describing. A primary source might be a journal, a letter, or a newspaper report. For example, in the last lesson you read a primary source from Eulalia Pérez.

Most of the information in this textbook, however, is from a secondary source. This kind of source is written by people who were not present at the events they describe. They got their information "secondhand."

Both kinds of information are important. A primary source can make us feel as though we were there. It can help us understand how one person thought about something. A secondary source may help us to see a broader view of events. It may give us more points of view on a subject.

Newberry Library

EXCERPT A

The Indians as well as the missionaries rise with the sun, and immediately go to prayers and mass, which lasts for an hour. During this time three large boilers [pots] are set on the fire for cooking a kind of soup, made of barley meal. . . . This sort of food, of which the Indians are extremely fond, is called *atole*. . . . After [the meal] they all go to work . . . some to dig in the garden, while others are employed in domestic occupations [jobs in the house], all under the eye of one or two missionaries.

USING THE SKILL

Read the two excerpts shown. Both give information about a visit to Mission San Carlos Borromeo by a French scientist named Jean François de La Pérouse (ZHAHN frahn SWAH DUH LAH PAY rooz). The journal he kept is used by many historians to learn about life at the mission. Excerpt A is from La Pérouse's journal. Excerpt B is from a book written in 1996 by Emily Abbink. Use the Helping Yourself box.

TRYING THE SKILL

Which of the two excerpts is a primary source? Which is a secondary source? Now think about the differences between them. Which gives you more of a feeling of actually being at the mission? Which places La Pérouse's journey in a broader view?

Both types of sources may express the writer's opinion, or point of view. If you were writing a report about this visit to the mission, how would each kind of source be helpful to you?

REVIEWING THE SKILL

1. What is the difference between a primary source and a secondary source?

2. If you wrote an article about your vacation, would it be a primary source or a secondary source? Why?

3. Is a biography a primary source or a secondary source?

4. How can both primary and secondary sources help us to understand history?

EXCERPT B

Mission San Carlos was only one of the stops for the French explorer La Pérouse. In 1785 he began a long voyage . . . in search of trade and scientific information. . . . He took careful notes of his findings and adventures. His travels took him to North America, Asia, and the South Pacific. In 1787, during his stay in . . . Asia, La Pérouse mailed his journal to France for safekeeping. His writings included detailed observations of Mission San Carlos.

The Granger Collection

Jean François de La Pérouse (above) visited Mission San Carlos Borromeo (left) in 1786.

125

CHAPTER 5 REVIEW

THINKING ABOUT VOCABULARY

Number a sheet of paper from 1 to 10. Beside each number write the word from the list that best matches the description.

adobe   missionary
alcalde   plaza
convert   presidio
frontier   pueblo
llavera   revolt

1. A farming town
2. A fort where soldiers lived
3. The "keeper of the keys" at a mission
4. The edge of an area that a group of people has settled
5. A brick made from clay and straw that has been dried in the sun
6. To change a person's religious beliefs
7. The mayor and judge of a pueblo
8. A central or square park
9. To resist with violence
10. A person who teaches religious beliefs to others who have different beliefs

THINKING ABOUT FACTS

1. Why did the Spanish set up missions in California?
2. What was the result of the "Sacred Expedition"?
3. Name the three types of Spanish settlements in California.
4. What happened to more than half of the Native American population in California? Why did this happen?
5. Give three reasons why Native Americans went to the missions.

THINK AND WRITE

WRITING A LOG
Suppose you are Gaspar de Portolá. Write a log describing what you find on your expedition to Monterey Bay.

WRITING AN ADVERTISEMENT
Design and write an advertisement that would interest people in settling in a pueblo.

WRITING A COMPARISON
Write a comparison of life in Native American villages in California and life at the missions.

APPLYING THINKING SKILLS

IDENTIFYING CAUSE AND EFFECT

1. What is a cause? What is an effect?
2. Serra founded a mission in San Diego. Was the large Kumeyaay population nearby a cause or an effect of this?
3. What were two causes of problems between missionaries and soldiers at the presidios?
4. Name three effects that living in missions had on Native Americans.
5. How might identifying cause and effect help you understand history?

APPLYING STUDY SKILLS

USING PRIMARY AND SECONDARY SOURCES

1. Explain the difference between a primary source and a secondary source.

2. Find two primary sources in the chapter.

3. Find two examples of information you think came from secondary sources.

4. Why are primary sources useful when studying history?

5. When is it helpful to understand the difference between primary and secondary sources?

Summing Up the Chapter

Use the following cause-and-effect chart to organize information from the chapter. When you have completed the chart, use it to answer the question "How did Spanish settlers change California?"

CAUSE	EFFECT
José Gálvez convinces the Spanish king of the need to settle California.	The Spanish return to California after 167 years.
The Spanish want to convert the Native Americans of California to the Roman Catholic religion.	
The Spanish need to protect the missions.	
	The Native Americans learn new skills, but they lose their freedom and way of life.

UNIT 2 REVIEW

THINKING ABOUT VOCABULARY

Number a sheet of paper from 1 to 10. Beside each number write a **C** if the underlined word is used correctly. If it is not, write the word that would correctly complete the sentence.

1. Harvest is the place where food is stored.

2. The alcalde was a Native American religious leader and healer.

3. The Northwest Passage was a sea route the English believed existed in North America.

4. A galleon is a ruler picked by a king.

5. A religion is the way a group worships the God or gods its members believe in.

6. A colony is the study of the tools and things people leave behind.

7. A mission was a Native American house with an open fire that men and boys sat around.

8. Longitude is how far north or south a place is from the equator.

9. Slavery is the practice of making a person the property of another.

10. The Spanish wanted to revolt Native Americans to their religious beliefs.

THINK AND WRITE

WRITING A PARAGRAPH
Write a paragraph that describes some of the ways the Native Americans' lives changed during the period of time covered in the unit.

WRITING ABOUT PERSPECTIVES
Write about Francis Drake's landing in California from the perspective of a sailor in Drake's crew and from that of a Miwok who met the crew.

WRITING A COMPARISON
Compare the explorations of Cabrillo and Portolá. In what ways were the reasons for the expeditions the same or different?

BUILDING SKILLS

1. **Notes and outlines** Read the section on pages 92–93 about Cermeño. Take notes as you read, and then write an outline.

2. **Latitude and longitude** Look at the map on page 99. Name the city closest to 118°W and 32°N.

3. **Primary and secondary sources** Suppose Junípero Serra had written an autobiography. Would this be a primary or secondary source?

4. **Cause and effect** Name two word clues or phrases that show cause and two that show effect.

5. **Cause and effect** Name one cause and one effect of the Miwok burning their land.

YESTERDAY, TODAY & TOMORROW

You have read about how the Europeans explored California. Today explorers are learning more about remote parts of the world, such as places above the Arctic Circle in Alaska. What might be some results of these explorations? What might happen if people lived in these cold places?

READING ON YOUR OWN

These are some of the books you could find at the library to help you learn more.

FIRE RACE: A KARUK COYOTE TALE
retold by Jonathan London
The story of how Coyote brought fire to the animals, including humans.

GOLDEN CITIES, GOLDEN SHIPS—EARLY SPANISH EXPLORERS OF CALIFORNIA
by Glen Dines
The story of the Spanish explorers of California.

HISTORIC COMMUNITIES: SPANISH MISSIONS
by Bobbie Kalman and Greg Nickles
A look at life in the missions from both Native American and Spanish points of view.

UNIT REVIEW PROJECT

Making a Poster

1. Working in groups, imagine you are one of the groups of people from the unit. Here are some suggestions for who you could be:
   • Hupa Native Americans
   • The crew of the *Golden Hind*
   • Members of the "Sacred Expedition"
2. Gather information about your group from your textbook and the library.
3. Think about the places you live or travel through, the foods you eat, and the clothes you wear. How will you show these things on your poster?

4. Create your poster by having each group member draw or cut out a picture about your group. Try to use a variety of materials, such as fabric, paint, crayons, or yarn.
5. Make sure you label each picture clearly.
6. Display your poster on the wall for the rest of the class to enjoy.

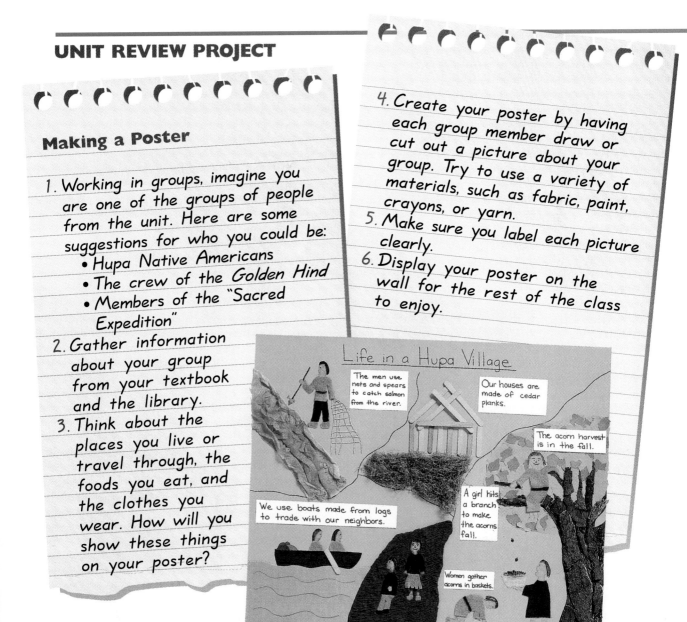

Life in a Hupa Village

The men use nets and spears to catch salmon from the river.

Our houses are made of cedar planks.

The acorn harvest is in the fall.

We use boats made from logs to trade with our neighbors.

A girl hits a branch to make the acorns fall.

Women gather acorns in baskets.

CATTLE YOKE (RIGHT)
CLIPPER SHIP (BELOW)
DISEÑO (BELOW RIGHT)

CALIFORNIA MUD
WAGON

New Flags Above California

"Everyone was welcome."

John Bidwell, 1841
See page 153.

WHY DOES IT MATTER?

In the early 1820s, California was owned by Spain. A chain of Spanish missions ran from San Diego to Sonoma. By 1850 the missions were closed and California was one of the United States. How did these changes happen? What did Californians think about them?

In Unit 3 you will read about the new flags that flew above California. You will also read about an incredible discovery that changed the lives of people throughout California.

CALIFORNIA GOLD MINER, 1850, AND GOLD NUGGET (ABOVE)

131

California, Here I Come

Word of California's riches traveled fast. In 1812 Russian fur traders established Fort Ross (far left) on the northern California coast. Furs attracted American trappers and explorers, such as Kit Carson (above). Mexican landowners, called rancheros, raised cattle on large estates. In 1846 war with Mexico broke out. Before the dust settled, gold was discovered at Sutter's Mill in 1848, luring thousands of adventurers to California to pan for gold. The Gold Rush was on! Soon Americans settled in towns like Bodie (background)—an 1870s boomtown turned ghost town today.

GEO JOURNAL

Did you come to California from someplace else? Do you know someone who did? Why do people still come to California to live?

CHAPTER 6

Mexican California

THINKING ABOUT HISTORY AND GEOGRAPHY

You have read how Spain claimed California and sent missionaries and soldiers to settle here. In Chapter 6 you will read how California became a part of Mexico. Read on to discover how life in California changed and how a new group of settlers began to arrive.

PACIFIC OCEAN

1834	1840	1846
SANTA CRUZ	**PINOLE POINT, CONTRA COSTA COUNTY**	**INDEPENDENCE, MISSOURI**
Mission Santa Cruz closes	**Cattle are rounded up at Rancho El Pinole**	**George and Tamsen Donner leave Missouri for California**

CANADA

UNITED
STATES

Pinole Point

Santa
Cruz

CALIFORNIA

Independence

Cahuenga Pass

MEXICO

1847

CAHUENGA PASS

**Bernarda Ruiz arranges
a peace meeting in the
Mexican War**

LAND GRANTS AND RANCHOS

Focus Activity

READ TO LEARN
How did life in California change when Mexico became a country?

VOCABULARY
land grant
rancho
diseño
diputación
tax

PEOPLE
Miguel Hidalgo
Estanislao
José Figueroa
Maria Juana de
 los Angeles
Ivan Kuskov

PLACES
Monterey
Fort Ross

READ ALOUD

On September 16, 1810, a priest named Miguel Hidalgo made a speech in the town of Dolores, in New Spain. He cried out, "Long live America. Long live the Catholic religion. And death to the Gachupines." By Gachupines he meant people born in Spain. Hidalgo's fiery words set off a long and bloody war to make New Spain a country free of Spanish rule.

THE BIG PICTURE

Like the American colonists in 1776, the people of New Spain had many complaints against their rulers. They disliked being ruled from a European country far away. Miguel Hidalgo convinced many Mexicans to go to war. They fought to become independent, or free, from Spain.

Why did they wish to be independent? Under Spanish government, people born in Spain were treated better than those born in the colony. They also controlled much of the wealth. Most people living in New Spain, however, were born in North America. They wanted to govern themselves.

The war for independence began in 1810. It did not end until 1821. The news of the war's end reached faraway California the following year. A crowd gathered at the presidio in Monterey, the capital. People shouted, "Long live Mexican independence!"

136

THE MISSION SYSTEM ENDS

Mexican Independence brought change to California. To begin with, California was no longer a part of Spain. It was now part of Mexico. Also many of Mexico's rulers did not support the missions the way Spanish rulers had. They felt that the missions had too much power. Others believed that the mission system had not treated the Native Americans fairly.

#2

They pointed to Native American revolts against the missions as proof that the mission system had failed. In 1828, for example, a Yokuts named Estanislao (e stahn ee SLOW) led a revolt against three missions. He sent a message to Mission San José: "We are rising in revolt . . . . We have no fear." The success of this and other revolts prevented the Mexicans from settling the San Joaquin Valley.

Dividing the Lands

In 1833 California got a new governor named José Figueroa (fee gay ROH ah). The following year Figueroa announced a plan to end the mission system. The mission priests could stay, and their churches could remain open. But the missions would lose their lands. Figueroa wanted to divide these lands equally between Native Americans and Mexican settlers. He believed that if they owned land, Native Americans

José Figueroa became governor in 1833. The Bell of Dolores (below) was rung when Mexico declared independence.

would be just as loyal to Mexico as new Mexican settlers.

Many people in California supported Figueroa's plan. Most of them did so because they hoped to gain control of the mission lands for themselves. When Figueroa's plan was carried out, few Native Americans ever got their land. Those who did soon lost or sold it to other settlers. Others tried to return to their old way of life but found that they no longer had the skills they needed to survive. Most ended up working for the settlers.

after closed #3

Lorenzo Asisara remembered what it was like for his Ohlone people when Mission Santa Cruz closed in 1834. "[We received] old horses and that were no longer productive [and] very old [sheep]." The mission lands they received "did not do the Indians any good."

137

Infographic
California Ranchos

The ranchos were the largest settlements in Mexican California. Each land grant could include an area up to 78 square miles. Some people got more than one grant. Ranchero families built *haciendas* (ah see **EN** dahs), or large homes. What was a *diseño* for?

Rancho	Owner	Location	Size (in square miles)
Santa Margarita	Pio and Andres Pico	San Diego County	209
Simi	Francisco Miguel and Santiago Pico	Ventura County / LA County	177
El Tejon	José Antonio Aguirre and Ignacio Del Valle	Kern County	153
Petaluma	Mariano Guadalupe Vallejo	Sonoma County	104
San Diego de Alcala Mission (Former Mission San Diego)	Santiago Argüello	San Diego County	92

Californio families used *diseños* (above and right) to map their land.

NEW SETTLEMENTS

Mexico's leaders gave some settlers huge pieces of land, known as land grants. Any Mexican citizen could ask for a land grant by applying in writing and following certain rules. Not everyone, however, received a land grant. Soldiers from presidios and already wealthy land owners got most of the land grants at first.

Only a few Native Americans received land grants. Maria Juana de los Angeles was one. Her husband had been a leader of the Luiseño. She received a grant when Mission San Luis Rey closed.

The Ranchos

De los Angeles used her land grant to create a rancho. A rancho was a ranch where cattle, horses, and other animals were raised. Five hundred ranchos were created during the years California was part of Mexico. Look at the Infographic. How big were the largest ranchos?

Mariano Guadalupe Vallejo was among the richest ranch owners. He owned the Rancho Petaluma. Vallejo was a ranchero, a man who owned a ranch. A woman who owned a ranch was a ranchera.

One of the things a ranchero or ranchera had to do to get a land grant was make a diseño (dee SE nyoh), or map. The diseño showed the rancho's borders. These borders might be marked with nothing more than a pile of stones or a clump of cactus.

The Granger Collection

CHANGES IN CALIFORNIA

Not everyone lived on ranchos. Many people lived in the pueblos.

Under the Spanish, pueblos such as Los Angeles had been small farming towns. Now they grew into important places for trade with other countries. Merchants—people who buy and sell goods—came to live in the pueblos. By 1835 Los Angeles had grown so much that the capital of California was moved here from Monterey. The dusty streets were lined with stores and wagons filled with goods.

Some Native Americans lived far from the Mexican settlements. They lived in their own communities, which the Mexicans called *rancherías* (ran cher EE ahs).

A Government for California

The governors of California acted as judges. They also made laws for the colony with the advice of the *diputación* (dee poo tah SYOHN). This was a group of wealthy or important citizens who were chosen by the settlers.

The *diputación* made decisions about roads, police, and city rules. It also placed taxes on cattle and crops. A tax is money people must pay to the government by law. The *diputación* did not have much power, though. It met only when the governor said it could.

Russians Build a Fort

Rancheros from Mexico were not the only people who had settled in California at this time. Mexico was afraid that other countries would build more settlements. One such settlement was Fort Ross, north of Bodega Bay.

Fur hunters led by Ivan Kuskov built Fort Ross in 1812. The hunters came to hunt sea otters, seals, and sea lions in the ocean. The sleek, waterproof fur of these animals was very valuable.

Some of the hunters, like Kuskov, were Russians. Because Russia is a very cold country, its people especially

Fort Ross, shown in an 1828 print (above), is now a State Historic Park.

liked the warm furs. Other hunters were hired by Kuskov from the Aleutian (uh LOO shun) Islands of Alaska. The Aleut hunters used skin canoes called *bidarkas*. The hunters killed so many otters and seals that few were left. Once most of the animals were gone, the Russians lost interest in California. They left Fort Ross in 1841.

WHY IT MATTERS

Under Mexico, life in California changed greatly. In the ranchos a new California culture began to take shape. You will learn more about the ranchos in the next lesson.

Reviewing Facts and Ideas

MAIN IDEAS

- Mexico became an independent country in 1821 after a war with Spain.
- California had a governor from Mexico and a local council known as a *diputación*.
- The missions closed in the 1830s.
- Five hundred ranchos were created in Mexican California.

THINK ABOUT IT

1. Why did the missions close?

2. Why did Russians build a settlement near Bodega Bay?

3. **FOCUS** How did California change after Mexico became a country?

4. **THINKING SKILL** What *caused* Mexico to give land in California to its citizens? What was one *effect* of that decision?

5. **WRITE** Imagine that you are a Native American at one of the missions about to be closed. Write a letter to the Mexican governor about your hopes for the future.

141

Focus Activity

READ TO LEARN
What was life at a rancho like?

VOCABULARY
vaquero
brand
import
export
Californio
mestizo
fiesta

PEOPLE
Prudencia Higuera

PLACES
San Pablo Bay

LIFE AT RANCHO EL PINOLE

READ ALOUD

"In the autumn of 1840 my father lived near what is now called Pinole Point, in Contra Costa County, California. I was then about twelve years old." So begins a true story about life on a California rancho. It was written by Prudencia Higuera. In this lesson you will learn about life on this and other California ranchos.

THE BIG PICTURE

Under Spanish rule, the missions were the most important settlements in California. Now the ranchos became the most important settlements. Each rancho was run almost like a small kingdom. The rancheros and rancheras had great power.

Many Native Americans went to work on the ranchos after the missions closed. Some were captured by the rancheros and forced to work. In fact, most of the people who cooked, cleaned, and took care of the ranchos were Native Americans. So were many of the vaqueros. A vaquero is a cowhand. "Without Indians," writes historian Andrew Rolle, "the ranchos could hardly have carried on." Yet the Native Americans who worked on ranchos were not paid for their work. They got food, clothing, and shelter. But they had few rights.

ROUNDUP

What was life at a rancho like? Imagine you are at a roundup at Rancho El Pinole. Roundups are held each autumn or spring. Sometimes they last a week or more. It is the most exciting time of year.

Prudencia Higuera recalled such a time in the autumn of 1840. One morning the vaqueros "went on horseback into the mountains and smaller valleys to round up all the best cattle."

The rancho is too large to fence, so the cattle roam it freely. In the roundup the vaqueros gather them together. The air is filled with clouds of dust as the vaqueros thunder by on their horses. Running before them is a herd of bellowing cattle. The vaqueros yell and wave their hats.

They chase the cattle into a corral, or pen, made of brush and sticks.

A vaquero lassos a young calf. He springs to the ground. Using a hot iron, he presses a brand, or mark, onto the calf's hip. The brand identifies the rancho to which the calf belongs.

Links to LANGUAGE ARTS

Cowboy Talk

Many of the words that cowboys use today came from the Spanish-speaking vaqueros. "Ranch," for example, sounds like the Spanish word *rancho*. "Lasso" comes from the Spanish *lazo*. "Lariat" comes from *la reata*, which means "rope."

Other words borrowed from the Spanish include "corral" and "bronco"— as well as "buckaroo," which is how the first English-speaking cowboys said "vaquero"! To learn more about the origins of these words, look them up in a dictionary.

Vaqueros lasso a steer during roundup (bottom). A fancy modern sombrero (right) recalls the hats once worn by vaqueros.

TRADE AND THE RANCHOS

Prudencia Higuera remembered one afternoon in 1840 when a man on horseback came riding to Rancho El Pinole. The rider reported that a great ship was sailing into San Pablo Bay. It was the first trading ship from the United States to enter the bay. How did Higuera's family feel about the visit?

Excerpt from an article written by Prudencia Higuera, 1890.

*We had a large number of **hides** and many pounds of **tallow** ready on the beach when the ship appeared. . . . The captain soon came to our landing with a small boat. . . . The captain looked over the hides, and then asked my father to get into the boat and go to the **vessel**. Mother was much afraid to let him go, as we all thought the Americans were not to be trusted unless we knew them well. . . .*

*He came back the next day, bringing four boat-loads of cloth, axes, shoes, fish-lines, and many new things. There were two **grindstones**, and some cheap jewelry. My brother had traded some deerskins for a gun and four toothbrushes, the first ones I had ever seen.*

hides: skins
tallow: cattle fat
vessel: ship
grindstones: stones used to sharpen a blade

The Hide-and-Tallow Trade

Why was the visit of a trading ship so exciting? The ranchos did not make many of their own goods. Trade was one of the ways they met their wants and needs. Ships from the United States and other countries brought imports. An import is something brought in from another country for sale or use. Trading ships also made stops in the countries of Chile and Peru in South America. Some went from California to Hawaii, the Philippine Islands, and Asia.

Richard Henry Dana was a sailor on a voyage from Boston to California in 1835. In his book *Two Years Before the Mast*, he described the cargo of his ship, the *Pilgrim*:

We had . . . teas, coffee, sugar, spices, raisins, molasses, hardware . . . clothing of all kinds, boots and shoes . . . shawls, scarfs, necklaces, jewelry,

Seaver Center for Western History Research, Natural History Museum of Los Angeles County

and combs . . . furniture; and in fact, everything that can be imagined, from Chinese fireworks to English cartwheels.

To buy these imports, the Californians traded their own **exports**. An export is something sold or traded to another country. Higuera described how her father's ranch exported cowhides and bags of tallow. Because the hides were traded for other goods, people called them "California banknotes." One hide was worth two or three dollars. They were used to make shoes, saddles, and other leather goods. The tallow was made into soap and candles.

Since only the hides and the fat were traded, the ranchos had a lot of meat left over. People on the ranchos ate fresh or dried beef at almost every meal.

Workers from the ranchos, using ox-drawn carts or mules, brought hides and tallow to the coast. The ships anchored far offshore. Sailors carried the heavy hides through the waves on their heads to small boats. The boats then transported the hides to the big ships.

Some captains crammed their ships with as many as 30,000 hides. Imagine how many pairs of leather shoes could be made from all those hides!

Traders exported the ranchos' goods to Boston. How did trade help them meet their wants and needs?

CALIFORNIA-BOSTON TRADE

In the 1800s fast clipper ships carried trade goods between California and Boston.

The Granger Collection

To California

🔗 Fishlines

／ Toothbrushes

☕ Tea and coffee

🔫 Axes and guns

👢 Shoes and boots

○ Jewels and combs

🍴 Knives and forks

🧂 Sugar and spices

👕 Cloths and Clothing

To Boston

✹ Hides

● Tallow

145

CALIFORNIOS

Under Spain, California had not been allowed to trade with other countries. As part of Mexico, however, trading was allowed, and new ideas came to California. A new culture came about. It was a blend of different peoples and ways of life.

The people of Alta, or upper, California, as California was known then, took pride in their new culture. They called themselves Californios, or Californians, rather than Mexicans. For them California was a special place.

Many of the great rancho owners were mestizos. A mestizo is a person who is part Spanish and part Mexican Indian. Some of the leading California families, such as the Tapias and the Picos, also were of African descent. Their ancestors had been brought to North America as enslaved people.

Running the Rancho

The rancho was not only a piece of land. It was a home to the ranchero's close family and relatives and all of the rancho's workers. The ranchero's wife usually was in charge of the home. She raised the children, tended the gardens, and kept the house in order. Most of the work was done by Native American women. Francisca Vallejo described some of the jobs done by the Native American women working for her:

> Six or seven serve in the kitchen, and five or six are always washing clothes . . . and . . . nearly a dozen are employed at sewing and spinning [making thread].

Because the ranchos were located far apart from one another, hospitality—or being generous to visitors—was very important. A traveler from the United States noted in 1841 that "every rancher's home was open to everyone, free."

Lively celebrations, or fiestas, were a big part of Californio life. Some were held to honor important family events, like weddings. More often, fiestas were held around religious holidays, such as days honoring saints or other holy figures.

Fiestas were a way for rancheros to show off their wealth and hospitality. They invited everyone

they could and provided all the food and drink. Spirited dancing and singing filled the fiesta, which could last for up to a week.

Restless California

Californios thought of themselves as loyal Mexicans. At the same time, they were proud of their way of life. When they felt the government in Mexico City was trying to control that way of life, Californios fought back. More than once they revolted and sent their governors back to central Mexico.

Californios often felt isolated, or separated from Mexico. California's capital at Monterey was almost 2,000 miles from Mexico City. Official letters could take as long as two years to make the journey. In addition, Mexico's long fight for independence had left it weak and divided. Often the central government in Mexico simply did not have the power to control events in distant California.

WHY IT MATTERS

The heritage of Mexican California is all around us. Names of cities such as Vallejo and of streets such as Pico Boulevard in Los Angeles remind us of our history. Just as the Mexican settlers were proud of the special land they called home, we are proud of our state today.

Reviewing Facts and Ideas

MAIN IDEAS

- The hide-and-tallow trade was important to California's economy.
- A new culture grew on the ranchos of Mexican California.

THINK ABOUT IT

1. Why did vaqueros brand cattle?

2. Why did people on the ranchos eat a lot of beef?

3. **FOCUS** What was life at a Californio rancho like?

4. **THINKING SKILL** *Classify* the items mentioned in the Primary Source on page 144. Which items meet people's needs? Which items meet wants?

5. **GEOGRAPHY** How did the climate and landforms make the Pacific Coast region a good place to raise cattle?

Students visit the Vallejo rancho in Petaluma (left). The Alta California Dance Company performs dances of the Californios' fiestas.

147

THE RODEO

There are about 25,000 cattle ranches in California today. Ranching today, of course, is far different from what it was during the 1830s. Yet the skills of the vaqueros are still celebrated in rodeos.

The first rodeos were simple contests at the end of a roundup. Today about 2,000 rodeos are held each year in the United States and Canada.

Some people today consider rodeos to be a cruel sport. Animals are sometimes hurt. The Rodeo Cowboys Association has strict rules to try to prevent cruelty.

Cowhands enjoy showing off their skills. Their rodeos help us appreciate this legacy of our past.

Frederic Remington painted a cowhand taming a wild horse in *Turn Him Loose, Bill*. Below, a rider tries to stay on a bucking bull at the Bill Pickett Rodeo.

In "bulldogging," shown above at the Salinas Rodeo, a cowhand tries to wrestle a young bull. A rider and horse race around a row of barrels in the barrel-racing event at a rodeo in Angels Camp.

NEW SETTLERS IN MEXICAN CALIFORNIA

READ ALOUD

"What a country this might be!" That's what Richard Henry Dana said about California. In Two Years Before the Mast, he praised its harbors, fertile soil, and mild climate. California seemed almost magical to visitors from the United States.

Focus Activity

READ TO LEARN
Why did people from the United States come to Mexican California?

VOCABULARY
trapper
pelt

PEOPLE
Jedediah Strong Smith
José Echeandía
Johann Sutter
John Bidwell
George Donner
Tamsen Donner

PLACES
Ebbets Pass
New Helvetia
Sacramento
Oregon Trail
Donner Lake

THE BIG PICTURE

Traders from the United States who came to Mexican California took away more than just cowhides and bags of tallow. They also carried home news of this beautiful land. Some later wrote books and articles about what they had seen. Their writings stirred people's interest in California.

People from the United States began settling in California in the 1820s. The Mexican government welcomed these early settlers. Some brought much needed skills, like carpentry or medicine. Others worked as traders, helping Californios deal with the Boston sea captains. Most became Mexican citizens after pledging loyalty to Mexico and converting to the Roman Catholic religion.

One of the first of these settlers was William Goodwin Dana, a cousin of Richard Henry. In 1828 William became a Mexican citizen and married Joséfa Carrillo. Nine years later the couple was granted Rancho Nipomo, near San Luis Obispo.

IN SEARCH OF FURS

Traders were not the only outsiders who were interested in California. Some trappers were, too. A trapper is someone who traps animals for their fur. The trappers were known as "mountain men."

The trappers often lived alone for months in cabins in the Rocky Mountains. Many hunted beaver. In the early 1800s the sleek, dark fur of the beaver was very valuable. Beaver pelts, or skins, are soft, warm, and waterproof. The pelts were used to make coats and hats.

The 1906 painting (above) shows Smith's party in the Mojave. Beaver were hunted for their valuable fur.

Each year the trappers sold their pelts at a gathering called a rendezvous (RAHN duh voo). In 1826 a rendezvous was held near Great Salt Lake, in what is now Utah. A trapper named Jedediah Strong Smith was there.

At the rendezvous Smith asked other trappers to go to California. He thought they could find lots of beaver there to trap. On August 16, 1826, Smith and 15 others set out for California. You can see their route on the map on page 154. They traveled southwest through the deserts of the Great Basin. They had never seen land like this before. Spikes of red rock stuck up into the pale sky. Their feet sank into the dry, loose soil.

In early October the party reached the Colorado River. Mojave people gave the travelers beans, corn, and pumpkins. Smith and his party were the first white Americans ever to make the long, dangerous journey to California overland.

151

SMITH IN CALIFORNIA

After resting among the Mojave, Smith's party set out again on November 10, 1826. They headed west, guided by two Native Americans who had left Mission San Gabriel.

For two weeks the party passed through the Mojave Desert. They crossed over the San Bernardino Mountains. Then they found a land of oak trees, grass, and sparkling streams.

On November 16 Smith and his men arrived at Mission San Gabriel. Father José Sánchez told them of a great valley to the north—the San Joaquin Valley. It was filled, he said, with all the beaver they could trap.

Before Smith could go there, he had to get permission. He and Peter Ranne, a young African American boy who worked for him, went to meet with the governor,

JEDEDIAH STRONG SMITH

José Echeandía (e che an DEE ah). Echeandía did not believe that Smith was only a trapper. He thought Smith was a spy and put him in jail. Smith promised to leave California. Then the governor let him go.

Smith believed that California included only the area of Mexican settlements. When the party reached the San Joaquin Valley, they thought they were out of California.

There, at last, they found what they were looking for. By April 1827 they had gathered over 1,500 pounds of beaver pelts. The party crossed through the Sierra Nevada at Ebbets Pass. This was the first known crossing over these high mountains.

Later in that year Smith returned to California. This time he traveled far up the coast into Oregon. His travels opened the way for other people from the United States.

NEW HELVETIA

People from the United States weren't the only ones coming to California. Other settlers began arriving from Europe. One was Johann Sutter from Switzerland.

Sutter left Switzerland because of business failings in 1834. He lived in St. Louis, Missouri, and in Santa Fe, New Mexico. He arrived in Monterey in July 1839.

In 1840 Sutter became a Mexican citizen. He was given a grant of 78 square miles. He picked a spot where the American River flows into the Sacramento River. There he built one of the largest settlements in the Sacramento Valley. He called it New Helvetia (hel VAY shuh). Helvetia is another name for Switzerland. It was near what is now Sacramento.

Sutter hired many Native Americans to work at New Helvetia. They tended herds of cattle and sheep. They grew grapes and other fruit in the orchards and did the weaving, spinning, and tanning. They helped build Sutter's Fort. You can see the fort below.

Around this time people from the United States began coming to California by land. Sutter was an important person to them. He welcomed the newcomers and helped them get settled. The first wagon train of settlers arrived in 1841. Its leader, John Bidwell, later had this to say:

Nearly everybody who came to California made it a point to reach Sutter's Fort. . . . Everyone was welcome— one man or a hundred, it was all the same.

THE OVERLAND ROUTE

New reports about California reached the United States each year. One trapper claimed it was "a perfect paradise." John Marsh, a doctor, wrote that it was "the most healthy country I have ever seen."

Wagon Trains

These reports led John Bidwell and hundreds of other settlers to head west. Once in California, most settlers built farms and ranches. Look at the map below. Find the various routes used by the settlers coming west.

Each family would put all its belongings into a large wooden wagon. The wagons would line up in a long train. The wagon trains sometimes took six months to reach California. Oxen or mules pulled the wagons over rough trails. If the settlers were lucky, they covered 20 miles a day. Crossing the deserts meant weeks of travel in scorching heat without fresh water. Then came the climb over high mountain passes with heavy wagons. One thing they had plenty of was danger.

The Donner Party

A party of about 90 settlers left Independence, Missouri, in the spring of 1846. George Donner led the party. They started out following the Oregon Trail, a well-known route. As they passed along the Platte River in June, Tamsen Donner, George's wife, wrote:

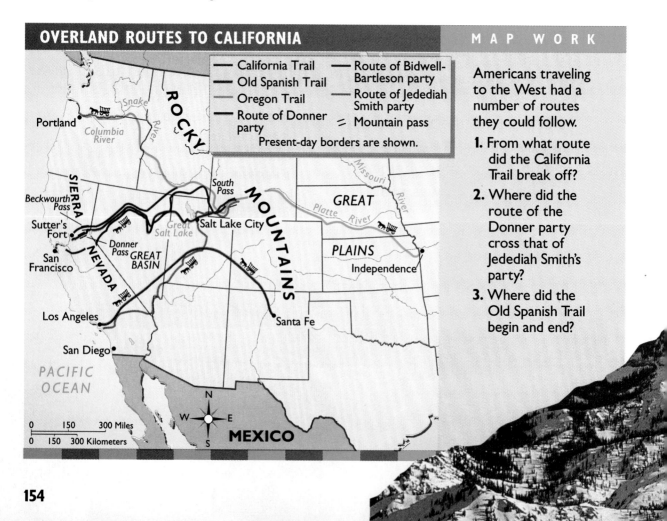

OVERLAND ROUTES TO CALIFORNIA

MAP WORK

Legend:
- California Trail
- Old Spanish Trail
- Oregon Trail
- Route of Donner party
- Route of Bidwell-Bartleson party
- Route of Jedediah Smith party
- Mountain pass

Present-day borders are shown.

Americans traveling to the West had a number of routes they could follow.

1. From what route did the California Trail break off?
2. Where did the route of the Donner party cross that of Jedediah Smith's party?
3. Where did the Old Spanish Trail begin and end?

We are now 450 miles from Independence. . . . I could never have believed we could have traveled so far with so little difficulty.

At Fort Bridger the Donner party decided to take a "shortcut" south around Great Salt Lake. This proved to be a big mistake. They lost time going through the Wasatch Mountains. Hauling their wagons over deep streambeds in the mountains was almost impossible.

By the time they reached the Sierra Nevada, winter was coming on. During the night of November 2, as they camped, a blinding snowstorm hit. That winter, 22 feet of snow fell in the mountains. The party was stranded near Donner Lake until February.

Finally, a rescue party from Sutter's Fort reached them. By then about 40 members of the party had died of cold and hunger. George Donner was too sick to travel. Tamsen Donner stayed with him as the rest of the party went to safety. Both the Donners died.

The doll (right) was owned by Patty Reed, who survived the Donner party's journey through the Sierra Nevada (below).

WHY IT MATTERS

The number of American settlers grew steadily in the 1840s. Most did not become Mexican citizens. They wondered if California might one day become part of the United States.

✔ **Reviewing Facts and Ideas**

MAIN IDEAS

- Trappers came to California in search of furs.
- Jedediah Strong Smith led the first party of Americans to reach California overland.
- The overland route was rough.

THINK ABOUT IT

1. Why were beaver pelts valuable?
2. Who founded New Helvetia?
3. **FOCUS** Why did people from the United States come to California?
4. **THINKING SKILL** What *effect* did reports like Richard Henry Dana's have on settlement of California?
5. **WRITE** Imagine that you traveled with the Donner party. Write a journal of your experiences.

STUDY SKILLS

Reading Time Lines

VOCABULARY

time line

WHY THE SKILL MATTERS

In this chapter you read about different events in Mexican California and the dates they took place.

To understand history, you need to know *when* events happened. You also need to know in which *order* they happened. Did the war for Mexican independence end before Governor Figueroa closed the missions? To help answer questions like this, you can use a time line. A time line is a diagram that shows when events took place. It also shows the amount of time that passed between events. The way a time line is drawn helps to give a sense of sequence, or order, to history.

USING THE SKILL

Look at the time line below. As you can see, the name of each event appears above or below the date it happened. The earliest event is on the left side. The most recent event is on the right.

Like most time lines, this one is divided into equal parts. Each part represents a certain number of years. Each part of the Mexican California time line represents 10 years.

Now read the time line from left to right. The first event is the end of the war for Mexican independence. The last event is the Donner party being stranded.

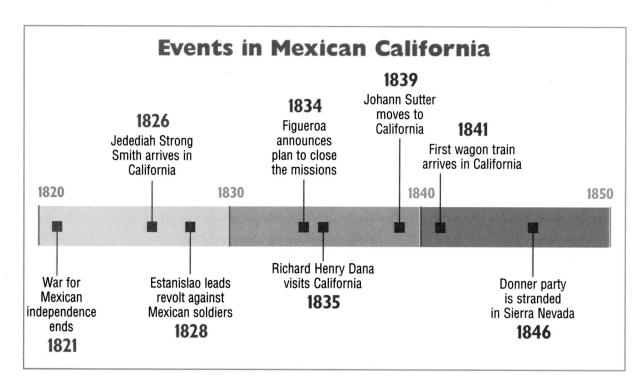

Events in Mexican California

1826 Jedediah Strong Smith arrives in California

1834 Figueroa announces plan to close the missions

1839 Johann Sutter moves to California

1841 First wagon train arrives in California

1820   1830   1840   1850

War for Mexican independence ends **1821**

Estanislao leads revolt against Mexican soldiers **1828**

Richard Henry Dana visits California **1835**

Donner party is stranded in Sierra Nevada **1846**

Which event took place between 1840 and 1846?

TRYING THE SKILL

Now read the time line of Events in California, the United States, and Mexico. As you can see, it has three tiers, or layers. Use the Helping Yourself box for hints on how to read the time line.

What period of history does the time line cover? How many years does each section cover? What event on the time line happened first? Did the American Revolution end before the Mexican Revolution?

HELPING Yourself

- **A time line** is a diagram that shows when historical events took place.
- **Note how much time is represented** by each part of the time line.
- **Read the events from left to right.**

REVIEWING THE SKILL

Use the information on the time line on this page to answer the following questions.

1. How does a time line help you to place events in the right order?
2. Which of the events on the time line took place in 1770?
3. How much time passed between the end of the American Revolution and the beginning of the Mexican Revolution?
4. In what other subjects would a time line be useful?

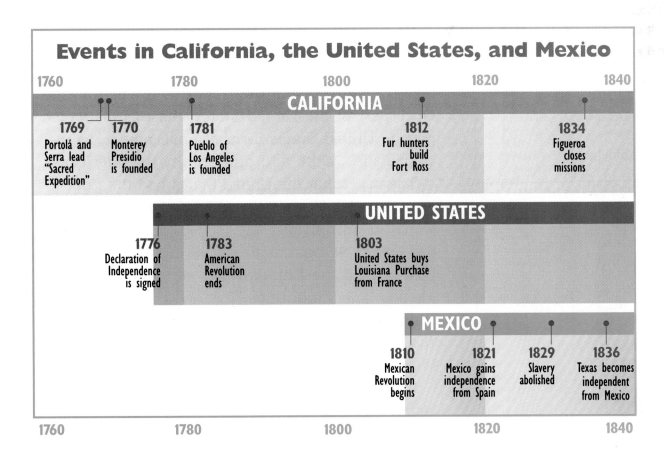

Events in California, the United States, and Mexico

| 1760 | 1780 | 1800 | 1820 | 1840 |

CALIFORNIA

1769 Portolá and Serra lead "Sacred Expedition"

1770 Monterey Presidio is founded

1781 Pueblo of Los Angeles is founded

1812 Fur hunters build Fort Ross

1834 Figueroa closes missions

UNITED STATES

1776 Declaration of Independence is signed

1783 American Revolution ends

1803 United States buys Louisiana Purchase from France

MEXICO

1810 Mexican Revolution begins

1821 Mexico gains independence from Spain

1829 Slavery abolished

1836 Texas becomes independent from Mexico

| 1760 | 1780 | 1800 | 1820 | 1840 |

1800   1815   1830   1845 1848   1860

RAISING THE BEAR FLAG

READ ALOUD

United States soldiers went into California in 1846. The Mexican military leader José Castro called upon the Californios to defend their land. He asked them "to give to the entire world an example of loyalty and firmness, maintaining . . . eternal [unending] hatred toward your invaders! Long live the Mexican Republic!"

THE BIG PICTURE

By the 1840s many Americans believed that the United States should grow all the way to the Pacific Ocean. The United States, they felt, had the right to take over other countries' lands in North America. Once part of the United States, these lands would get the United States form of government, as well as provide wealth and opportunity to Americans.

The belief that the United States had the right to claim new lands was called Manifest Destiny. These words mean "obvious fate." James K. Polk shared this idea. Polk became President in 1845. President Polk wanted the United States to gain Texas, New Mexico, and California. Texas was an independent country that had broken away from Mexico in 1836. But New Mexico and California were part of Mexico.

If the United States took over these lands, it would reach all the way from the Atlantic Ocean to the Pacific Ocean. But how could this happen?

Focus Activity

READ TO LEARN
How did California become part of the United States?

VOCABULARY
republic
Bear Flag Revolt
Mexican War
Treaty of Guadalupe Hidalgo

PEOPLE
John C. Frémont
Jessie Frémont
José Castro
Mariano Guadalupe Vallejo
Stephen Watts Kearny
Andrés Pico
Bernarda Ruiz

PLACES
Dominguez Rancho
San Pascual
Cahuenga Pass

A REVOLT BEGINS

Captain John C. Frémont was an officer in the United States Army. His wife, Jessie Frémont, was a writer. In the 1840s John led journeys in the American West. He and Jessie wrote exciting books about his travels. Their books presented him as a brave hero.

John and Jessie Frémont wrote books about the West. The flag (bottom) is an 1896 copy of William Todd's original bear flag.

John Frémont came to California on December 9, 1845. With him were 60 armed men. He met with Colonel José Castro at Monterey. Colonel Castro ordered them out of California.

Frémont Returns

After crossing into Oregon, however, Frémont ordered his men to turn back. Frémont's return was welcomed by some American settlers. He had spread rumors that Castro would make the settlers, too, leave California.

Then Frémont encouraged a band of about 30 people to rebel, or make a revolt. They surrounded the home of Colonel Mariano Guadalupe Vallejo, in Sonoma. Vallejo was one of California's most important citizens. On the morning of June 14, 1846, the rebels captured him. Frémont ordered him held prisoner.

The rebels declared California to be independent from Mexico. They raised a flag over Sonoma. The flag, made by William Todd, had a drawing of a grizzly bear, the strongest animal in California. Printed on the flag were the words CALIFORNIA REPUBLIC. A republic is a government in which people choose leaders to represent them. This event was the start of the Bear Flag Revolt.

CALIFORNIA REPUBLIC.

159

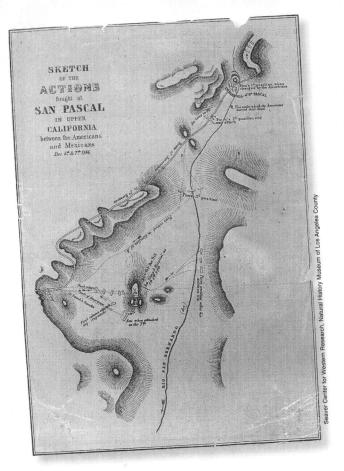

SKETCH OF THE ACTIONS fought at SAN PASCAL IN UPPER CALIFORNIA between the Americans and Mexicans Dec 6th & 7th 1846.

Seaver Center for Western Research, Natural History Museum of Los Angeles County

The Battle of San Pascual, shown on the map at left, ended in victory for the Californios.

WAR WITH MEXICO

On May 13, 1846, the United States and Mexico went to war. Fighting broke out along the Rio Grande River in an area claimed by both countries. President Polk hoped a quick war would gain Texas and California for the United States.

The Mexican War reached California on July 7. On that day United States Navy ships, led by John Drake Sloat, landed at Monterey. With Sloat were 250 soldiers. Sloat claimed that California was now "a portion [part] of the United States." The Bear Flag rebels soon joined Sloat's soldiers.

The Californios Strike Back

More troops landed at Los Angeles in August. At first they met no fighting. Then, on October 8, Californio soldiers led by José Antonio Carrillo attacked. The Californios had horses, long wooden lances, and rifles. They also had a cannon that a woman named Inocencia Reyes had hidden from the Americans in her garden. The Californios won a battle with the Americans at Dominguez Rancho.

Soon more American soldiers came overland from Kansas with General Stephen Watts Kearny. Before dawn on December 6, Kearny's group of about 100 soldiers attacked 150 Californios camped near the village of San Pascual. The Americans were tired, hungry, and weak from their long journey. They were not in shape to fight.

Andrés Pico, the Californio leader, allowed the Americans to move forward through the fog and rain. John Griffin was a doctor with Kearny's army. He described what Pico's men did next:

They came at us . . . with their lances—being mounted on swift horses—and most of our [guns] . . . missed fire from the rain . . . our advance was perfectly at their mercy [under their power].

The Californios won the battle. About 20 Americans were killed. The Californios were hardly hurt at all.

Infographic

The War in California

American settlers began the Bear Flag Revolt in June 1846. The Mexican War soon came to California. At first the Californios won several battles against American soldiers. What happened during the war in California?

CARRILLO

Sonoma
A group of American settlers start the Bear Flag Revolt on June 14, 1846.

Monterey
United States Navy Commodore John D. Sloat captures the capital of Mexican California on July 2, 1846.

Cahuenga Pass
On January 13, Californios surrender to United States forces, ending fighting in California.

Los Angeles
On August 13, 1846, United States forces capture Los Angeles. On September 26, Californios retake Los Angeles.

Dominguez Rancho
On October 9, 1846, Californios led by José Antonio Carrillo again defeat United States forces near Los Angeles.

KEARNY

San Pascual
On December 6, 1846, Californios led by Andrés Pico defeat United States forces under General Kearny.

PICO

Andrés Pico and John C. Frémont sign a treaty at Cahuenga Pass.

AFTER THE WAR

The Californios lost their struggle against the Americans. The Americans won because they had more soldiers, weapons, and ammunition.

A woman in Santa Barbara helped to bring the fighting to an end. Bernarda Ruiz told Frémont that she wanted peace in California. Ruiz offered to set up a meeting between Frémont and Pico. The meeting took place at Cahuenga (cah WENG uh) Pass, near Los Angeles. There, on January 13, 1847, the Californios surrendered. The fighting in California was over.

A Treaty Is Signed

The Mexican War continued for another year in Texas and Mexico.

The war finally ended when officials from the United States and Mexico signed the Treaty of Guadalupe Hidalgo on February 2, 1848. A treaty is an agreement to make peace.

In the treaty Mexico gave to the United States more than 525,000 square miles of land, known as the Mexican Cession. The treaty also promised to protect the rights of people who lived in the Mexican Cession. What rights did it promise the Mexicans?

MANY VOICES
PRIMARY SOURCE

Excerpt from
the Treaty of Guadalupe Hidalgo,
signed in 1848.

*Mexicans now established in **territories** previously belonging to Mexico, and which remain for the future within the limits of the United States . . . shall be free to continue where they now **reside**, or to remove at any time to the Mexican Republic. . . . Those who shall prefer to remain in the said territories may either retain the title and rights of Mexican citizens, or acquire those of citizens of the United States. . . .*

In the said territories, property of every kind, now belonging to Mexicans established there, shall be . . . respected . . . as if [it] belonged to citizens of the United States.

territories: lands owned by a country
reside: live in

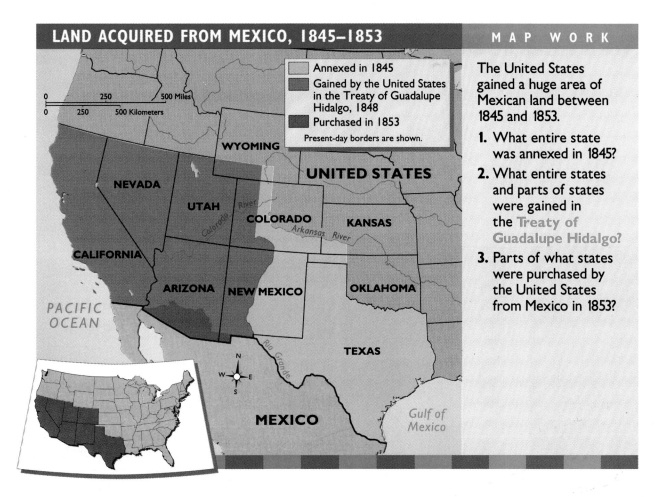

MAP WORK

Annexed in 1845

Gained by the United States in the Treaty of Guadalupe Hidalgo, 1848

Purchased in 1853

Present-day borders are shown.

0   250   500 Miles
0   250   500 Kilometers

WYOMING

NEVADA

UTAH

Colorado River

COLORADO

Arkansas River

KANSAS

UNITED STATES

CALIFORNIA

ARIZONA

NEW MEXICO

OKLAHOMA

PACIFIC OCEAN

Rio Grande

TEXAS

N W E S

MEXICO

Gulf of Mexico

The United States gained a huge area of Mexican land between 1845 and 1853.

1. What entire state was annexed in 1845?

2. What entire states and parts of states were gained in the Treaty of Guadalupe Hidalgo?

3. Parts of what states were purchased by the United States from Mexico in 1853?

WHY IT MATTERS

The Treaty of Guadalupe Hidalgo made California part of the United States. Many Americans believed that our country had now achieved its Manifest Destiny. For Mexico the war with the United States was a great loss. It had to give up about half its land.

✓ Reviewing Facts and Ideas

MAIN IDEAS

- John C. Frémont encouraged American settlers in California to start the Bear Flag Revolt.

- American and Mexican forces fought in California during the Mexican War.

- Bernarda Ruiz helped set up a meeting at Cahuenga Pass that ended the fighting in California.

- The Treaty of Guadalupe Hidalgo gave the Mexican Cession, including California, to the United States.

THINK ABOUT IT

1. How did the Bear Flag Revolt begin?

2. Who were three of the military leaders of the Californios?

3. FOCUS How did California become part of the United States?

4. THINKING SKILL Make a _conclusion_ about why the American settlers welcomed Frémont's soldiers.

5. GEOGRAPHY Look at the map above. In what year did California become part of the United States?

163

CITIZENSHIP VIEWPOINTS

Seaver Center for Western Research, Natural History Museum of Los Angeles County

California was the thirty-first state to join the United States, but the flag still had only 28 stars in 1850.

WHAT DID CALIFORNIANS THINK ABOUT JOINING THE UNITED STATES?

In 1846 the Mexican War broke out. The United States declared that it owned California.

The feelings of people in California were divided. Many Californios were angry at the United States. Juan Bautista Alvarado disliked the way Mexico governed California. Yet he did not want his land to be forced to join another country.

Some Californios, however, felt differently. Mariano Guadalupe Vallejo felt little connection to the rest of Mexico. He believed the Californios would be better off in the United States.

As believers in Manifest Destiny, most American settlers felt that the United States had the right to take over California. Lansford W. Hastings thought that the Mexican government should not try to stop American settlers from coming to California.

Native Americans served on both sides of the conflict. A group of people who were probably Tongva helped the Mexicans defend Los Angeles. On the other side, 40 Native Americans helped John C. Frémont.

Read the three different viewpoints about California joining the United States. Then answer the questions that follow.

Three DIFFERENT Viewpoints

1 JUAN BAUTISTA ALVARADO
Former President of the California *Diputación*
Excerpt from his book *Historia de California*, 1876

Despite my strong and powerful reasons to complain against Mexico, which had for so many years been our oppressor *[mistreated us]* . . . we preferred to undertake a life of shortages *[and]* uncertainty . . . until [Mexico] triumphed . . . in this lopsided *[uneven]* contest . . . provoked *[started]* by its powerful neighbor.

". . . we preferred to undertake a life of shortages [and] uncertainty. . . ."

2 LANSFORD W. HASTINGS
United States settler
Excerpt from a letter to John Marsh, 1846

What . . . folly *[foolishness]* it is for the natives of the Californias to attempt to check *[stop]* the emigration [from the United States] to this country. They might just as well attempt to arrest the thundering wheels of time [or] to resist the mighty waters' flow.

". . . folly . . . to check the emigration. . . ."

3 MARIANO GUADALUPE VALLEJO
Northern Military Commander of Mexican California
Excerpt from a speech, 1846

Gentlemen, I am of the opinion that . . . only one thing remains to be done and that is to declare the annexation of our country to the United States. . . . Only in this way will we be able to overcome the ills *[problems]* that hold us back from developing our resources.

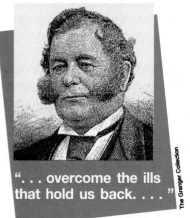

". . . overcome the ills that hold us back. . . ."

BUILDING CITIZENSHIP

1. What was the viewpoint of each person?
2. In what ways are some of the viewpoints alike? In what ways are the viewpoints different?
3. What other viewpoints might people have had on this issue?

SHARING VIEWPOINTS

Suppose you and your classmates were living at the time of the American annexation of California. Discuss what you agree with about these viewpoints. Then, as a class, write two statements that all of you could have agreed with about California joining the United States.

CHAPTER 6 REVIEW

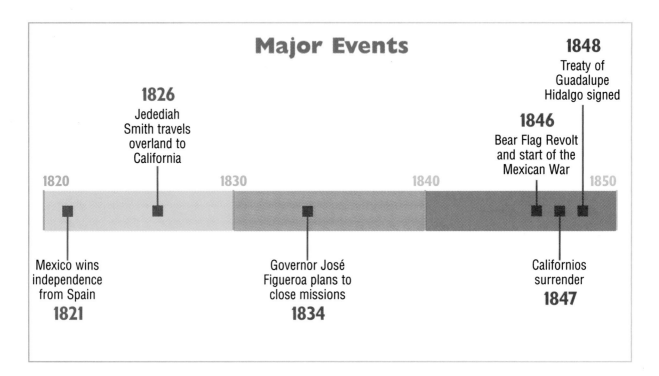

Major Events

1848
Treaty of Guadalupe Hidalgo signed

1826
Jedediah Smith travels overland to California

1846
Bear Flag Revolt and start of the Mexican War

1820　　　1830　　　1840　　　1850

Mexico wins independence from Spain
1821

Governor José Figueroa plans to close missions
1834

Californios surrender
1847

THINKING ABOUT VOCABULARY

Number a sheet of paper from 1 to 5. Beside each number write the word from the list below that best completes the sentence.

diseño　　republic　　trapper
import　　tax

1. Someone who catches animals for their fur is a _____.

2. A map showing a rancho's border was called a _____.

3. Money people must pay to the government by law is a _____.

4. An _____ is something brought in from another country for sale or use.

5. A government in which people choose leaders to represent them is a _____.

THINKING ABOUT FACTS

1. Why did Mexican leaders want to close the missions?

2. Who received land grants?

3. Where was California's capital moved to?

4. What were California's two main exports?

5. Why did Californios dislike the Mexican governors?

6. What were beaver pelts used for?

7. Why did Echeandía put Jedediah Smith in jail?

8. What was on the flag made by William Todd?

9. Why did the Americans win the war in California?

10. What did Mexico give up and get in the Treaty of Guadalupe Hidalgo?

THINK AND WRITE ✐

WRITING A STORY

Write a story that describes what happened at a roundup.

WRITING A LOG

Suppose you are Jedediah Smith. Write a log of your trip to California.

WRITING AN EXPLANATION

Write a paragraph explaining how the Mexican War affected life in California.

APPLYING STUDY SKILLS

READING TIME LINES

1. How many years does the time line on the opposite page cover?

2. In what year did Jedediah Smith make his trip to California?

3. When did the Bear Flag Revolt take place?

4. About how long after the Bear Flag Revolt did California officially become part of the United States?

5. How are time lines useful in studying history?

Summing Up the Chapter

Use the following time line to organize information from the chapter. Copy the time line on a piece of paper. Then fill in a major event from our state's history for each date on the time line. When you have filled in the time line, use the information to write an answer to the question "How did California change in the early and middle 1800s?"

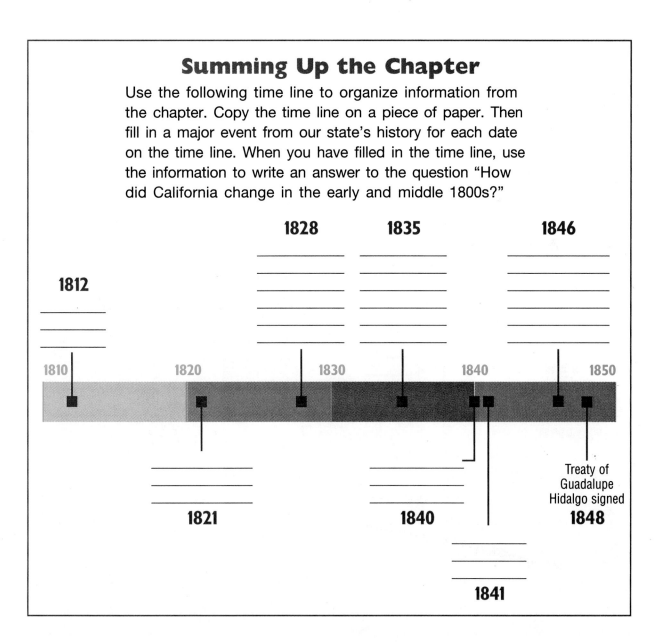

1812

1828

1835

1846

1810   1820   1830   1840   1850

1821

1840

1841

Treaty of Guadalupe Hidalgo signed
1848

CHAPTER 7

The Golden State

THINKING ABOUT HISTORY AND GEOGRAPHY

You read how California became a part of the United States in 1848. In Chapter 7 you will read about another event that occurred in 1848. Read on to find out what that event was and how it led to a new California.

1848
COLOMA

Men working for Johann Sutter discover gold

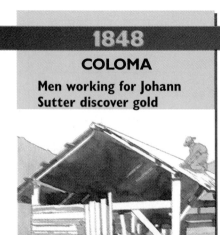

1849
MONTEREY

José Antonio Carrillo speaks at the constitutional convention

1851
RICH BAR

Dame Shirley writes letters about life in gold-mining camps

168

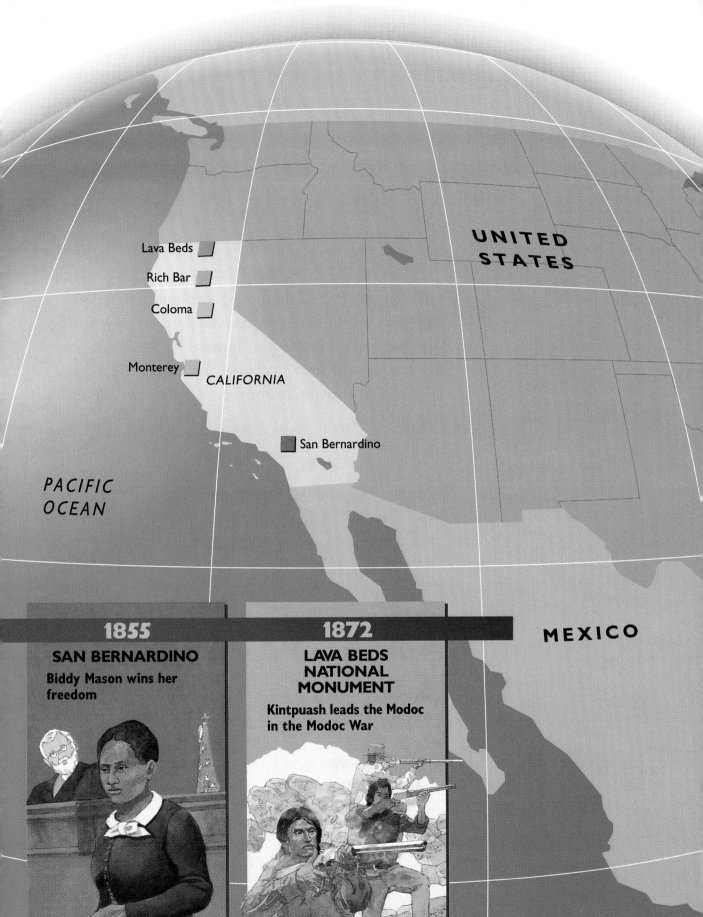

Lava Beds

Rich Bar

Coloma

Monterey

CALIFORNIA

UNITED
STATES

San Bernardino

PACIFIC
OCEAN

MEXICO

1855

SAN BERNARDINO

Biddy Mason wins her freedom

1872

LAVA BEDS NATIONAL MONUMENT

Kintpuash leads the Modoc in the Modoc War

THE GOLD RUSH

READ ALOUD

Early on the morning of January 24, 1848, James Marshall's eye was suddenly "caught by something shining in the bottom of the ditch. . . . [It] was about half the size and shape of a pea. It made my heart thump, for I was certain it was gold."

Focus Activity

READ TO LEARN
How did the discovery of gold change California?

VOCABULARY
Gold Rush
Forty-Niner
isthmus
pass
mother lode

PEOPLE
James Marshall
James Beckwourth

PLACES
American River
Sutter's Mill
Isthmus of Panama
Beckwourth Pass

THE BIG PICTURE

In the last chapter you read about the settlers from the United States who started to come to California in the early 1840s. James Marshall was one of those settlers. In 1847 Johann Sutter hired Marshall to build a sawmill. A sawmill is a place where trees are cut into boards for building. Sutter hoped to sell the boards to the many new settlers. Marshall found a spot along the south fork of the American River near the Maidu village of Coloma. While building the sawmill, known as Sutter's Mill, Marshall made his exciting discovery.

Sutter wanted Marshall and the Native Americans working with him to keep the discovery a secret. It was too late, however. News of the discovery spread. Soon, not only New Helvetia but all of California would change forever.

The Granger Collection

THE RUSH IS ON

In the months after Marshall's discovery, people from all over California went to mine, or dig, for gold. This rapid movement of people in search of gold is known as the Gold Rush. Soldiers, sailors, blacksmiths, bakers—people simply stopped what they were doing and left. "All were off for the mines," reported Walter Colton, alcalde of Monterey, "some on horses, some on carts, and some on crutches."

The urge to get rich struck some like a sickness. People called it "gold fever." An early San Francisco newspaper complained:

> The whole country . . . from the seashore to the base of the Sierra Nevada, resounds [rings out] with the sordid [unpleasant] cry of "gold! Gold!! GOLD!!!"

Almost 1,300 of the miners in 1848 were Californios. More than half the miners were Native Americans. They often worked for American settlers or Californios and got little in return.

News of the discovery quickly spread. American settlers from Oregon hurried south. People from Mexico, Peru, Chile, and Hawaii joined the rush a few months later.

By the end of 1848, about 6,000 miners were at work in California. They were the lucky ones. They had only a few basic tools and a willingness to work very hard. Yet they managed to find about $10 million worth of gold. That would be about $2 billion at today's prices.

California Historical Society

James Marshall (far left) found gold while building Sutter's Mill (center). Posters advertising ships (above) attracted gold seekers to California.

171

THE FORTY-NINERS

The fantastic tales of gold reached newspapers in the eastern United States. Cautious people doubted such stories. On December 5, 1848, however, President James K. Polk swept away the doubts. He told Congress that the reports of gold in California were true. By the spring of 1849, many people in the eastern United States were making ready to leave for California.

Three Routes Westward

The gold seekers who left for California in 1849 were called Forty-Niners. Most were from the eastern United States. Many also came from China, Australia, and Europe. Look at the map on this page to see the main routes the Forty-Niners took.

Most early Forty-Niners came by sea. The longest route from the eastern United States was around South America. This trip of 18,000 miles took five to eight months. Rounding Cape Horn was the most difficult part of the voyage. Storms there sent many ships to the bottom of the sea.

A second sea route covered just 5,000 miles. It involved crossing the Isthmus of Panama. An isthmus is a narrow stretch of land with water on both sides. This route took between three and five months. The main difficulty was crossing the tropical forests of Panama. Along the way, many Forty-Niners became ill and died from diseases.

The overland route to California was the shortest—only 2,000 miles. It usually took three or four months. It was also the way that most of the Forty-Niners came. About twice as many came overland as came by sea.

Hardships on the Overland Trail

Forty-Niners on the overland trail gathered in Missouri. There they waited for the good weather of the late spring to start their journey.

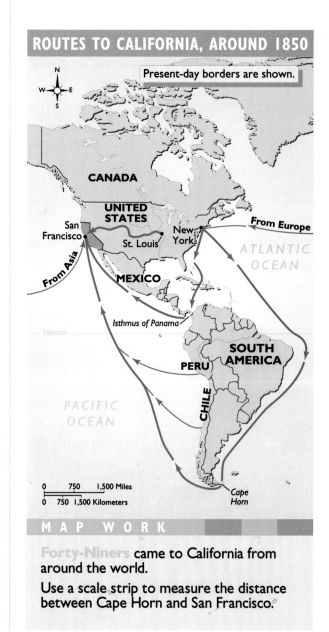

ROUTES TO CALIFORNIA, AROUND 1850

Present-day borders are shown.

MAP WORK

Forty-Niners came to California from around the world.

Use a scale strip to measure the distance between Cape Horn and San Francisco.

Miners (above) were aided by "mountain men" like James Beckwourth (left).

There were no roads, only rough trails. There were no stores. Everything they needed, they had to bring with them. Crossing a stream or river could be dangerous, and there were dozens to cross. When Sallie Hester's party came to the Platte River, for example, it

> had a great deal of trouble swimming [the] cattle across. . . . A number of accidents happened here. A lady and four children were drowned.

Forty-Niners worried that Native Americans would attack. After all, they were crossing Native American land without permission. But Native Americans did not often bother the gold seekers.

In the deserts Forty-Niners battled heat and thirst. One weary traveler later remembered the "tramp of men and beasts, worn out with heat and famished [starving] for water." It was during the Gold Rush that Death Valley got its name. Some groups of Forty-Niners who tried to use Death Valley as a shortcut never came out.

The Sierra Nevada was the final challenge. Its high passes, or narrow gaps between the mountains, were difficult to cross. James Beckwourth made the trip easier. Beckwourth was born in slavery in Virginia. He became one of the most famous "mountain men" in the West. In 1851 Beckwourth found a new pass through the northern Sierra. Beckwourth Pass made this part of the journey safer for the gold seekers.

The Forty-Niners took all these risks because of the chance to get rich in California. Along the trail, they kept their hopes up singing songs like the one on the next page.

OH, CALIFORNIA!

I soon shall be in Fri-is-co and there I'll look a-round, And

when I see the gold lumps there, I'll pick them off the ground, I'll

scrape the moun-tains clean, my boys, I'll drain the ri-vers dry. A

pock-et-ful of rocks bring home, so bro-thers don't you cry!

Oh Ca-li-for-nia, that's the place for me. I'm

bound for San Fran-cis-co with my wash-bowl on my knee.

ARRIVING IN CALIFORNIA

When the gold seekers arrived in California, they often felt proud and thankful. Charles Glass Gray came overland in 1849. He celebrated his arrival by sleeping in a bed for the first time in months. Gray was glad to be off the trail "for I have suffered enough already I think."

Arriving in California could also bring disappointment. Groups that had formed along the trail now broke up. Gray felt a sense of "loneliness . . . in this land of strangers."

The miners soon headed for the mother lode. This was a gold-rich area in the central Sierra Nevada foothills. There they faced a tough time striking it rich. By the end of 1849, more than 40,000 miners were working the mother lode. As you will learn in the next lesson, many miners came away disappointed.

MOTHER LODE

Forty-Niners played banjos, like the one at right, to entertain themselves in the camps.

Oakland Museum of California

WHY IT MATTERS

Before the Gold Rush, California was a land of ranches, small towns, and Native American villages. News of the gold discovery brought thousands of people from across the country and around the world. California changed overnight into a land with several bustling cities and a booming population.

✓ Reviewing Facts and Ideas

MAIN IDEAS

- James Marshall discovered gold at Sutter's Mill in 1848.
- The Gold Rush brought people all over the world to California.
- Forty-Niners from the eastern United States came by three main routes.

THINK ABOUT IT

1. What portion of the miners in 1848 were Native Americans?
2. Why were the Forty-Niners willing to take the risks of coming to California?
3. **FOCUS** How did the discovery of gold change California's population?
4. **THINKING SKILL** *Compare and contrast* the three routes from the eastern United States.
5. **WRITE** Imagine that you have just arrived in California in 1849. Write a letter to a friend describing your trip, the people you met, and what you plan to do.

STUDY SKILLS

Reading Line and Circle Graphs

VOCABULARY

graph
line graph
circle graph

WHY THE SKILL MATTERS

In the last lesson you read about the beginning of the Gold Rush. You learned that thousands of people came to California to look for gold. About how many people were in California by 1850?

You can answer this question by looking at a graph. A graph is a special diagram that shows information in a clear way. A graph uses pictures to tell you a lot with only a few words.

USING LINE GRAPHS

Look at the graph on this page. It is a line graph. A line graph shows how something has changed over time. A line graph often shows an increase or decrease in number.

Start by reading the title. The title tells you that this is a graph of the population in California from 1845 to 1890.

Read the label at the left side of the graph. This gives the number of people. The dates at the bottom of the graph tell you the years that the population was measured.

Trace the line with your finger. Each dot on the line stands for the number of people in California during a particular

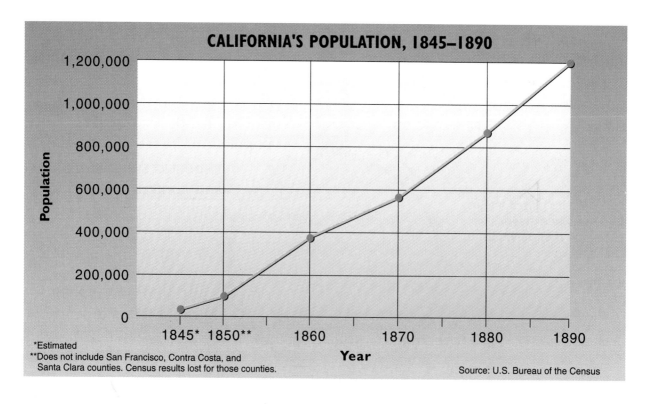

CALIFORNIA'S POPULATION, 1845–1890

*Estimated
**Does not include San Francisco, Contra Costa, and
Santa Clara counties. Census results lost for those counties.

Source: U.S. Bureau of the Census

year. As you can see, the population increased sharply between 1845 and 1850, when the Gold Rush started. But you can also see that California's population continued to grow very fast.

USING CIRCLE GRAPHS

Unlike a line graph, a circle graph does not show how things change over time. A circle graph shows how parts of something fit into the whole. Because each part may look like a slice of a pie, a circle graph is sometimes called a pie graph.

Read the title of the graph. This circle graph shows the numbers of California

HELPING Yourself

- **Line graphs** show how a piece of information changes over time.
- **Circle graphs** show how the parts fit into the whole.
- Study the title, key, and labels.
- Use the **graphs** to compare facts or figures.

workers in 1860. The "slices" show the different jobs that groups of workers had in California in 1860. They also show which type of job was most common at the time. You can tell that the largest group was the miners because this is the largest slice of the graph.

TRYING THE SKILL

Look again at the line graph of the population in California from 1845 to 1890. How many people lived in California in 1870? How many lived here in 1890?

Now study the circle graph of California workers in 1860. Were there more laborers or farmers? Were there more merchants or manufacturers?

REVIEWING THE SKILL

1. During which ten-year period did the population of California rise the least? What did you do to find the answer?

2. What can you conclude from the line graph about the population of California between the years 1850 and 1860?

3. How do line and circle graphs differ? How do graphs make it easier for you to understand information?

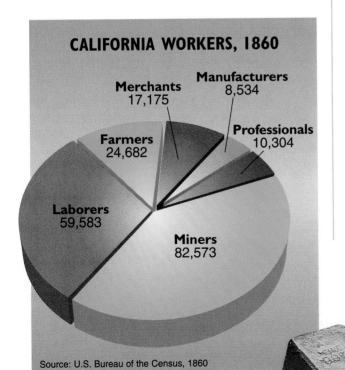

CALIFORNIA WORKERS, 1860

Manufacturers 8,534
Merchants 17,175
Professionals 10,304
Farmers 24,682
Laborers 59,583
Miners 82,573

Source: U.S. Bureau of the Census, 1860

177

The Granger Collection

LIFE IN THE GOLD RUSH

Focus Activity

READ TO LEARN
What was life in the Gold Rush like?

VOCABULARY
placer
panning
hydraulic mining

PEOPLE
Levi Strauss
Dame Shirley

PLACES
San Francisco
Sacramento
Stockton

READ ALOUD

*It's four long years since I reached this land
In search of gold among the rocks and sand;
And yet I'm poor when the truth is told,
I'm a lousy miner, I'm a lousy miner
In search of shining gold.*

Songs like this one tell of the bad luck that many miners had during the Gold Rush.

THE BIG PICTURE

Gold attracted a flood of newcomers to California. They changed everything. New cities started up. Old ones grew quickly. Old ways of life died out— sometimes violently—and new ways began.

The gold seekers came to California hoping to become rich. Most were disappointed. Only about 1 out of every 20 gold seekers returned home richer than when he left. Those who stayed on began the job of building California.

BOOMING CITIES

As miners poured into California, new cities sprang up. The biggest boom town of all was San Francisco. A young reporter from New York named Bayard Taylor described the city in September 1849.

On every side stood buildings of all kinds, begun or half-finished, and the greater part of them [just] canvas sheds, open in front and covered with all kinds of signs in all languages.

Hundreds of abandoned ships crowded the waterfront. Their crews had left them to go to the gold fields. San Franciscans pulled many of the ships onto land and turned them into shops and houses.

From just 600 people in 1848, San Francisco grew to 25,000 in 1849. By 1852 there were over 30 churches and 40,000 people in San Francisco. Peruvians, Chileans, Australians, Chinese, French, Italians, Irish, Americans—people came from around the world. Most were men. There were ten men for each woman.

San Francisco soon became a center of banking and business. Shopkeepers there grew rich selling

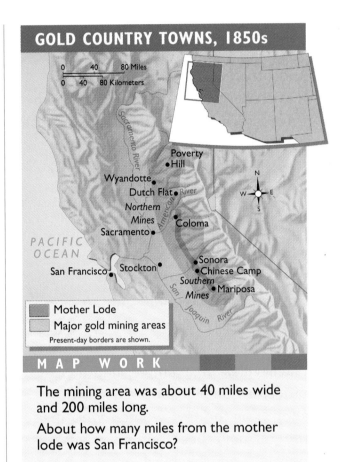

GOLD COUNTRY TOWNS, 1850s

Mother Lode
Major gold mining areas
Present-day borders are shown.

MAP WORK

The mining area was about 40 miles wide and 200 miles long.

About how many miles from the mother lode was San Francisco?

food, clothing, and mining tools. Levi Strauss, a Jewish settler from Germany who came to San Francisco in 1853, was one such shopkeeper. He bought goods from the eastern United States and sold them to shopkeepers in other parts of California. His success showed that there was often more money in supplying the needs of the miners than in mining itself.

San Francisco Maritime Museum

DIGGING FOR GOLD

Most of the clothes, shoes, tools, and other goods a miner needed had to be brought all the way from the eastern United States. They came by ship to San Francisco. From there goods moved to two supply centers. Sacramento served the northern mining towns. Stockton served the southern mining towns.

Mining Camps and Towns

In the mother lode, mining camps started wherever gold was found. These grew quickly into towns. Placerville, for example, had a post office, a butcher shop, and a tool shop. For the few women who made the journey, these mining towns offered good business opportunities. Some women started bakeries, laundries, and rooming houses. Others, like Luzena Stanley Wilson, started restaurants to feed the miners.

Often miners would name towns after their homes. Sonora was named by gold seekers from Mexico. A group of Wyandot Native Americans from Kansas named their town Wyandotte. Chinese Camp is a reminder of the miners who came from China.

Other towns got more colorful names. Why, do you suppose, did miners name towns Poverty Hill, Skunk Gulch, or Murderers Bar?

In the Diggings

The miners' dreams of easy wealth soon faded. Looking for gold was hard work. Mostly they dug with a pick and shovel. Six days a week the miners worked their small claims. They worked for long hours knee-deep in icy cold streams and rivers. Their backs ached. Their feet grew numb while their faces blistered in the sun.

Most of the gold taken from California in the early years was placer gold. *Placer* is a Spanish word meaning "a sandy stream bank."

A miner would scoop some dirt into a shallow pan. Next, he would fill the pan with water. Carefully swishing the pan around, the miner spilled out the water and dirt. If there was any gold, it would stay in the pan because it was very heavy.

This process of mining, called panning, was hard, tiring work. Look at the diagram to see some other ways miners looked for gold.

DID YOU KNOW?

What is gold used for?

When you talk into the phone, do you know you are talking into a thin layer of gold? Or when you plug in a TV or VCR, do you know the plug is coated with gold?

Gold is used for a lot of things. It is very strong. A single ounce of gold can be pulled into a wire 50 miles long and thinner than a human hair!

Today most gold continues to be used the way it has always been used—to make jewelry.

Înfographic

Mining for Gold

Miners developed a number of clever devices to help them do their job more easily. But the basic idea stayed the same as in panning. Water and constant motion were used to separate gold from dirt.

THE ROCKER

One miner shovels dirt into the top box, another pours in water and moves the rocker back and forth.

Water washes dirt through holes in the box.

A canvas screen slows the water.

Gold sinks behind wooden bars. Muddy water flows out.

Wooden wing dam stops water.

THE LONG TOM

Sluice brings water to long tom.

Long tom separates gold from dirt. It does not need to be rocked.

Miners shovel dirt into long tom.

A MINER'S LIFE

As you read earlier, most of the people who came to California in the Gold Rush were men. One of the women who made the journey was Louise Clappe, who was known as Dame Shirley. She and her husband lived in a mining camp called Rich Bar, along the Feather River, in 1851 and 1852. She wrote a series of letters to her sister Molly in New England. The letters were published in 1854 under the name Dame Shirley.

The Shirley Letters

About a thousand men—and only four women—lived in Rich Bar when Dame Shirley arrived in September 1851. She met one miner who had not spoken to a woman for two years!

In her letters Dame Shirley often complained that the miners drank liquor, fought, and gambled. She disapproved when miners from the United States attacked miners from Mexico. Yet she also felt sorry for these miners, too. She knew how difficult it was for them to be far from their homes and families. They had little to do besides work, and the work could be boring and dangerous. One young man had his leg crushed by a falling boulder, or large rock. Dame Shirley wrote that "similar [accidents] happen very often."

Miners visited towns like Placerville (left) but mostly worked their claims.

182

She also understood the disappointment many of the miners faced.

A man may work . . . for many months, and be poorer at the end of the time than when he commenced [began]; or he may "take out" thousands in a few hours. . . . And yet, I cannot help remarking that almost all with whom we are acquainted [know] seem to have lost.

Many miners never found more than $8 worth of gold a day. That was more than they earned back home. But prices in California were much higher. A loaf of bread that sold for 5 cents in New York cost 50 to 75 cents in California. A blanket cost $40. Eggs sold for $5 each. Miners used up their money quickly.

Dame Shirley's letters tell us a lot about everyday life during the Gold Rush. In the following letter, for example, she describes the interior of her simple cabin to her sister Molly. How would you feel entering such a cabin?

MANY VOICES
PRIMARY SOURCE

Excerpt from a letter written by Dame Shirley on October 7, 1851.

Enter my dear; you are perfectly welcome; besides, we could not keep you out if we would, as there is not even a latch on the canvas door. . . .

The room into which we have just entered is about twenty feet square. It is lined over the top with white cotton cloth . . . which being sewed together only in spots, stretch[es] apart in many places, giving one a birds-eye view of the shingles above. . . .

The fireplace is built of stones and mud . . . ; contrary to the usual custom, it is built inside . . . and you may imagine the queer [strange] appearance of this unfinished pile of stones, mud and sticks. . . .

I must mention that the floor is so uneven that no article of furniture gifted with four legs pretends to stand upon but three at once, so that the chairs, tables, etc., remind you constantly of a dog with a sore foot.

CALIFORNIA GOLD PRODUCTION, 1848–1860

Gold produced (in millions of dollars) vs. Year

Source: *California Gold* by Rodman W. Paul

GRAPH WORK

California gold production reached its peak in 1852.

About how much did it drop by between 1852 and 1857?

CHANGES IN THE GOLD FIELDS

In mining camps there were no police or judges to keep law and order. The miners had to make and follow their own rules. Unfortunately the miners' rules did not treat everyone equally.

Conflict

The gold country was the homeland of thousands of Miwok, Nisenan, Yokuts, and other Native Americans. The miners swarmed across their land. Without knowing it, they brought diseases that killed many Native Americans. They also ruined the resources that the Native Americans needed to live.

Starving, the Indians stole the cattle and supplies of the newcomers. Some of the miners attacked Native American villages. They killed men, women, and children. Between 1848 and 1880, at least 4,500 Native Americans were murdered.

Unfair Taxes

Miners from the United States were often jealous of miners from other countries. In 1850 and 1852 they got the government to pass a tax against foreign miners, especially Mexicans and Chinese. These unfair taxes made it difficult for foreign miners to make any money. Within a year of the 1852 tax, nearly 10,000 miners had returned to Mexico.

Environmental damage caused by hydraulic mining (above left) can still be seen today near Nevada City (above).

Between 1852 and 1870, half of all state taxes were paid by Chinese, who were only a small part of our state's population.

Hydraulic Mining

Placer gold was easy to find. Once it was gone, however, miners had to dig deeper. In 1853 hydraulic (hī DRAW lihk) mining was invented. Miners used hoses to shoot water at hillsides thought to have gold. Hydraulic mining damaged the environment. It washed away hill-

sides, clogged streams, and killed fish. The land was scarred forever.

Hydraulic mining changed life for the miners. Only large companies could afford the costly hydraulic mining tools. Soon most miners became workers for these companies instead of mining for themselves. Mining was no longer an adventure. Now it was just a job.

WHY IT MATTERS

The Gold Rush was the first of many great booms in California history. While most miners failed to make a fortune, the Gold Rush helped to make California a land of golden opportunity for people around the world.

✓ Reviewing Facts and Ideas

MAIN IDEAS

- San Francisco grew rapidly.
- Mining for gold was hard work.
- Not everyone was treated fairly.

THINK ABOUT IT

1. Name three important cities in California during the Gold Rush.
2. How were miners from Mexico and China treated unfairly?
3. **FOCUS** What was life in the Gold Rush like?
4. **THINKING SKILL** What *questions* would you ask Dame Shirley?
5. **GEOGRAPHY** Look at the map of Gold Country Towns on page 179. In which region of California are most of these towns located?

CALIFORNIA FASHION
BLUE JEANS

You may be wearing a legacy from the Gold Rush and not even know it!

We all like to wear blue jeans because they are comfortable, they last a long time, and they look good. Look in any magazine—you will probably see someone wearing them.

Blue jeans were invented in California in 1872. Levi Strauss, the successful San Francisco merchant you read about in Lesson 2, went into business with a Nevada tailor named Jacob Davis. Strauss and Davis made blue jeans for the tough life of the mines.

They used *denim*, a strong cloth named after the town of Nimes (NEEM) in France, where it was made. Before long the partners had factories making thousands of pairs of blue jeans.

Today, in almost any country, you may see people wearing jeans in all colors. California gave the world one of its favorite pairs of pants.

Jacob Davis (above) invented a way to fasten the pockets of jeans with metal rivets so they would not tear off during hard work. He went into business with Levi Strauss (right).

Levi Strauss sold his clothes mostly to miners and other laborers, as the ad shows (below). Today jeans come in every color of the rainbow.

A NEW STATE

READ ALOUD

Portsmouth Square in San Francisco was filled with a meeting of restless people. They had gathered on a fine June day in 1849 to demand a new government. They wanted "the great and growing interests of California [to] be represented in the . . . United States."

THE BIG PICTURE

Why were these San Franciscans restless? After the Mexican War, California became part of the United States. But it was not yet a state. Californians did not vote for, or choose, their leaders. Instead, five different military governors led California in only ten months! These governors mostly followed the old Mexican laws. Few American settlers, however, knew these laws. They wanted to have a say in making their own laws.

Bennett Riley was the last military governor. On June 3, 1849, he announced plans for a meeting to be held in Monterey in three months. He called on Californians to pick some representatives, or people who would speak for them, to attend the meeting. This meeting would be the first step in forming a state government for California.

California's constitution (far right) was written at Colton Hall. It was published in both English and Spanish.

Focus Activity

READ TO LEARN
How did Californians form a state government?

VOCABULARY
representative
convention
constitution
legislature
capital
Compromise of 1850

PEOPLE
Bennett Riley
José Antonio Carrillo
Peter Burnett
Henry Clay
Biddy Mason

PLACES
Monterey
San Jose

MAKING A CONSTITUTION

The convention began on September 1, 1849, in Monterey's Colton Hall. A convention is a formal meeting for a special purpose. The goal of the convention was to plan a new constitution (kahn stih TOO shun). A constitution is a plan of government.

Of the 48 delegates, or representatives, at the meeting, most were Americans who had come to California before the Gold Rush. All the delegates were men. No women or African Americans were allowed to take part. Only eight of the delegates were Californios, including José Antonio Carrillo. He spoke up for the large land holders. They were afraid any new government would tax them unfairly.

The issue of California's eastern border divided the convention. Some delegates wanted it to extend to the Great Salt Lake. The majority, however, thought a border set along the Sierra Nevada and the Colorado River made more sense. Such a border would be accepted by the Congress in Washington, D.C.

A Free State

Surprisingly, all the delegates quickly agreed not to allow slavery in the California. Slavery is the practice of owning a person as property. The United States was divided over slavery at this time. Some states allowed it. Others did not.

In California miners opposed slavery. They felt that having slaves gave some miners an unfair advantage in the search for gold. Since miners were the largest group in California at this time, the convention followed their wishes.

The delegates also decided, however, that only white male citizens should be allowed to vote. The Californios objected. Some had Native American ancestors. They might lose their right to vote under this rule. Pablo de la Guerra called it "a great injustice."

California State Archives

189

THE 31ST STATE

On November 13, 1849, the people of California approved their constitution. They picked people to serve in the state government. They voted for representatives to the state legislature (LEJ ihs lay chur). A legislature is a group of representatives who make laws.

Peter Burnett, a lawyer from Oregon, was picked to be the first governor. The governor's job is to carry out the laws made by the state legislature.

The legislature met in San Jose, the state's new capital. A capital is where a government meets. The legislators picked William Gwin and John C. Frémont to be California's senators. They would represent Californians in the United States Senate.

The Compromise

In Washington, D.C., Senators Gwin and Frémont asked the government to make California one of the United States. This was not an easy decision.

The country was split over slavery. Half the states, in the North, were free states. Slavery was not allowed in these states. The other half, in the South, allowed slavery. If California was admitted as a free state, the balance would change. Southern senators did not want California to join the country as a free state. Senators from the free states said that it should.

The arguments went on for months. Then Senator Henry Clay of Kentucky thought of a compromise, or agreement. In the Compromise of 1850,

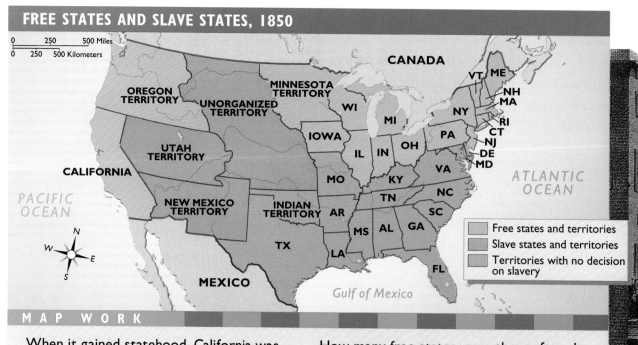

FREE STATES AND SLAVE STATES, 1850

Free states and territories
Slave states and territories
Territories with no decision on slavery

MAP WORK

When it gained statehood, California was a free state. That meant it did not allow slavery.

How many free states were there after the Compromise of 1850? How many slave states?

California would join as a free state. But the Compromise included a law the Southern states wanted, too. The Fugitive Slave Law said that police in free states had to help capture and return enslaved people who had escaped from the South.

The Granger Collection

Statehood

The Compromise of 1850 opened the way for California to become a state. On September 9, 1850, President Millard Fillmore signed the law making California the 31st state.

The news reached San Francisco on October 18. The city went wild! On October 29 a grand parade was held. Town marshals in red scarves led the way. Chinese marched beneath a blue silk banner. Californios carried a streamer with 31 stars.

A Fight for Freedom

In the 1850s about 2,500 African Americans lived in California. Some were free people who had come from the Northern states. Others were brought in slavery from the South.

Biddy Mason was among those who came to California as an enslaved person. Mason was born in Georgia. Her owner, Robert Smith, brought Mason and her three daughters to California in 1851. Smith did not tell Mason that slavery was against the law in California. He continued to force her to do what he wanted or be punished.

In 1855 Smith told Mason to go with him to Texas. Slavery was allowed in Texas. Once Mason and her family were there, they would lose the chance to be free. But it was against California law to trick someone into going to a slave state. Mason refused to go. When the local sheriff learned of Smith's plan, Smith was arrested.

Judge Benjamin Hayes said that Mason was a free person. He said that under California's constitution, she and her family "are entitled to their freedom and are free forever."

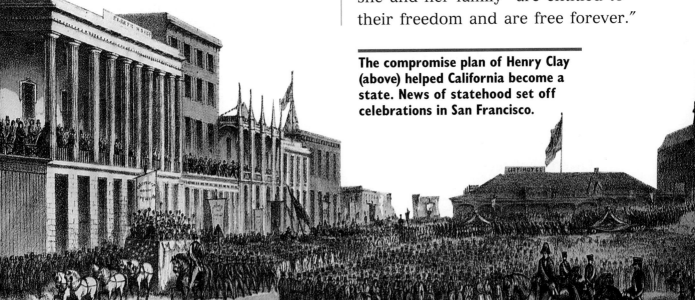

The compromise plan of Henry Clay (above) helped California become a state. News of statehood set off celebrations in San Francisco.

The Granger Collection

MASON HELPS OTHERS

Biddy Mason and other African Americans continued to fight for their rights. In 1855 they organized a Convention of Colored Citizens. *Colored* was a term used to describe African Americans. The convention asked the state government to give African Americans the right to vote.

Mason moved to Los Angeles, where she worked as a nurse. She was one of the first African American women to buy land in that city. She also became famous for being generous. She helped many people in need. Once, during a flood, she paid for the groceries of people whose homes had been flooded. Her great-granddaughter remembered that Mason was fond of saying:

If you hold your hand closed . . . nothing good can come in. The open hand is blessed, for it gives . . . even as it receives.

Biddy Mason (above) was a leading Los Angeles citizen.

WHY IT MATTERS

California entered the Union as a free state in 1850. Yet not all citizens were treated the same. African American men won the right to vote in 1870. It was not until 1911 that California women, black and white, got the right to vote. Native Americans became citizens in 1924. Some Californians from Asia were not allowed to become citizens or to vote until 1952. In every case, citizens worked hard for these rights. Working to make our state a better, fairer place is part of why we learn about citizenship.

✔// Reviewing Facts and Ideas

MAIN IDEAS
- A convention in Monterey created the California constitution.
- California entered the United States as the 31st state in 1850.
- The Biddy Mason case made all African Americans in California free people.

THINK ABOUT IT
1. Name two decisions the constitutional convention had to make.
2. Where was California's first state capital?
3. **FOCUS** How did Californians form a state government?
4. **THINKING SKILL** Name one *cause* and one *effect* of the Compromise of 1850.
5. **WRITE** Write a poem about the life of Biddy Mason. Use as many details of her life as possible.

CITIZENSHIP
MAKING A DIFFERENCE

Get Out to Vote

SAN JOSE—Analisa Castaneda is 14 years old, but she voted in the 1996 election for President. So did Dante Randazzo, age 12, and his sister Liana, age 10. Each of them also voted for Californians running for offices in state government.

By law, Americans have to be 18 years old to vote. Yet none of these young voters was breaking the law. They were among the thousands of people in Santa Clara County who took part in a program called Kids Voting. On election day Analisa and Dante and Liana went to the polls, or voting places, with their parents. Their votes were added up and reported. But they did not count in the official totals.

The goal of Kids Voting, explains Analisa, "is to get kids involved in learning more about their government. It's also a way for us to get our parents interested in voting."

The students started getting involved months before election day. At over 400 schools in Santa Clara County, students took time to learn about candidates and issues. In March 1996, 6,500 students met in the San Jose Arena for a one-day Kids Vention, a political convention, or gathering, for kids. Candidates for government office came to speak.

The students also debated and voted on issues. "One of the hottest debates," said Dante, "was over the question of whether students should be required to wear uniforms to school. During the voting at Kids Vention, I learned that what may seem right to you may not seem right to someone else. The voting may not always go your way. But if you don't vote, you don't have any chance of influencing the outcome."

Analisa believes that Kids Voting will change the way young people think about voting. "It will definitely result in more Americans voting in the future," she says, "because kids are learning that their vote can make a difference."

" . . . their vote can make a difference."

Analisa M. Castaneda

1840   1850 1851   1881

Society of California Pioneers

UNREST IN CALIFORNIA

Focus Activity

READ TO LEARN
How did Native Americans and Californios lose their lands?

VOCABULARY
vigilante
reservation
Modoc War
squatter

PEOPLE
Kintpuash
Helen Hunt Jackson
Mariano Guadalupe Vallejo

PLACES
Lava Beds National Monument

READ ALOUD

"Cheating, robbing, breaking promises . . . are clearly things which must [stop]." These are the words of Helen Hunt Jackson. Her 1881 book A Century of Dishonor *criticized the way Native Americans had been treated by the United States. She felt that United States citizens were not being true to their own beliefs, in California or elsewhere.*

THE BIG PICTURE

Even with a new state government, the 1850s were a time of unrest in California. Some of the new laws were unfair. They protected United States citizens. But they did not always protect Native Americans, Mexicans, African Americans, Californios, or people from Asia, Europe, and Australia.

Crime, too, was a big problem in California. The police were not strong enough to punish criminals. In San Francisco and in other places around the state, citizens calling themselves vigilantes (vihj uh LAN teez) responded. They arrested and punished people they claimed were criminals. But often the vigilantes simply arrested people they thought of as enemies, even if they had not broken the law. By taking the law into their own hands, the vigilantes were breaking the law themselves.

THE MODOC WAR

The United States government made 18 treaties with California's Native Americans in 1851 and 1852. Each treaty promised to create large reservations, or land set aside for Native Americans to live on.

The large reservations were never set aside, however. Settlers ignored the Native Americans' rights to their lands. In some cases, soldiers forced native people off their lands.

Kintpuash Leads His People

In 1872 about 150 Modoc tried to return to their lands in northern California. Their leader was Kintpuash (KIHNT poo ash), known also as Captain Jack. Using guns and cannons, soldiers attacked the Modoc. Kintpuash led his people bravely. They hid in the rough land now known as Lava Beds National Monument, in eastern Siskiyou County. After six months, the Modoc were driven back to a reservation in southern Oregon. The Modoc War was over. Kintpuash was hanged.

Events like the Modoc War led Helen Hunt Jackson to write her famous book. Jackson sent copies to the United States Congress. Printed in red on the cover were these words: "Look upon your hands! They are stained with the blood of your relations [fellow people]."

Helen Hunt Jackson criticized treatment of Native Americans.

The Granger Collection

CALIFORNIA NATIVE AMERICAN TREATIES, 1853

OREGON

0   75   150 Miles
0   75   150 Kilometers

N W E S

NEVADA

Sacramento

Stockton

San Francisco

San Joaquin River

Sacramento River

PACIFIC OCEAN

Los Angeles

San Diego

MEXICO

Legend:
- Lands ceded, or given, by Native Americans
- Lands promised to Native Americans

MAP WORK

California's Native Americans were promised large reservations that they never received.

In what part of the state were most reservations to be located?

A CENTURY OF DISHONOR

A SKETCH
OF THE UNITED STATES GOVERNMENT'S DEALINGS
WITH SOME OF THE INDIAN TRIBES

By HELEN JACKSON (H. H.),

THE CALIFORNIOS' LAND TROUBLES

In Chapter 6 you learned about the Treaty of Guadalupe Hidalgo. You read that it promised to protect "property of every kind" belonging to the Mexican people. That included the huge rancho lands held by the Californios.

Many American settlers believed that after the Mexican War, all the lands in California belonged to the United States. They felt this allowed them to settle on the Californios' lands without permission. These settlers were squatters.

When Californios tried to remove them, the squatters sometimes struck back using force. The Peralta family, who owned most of the eastern shore of San Francisco Bay, had its trees cut down and its cattle killed. One day squatters blocked the doors to the Peralta home. The frightened family was forced to leave.

The Land Commission

In 1851 the government in Washington, D.C., formed a group called the Land Commission. Its goal was to settle the problems of land ownership. Rancheros met with the commission. They tried to prove that they owned their lands.

The commission found that the Californios owned most of what they claimed. The decisions were slow in coming, however. It often took 17 years to prove ownership! It was also costly. The rancheros needed lawyers to represent them. By the time the commission made its decisions, many Californios had been forced to sell their land to pay their lawyers.

Apolinaria Lorenzano, once the owner of three ranchos, lost all of her lands. In 1878 she said, "I find myself in the greatest poverty, living by the favor of God and from handouts."

Mariano Guadalupe Vallejo lost his Soscol rancho to squatters. Read what he later said about the Californios losing their lands. Why did he think there was no use complaining?

The Seaver Center

Californio families like these fought for many years to keep their lands.

**Excerpt from the memoir of
Mariano Guadalupe Vallejo, 1875.**

*The time has not yet arrived for
commenting on or judging the
actions of the **authorities** that
have governed the country during the past twenty years. . . .
I declare [say] that despite the
Treaty of Guadalupe Hidalgo,
the North Americans treated
the Californios like a **conquered**
people and not like citizens. . . .*

*But what does this matter to
the **conqueror**? He looks after
his own interests and not ours,
a trait . . . that I condemn in a
government that had promised
to respect . . . our rights and to
treat us like sons and daughters,
but of what use is it to
complain?*

authorities: government
conquered: defeated in war
conqueror: winner of a war

California State Library

WHY IT MATTERS

In spite of the loss of their lands,
Native Americans and Californios
remained in California. Their legacy
is an important part of what makes
California special.

✓✓ Reviewing Facts and Ideas

MAIN IDEAS

- Vigilantes took the law into their
  own hands.
- Kintpuash led the Modoc in a war
  to keep their lands in California.
- Many Californios lost their lands
  to squatters.

THINK ABOUT IT

1. In what way were the vigilantes
   breaking the law?

2. What was the purpose of the Land
   Commission?

3. **FOCUS** How did Native Americans
   and Californios lose their lands?

4. **THINKING SKILL** Why, do you
   think, did Kintpuash and the
   Modoc make the *decision* to fight
   for their land? What alternatives
   might they have had?

5. **GEOGRAPHY** Why, do you think,
   did squatters want the Californios'
   lands?

THINKINGSKILLS

Making Conclusions

VOCABULARY
conclusion

WHY THE SKILL MATTERS

In the last lesson you read about how Native Americans in California lost their lands. You read that newcomers came in and took Native American lands by force. You also learned that the government made promises to set aside large amounts of land for Native Americans but did not keep its promises. You might think about these facts and decide that Native Americans in California were treated unfairly.

When you put together several pieces of information and decide what they mean, you are making a conclusion. A conclusion does not repeat specific facts. Instead it adds up these facts and tells how they are connected.

USING THE SKILL

In Lesson 3 you learned about Biddy Mason. Read each of the following statements:

- Biddy Mason helped people as a nurse.
- Biddy Mason fought for the rights of African Americans.
- Biddy Mason helped people in need.

First ask yourself, "What do all these statements have in common?" All of these statements have the common theme that Biddy Mason helped people. Now state this common theme in your own words. A conclusion you might make is "Biddy Mason was a generous person." This conclusion connects all three statements. It takes the common theme behind the statements and says it in a sentence.

Bancroft Library

198

TRYING THE SKILL

You have practiced drawing a conclusion about what sort of person Biddy Mason was. Now read the following statements about being a gold miner. Then make a conclusion from the statements. Use the Helping Yourself box for hints.

- Gold miners were often lonely and far from their family and friends.

- Gold miners had to work very hard to find any gold.

- Gold mining could be dangerous.

- Gold miners had to pay high prices for goods like clothes and food.

What common theme or meaning did you find in all four statements? How do they add up to a conclusion? What conclusion can you make about being a gold miner during the Gold Rush?

REVIEWING THE SKILL

1. How did you reach your conclusion?

2. What did the four statements suggest about being a gold miner? How do you know?

3. If you were a gold miner in the 1850s and came to the same conclusion, what would you do?

4. How might making conclusions help you to learn about history?

Letters (left) were often the only way for lonely miners to hear news of their families.

Superstock/The Huntington Library

199

CHAPTER 7 REVIEW

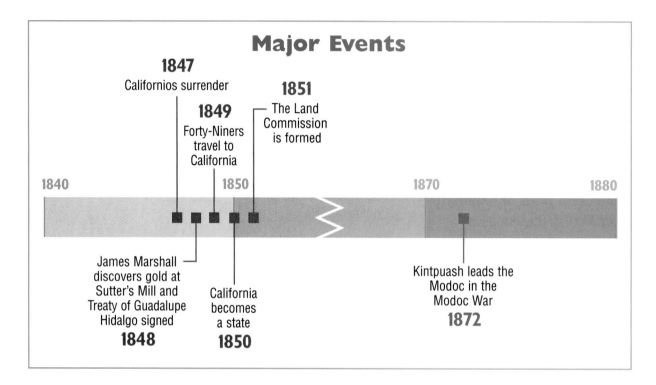

Major Events

1847
Californios surrender

1849
Forty-Niners travel to California

1851
The Land Commission is formed

1840   1850   1870   1880

James Marshall discovers gold at Sutter's Mill and Treaty of Guadalupe Hidalgo signed
1848

California becomes a state
1850

Kintpuash leads the Modoc in the Modoc War
1872

THINKING ABOUT VOCABULARY

Number a sheet of paper from 1 to 10. Beside each number write the word from the list that best matches the definition.

capital   isthmus   pass
constitution   mother lode   reservation
convention   panning   squatter
Forty-Niner

1. A narrow gap between mountains
2. A gold seeker who came to California
3. The place where government meets
4. A narrow stretch of land with water on both sides
5. A gold-rich area
6. A way to mine gold
7. A settler without permission
8. Land set aside for Native Americans
9. A formal meeting for a special purpose
10. A plan of government

THINKING ABOUT FACTS

1. Name three routes of Forty-Niners.
2. How many gold seekers got rich?
3. What happened on September 1, 1849?
4. What was the Compromise of 1850?
5. What did the Land Commission do?

THINK AND WRITE

WRITING A LETTER
Suppose you are a Forty-Niner traveling overland to California. Write a letter describing your experiences along the way.

WRITING AN ARTICLE
Suppose you are a journalist writing about Gold Rush mining towns. Write an article describing what miners' lives are like.

WRITING AN EXPLANATION
Write a paragraph explaining why Californios were angry over losing their land.

APPLYING THINKING SKILLS

MAKING CONCLUSIONS

1. What is meant by making conclusions?

2. What steps would you follow when making a conclusion?

3. Read "Changes in the Gold Fields" on page 184. What conclusion can you make about the fairness of these rules?

4. Read "The Californios' Land Troubles" on page 196. What conclusion can you make about how the Californios felt about the Land Commission?

5. Why is it important to make conclusions about what you read?

APPLYING STUDY SKILLS

READING CIRCLE AND LINE GRAPHS

1. Describe the difference between a line graph and a circle graph.

2. Look at the line graph on page 176. What was the approximate population of California in 1860?

3. Look at the circle graph on page 177. What type of job was least common in California in 1860?

4. What kind of graph would you use to show the types of sports played by you and your friends?

5. How do graphs make some information easier to understand?

Summing Up the Chapter

Use the following spider map to organize information from the chapter. Write at least one piece of information in each blank circle. When you have filled in the map, use it to write a paragraph that answers the question "How did American settlers change California?"

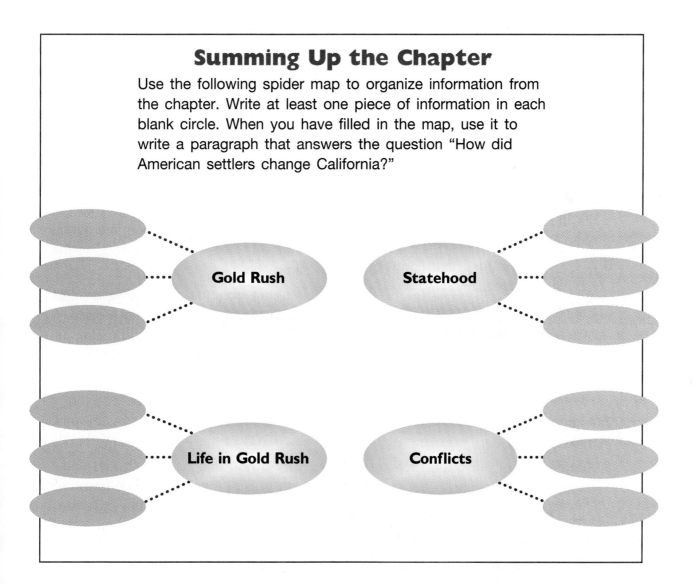

Gold Rush

Statehood

Life in Gold Rush

Conflicts

UNIT 3 REVIEW

THINKING ABOUT VOCABULARY

A. Write a sentence for each pair of words below. Include details that give clues to the meaning of both words.

1. diseño, land grants
2. import, export
3. representatives, convention
4. placer, panning
5. capital, legislature

B. Number a sheet of paper from 1 to 10. Next to each number write the word or term from the list above that best completes the sentence.

1. The _____ is where the government meets.

2. An _____ is something brought in from another country for sale or use.

3. Most of the gold found in California during the early years of the Gold Rush was _____ gold.

4. A _____ was a map that showed a rancho's borders.

5. People who speak up for you in government are _____.

6. Huge pieces of land that were given away after the missions were closed were _____.

7. A group of representatives who make laws is a _____.

8. Something sold or traded to another country is an _____.

9. _____ is a process of mining.

10. A formal meeting for a special purpose is a _____.

THINK AND WRITE

WRITING ABOUT PERSPECTIVES
Imagine you are a settler from a state such as Ohio or Massachusetts who settled in California in the 1840s. Explain why the settlers believe the United States has a right to California. Do you think this is a fair belief?

WRITING A COMPARISON
Write a paragraph that describes life for Californios before and after the Mexican War.

WRITING AN ADVERTISEMENT
Suppose you are the owner of a mining company. Design and write an advertisement encouraging miners to work for you.

BUILDING SKILLS

1. **Time lines** How are time lines helpful when studying history?

2. **Time lines** Draw a time line that goes from 1800 to 1880. Place five events that you read about in Unit 3 on the time line.

3. **Making conclusions** You have read about California becoming a state. What conclusions can you make about how people felt at this time?

4. **Circle and line graphs** Using the graph on page 176, what was the approximate population of California in 1870?

5. **Circle and line graphs** Would you use a circle graph or a line graph to show your height over the past five years?

YESTERDAY, TODAY &
TOMORROW

You have read about the problems that occurred when people wanted land that others claimed. Suppose countries decide to build cities on the moon. Why might it be a good idea for people from different countries to cooperate with one another? What might happen if people do not cooperate?

READING ON YOUR OWN

These are some of the books you could find at the library to help you learn more.

NINE FOR CALIFORNIA
by Sonia Levitin
A family's 21-day journey from Missouri to California by stagecoach.

VALLEJO AND THE FOUR FLAGS—
A TRUE STORY OF OLD CALIFORNIA
by Esther J. Comstock
California's history from Spanish days to United States rule told through the story of Mariano Guadelupe Vallejo.

THE BALLAD OF LUCY WHIPPLE
by Karen Cushman
The story of a young girl who lives in a Gold Rush mining town.

UNIT REVIEW PROJECT

Write an Historical Newspaper

1. Working in groups, imagine you are writing your own historical newspaper. Take a look at a newspaper to see what types of articles it includes.
2. Working in a group, choose three news items from the following list:
   - The Mexican War for Independence
   - The founding of Fort Ross
   - A roundup on a rancho
   - The Donner party
   - The Bear Flag Revolt
   - The Mexican War
   - Treaty of Guadalupe Hidalgo
   - The Gold Rush
   - Statehood

3. Decide which articles you will write, and then gather information from your textbook and the school library. Remember to report the facts.
4. Choose a name for your newspaper. You may want to include illustrations, a comic strip about California, or advertisements relating to California.
5. Present your newspaper to the class.

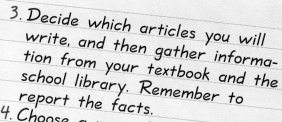

RUSSIAN
IMMIGRANTS IN
SAN FRANCISCO,
1923 (RIGHT)
PONY EXPRESS
LETTER (BELOW)

GOLDEN SPIKE
(ABOVE)
1959 CAR (BELOW)

California, the United States, and the World

"The chosen spot of all this earth . . ."

Luther Burbank
See page 246.

WHY DOES IT MATTER?

In the last 150 years California has grown to become one of the most important places on Earth. It has become the home for millions of people from around the world. How did these changes happen? What decisions—large and small—did people make to bring this about? What has our state gained? What has it lost?

Read on. In Unit 4 you will discover the exciting story of how California gained its place in the world.

ADVERTISEMENT FOR CALIFORNIA LAND, 1870, AND PROTEST BUTTON (ABOVE)

205

Adventures
with
NATIONAL
GEOGRAPHIC

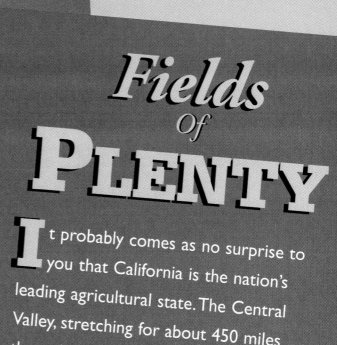

Fields Of PLENTY

It probably comes as no surprise to you that California is the nation's leading agricultural state. The Central Valley, stretching for about 450 miles through the center of our state, is one of the world's greatest farming areas. The proof is in the lettuce, the peaches, the tomatoes—and more. Our state ranks first in the production of these and many other crops. Grapes, almonds, garlic, strawberries, oranges, walnuts, plums—the bounty of our fields offers abundant proof that California is a growing state.

GEO JOURNAL

What is your favorite kind of produce from our state's fields of plenty? Where is it grown? How does it get to your table?

CHAPTER 8

Bringing the World to California

THINKING ABOUT HISTORY AND GEOGRAPHY

California became a state in 1850. Linking California to the rest of the United States, however, was a big problem. How could goods, people, and information be moved across such huge distances quickly and cheaply? Read on to learn about the different ways Californians met this challenge and how these changes in transportation led to changes in our state's population, government, and economy.

PACIFIC OCEAN

1851	1861	1869
SANTA CRUZ	**WASHINGTON, D.C.**	**PROMONTORY, UTAH**
Charlotte Parkhurst becomes a stagecoach driver	First telegraph message from San Francisco reaches Washington, D.C.	Chinese and Irish workers race to finish the transcontinental railroad

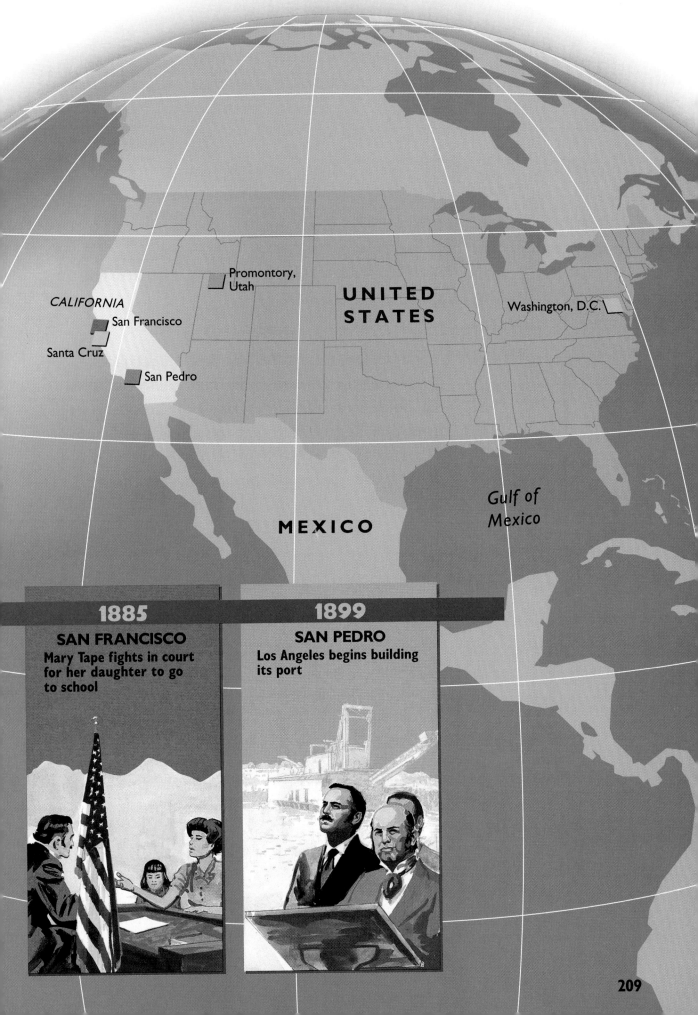

CALIFORNIA

San Francisco

Santa Cruz

San Pedro

Promontory,
Utah

UNITED
STATES

Washington, D.C.

MEXICO

Gulf of
Mexico

1885

SAN FRANCISCO
Mary Tape fights in court for her daughter to go to school

1899

SAN PEDRO
Los Angeles begins building its port

Los Angeles County Museum of Natural History, Seaver Center

PONIES, TELEGRAPHS, AND RAILROADS

Focus Activity

READ TO LEARN
How did new forms of transportation and communications help California?

VOCABULARY
transportation
technology
communication
telegraph
engineer
transcontinental

PEOPLE
Charlotte Parkhurst
Samuel F. B. Morse
Theodore Judah

PLACES
St. Joseph, Missouri
Folsom

READ ALOUD

On October 10, 1858, the first stagecoach— a car pulled by horses—reached California from St. Louis. A reporter described the scene: "As the coach dashed . . . through the crowds, the hats of the spectators were whirled in the air and the hurrah was repeated from a thousand throats."

THE BIG PICTURE

Why were people excited about a stagecoach? You learned in the last chapter that each of the routes from the East Coast to California took months of difficult travel. Deserts, mountains, and fast rivers caused great danger for travelers. The distance isolated, or separated, California from the East.

As the population of California grew, the need for faster transportation grew. Transportation is the movement of people and goods. Merchants in the East wanted to send goods to California. New Californians wanted to hear the latest news from home. How would the transportation problem be solved?

A ROUGH RIDE

Charlotte Parkhurst came to San Francisco hoping to drive a stagecoach route. The stagecoach companies, however, hired only men as drivers. So Parkhurst put on men's clothing and applied for the job as "Charley" Parkhurst.

She became one of the best stagecoach drivers in California. She worked for Wells, Fargo and Company, driving a four-horse team between Santa Cruz and San Jose. When she died in 1879, the *San Francisco Morning Call* said that it was an honor to ride in a coach "when the fearless Charley Parkhurst held the reins."

Stagecoaches began crossing the continent to California in 1858. They carried riders and mail on a journey of more than 2,800 miles. The coaches traveled from Tipton, Missouri, to San Francisco in about three weeks.

It took a strong back and a strong stomach to make the trip. The coaches bounced along roads that were little more than bumpy trails. The writer Mark Twain described a stagecoach trip to California. How would you like to be one of the passengers?

Stagecoaches, like the one below, helped link California to the rest of the United States.

MANY VOICES
LITERATURE

Excerpt from *Roughing It*, written by Mark Twain in 1872.

We began to get into country, now, threaded here and there with little streams. These had high, steep banks on each side, and every time we flew down one bank and scrambled up the other, our party inside got mixed somewhat. First we would all be down in a pile at the forward end of the stage . . . and in a second we would shoot to the other end, and stand on our heads. And we would sprawl and kick . . . and probably say some hasty thing, like: "Take your elbow out of my ribs!— can't you quit crowding?"

country: countryside

The Granger Collection

211

The Pony Express could deliver the mail from St. Louis to Sacramento twice as fast as a stagecoach.

PONY EXPRESS!

CHANGE OF

REDUCED RATES!

Days to San Francisco!

LETTERS

WILL BE RECEIVED AT THE

OFFICE, 84 BROADWAY, NEW YORK,

Up to 4 P. M. every TUESDAY.
AND
Up to 2½ P. M. every SATURDAY.

Which will be forwarded to connect with the PONY EXPRESS leaving ST. JOSEPH, Missouri,

Every WEDNESDAY and SATURDAY at 11 P. M.

TELEGRAMS

to Fort Kearney on the mornings of MONDAY and FRIDAY, will connect with PONY leaving St. Joseph, WEDNESDAYS and SATURDAYS.

EXPRESS CHARGES.

LETTERS weighing half ounce or under.......... $1.00
For every additional half ounce or fraction of an ounce 1.00
In all cases to be enclosed in 10 cent Government Stamped Envelopes,
And all Express CHARGES Pre-paid.

☞ PONY EXPRESS ENVELOPES For Sale at our Office.

New York, July 1, 1861.

WELLS, FARGO & CO., Ag'ts.

SLOTE & JANES STATIONERS AND PRINTERS, 89 FULTON STREET, NEW YORK

PONIES AND CAMELS

"Pony Bob" Haslam was drenched to the skin. The wind bit into his face. His pony had raced for nearly 10 miles. Yet he never once slowed his breakneck speed.

Through the darkness, Haslam saw the lighted window of an adobe cabin. Standing at the rail was another pony, saddled and ready to go. When he reached the cabin, Haslam leaped to the ground. In a flash he pulled the leather pouch from his pony and threw it across the saddle of the other pony. Then he was off again, disappearing into the night.

"Pony Bob" Haslam worked for a service called the Pony Express. Its job was to carry the mail across the country as quickly as possible.

Another rider was George Monroe, an African American, who rode from Merced to Mariposa.

The Pony Express began business in 1860. On April 3 the first rider left St. Joseph, Missouri, with a bag of mail. Ten days later, another rider and his pony carried that mail into Sacramento.

After the rider got to Sacramento, he traveled with his pony by river-boat to San Francisco. The city welcomed him with a big party. This one was even grander than the one that greeted the first overland stage-coach in 1858. The *San Francisco Bulletin* reported that

The crowds cheered till their throats were sore; the band played as if they would crack their cheeks. . . . As the pony

trotted into line, [a woman] tore the ribbons from her bonnet and tied them around his neck. . . . Long live the Pony!

Everything about the Pony Express was set up for speed. There were about 80 riders. Each rider rode about 75 miles, stopping to change ponies about every 20 or 30 miles. Just 2 minutes were allowed to make the change! The riders wore close-fitting clothes to help them move quickly. Their leather pouches held no more than 20 pounds of mail. Inside, the letters were wrapped in oiled silk to keep them dry.

The Pony Express allowed news to reach California from the eastern United States faster than ever before. It could deliver a letter twice as fast as a stagecoach. But the cost was high—as much as $10 an ounce.

The Pony Express was in business for only about 18 months. Yet these riders—and their fast ponies—live on in our memory. We still admire their bravery and skill in bringing the world to California.

Camels Across the Desert

Another try at linking the West Coast and the East Coast used animals much slower than ponies. In 1857 the United States Army began using camels to carry goods in the deserts of the Southwest. Camels are

four-legged animals that live in deserts. They store water in their bodies, so they need to drink less often than other animals.

The camels came from the Middle East. A man named Haiji Ali (HĪ jee AH lee) came from the country of Syria to drive the camels. He herded them across New Mexico and Arizona. They crossed one stretch of land without stopping for water in 36 hours. The first camel "train" arrived in Los Angeles in January 1858.

Ponies and camels were used for only a short time. Better transportation and communication came with new technology. Technology is the use of skills, ideas, and tools to meet people's needs.

For a time camels crossed the deserts of the Southwest, bringing goods to California.

NEW TECHNOLOGIES

Technology made communication throughout the country much easier. Communication is the exchange of information between people.

The Telegraph

Samuel F. B. Morse, a painter and inventor, changed communication forever. He came up with a way to send messages long distances. His invention, the telegraph, sends an electrical code through a wire.

Before the telegraph, messages could travel only as fast as a person or animal could carry them. Morse's telegraph could send a message thousands of miles in one second.

Using the telegraph was expensive, however. Messages had to be kept short. The telegraph wires sometimes broke. Then no messages could be sent at all.

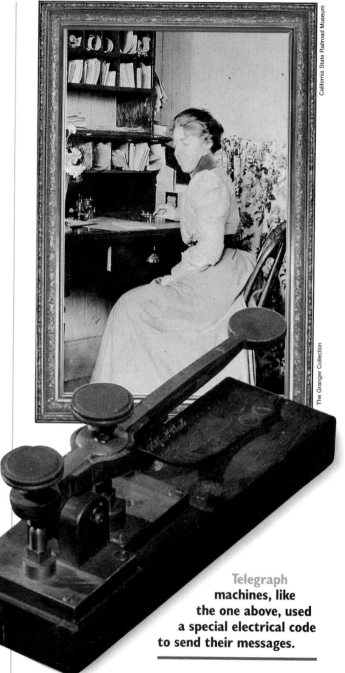

California State Railroad Museum

The Granger Collection

Telegraph machines, like the one above, used a special electrical code to send their messages.

Links to LANGUAGE ARTS

What's the Code?

To send messages on his telegraph, Morse wrote a special code. It is known as the Morse code. Morse code uses dots, dashes, and spaces to create messages. Each letter of the alphabet has its own pattern of dots and dashes. For instance, three dots stand for the letter *s*. Spaces of different lengths separate letters and words.

Look up *Morse code* in a reference source and write out a message. Exchange messages with a partner and decode his or her message.

Cross-country Message

On October 24, 1861, workers completed a telegraph line across the country. That day the first message was sent from San Francisco to Washington, D.C. Two days later, the Pony Express went out of business. The telegraph made the Pony Express a thing of the past.

Theodore Judah's Plan

Another new technology was the railroad. Railroads use a track of two rails to guide trains of cars along a route very fast. Steam-powered trains began running in the United States around 1830.

Theodore Judah was a young engineer with a strong imagination. An engineer is someone skilled in designing and building things. Judah came to California from New York in 1854. He helped build a railroad from Sacramento to Folsom. This was the first railroad on the West Coast.

In California, Judah dreamed of building a railroad across the country. It would be a transcontinental railroad. *Transcontinental* means "across the continent." Nowhere in the world was there

Theodore Judah hoped to build a transcontinental railroad reaching California.

California State Railroad Museum

such a railroad. But Judah was not worried. He knew that he could figure out a way to build it. You will read how he did in the next lesson.

WHY IT MATTERS

The stagecoach, Pony Express, and telegraph all brought California closer to the rest of the country. Today communications technologies like fax machines, satellites, and E-mail bring us closer together than ever before. What new technologies do you suppose will shape our future?

Reviewing Facts and Ideas

MAIN IDEAS

- Stagecoach travel to California began in 1858.
- The Pony Express carried mail across the country in 10 days.
- Samuel Morse's telegraph was the fastest form of communications invented at that time.

THINK ABOUT IT

1. How long did it take stagecoaches to reach California from Missouri?
2. Why was the telegraph faster than the Pony Express?
3. **FOCUS** Why did people need better transportation to California?
4. **THINKING SKILL** Identify some *causes* and *effects* of the building of telegraph lines.
5. **WRITE** Imagine that you are a reporter in 1861. Write an editorial about the first transcontinental telegraph message.

Reading Elevation Maps

VOCABULARY

elevation

WHY THE SKILL MATTERS

When Theodore Judah began planning the transcontinental railroad, he needed to select a route. How would he know which route to pick? A physical map of the United States like the one on pages R14–R15 would have shown him some things. One of the things that it shows is the location of the Rocky Mountains and the Sierra Nevada. But it would not have shown him other things, such as the height of the various mountains.

For this kind of information, you would need an elevation map. Elevation is the height of the land above sea level. Elevation at sea level is 0 feet.

An elevation map uses colors to show elevations. Look at the map key on this page. It tells you, for example, that all the places colored yellow are between 3,000 and 7,000 feet (1,000 and 2,000 meters) above sea level. The other colors show different elevations.

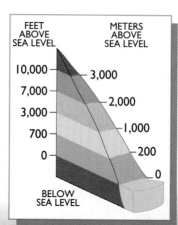

USING THE SKILL

Try using an elevation map to trace the route of the transcontinental railroad in California. The railroad begins in Sacramento, located in the middle of the Central Valley. Find Sacramento on the map on the opposite page. What color is the area where the railroad begins? Check the map key to find out what elevation this color represents. You can see that the railroad begins between sea level and 650 feet.

Follow the railroad's route. You can see that it passes through areas of higher elevation as it moves east. These are the foothills of the Sierra Nevada. Then it crosses Donner Pass, northwest of Lake Tahoe.

Of course, elevation maps tell us about many things besides mountains. For example, they give us important information about valleys.

In Chapter 1 you learned that a valley is a flat or V-shaped area between two mountain ranges. You also learned that the largest valley in California is the Central Valley. It has many farms. On the map the Central Valley is colored dark green. If you wanted to find other valleys in California with farms, you might look for other areas that are colored dark green. What valleys can you find that are colored dark green? Can you find valleys that are not colored dark green?

TRYING THE SKILL

You have used the map to trace the route of the transcontinental railroad in California. Now use the elevation map to trace the path of the Sacramento River.

At what elevation does the Sacramento River begin? In which direction does it flow? When it gets to the Central Valley, is the Sacramento River at a higher, a lower, or the same elevation as when it started? Why, do you think, is that? Into what body of water does the Sacramento River flow?

Elevation maps have many uses today. Engineers planning new roads and highways use elevation maps, just as Judah did. If you plan a hike into the mountains, an elevation map will help you find a good trail.

HELPING Yourself

- **Elevation** maps show how high the land is above sea level.
- Study the map key to see which colors stand for different elevations on the map.

REVIEWING THE SKILL

Now use the elevation map to answer the following questions. Use the Helping Yourself box for hints.

1. What is elevation?

2. What is the elevation of the highest point in California? What is the elevation along the coast?

3. In what color would this map show the Sierra Nevada foothills at 2,000 feet?

4. How does an elevation map help us learn about California's environment?

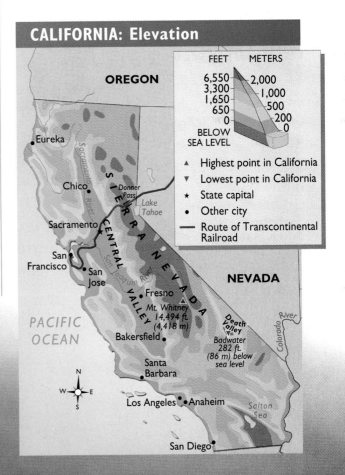

CALIFORNIA: Elevation

FEET	METERS
6,550	2,000
3,300	1,000
1,650	500
650	200
0	0
BELOW SEA LEVEL	

▲ Highest point in California
▼ Lowest point in California
★ State capital
• Other city
— Route of Transcontinental Railroad

OREGON

Eureka
Chico
Sacramento
San Francisco
San Jose
Fresno
Mt. Whitney 14,494 ft (4,418 m)
Bakersfield
Santa Barbara
Los Angeles • Anaheim
San Diego

Donner Pass
Lake Tahoe

PACIFIC OCEAN

NEVADA

Death Valley
Badwater 282 ft (86 m) below sea level

Colorado River
Salton Sea

N W E S

217

PLANNING THE RAILROAD

READ ALOUD

Building a transcontinental railroad was Theodore Judah's great dream. Wherever he went, he "read, talked and studied the problem." As he told his wife, Anna, "It will be built, and I'm going to have something to do with it."

Focus Activity

READ TO LEARN
How did the transcontinental railroad get built?

VOCABULARY
investor
Central Pacific Railroad
Big Four

PEOPLE
Leland Stanford

PLACES
Dutch Flat
Promontory, Utah

THE BIG PICTURE

Theodore Judah knew that building a railroad to link the eastern United States to California was not going to be easy. His first challenge was to find a route through the Sierra Nevada that would be flat enough for a train to climb. In 1860 Judah found a route, near Dutch Flat. It rose slowly over a long distance until it reached the Donner Pass. It was perfect. But who would pay to build the railroad?

By 1861 the country's divisions over slavery led to a great conflict known as the Civil War. How could a great railroad be built across the continent in the middle of a war?

THE RAILROAD ACTS

Theodore Judah brought his plan to a group of Sacramento merchants. In a room above a hardware store, he explained how a transcontinental railroad could be built.

Four of the merchants were interested in Judah's plan. Leland Stanford, Charles Crocker, Collis Huntington, and Mark Hopkins agreed to become investors in the Central Pacific Railroad. An investor is someone who puts money into a business, hoping to make more money if the business is successful. The four investors in the Central Pacific became known as the Big Four. Leland Stanford became the railroad's president.

Judah and the Big Four knew they did not have enough money to build the railroad themselves. In the fall of 1861, Judah traveled to Washington, D.C. There he helped convince Congress to pass the Pacific Railroad Act of 1862. When President Abraham Lincoln signed the act, it became a law.

The law said the United States government would loan money to the Central Pacific and another railroad, the Union Pacific. Together these companies would build the transcontinental railroad. The government also gave the railroads 10 square miles of land on each side of the track for each mile of track they laid. Ten square miles is about the size of the city of Berkeley! Another law passed in 1864 made the offer even more generous. Within ten years, the Big Four had become the richest and most powerful people in California.

Leland Stanford (left) was one of the Big Four. Building of the Central Pacific Railroad (below) started in Sacramento in 1863.

THE RACE IS ON!

Construction of the railroad began in Sacramento on January 8, 1863. Soon, however, Theodore Judah and the Big Four began to disagree. Judah wanted to build the railroad well. The Big Four tried to cut costs so that they could make more money.

Judah hoped to find other investors to take the place of the Big Four. But he died suddenly in November 1863. The Big Four now were in complete control of the railroad.

It took six years to build the railroad. People from around the world worked on the job. Most came from China and Ireland. Look at the map below. It shows the route of the transcontinental railroad. Tracks were laid eastward from Sacramento by Central Pacific workers and westward from Omaha, Nebraska, by Union Pacific workers.

Each company raced to lay as many miles of track as possible. The more track each company laid, the more land and money it got from the government.

At first the Union Pacific had an advantage. It could bring its supplies and machines on the railroad as it built it. The Central Pacific, however, had to bring rails, trains, and equipment by boat to San Francisco. It also had to face the Sierra Nevada. Central Pacific workers spent almost three

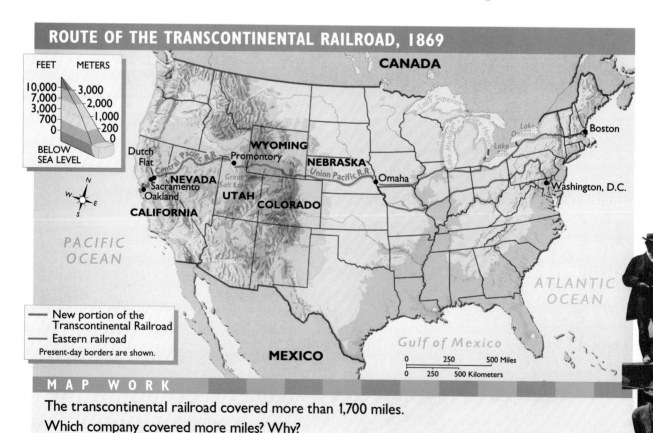

ROUTE OF THE TRANSCONTINENTAL RAILROAD, 1869

FEET / METERS
10,000 / 3,000
7,000 / 2,000
3,000 / 1,000
700 / 200
0 / 0
BELOW SEA LEVEL

— New portion of the Transcontinental Railroad
— Eastern railroad
Present-day borders are shown.

CANADA
Boston
Washington, D.C.
Omaha
NEBRASKA
Union Pacific R.R.
WYOMING
Promontory
Dutch Flat
Central Pacific R.R.
NEVADA
Sacramento
Oakland
CALIFORNIA
UTAH
Great Salt Lake
COLORADO
PACIFIC OCEAN
ATLANTIC OCEAN
Gulf of Mexico
MEXICO
Lake Superior
Lake Michigan
Lake Huron
Lake Ontario
Lake Erie

0 — 250 — 500 Miles
0 — 250 — 500 Kilometers

MAP WORK

The transcontinental railroad covered more than 1,700 miles. Which company covered more miles? Why?

years carving a path through the rugged mountains.

Finally the Central Pacific got over the mountains into Nevada. Then the race really began. Building teams worked at an incredible rate. One day the Union Pacific laid 6 miles of track. The next day the Central Pacific laid 7. By April 28, 1869, the two railroads were only 26 miles apart. That day workers for the Central Pacific set a new record. They laid more than 10 miles of track in a single day!

The Golden Spike

Finally, on May 10, 1869, the two railroads met at Promontory, Utah. Workers, reporters, and settlers formed a crowd. Leland Stanford came forward. He held a silver hammer and a spike made of California gold. He drove the golden spike into the railroad tie. A telegraph operator sent the message "The last spike is driven! The Pacific Railroad is complete!"

WHY IT MATTERS

California became a state in 1850. Yet it took the transcontinental railroad to link California to the rest of the United States.

✓ Reviewing Facts and Ideas

MAIN IDEAS

- The government loaned money and gave land to help build a transcontinental railroad.
- The transcontinental railroad was completed in 1869.

THINK ABOUT IT

1. Who were the Big Four?
2. What kind of help did the Pacific Railroad Act of 1862 give?
3. **FOCUS** How did the transcontinental railroad get built?
4. **THINKING SKILL** *Compare and contrast* the attitudes of Judah and the Big Four toward the railroad.
5. **GEOGRAPHY** Look at the map on page 220. Is Promontory farther from Sacramento or from Omaha?

Crowds (below) celebrated the driving of the golden spike (previous page).

1850 1860 1885 1890 1910 1930

IMMIGRANTS BUILD THE RAILROAD

READ ALOUD

Arr Sing has heard many stories about California. It is far from his home in China, but Arr Sing wants to go. When a government official asks him why, Arr Sing is ready with his answer: "Because America is a rich land, and I will have the chance to earn a good living."

THE BIG PICTURE

You learned in the last lesson that the transcontinental railroad was built by people from around the world. Most were immigrants. An immigrant is a person who comes to a new country to live. As many as 12,000 Chinese immigrants worked on the Central Pacific Railroad. Some had been miners earlier. Others came from China.

The Union Pacific Railroad was built mainly by immigrants from Ireland. Crops in Ireland had failed. Many people were dying of hunger. Like Arr Sing, Irish immigrants came looking for a better life. Many stayed in California.

GAM SAAN

Imagine that you are a young man like Arr Sing. Your village of Shanjing is in the Guangdong province of China. In the fall of 1865, you read a poster sent by a railroad company. The poster says, "Come over and help! We have money to spend, but no one to earn it."

You have heard of California. It is the land you know as Gam Saan, or "Gold Mountain." Friends from your village went there in the Gold Rush. Should you leave behind your family and everything you know to go work in this new land?

Your own country has been at war for 15 years. The government just raised your taxes. You earn about $5 each month. The poster promises that you will earn six times that much in Gam Saan! If you earn enough money in California, you can return to China a wealthy man.

You board a ship at the port of Hong Kong. The trip across the Pacific Ocean will take as long as 60 days. It is crowded, and most of your time is spent below the deck. Meals are almost always rice. The pork brought on board has gone bad.

Finally you get to San Francisco. Now you must travel by riverboat to Sacramento. There you are crowded into a dark, smoky freight car. Your thoughts return to home. A railroad worker whose name we do not know wrote this letter to his wife. How does he feel about being far from her?

MANY VOICES PRIMARY SOURCE

Excerpt from a letter by a Chinese worker in California, c. 1870.

*I*t has been several autumns now since your dull husband left you for a far remote **alien** land. Thanks to my **hearty** body I am all right. Therefore stop your . . . worries about me.

Yesterday I received another of your letters. I could not keep tears from running down my cheeks when thinking . . . back to the time of our **separation**.

---

alien: foreign
hearty: strong
separation: parting

Immigrants, like the **Ah Quin family of San Diego (left), helped California grow.**

WORKING ON THE RAILROAD

The train lurches to a stop. You jump down to the frozen ground. Snowy peaks tower above you. You shiver in the cold mountain air.

You are put with a group of 30 other workers. The group's leader warns you in Cantonese, a Chinese language: *Jo lui ja*, meaning "We work like mules." The leader explains that you will be paid $30 each month. But you will have to pay for your meals. "White workers," he says angrily, "get all their meals free."

Ledges and Tunnels

At sunrise your work begins. You step into a large basket that lowers you over a steep cliff. Your job is to help carve a ledge into the face of the cliff. Other workers will lay track after the ledge is finished.

You look up. If the rope holding the basket breaks, you will surely die. You reach the narrow ledge. You begin chipping at the stone with a hammer and chisel.

At sunset, after 12 hours of work, you return to camp exhausted. The cook has heated water for washing. You hand over your clothes. Dinner is the only thing that reminds you of home—rice, bamboo shoots, mushrooms, and dried oysters.

In the weeks ahead, you are given other jobs. A hand drill and black gunpowder help with building the ledge. But the gunpowder is dangerous. You must be pulled up quickly after you light the fuse.

In the spring of 1866, you begin work on a tunnel near the peak. The rock is so hard that gunpowder hardly works. A new explosive, nitroglycerin (ni truh GLIHS ur ihn), only makes the job more dangerous. Many workers' lives are lost.

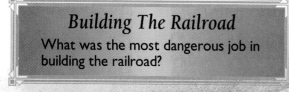

Building The Railroad

What was the most dangerous job in building the railroad?

Laying the rails

Setting the ties

Grading the rail bed

During the winter of 1866–1867, more than 40 blizzards hit the Sierra Nevada. A snowbank crashes down and buries 20 of your friends. Dozens more die in other accidents. Still the work goes on.

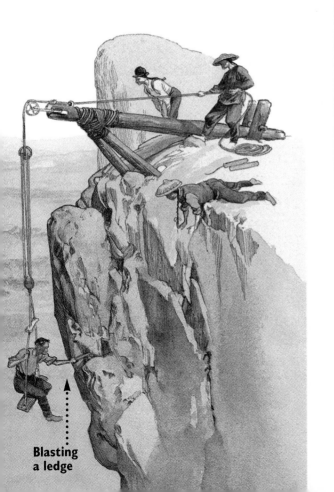

Blasting a ledge

Chinese immigrant workers built many railroad bridges across mountain passes in the Sierra Nevada.

Protest

By June 1867 you and 5,000 other workers have had enough. You put down your tools and refuse to work. You demand $10 more a month. That will be enough at least to cover the cost of your meals. You also demand a shorter workday. You want to be treated the same as the white workers.

The railroad bosses refuse to meet your demands. You try to hold out. But when the railroad cuts off your food supply, you have no choice. You must return to work.

Two years later, you are standing in the crowd at Promontory, Utah. The last spike is driven. "How strange," you think. "No one remembers to thank us for our work."

BUILDING A COMMUNITY

After the railroad was completed, many workers like Arr Sing settled in San Francisco. By 1870 the city's Chinese population was more than 12,000. In Chinatown, a six-block area stretching from California Street to Broadway, people kept some of the customs they had in China. For example, residents celebrated Chinese New Year with firecrackers and a colorful dragon parade.

Chinese immigrants also settled in other towns. Some worked on farms. Others built canals, ditches, and dams to turn Central Valley wetlands into farmland. Some of their children founded the town of Locke in 1915. It is the only town in our country founded by Chinese.

"The Chinese Must Go"

Hard times hit California in the 1870s. Many people lost their jobs. Some white workers blamed their troubles on the Chinese immigrants. Denis Kearney was a leader of those who were against the Chinese. Kearney was an Irish immigrant. He made fiery speeches saying that Chinese immigrants got jobs because they worked for less pay. Kearney ended his speeches with the cry "The Chinese must go!"

Feelings of people like Kearney led to discrimination (dih skrihm uh NAY shun). Discrimination is an unfair difference in the way people are treated. In 1871 Chinese were barred from San Francisco public schools. The state would not hire Chinese after 1879.

In 1882 the United States Congress passed the Chinese Exclusion Act. This law excluded, or kept out, Chinese immigrants. No other group of immigrants at this time suffered this discrimination.

San Francisco's street lamps and road signs show the city's Chinese heritage.

THE TABLES TURNED.
How our Streets will look next Summer as the result of the Chinese invasion.

The Granger Collection

This political cartoon shows the discrimination Chinese workers faced.

Mary Tape

Chinese Californians fought against these acts of discrimination. For instance, Chinese immigrants had to pay a special tax to the government. Ling Sing of San Francisco went to court. He argued that this tax was not allowed in our country's Constitution. He won the case, and the tax was ended.

In 1885 Joseph and Mary Tape took the San Francisco schools to court. Their eight-year-old daughter, Mamie, was not allowed to go to public school because she was Chinese. "Will you please tell me," Mary Tape asked the school officials, "is it a disgrace to be born a Chinese?" The court told the school officials to admit Mamie. Instead, the officials made a separate school only for Chinese. Years later, this, too, was found to be against our laws.

WHY IT MATTERS

The immigrants were great builders. They built more than the transcontinental railroad. Despite the discrimination they faced, they built new communities and new lives in California. The heritage of Chinese and Irish immigrants is part of what makes California special.

Reviewing Facts and Ideas

MAIN IDEAS

- Immigrants from China and Ireland built the transcontinental railroad.
- Work on the railroad was hard and dangerous.
- Chinese immigrants settled in San Francisco's Chinatown and other California communities.

THINK ABOUT IT

1. In what ways was railroad work dangerous?

2. Define the Chinese Exclusion Act.

3. **FOCUS** Why did people from other countries come to the United States to build the railroad?

4. **THINKING SKILL** If you were a railroad worker and were being treated unfairly by your boss, what would you *decide* to do? Describe how you made this decision.

5. **GEOGRAPHY** Why was the Sierra Nevada hard for Central Pacific Railroad workers to build on?

227

Martial Arts

Martial means "warlike," and long ago some martial arts were part of training for war. Others may have roots in religious exercises that taught discipline and concentration. Today people practice martial arts as sports—for fun, exercise, and self-defense.

The first martial art taught in this country was *kung fu*. It was brought here by Chinese immigrants in the mid-1800s. At first kung fu teachers taught only Chinese Americans. Then in 1964 a teacher in Los Angeles opened his school to everyone. Soon Americans all over the country were learning kung fu.

Other Asian immigrants brought martial arts. From Japan came *judo,* which means "gentle way," and *karate*. Koreans brought *tae kwan do* (TĪ KWAHN DOH). These sports now enjoyed by millions of Americans are a legacy from countries in Asia.

The boy (above) is competing in kickboxing. He wears special pads to prevent injury. The college students (below) are practicing judo, a Japanese martial art invented in the 1890s. It uses timing and skill over brute strength.

Many older people practice t'ai chi (TĪ JEE) to stay fit (below). It calls for graceful movement and deep concentration. The students (bottom) are learning karate. Colored belts show different levels of skill.

CITIZENS TAKE ACTION

READ ALOUD

Katherine Philips Edson believed that everyone should have a voice in government. She fought long and hard for women's right to vote. When California women won that right in 1911, Edson wrote a friend: "The whole world seems to be opened up to us."

THE BIG PICTURE

The railroad helped California grow. In the 20 years after the railroad was completed, our state's population more than doubled. The Big Four sold people land that the government had given them for free. They used their wealth to make themselves even more powerful.

The Big Four had a lot of say in the government by unfair means. Our country is a democratic republic. In this form of government, citizens elect representatives to make decisions for them. Many Californians feared that the government no longer represented the citizens. Instead, representatives made decisions that would help the powerful railroad. What would Californians do?

Focus Activity

READ TO LEARN
How did people work to change California's government around 1900?

VOCABULARY
democratic republic
bribe
reformer
initiative
political party
suffrage
minimum wage

PEOPLE
Abraham Ruef
Hiram Johnson
Katherine Philips Edson
Delilah Beasley

PLACES
San Pedro

"THE OCTOPUS"

The Big Four owned much of California's transportation. They controlled the waterfront in San Francisco Bay Area. They built a rail line through the Central Valley. They finished another transcontinental railroad, which stopped in Los Angeles. In 1884 they named their whole railroad system the Southern Pacific Company.

Farmers and merchants were angry. If they wanted to ship their goods, they had to pay the Southern Pacific's high fees. They called the railroad "the octopus." They said that its many "arms" were choking the state. But when they complained to the government, nothing happened.

Why not? The Southern Pacific was giving bribes to officials, or government workers. A bribe is money paid to an official to do something. Representatives made laws that helped the railroad. Judges decided lawsuits in the railroad's favor.

Leland Stanford was the president of the railroad. He served as California's governor and, later, one of its United States senators. He used his government jobs to make laws that helped his own company. Today that is against the law.

Californians tried to fight against the railroad's hold on government. One important early success occurred in Los Angeles. In the 1890s the

The Southern Pacific "octopus" (above, in an 1882 political cartoon) seemed to reach into every area of California's life, including government.

people of the city wanted to build a new harbor at the town of San Pedro. The Southern Pacific owned land at Santa Monica and wanted a new harbor to be built there instead. Los Angeles fought for nearly ten years before the city won the right to build its harbor at San Pedro.

CLEANING UP GOVERNMENT

California was not the only state where large businesses controlled the government. Citizens around the country took action. They were known as reformers. Reformers wanted to improve the way government was run.

The Fall of "Boss" Ruef

In San Francisco the reformers took action against Abraham Ruef (ROOF). Ruef was not a government official. He was a political "boss" who ran the city as though he were a king. He used the money he got from big businesses to bribe city officials. The city officials then did what Ruef told them to do. For example, they hired a streetcar company that had paid a bribe to Ruef.

On April 18, 1906, a huge earthquake struck San Francisco. As you read in Chapter 1, the earthquake started fires that destroyed much of the city. City hall lay in ruins. Ruef and his friends stole some of the money that people had sent to help San Francisco.

San Franciscans were angry. The reformers led the fight to clean up the government. Within months, Ruef, Mayor Eugene Schmitz, other city officials, and the businessmen who bribed them were arrested. Their trials lasted more than two years. A young lawyer from Sacramento named Hiram Johnson presented the case against them. But in the end, only Ruef went to jail.

Reform Around the State

Citizens in Los Angeles also fought for reform. In 1903 the city voted in a new city charter, or basic law. It had several important reforms. The initiative (ih NIHSH uh tihv), for example, allowed citizens to suggest laws and then vote on them.

Hiram Johnson (right) fought "bosses" like Abraham Ruef (above).

REGULAR PROGRESSIVE NOMINATIONS
FOR PRESIDENT
THEODORE ROOSEVELT
OF NEW YORK.
FOR VICE-PRESIDENT
HIRAM JOHNSON
OF CALIFORNIA.

In 1910 Southern California reform leaders asked Hiram Johnson to run for governor. Johnson agreed. Everywhere he went, he promised to "kick the Southern Pacific Railroad out of [government]." He said Californians were through "pick[ing] our own pockets to bribe ourselves with our own money!"

Johnson and many other reformers won election in 1910. The following year the legislature passed laws to correct unfair practices in business and government. See the chart for some of the reform laws passed in 1911.

Other states passed laws like these. Johnson hoped to bring reformers everywhere together. Reformers would make a new political party, the Progressives. A political party is a group of people who share similar ideas about government. In 1912 Johnson became the Progressive party's choice for Vice President. Theodore Roosevelt was the party's choice for President. Although Roosevelt and Johnson lost, they kept working for reform.

The Limits of Reform

Most of the reformers were from families that had lived in the United States for many years. Some of

them blamed the problems in government on recent immigrants who had voted for bosses like Ruef. Some reformers wanted laws against newcomers from Japan. In 1913, for example, a law barred Asian immigrants from owning land in California.

PROGRESSIVE LAWS IN CALIFORNIA

1911

- Law gives California Railroad Commission the power to set railroad rates

- Law gives California Railroad Commission the power to set rates for services like gas and electricity

- Initiative law gives voters a way to create laws directly

- Recall law allows voters to remove elected officials from office

- Women's suffrage law gives women the right to vote in California

- 8-hour day law limits the workday for women

1913

- Law sets minimum wage for women and children

- Pure milk law regulates how milk products are made

CHART WORK

Progressives helped pass many reform laws.

What law listed on the chart above changed the way laws can be made in California?

233

IMPROVING LIFE IN CALIFORNIA

Reformers helped clean up California's government. They also worked to improve the lives of Californians in other ways. One tireless reformer was Katherine Philips Edson. You read her words in the Read Aloud.

Katherine Philips Edson

Edson began her fight for reform in Los Angeles during the early 1900s. Children were becoming ill from drinking bad milk. As a mother of two children, Edson was upset. She and other women demanded the government test milk to make sure it was safe. In a letter she asked:

If the milk supply is in the hands of politicians, how can a woman who wants to do the right thing by her babies stay at home and keep quiet?

Edson's efforts soon paid off. The city hired inspectors to test all the milk sold in Los Angeles.

Edson also worked for women's suffrage. Suffrage is the right to vote. Women were not allowed to vote in California at this time. Edson met with representatives in Sacramento. She got them to vote for women's suffrage. In 1911 California became the sixth state to grant women's suffrage.

In 1912 Governor Johnson asked Edson to study working conditions in California. Women and children were working 10 to 12 hours a day, often in an unhealthy environment. They were usually paid less than 15 cents an hour.

Edson led the fight to improve working conditions. In 1913 she

Katherine Philips Edson (above) and other reformers fought for women's right to vote, or suffrage (below).

helped pass a minimum wage law for women and children. A minimum wage is the lowest amount of money that a business can pay its workers. Today we have minimum wage laws for all workers, including men.

The Power of the Press

Another citizen who worked to make life better was Delilah Beasley. Born in Ohio, Beasley came to California in 1909. She studied the history of African Americans. After years of study, she wrote *The Negro Trailblazers of California*. Beasley also wrote about the lives of African Americans of her time. In 1923 she began writing a weekly column for the *Oakland Tribune* newspaper. Her stories covered the events and achievements of the African American community. They also called for an end to many forms of discrimination.

WHY IT MATTERS

Citizens play an important role in a democratic republic. They elect the leaders of government. If government is not working correctly, they can change it and help improve people's lives.

Reviewing Facts and Ideas

MAIN IDEAS

- The Southern Pacific paid bribes to government officials in California.

- Hiram Johnson and other reformers passed the initiative and other laws to clean up California's government.

- Reformers worked to improve the lives of California's people.

THINK ABOUT IT

1. How did the Southern Pacific influence government?

2. What did Hiram Johnson promise to do if elected governor?

3. **FOCUS** How did people work to change California's government around the turn of the century?

4. **THINKING SKILL** List three *questions* you would ask Hiram Johnson.

5. **WRITE** Imagine that you are going to shoot a film about the life of Delilah Beasley. Do some research in the library. Write an outline of your script.

CHAPTER 8 REVIEW

Major Events

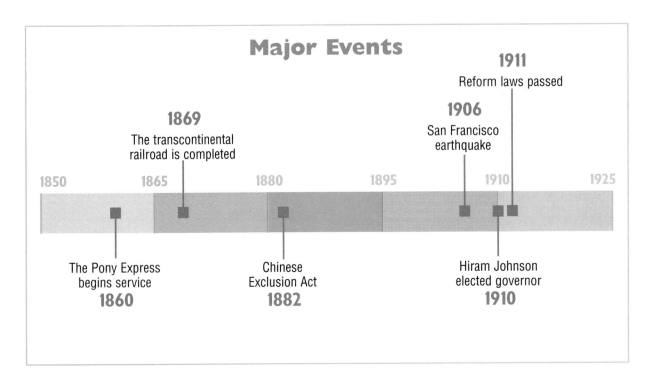

1911
Reform laws passed

1906
San Francisco
earthquake

1869
The transcontinental
railroad is completed

1850   1865   1880   1895   1910   1925

The Pony Express
begins service
1860

Chinese
Exclusion Act
1882

Hiram Johnson
elected governor
1910

THINKING ABOUT VOCABULARY

Number a sheet of paper from 1 to 5. Next to each number write the word from the list that best matches the definition.

bribe
discrimination
elevation
suffrage
transportation

1. Money given to an official to get him or her to do something
2. The right to vote
3. An unfair difference in the way people are treated
4. The movement of people and goods
5. The height of land above sea level

THINKING ABOUT FACTS

1. What did Theodore Judah and the "Big Four" disagree about?
2. Why were Chinese immigrants discriminated against?
3. What did Samuel F. B. Morse invent? Why was it important?
4. How did the minimum wage law help women and children?
5. Which groups of immigrants worked to build the transcontinental railroad?
6. Why did the Pony Express go out of business?
7. How did the reformers help to "clean up" California's government?
8. Name the railroad companies that built the transcontinental railroad.
9. Why did the railroad companies work quickly?
10. How did Katherine Philips Edson help children?

THINK AND WRITE

WRITING A DESCRIPTION

Write a paragraph describing what the Pony Express was and how it worked.

WRITING A LETTER

Suppose you are Theodore Judah. Write a letter encouraging business people to invest in the transcontinental railroad.

WRITING A JOURNAL

Suppose you are a Chinese immigrant in San Francisco in 1870. Write a journal entry describing what life is like.

APPLYING GEOGRAPHY SKILLS

READING ELEVATION MAPS

1. What tells you this is an elevation map?

2. What landform in California has the highest elevation?

3. What color on this map shows a landform 2,000 feet above sea level?

4. In what elevation range is Fresno?

5. Why were elevation maps necessary in building the transcontinental railroad?

CALIFORNIA: Elevation

Summing Up the Chapter

Use the following word map to organize information from the chapter. Write at least one piece of information in each blank circle. When you have filled in the map, use it to write a paragraph that answers the question "How did new technology change California?"

Transportation and Communications

Transcontinental Railroad

Citizens Take Action

CHAPTER 9

Growing California

THINKING ABOUT HISTORY AND GEOGRAPHY

The transcontinental railroad helped our state grow. Farmers began to sell their crops all over the country. Cities built large projects that brought water from the distant mountains. Even in hard times, California offered a chance for diverse people to build better lives in new communities. Read on to learn more about the growth of California.

1873
RIVERSIDE

Luther and Eliza Tibbets plant the first navel orange trees in California

AROUND 1920
HETCH HETCHY VALLEY

Workers build the O'Shaughnessy Dam

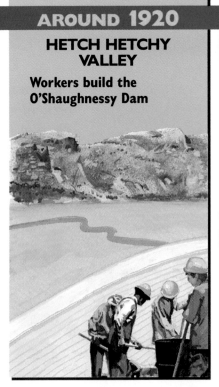

AROUND 1936
ALONG ROUTE 66 IN NEW MEXICO

"Okies" head to California, fleeing the Dust Bowl

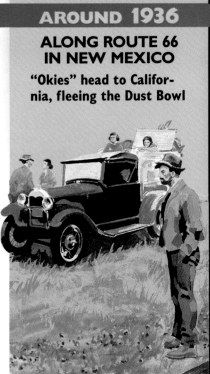

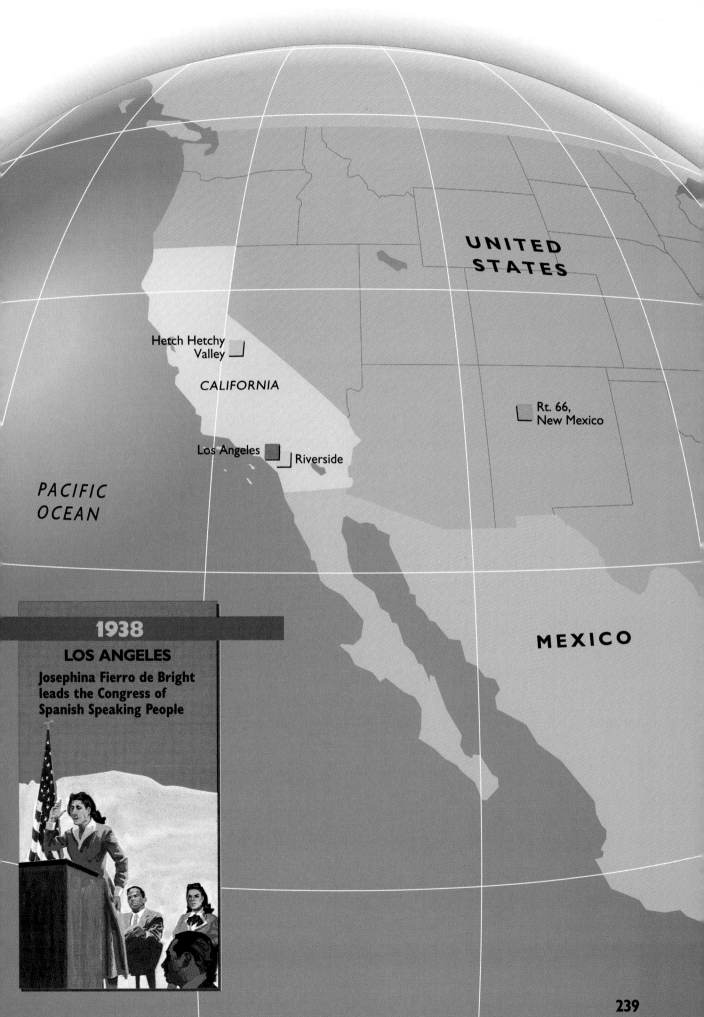

UNITED
STATES

Hetch Hetchy
Valley

CALIFORNIA

Rt. 66,
New Mexico

Los Angeles ☐ Riverside

PACIFIC
OCEAN

MEXICO

1938

LOS ANGELES

Josephina Fierro de Bright
leads the Congress of
Spanish Speaking People

1860   1920   1940

RICHES OF THE EARTH

READ ALOUD

It's always orange day in California,
Forget your winter snow,
Come out and see them grow.

By the early 1900s, California was known for sunshine and endless orange groves. Songs, like the one above, celebrated the Golden State's good fortune and lured visitors.

THE BIG PICTURE

In the 1860s farming started to become a big business in California. Transportation links to places outside California meant that California's farmers could grow food for sale in faraway markets. A market is a place where goods are bought and sold.

With so much money to be made by farming, Californians began making more changes to the natural environment. Wetlands were drained. Ways were found to channel streams and rivers toward farmlands. Farmers planted new types of crops. Scientists developed ways to grow more food. Inventors created machines to harvest the crops more easily. By the early 1900s, people in much of the country were enjoying food from California's farms.

Focus Activity

READ TO LEARN
How did California become the leading agricultural state in the country?

VOCABULARY
market
drought
tractor
refrigeration

PEOPLE
Benjamin Holt
Luther Tibbets
Eliza Tibbets
Luther Burbank

PLACES
Stockton
Riverside
Santa Rosa
Davis

CATTLE AND WHEAT

As it had been in the days of the Californio rancheros, cattle ranching continued to be an important agricultural business in the late 1800s. One of the biggest ranchers during that time was Henry Miller. He bought swampy land in the San Joaquin Valley and drained it to make it good for ranching. He and a partner owned more than 1,500 square miles!

Miller and other ranchers in the late 1800s began raising many cows for milking. Today California is first among the states in dairy production and sixth in beef production.

Wheat

In the early 1860s a bad drought (DROWT) hurt ranchers. A drought is a long period with very little rain. With no grass to eat, many cattle died. When the drought ended, many farmers decided to grow wheat instead. Wheat was a perfect crop for the flat lands and dry summers of the Central Valley. For the next 30 years, wheat was the most important crop in our state.

New farm machines helped wheat farmers and other farmers harvest their crops more easily. Many were made in Stockton, an important center for making farm machines. Benjamin Holt invented one of the most important of these farm machines. In 1904 Holt invented the first "caterpillar track" tractor. A tractor is a small, powerful vehicle for pulling farm machinery. Holt's caterpillar tractor ran on its own track instead of wheels. That allowed the tractor to keep moving without getting stuck in the mud.

Farmers still use Benjamin Holt's caterpillar tractor to pull machinery.

Early refrigerated railroad cars (below) used ice (right) to keep produce fresh.

NEW CROPS

California farmers of the early 1900s knew that fruits and vegetables grow well in the state's sunny climate. Unlike wheat, however, fruits and vegetables spoil, or go bad, quickly. Farmers needed a way to get these crops quickly to markets in the eastern United States so they would not spoil.

Refrigeration

The answer was to ship fruits and vegetables in fast railroad cars that could be kept cool. Food that is kept cool will not spoil as quickly. That is why we keep our food in refrigerators. Keeping food cool to preserve it is called refrigeration.

Experiments with refrigerated railroad cars started in the 1860s. It was not until the 1880s, however, that refrigerated railroad cars started making regular trips. Each railroad car had huge ice blocks placed at either end. When the ice blocks melted, new blocks of ice would be put into the cars to keep the food cold.

Oranges in Southern California

In 1870 a man named John Wesley North planted orange trees on land he owned near Riverside. The trees grew well in the hot, sunny climate. They also needed a lot of water.

North solved this problem through irrigation. Irrigation uses ditches or pipes to bring water to dry land. You may remember from Chapter 3 that the Cahuilla used irrigation to grow crops in the Colorado Desert. North's success at bringing water from the Santa Ana River to his land made the land very valuable.

But it was Luther and Eliza Tibbets who helped make orange growing a big business in Southern California. In 1873 the Tibbetses introduced a new, better kind of orange tree to California. The navel orange tree came from Brazil in South America. Its fruit was juicy, delicious, and seedless. Eliza spent long hours making sure the trees grew strong and healthy. Soon many other farmers in Southern California were growing what they called Riverside navels.

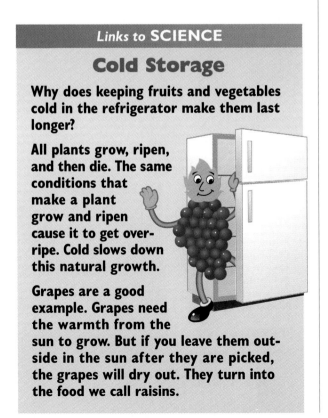

Links to SCIENCE

Cold Storage

Why does keeping fruits and vegetables cold in the refrigerator make them last longer?

All plants grow, ripen, and then die. The same conditions that make a plant grow and ripen cause it to get over-ripe. Cold slows down this natural growth.

Grapes are a good example. Grapes need the warmth from the sun to grow. But if you leave them outside in the sun after they are picked, the grapes will dry out. They turn into the food we call raisins.

CALIFORNIA FARMING AROUND 1920

OREGON

IDAHO

- Eureka

Beef and dairy
Oranges
Grains
Grapes
Irrigated farmland

Santa Rosa

Sacramento ★

Mono Lake

NEVADA

San Francisco

Stockton

San Jose

San Joaquin River

Salinas

Fresno

Bakersfield

PACIFIC OCEAN

Los Angeles

Riverside

San Diego

Imperial Valley

MEXICO

0   75   150 Miles
0   75   150 Kilometers

N
W   E
S

MAP WORK

By the 1920s California farmers were growing many different crops.
Near what cities were grapes grown?

Harvest Labor

Many of the people who did the hard work of harvesting California's crops were immigrants. They came from China, Mexico, the Philippines, Japan, India, and other countries. Native Americans continued to harvest crops also. Without these farmworkers, California's farmers could not have been nearly so successful. Even so, the farmers did not always treat the farmworkers fairly.

infographic

From the Farm to Your Table

You have read a lot about California's farms. But most of us do not buy our food right at the farm. Instead, we buy our food at a store. How does food get from the farm to the store? It is a long journey. Read on to learn how a typical farm product—the tomato—moves from farm to table.

One

Tomatoes grow from seeds. Often these seeds are first planted indoors. After a few weeks, the new plants, or seedlings, are transplanted outdoors.

Two

It takes almost 3 months for tomatoes to ripen. Those going directly to the market are picked by hand. The rest are picked by machine.

Five

At homes across the United States and around the world, California tomatoes become part of meals enjoyed by millions of families.

Four

At the supermarket you can find tomato products such as soup, salsa, ketchup, canned tomatoes, and juice.

Three

Tomatoes are shipped by trucks to factories. There they are processed, or made into other products, such as soup.

245

SCIENCE AND FARMING

Technology and science have also played key roles in the success of California agriculture. As you have seen, new crops and inventions helped to make the state's farms more productive.

Luther Burbank

One person who led the way in using science to help farming was Luther Burbank. Burbank was born on a farm in Massachusetts in 1849. He was always fascinated by plants.

In 1875 Burbank moved to California and settled in Santa Rosa. He called the city "the chosen spot of all this earth" because of its rich soil and pleasant climate. There Burbank experimented with plants from around the world. He grew them in a way to bring out the new features he wanted. For example, he hoped to get plants that grew faster and produced more food.

In all, Burbank developed about 800 new kinds of plants while living in Santa Rosa. Many, including special types of plums, are still grown by California farmers today.

Agriculture Today

Science continues to be important to California agriculture. Scientists at the University of California at Davis, for example, are famous for their advances in agricultural science. They invented a tree-shaking machine to help harvest fruit.

Today California is the number one agricultural state in the United States. Its farmers produce over $24 billion worth of products each year. Look at the chart on the next page to see some of our state's leading agricultural products.

UC Davis agricultural scientists today (right) follow Luther Burbank's example.

Univ. Calif./Davis

Unfortunately, farming has also changed or damaged our environment. Too much irrigation, for example, has left some fields choked with salt and dangerous chemicals. Plants and animals have lost their homes when land has been cleared.

In recent years California farmers have worked to fix some of these problems. Rice farmers in the Sacramento Valley, for example, now provide winter homes for birds.

WHY IT MATTERS

California's fresh fruits and vegetables are enjoyed across the country. Everyone shares in California's harvest.

✓ Reviewing Facts and Ideas

MAIN IDEAS

- Refrigeration and irrigation allowed California's farmers to grow new crops.
- California's orange-growing industry began in Riverside in the 1880s.
- Science and technology are keys to the success of California agriculture.

THINK ABOUT IT

1. Why did many farmers first plant wheat in the 1860s?
2. Name one kind of orange grown in California.
3. **FOCUS** How did California become the leading agricultural state in our country?
4. **THINKING SKILL** Why, do you suppose, have some California farmers made the _decision_ to repair the damage that farming has done to the environment?
5. **GEOGRAPHY** Look at the map of California farming on page 243. Which part of our state grew the most oranges in 1920?

TOP TEN CALIFORNIA FOOD PRODUCTS (1995)

Ranking	Product	Dollar Value
1	Dairy	$3,078,000,000
2	Grapes	1,839,000,000
3	Beef	1,290,000,000
4	Lettuce	987,000,000
5	Almonds	858,000,000
6	Tomatoes	672,000,000
7	Strawberries	552,000,000
8	Oranges	458,000,000
9	Chickens	384,000,000
10	Rice	318,000,000

CHART WORK

California farmers are leading producers of many crops.

Which food products had a value greater than $1,000,000,000 in 1995?

Source: Calif. Dept. of Food and Agriculture

247

STUDYSKILLS

Using Reference Sources

VOCABULARY

reference source   encyclopedia
dictionary   CD-ROM
guide word   Internet

WHY THE SKILL MATTERS

In the last lesson you read about the refrigerated railroad car, irrigation, and Luther Burbank. You might like to find out more about any of these topics— let's say, the importance of irrigation.

You could find the information you want in reference sources. These are books and other sources that contain facts about many different subjects. They can be found in a special part of the library called the reference section.

USING A DICTIONARY

To begin, you might want to know the exact meaning of the word *irrigation*. To find out, you would look in a dictionary. A dictionary gives the meanings of words. It shows how to pronounce and spell each word. Sometimes a dictionary explains where a word comes from or uses it in a sentence.

The words in a dictionary are arranged in alphabetical order. To make your work faster, you can refer to the guide words. These appear at the top of each page of the dictionary. They tell you the first and last words that are defined on that page.

Look at the guide words on the sample dictionary page. According to them, what is the last word to be defined on the page? Would the word *invention* appear on this page? Now find the word *irrigation*. What does this word mean?

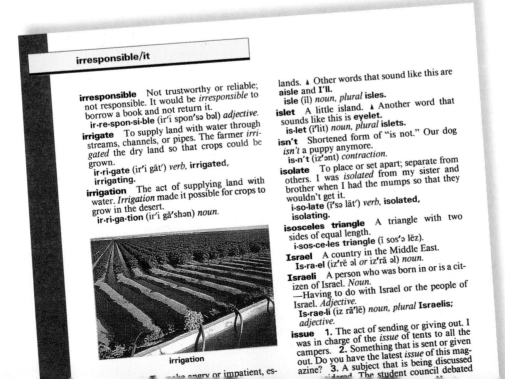

irresponsible/it

irresponsible Not trustworthy or reliable; not responsible. It would be *irresponsible* to borrow a book and not return it.
ir·re·spon·si·ble (ir′i spon′sə bəl) *adjective.*
irrigate To supply land with water through streams, channels, or pipes. The farmer *irrigated* the dry land so that crops could be grown.
ir·ri·gate (ir′i gāt′) *verb,* **irrigated, irrigating.**
irrigation The act of supplying land with water. *Irrigation* made it possible for crops to grow in the desert.
ir·ri·ga·tion (ir′i gā′shən) *noun.*

lands. ▲ Other words that sound like this are **aisle** and **I'll.**
isle (īl) *noun, plural* **isles.**
islet A little island. ▲ Another word that sounds like this is **eyelet.**
is·let (ī′lit) *noun, plural* **islets.**
isn't Shortened form of "is not." Our dog *isn't* a puppy anymore.
is·n't (iz′ənt) *contraction.*
isolate To place or set apart; separate from others. I was *isolated* from my sister and brother when I had the mumps so that they wouldn't get it.
i·so·late (ī′sə lāt′) *verb,* **isolated, isolating.**
isosceles triangle A triangle with two sides of equal length.
i·sos·ce·les triangle (ī sos′ə lēz).
Israel A country in the Middle East.
Is·ra·el (iz′rē əl *or* iz′rā əl) *noun.*
Israeli A person who was born in or is a citizen of Israel. *Noun.*
—Having to do with Israel or the people of Israel. *Adjective.*
Is·rae·li (iz rā′lē) *noun, plural* **Israelis;** *adjective.*
issue **1.** The act of sending or giving out. I was in charge of the *issue* of tents to all the campers. **2.** Something that is sent or given out. Do you have the latest *issue* of this magazine? **3.** A subject that is being discussed ... The student council debated

irrigation

USING AN ENCYCLO-PEDIA, A CD-ROM, OR THE INTERNET

Another useful reference book is the encyclopedia. This book or set of books gives information about people, places, things, and events. Like a dictionary, the topics in the encyclopedia are arranged in alphabetical order. Most encyclopedias also use guide words.

Suppose you want to learn even more about irrigation. You would look in the encyclopedia volume, or book, with *I* on the spine. Which volume would you look in to learn more about Luther Burbank?

Two newer kinds of reference sources are the CD-ROM and the Internet. A CD-ROM is a compact disc that you "read" with the aid of a computer. Like an encyclopedia, a CD-ROM contains facts about many subjects. It also may include sounds, music, and even short movies! The Internet is a computer network. With a computer that has an Internet connection, you can "visit" sources of information such as libraries, schools, or government offices. Your teacher or librarian will help you use these types of reference sources.

HELPING Yourself

- **Reference sources** have information about many subjects.

- **A dictionary** gives the meanings of words. An **encyclopedia** gives information on people, places, things, and events.

- Look up a subject using a **guide word** or title.

TRYING THE SKILL

You have practiced using reference sources. Now suppose you want to write a report on the use of chemical pesticides in farming. What is a pesticide? What reference source would you use to find out? How would you find out more about pesticides? See the Helping Yourself box for hints.

REVIEWING THE SKILL

1. What is a reference source?

2. Which reference source would you use to find the meaning of the word *drought*?

3. Some encyclopedias have guide words instead of letters. Suppose you had a volume covering everything from *machinery* to *Oklahoma*. Would it contain an article about oranges?

4. When are reference sources useful to students?

249

WATER FROM THE MOUNTAINS

READ ALOUD

On November 5, 1913, thousands gathered to see the first water from the Owens Valley flow into Los Angeles. The man who had made it possible, William Mulholland, rose to make a speech. "There it is," he told the crowd. "Take it." Three hundred million gallons of water a day thundered down the aqueduct.

Focus Activity

READ TO LEARN
How did Californians meet their need for water?

VOCABULARY
canal
aqueduct
dam
reservoir
hydroelectric power

PEOPLE
George Chaffey
William Mulholland
Mary Austin
John Muir

PLACES
Imperial Valley
Owens Valley
Hetch Hetchy Valley

THE BIG PICTURE

Water is California's most important natural resource. We cannot live without it. We need it to grow our food, and we use it to run our factories. But most of the state is dry. It receives less than 20 inches of rain a year. Only the mountain regions and the far north coast get large amounts of precipitation.

One of our state's biggest challenges has been bringing the water from where it falls as precipitation to where it can be used in farms, cities, and factories. Californians have found amazing solutions to this problem. The solutions have allowed our population, farms, and factories to grow. These solutions have also created new problems for the environment. California will need to face its water challenges for years to come.

CREATING THE IMPERIAL VALLEY

As you read in Chapter 3, the Cahuilla people farmed in the Colorado Desert for thousands of years. Early American settlers, however, thought the area was too dry to grow anything there.

George Chaffey

In 1900 George Chaffey set out to change that idea. He worked as an engineer for a company that bought and sold land. The company wanted to bring water to the area and then sell land to farmers.

Chaffey started by giving the area a new name. He thought the Imperial Valley would sound much better to farmers than the Colorado Desert. Next, he hired workers to build a 70-mile canal that brought water from the Colorado River to the desert. A canal is a waterway built by people.

Chaffey's project was a huge success. By 1902 more than 2,000 people were living in the valley. In 1905 Chaffey left the company. Trying to get more water, the canal's owner caused a huge flood. The flood created what we know as the Salton Sea.

Today the valley is famous for its lettuce, cantaloupes, and other crops. The All-American Canal and the Coachella (koh CHE luh) Canal, both finished in the 1940s, have since replaced Chaffey's canal.

The Salton Sea flood lasted two years (below). Today date trees grow in the Imperial Valley (left).

WATER FOR CITIES

In the early 1900s Los Angeles was growing so fast that city leaders thought it might soon run out of water. They thought a canal might be the answer.

Los Angeles Aqueduct

In 1902 an Irish immigrant named William Mulholland became chief engineer for Los Angeles. He soon formed plans to bring the waters of the Owens River to Los Angeles. The Owens flowed through the Owens Valley, a high mountain valley over 200 miles northeast of Los Angeles.

Los Angeles secretly bought much of the land in Owens Valley. Settlers in the valley had thought the United States government was going to irrigate the valley for farming. Now they found they were wrong. The settlers began to oppose Los Angeles's plan.

In 1907 Los Angeles voted to build an aqueduct (AK wuh dukt). An aqueduct is a canal or pipe for bringing water from a faraway source. Work began in 1908. Five thousand men spent five years on the job. They dug 142 tunnels through mountains and cut canals through deserts.

Triumph and Disaster

To the people of Los Angeles, Mulholland was a hero. The city continued to grow very quickly. By 1920 it had over 575,000 people, passing San Francisco as the largest city in the state.

For the Owens Valley, the Los Angeles Aqueduct was a disaster. Without water, farms failed, people moved away, and Owens Lake dried up. In her 1903 book *The Land of Little Rain,* Mary Austin described the air in the Owens Valley as the "cleanest . . . to be breathed anywhere in God's world." Today dust blows off the dried-out Owens Lake and makes the air there unhealthy to breathe.

L.A. Dept. of Water and Power

William Mulholland (above) led workers in building the Los Angeles Aqueduct (left).

252

The Hetch Hetchy Valley is seen in 1917 (left). Today (below) a reservoir supplies San Francisco with water.

The Hetch Hetchy Fight

In the early 1900s San Francisco was also a growing city that believed it needed more water. City officials decided that the Tuolumne (too AH luh mee) River offered the best source. The river flowed through the beautiful Hetch Hetchy Valley, inside Yosemite National Park. The city wanted to build a dam, or wall built across a river, to create a large reservoir (REZ ur vwahr). A reservoir is a natural or human-built lake used to store water. The reservoir would flood the valley, which angered many people.

One of these people was John Muir, an immigrant who came from Scotland. Muir had been an important voice in preserving California's natural environment. In Chapter 1 you read how he helped to create Yosemite National Park. Muir thought that flooding what he called

one of the most beautiful gorges [mountain valleys] of the Sierras . . . a tremendous price for the nation to pay for San Francisco's water.

Muir and others fought long and hard to defeat the dam. They pointed out that the dam could be built just as well in other places. But in 1913 the United States Congress approved the Hetch Hetchy plan.

It took nine years to build the dam. However, San Francisco did not start getting water from it until 1934, when an aqueduct carrying the water from the reservoir to the city was finally completed. The Hetch Hetchy Aqueduct today remains the major source of water for the people of San Francisco.

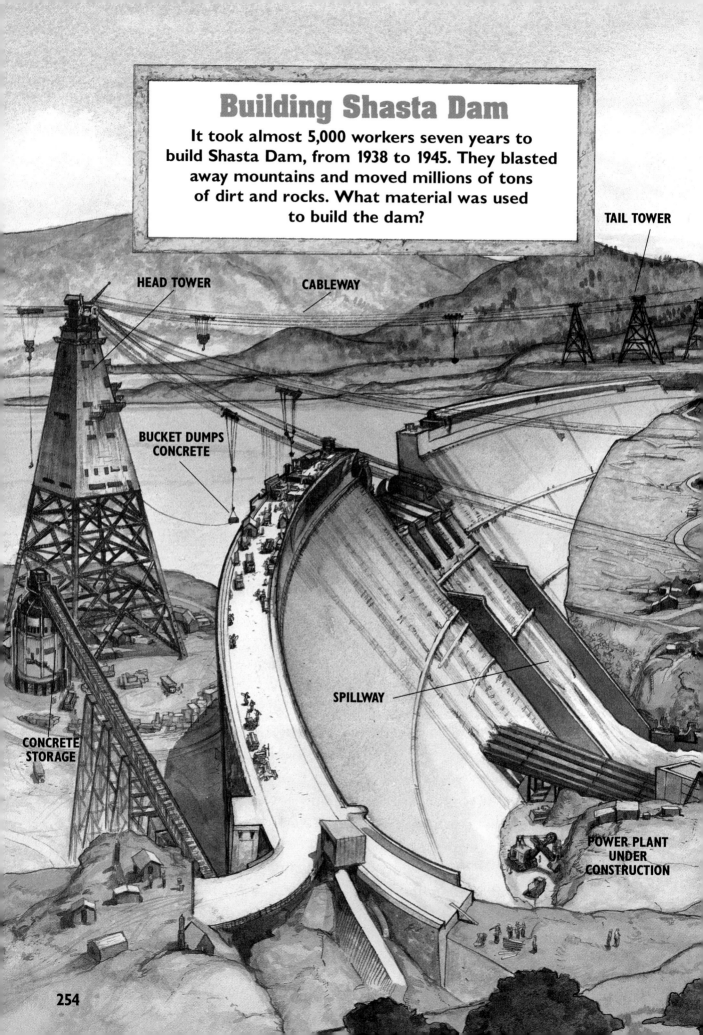

Building Shasta Dam

It took almost 5,000 workers seven years to build Shasta Dam, from 1938 to 1945. They blasted away mountains and moved millions of tons of dirt and rocks. What material was used to build the dam?

TAIL TOWER

HEAD TOWER

CABLEWAY

BUCKET DUMPS CONCRETE

CONCRETE STORAGE

SPILLWAY

POWER PLANT UNDER CONSTRUCTION

SHASTA DAM

There are many other dams in California besides the one you have just read about. The largest is Shasta Dam. In fact, Shasta Dam is the second largest dam in our country. Over 600 feet high, it is more than three times the height of Niagara Falls!

What Does a Dam Do?

Humans need water all year round. In dry places like California, however, most of the rain and snow falls during the winter months. Dams store, or hold, water in a reservoir. They release water when people need it.

Many dams are also built to produce hydroelectric power. Hydroelectric power is electricity created by water flowing in rivers. Water rushes through openings in the dam. Inside the dam, it spins machines called turbines. The spinning turbines create electricity. Each year Shasta Dam produces enough hydroelectric power to run a city the size of Long Beach.

A Long Journey

Water leaving Shasta Dam starts a long journey. Some of it is directed into a human-built canal that irrigates the farms of the western Sacramento

Central Valley Project control room (above) monitors water flow.

Valley. Some of it flows down the natural channel of the Sacramento River. This water used to flow from the Sacramento Delta to the Pacific Ocean. Today a huge pump sucks much of the water from the Delta and sends it south. Some water makes it as far as Riverside County. That means it has traveled over 650 miles.

Dams and the Environment

Dams change the environment. Freshwater fish can be especially hard hit. A dam's great height, for example, can make it almost impossible for fish to return to the places where they lay eggs.

In recent years the officials who run Shasta Dam have tried to help the fish. They release water from the dam into the river as the fish return, making it easier for the fish to swim upstream. At other dams, "stairs" have been built so the fish can "climb" past the dams.

But officials cannot help the plants and animals that once lived on the lands flooded by the dam. Once their land is gone, it is gone. The trees and plants have died. The bears, eagles, river otters, and other animals have been crowded into smaller areas, or they have died. Many people believe that big dams should no longer be built in California.

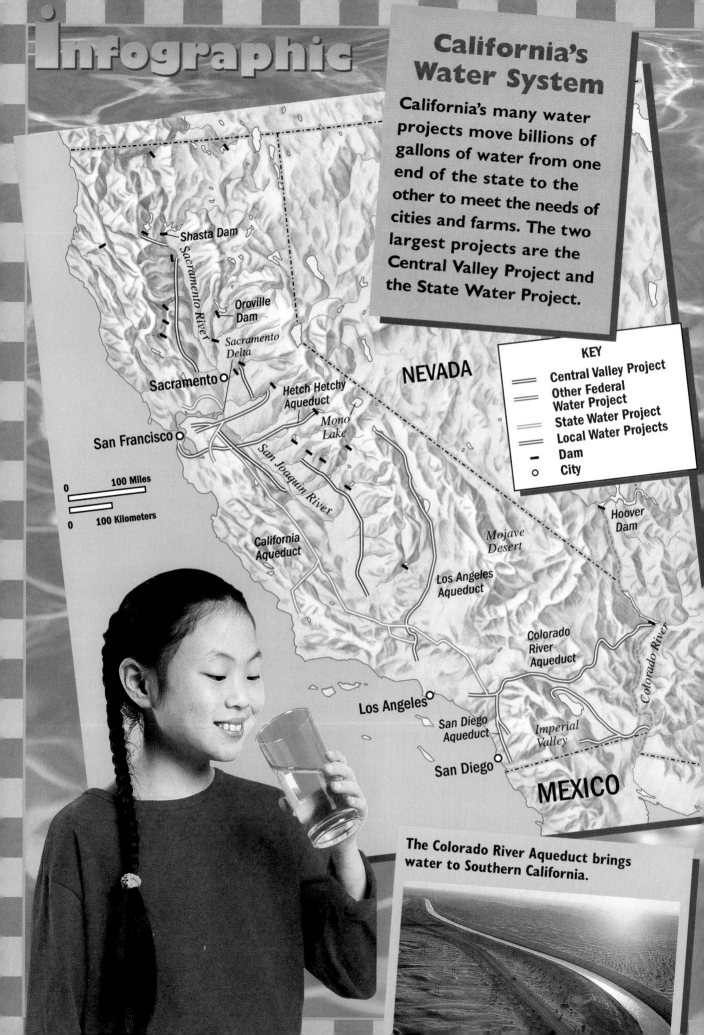

Infographic

California's Water System

California's many water projects move billions of gallons of water from one end of the state to the other to meet the needs of cities and farms. The two largest projects are the Central Valley Project and the State Water Project.

KEY
- Central Valley Project
- Other Federal Water Project
- State Water Project
- Local Water Projects
- Dam
- City

Shasta Dam

Sacramento River

Oroville Dam

Sacramento Delta

Sacramento

NEVADA

Hetch Hetchy Aqueduct

Mono Lake

San Francisco

San Joaquin River

100 Miles

100 Kilometers

California Aqueduct

Mojave Desert

Hoover Dam

Los Angeles Aqueduct

Colorado River Aqueduct

Colorado River

Los Angeles

San Diego Aqueduct

Imperial Valley

San Diego

MEXICO

The Colorado River Aqueduct brings water to Southern California.

At 754 feet, the Oroville Dam is the highest dam in the country.

A California Aqueduct pumping station lifts water over the Tehachapi Mountains.

Generators at Hoover Dam produce huge amounts of hydroelectric power.

WHY IT MATTERS

California's huge water projects allowed our state to lead the country in population, farming, and industry. They have also changed the natural environment and set off bitter conflicts. Because water is so important in California, it is likely that the conflicts will continue in the future.

✓✓ Reviewing Facts and Ideas

MAIN IDEAS

- Irrigation changed the Colorado Desert into valuable farmland.
- Los Angeles and San Francisco used water from the Sierra Nevada to grow.
- Dams store water for people to use, but they can damage the environment.

THINK ABOUT IT

1. Why did George Chaffey change the name of the Colorado Desert to the Imperial Valley?

2. Why did farmers in the Owens Valley oppose the Los Angeles Aqueduct?

3. **FOCUS** How have Californians met their needs for water?

4. **THINKING SKILL** Based on what you have read in this chapter, _make a prediction_ about what Los Angeles would be like today if the Los Angeles Aqueduct had not been built.

5. **WRITE** Write a letter to a friend in which you explain John Muir's ideas about protecting the environment. Are these ideas important today or not?

CITIZENSHIP
VIEWPOINTS

If we are careful about how we use water, we will have enough even to cool us off on a hot day.

HOW SHOULD CALIFORNIA'S WATER RESOURCES BE SHARED?

In California water is a precious resource that we all need to share. But determining how it should be shared can be difficult. How much water should be set aside for people and how much for plants and animals? How do we keep that water safe to drink?

In Southern California officials are looking for ways to stretch their water supply. Myriam Cardenas feels that dry areas should learn to recycle water. People who work in agriculture, such as Roger Duncan, are concerned about our state's growing population. They are afraid that California's farms will suffer if large cities use too much water. People who are concerned with the environment, like Glenda Humiston, think that the sources of water should be protected so that our water supplies will not run out or become polluted.

Read and consider three viewpoints on this issue. Then answer the questions that follow.

Three DIFFERENT Viewpoints

1

MYRIAM CARDENAS
Water chemist, Los Angeles
Excerpt from interview, 1997

Because farmers can buy water cheaply, they have not learned to use water more efficiently *[with as little waste as possible]*. People in cities like Los Angeles need water, too. Southern California is trying to become more self-sufficient in its water use. One way to do this is through water recycling—cleaning up dirty water so it can be put on lawns and gardens.

"... become more self-sufficient ..."

2

ROGER DUNCAN
Farm adviser, Modesto
Excerpt from interview, 1997

There needs to be a reliable source of water for agriculture. Farming provides a large number of jobs in farming and in related businesses. There is more and more pressure to claim water from the Central Valley to support the growing population in Southern California.

"... needs to be a reliable source of water for agriculture."

3

GLENDA HUMISTON
Natural resource consultant, Rio Nido
Excerpt from interview, 1997

We need to use our water resources so that they are here for the long run. We must find a way to protect the rivers and lakes in the north that provide water for the south. Ensuring water quality requires considering the needs of trees, plants, and fish along with the needs of people. Building a dam to create water for irrigation may block off a stream where fish are spawning *[laying eggs]*.

"... use our water resources so that they are here for the long run."

BUILDING CITIZENSHIP

1. What is the viewpoint of each person?
2. In what ways do the viewpoints agree? How do they disagree?
3. What other viewpoints might people have on this issue? How could you find out more about this issue in your community?

SHARING VIEWPOINTS

Discuss what you agree with or disagree with about these and other viewpoints. Make a chart showing the various ways water resources are used in California. Then, as a class, write two statements about using water resources that all of you can agree with.

FARMWORKERS BUILD COMMUNITIES

Focus Activity

READ TO LEARN
How did immigrants from Mexico build communities in California?

VOCABULARY
migrant labor
strike
barrio
mutualista
deport
Great Depression
New Deal
Dust Bowl

PEOPLE
Josefina Fierro de Bright
Franklin Delano Roosevelt
John Steinbeck

PLACES
Los Angeles
Bakersfield

READ ALOUD

The letters came from family and friends in the United States. They said: "Come! Come! It is good here." Jesus Garza was one who came. "I heard a lot about the United States," he said. "It was my dream to come."

THE BIG PICTURE

In Lesson 1 you read that most farmworkers were immigrants who came to California to make a better life. In the early 1900s many of those immigrants came from Mexico. They came to escape war and poverty in their homeland. Some returned to Mexico after a short time. Others stayed, finding jobs where they could—in the fields, in factories, and on the railroads. Life in the United States was not always easy for these new Californians. Yet they built strong communities and made our state a better place.

WORKING THE FIELDS

In 1915 Pablo Mares decided to leave Mexico and come to the United States. The Mexican Revolution, which had begun five years earlier, had made it "impossible to live [in my country]." Mares was part of a huge wave of immigrants. Between 1910 and 1930, almost one of every ten Mexicans came to the United States. That was more than one million people!

Like Pablo Mares, many of the immigrants became farmworkers. Whole families—children as well as parents—often worked in the fields as migrant labor. That meant they moved from place to place to harvest different crops as they ripened.

Life was hard for migrant workers. In the Imperial Valley the family of Anatascio Torres lived in a shack made of heavy cloth and palm branches. Clean, running water was rare. The children often got sick from drinking dirty water.

Fighting for Rights

Wages were low for all farmworkers. Mexican workers, however, were paid 50 cents to $1 less each day than other workers. Farm owners often tried to force wages even lower.

Mexican and other workers organized strikes to demand better treatment. A strike is when workers stop working until the business owners meet their demands. Lydia Ramos joined a big strike in the San Joaquin Valley in 1933. She did so, she said, because she "believe[d] in justice . . . equality and justice."

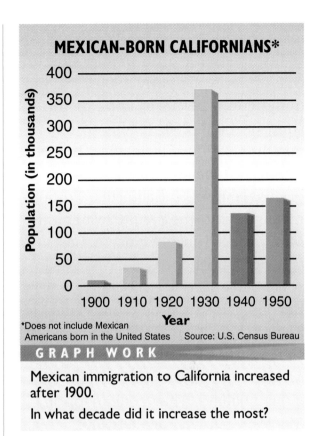

MEXICAN-BORN CALIFORNIANS*

Bar graph showing Population (in thousands) by Year

*Does not include Mexican Americans born in the United States

Source: U.S. Census Bureau

GRAPH WORK

Mexican immigration to California increased after 1900.

In what decade did it increase the most?

Farmworkers picking lettuce.

BUILDING COMMUNITIES

For many Mexican immigrants to California in the early 1900s, leaving home could be hard. Look at the song on page 263. It tells of one person's sadness at leaving home.

But, fortunately, for these immigrants, coming to California did not mean leaving their culture behind. Many settled in barrios. A barrio is a neighborhood where Mexican Americans have lived for many years. Barrios helped the newcomers feel at home. There they found people who spoke Spanish. They could celebrate Mexican Independence Day and religious holidays. They could shop in Mexican markets, or *mercados*.

Mutualistas

Each of the barrios had its own mutualistas (moo too ah LEE stahs). A *mutualista* was a group of Mexican Americans who helped other Mexican Americans. The *mutualistas* helped immigrants find jobs and fight for their rights. Some ran schools and started libraries. Others worked to end overcrowding in barrios caused by housing discrimination.

In the 1930s, as you will read on page 264, jobs were scarce all over the United States. Many Californians began to complain. They felt that Mexican immigrants were taking away the jobs of other Americans.

Mutualistas tried to protect immigrants. But the government began to deport Mexican immigrants, or force them to leave. Some were in the United States illegally. Others were United States citizens. Between 1931 and 1933, as many as 100,000 Mexicans were sent across the border from California to Mexico.

One of the strongest defenders of immigrant rights was Josefina Fierro de Bright. She was the first president of the Congress of Spanish Speaking People. This group was founded in Los Angeles in 1938 by labor leader Luisa Moreno. It called for an end to discrimination. Under Bright's leadership, the congress also fought for better housing and healthcare for Mexican immigrants.

Josefina Fierro de Bright helped many immigrants in California.

El quelite
The Village

Mexican Folk Song
English Words by MH

At the edge of a green *que - li - te,* I stopped a- while there to

sleep. A roos - ter cried out and woke me. He sang a "qui qui ri

qui." I don't sing be - cause I'm a - ble, nor be - cause _ my voice is

good. I sing be - cause I feel joy __ in my land _ and for - eign

lands. To - mor - row I will be leav - ing, and who can tell where I'll

be? But here is my con - so - la - tion: that some - one re - mem - bers me.

THE GREAT DEPRESSION

As you have read, the 1930s were a time of hardship in many countries. This period is known today as the Great Depression. Many businesses failed. Millions of people lost their jobs, homes, and farms. In California alone, one out of every five people in 1934 needed money from the government just to survive.

President Franklin Delano Roosevelt took action. While he was President, the government began programs to help people get through the hard times. They are known together as the New Deal. Many programs put people to work.

Construction workers built parks, bridges, and dams. Shasta Dam, for example, was built by citizens working for the government in the New Deal. Artists painted murals, or wall paintings, on many public buildings. Young people built trails through the forests and worked to preserve the environment. California benefited in many ways from the programs of the New Deal.

The "Okies"

The Great Depression hit hardest in the Great Plains part of our country. A bad drought lasting seven years turned the land there into dust. Farms were ruined and many animals died. An area half the size of California became known as the Dust Bowl.

In the 1930s more than 350,000 people left the Dust Bowl and migrated, or moved, to California. So many came from Oklahoma that

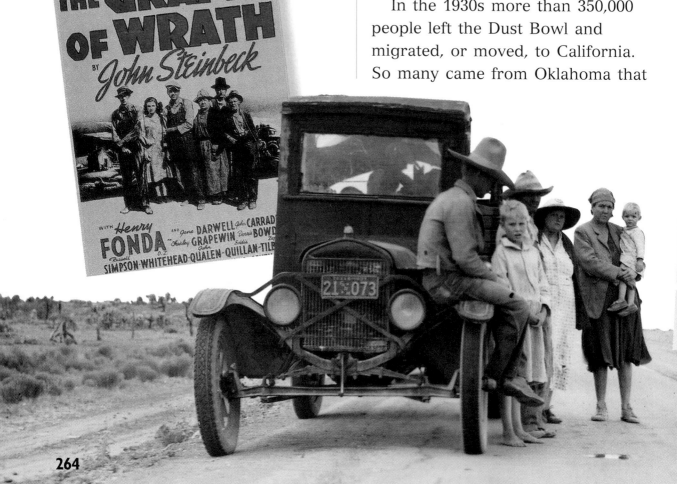

DARRYL F. ZANUCK'S Production of

THE GRAPES OF WRATH

BY John Steinbeck

WITH Henry FONDA AND Jane DARWELL John CARRAD Charley GRAPEWIN Doris BOWD Russell SIMPSON · O.Z. WHITEHEAD · John QUALEN · Eddie QUILLAN · Zeffie TILB

they became known as "Okies." John Steinbeck wrote a book called *The Grapes of Wrath* about the migrants' journey to California. A character in the book, named Ma Joad, expressed the hopes of many real people:

> I like to think how nice it's gonna be, maybe, in California. Never cold. An' fruit ever'place, an' people just bein' in the nicest places . . . that is, if we all get jobs an' all work.

When the Dust Bowl migrants arrived in California, they often faced discrimination. Many Californians thought the newcomers would take their jobs. They even tried to pass a law to keep "Okies" out. That kind of law is illegal in our country. Like Mexican farmworkers, the Dust Bowl migrants went on many strikes to earn enough money to live.

Most of the newcomers from the Middle West settled in the Central

The *Grapes of Wrath* movie poster (far left) shows one of the hardships that "Okie" families (above and left) faced.

Valley. In cities like Bakersfield they built strong communities. Though times in California were hard, they were determined to make a better life for themselves.

WHY IT MATTERS

In the early 1900s large numbers of Mexican immigrants came to California to work as farm laborers. They created strong communities. Today one out of every five Californians has a Mexican heritage.

✓✓ Reviewing Facts and Ideas

MAIN IDEAS

- Immigration from Mexico increased in the early 1900s.
- Mexican immigrants built strong communities in California that helped make our state a better place.
- Many people from the Great Plains came to California in the 1930s to escape the Dust Bowl.

THINK ABOUT IT

1. How were Mexican farmworkers treated unfairly?

2. Name one New Deal project.

3. **FOCUS** How did immigrants from Mexico build communities in California?

4. **THINKING SKILL** *Compare and contrast* the experiences of the Mexican immigrants and the "Okies."

5. **GEOGRAPHY** Look up the *Dust Bowl* in an encyclopedia. List the states that made up the Dust Bowl.

MURALS

Diego Rivera, "The Making of a Fresco Showing the Building of a City," San Francisco Art Institute

Murals are one of California's most colorful legacies. A mural is a picture or design that decorates a wall.

Artists have been painting murals for centuries. In the early 1900s artists in Mexico City began painting huge murals showing scenes from Mexican history and legends.

One of the most famous Mexican muralists of this time was Diego Rivera. Rivera came to California in the 1930s. The murals he painted here have inspired many California artists to paint murals also.

Today you will see murals in many cities around our state. You can find them in government buildings, like post offices and city halls. You can also find them on buildings in neighborhoods much like your own. Who knows? Maybe there is a mural right near where you live.

Diego Rivera painted *The Making of a Fresco Showing the Building of a City* (above) in San Francisco in 1931. It inspired California artists to paint murals.

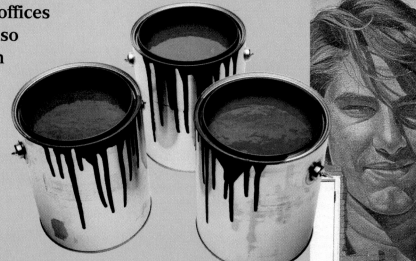

Many murals, like this one in San Francisco (below), show colorful scenes of everyday life. A mural decorates the city courthouse in Lompoc (bottom).

Brooke Fancher, "Tuzuri Watu: We Are a Beautiful People"

Richard Wyatt, Jr., asst. Richard Wyatt, Sr., "Tribute to the People of Lompoc"

CHAPTER 9 REVIEW

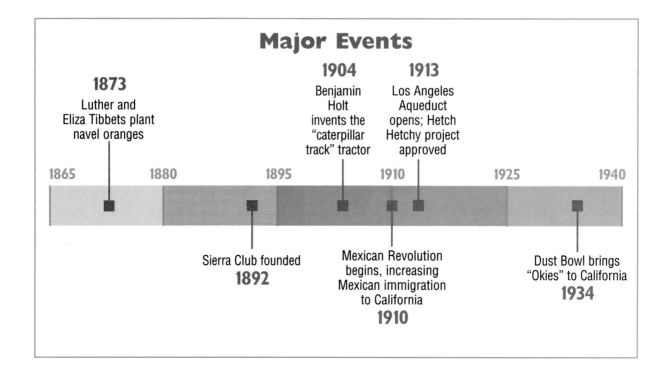

Major Events

1873
Luther and Eliza Tibbets plant navel oranges

1904
Benjamin Holt invents the "caterpillar track" tractor

1913
Los Angeles Aqueduct opens; Hetch Hetchy project approved

1865   1880   1895   1910   1925   1940

Sierra Club founded
1892

Mexican Revolution begins, increasing Mexican immigration to California
1910

Dust Bowl brings "Okies" to California
1934

THINKING ABOUT VOCABULARY

Number a sheet of paper from 1 to 10. Beside each number write **C** if the underlined term is used correctly. If it is not, write the term that would correctly complete the sentence.

1. A <u>canal</u> is a natural or human-built lake used to store water.

2. A *mutualista* is a place where goods are bought and sold.

3. The <u>Great Depression</u> created programs that put people to work.

4. Keeping food cool to preserve it is called <u>refrigeration</u>.

5. A period with very little rain is a <u>drought</u>.

6. A <u>dam</u> is a waterway built by people.

7. Workers who move from place to place to harvest crops are known as <u>barrios</u>.

8. Workers on <u>strike</u> stop working until business owners meet their demands.

9. A pathway or pipe built for bringing water from faraway sources is an <u>aqueduct</u>.

10. When a government wants to force people to leave, it will <u>deport</u> them.

THINKING ABOUT FACTS

1. Why was it important to find ways to bring water to different parts of California?

2. Name two inventions that helped California farmers. Explain how they were helpful.

3. Why did orange growing become an important business in California?

4. How did barrios help Mexicans feel like they were at home?

5. What led the "Okies" to migrate to California?

THINK AND WRITE ◄ ▤ ▶

WRITING ABOUT PERSPECTIVES
Write about the ways in which building dams in California is good and bad. Do dams do more good than harm? Explain why or why not.

WRITING AN EXPLANATION
Write a paragraph explaining how science and technology helped agriculture in California.

WRITING A COMPARISON
Compare the experiences of Mexican immigrants and the "Okies" in California in the early 1900s.

APPLYING STUDY SKILLS

USING REFERENCE SOURCES

1. What are reference sources?
2. What reference source would you use to find the exact meaning of the word *turbine*?
3. Which type of source could you use to find information about the Mexican War—and perhaps hear sounds and music?
4. What book reference would you use to find out when the Great Depression started and ended?
5. How might reference sources be helpful when you are studying history?

Summing Up the Chapter

Use the following cause-and-effect chart to organize information from the chapter. Fill in the blank spaces. When you have completed the chart, use it to write a paragraph titled "How did the growth and success of agriculture affect California?"

CAUSE	EFFECT
Refrigeration is developed.	Vegetables and fruits can be sold to distant places.
	Agriculture is successful in California.
Irrigation systems are developed.	
Drought creates Dust Bowl.	

CHAPTER 10

Building California

THINKING ABOUT PEOPLE AND HISTORY

Great changes happened in California after 1900. Many new immigrants came to our state, bringing new ideas and skills. The opening of the Panama Canal in 1914 spurred further growth in business and immigration. In the 1920s new industries started. World War II brought a terrible time to some Californians but changed our state's economy forever. Read on to find out more about these events and how they changed California.

1911
SOLVANG

Danish immigrants found a town

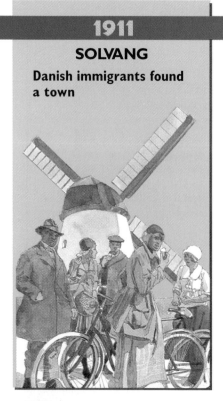

1913
HOLLYWOOD

Cecil B. DeMille directs the first full-length film

1942
OWENS VALLEY

Jeanne Wakatsuki Houston is sent to the Manzanar internment camp

UNITED
STATES

Sacramento ■

CALIFORNIA

■ Owens Valley

■ Delano

Solvang ▢

▢ Hollywood

PACIFIC
OCEAN

MEXICO

1963
SACRAMENTO
William Byron Rumford calls for fair housing

1965
DELANO
Grape pickers, led by Chavez and Huerta, go on strike

1900 **1906** **1927** 1940 1960 1980

California State Parks/Tom Myers

Focus Activity

READ TO LEARN
How did immigrants contribute to California in the early twentieth century?

VOCABULARY
mutual aid society

PEOPLE
Abiko Kyutaro
Ernest Bloch
Pedro Flores

PLACES
Yamato Colony
Angel Island
Solvang

NEWCOMERS BUILD CALIFORNIA

READ ALOUD

A Russian immigrant named Serge Nicholas was excited to move to California. "I was looking forward to coming to America," he said. "I had an impression . . . that this is a country where, if it rains, gold pours out of the skies and fills your pockets. . . . I expected a band to meet us at the San Francisco pier."

THE BIG PICTURE

Immigrants have been coming to California throughout its history. You have read how the Gold Rush brought a wave of immigrants. People from Europe, Asia, and South America came to California then. In the early 1900s immigration increased. The opening of the Panama Canal in 1914 helped bring many immigrants to California. It made the trip here from Europe much shorter. In all, between 1900 and 1930, nearly 19 million immigrants came to the United States.

As you read in Chapter 9, Mexicans were the largest group of immigrants to our state in the early 1900s. But people from Britain, Germany, Italy, Canada, Ireland, Russia, Sweden, China, Japan, the Philippines, and other countries came in large numbers also. These immigrants brought new ideas and new ways of living to our state and to our country.

California State Parks/Tom Myers

AN IMMIGRANT'S STORY

Abiko Kyutaro (kyoo ta roh) ran away from home when he was just 14. In 1885 he came by steamship to San Francisco. When he arrived in the city, he had only $1 in his pocket. He worked in several different jobs. Soon he had enough money to open a cafe and a laundry. He also began publishing *Nichibei Shimbun*, which means "Japanese American Newspaper."

Kyutaro encouraged other Japanese Americans to put down roots in California. In 1906 he founded an agricultural community in the San Joaquin Valley. He named it the Yamato Colony. *Yamato* is an old name for Japan. He said:

> *We believe that the Japanese must settle permanently with their countrymen on large pieces of land if they are to succeed in America.*

Challenges to Immigrants

Some immigrants to California faced discrimination. Farmers in our state became jealous of the success of the Yamato Colony. In 1913 these farmers got the state government to make a law that stopped Japanese immigrants from owning land in California. This was called the Alien Land Law.

Chinese people faced discrimination as well. In the 1920s and 1930s, many of them who wanted to immigrate to California had to wait at a place called Angel Island in San Francisco Bay. Here they stayed until immigration officials decided whether they should be allowed into the country. There was nothing to do on the island. One woman, Mrs. Chan, remembers, "People cried when they saw others [leaving]. . . . I must have cried a bowlful during my stay at Angel Island."

California Historical Society, San Francisco. FN-18240

In the early 1900s Chinese immigrants, such as these (right), passed through Angel Island (below).

273

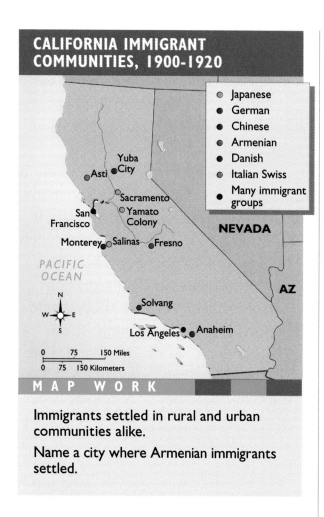

- Japanese
- German
- Chinese
- Armenian
- Danish
- Italian Swiss
- Many immigrant groups

Yuba City
Asti
Sacramento
San Francisco
Yamato Colony
NEVADA
Monterey Salinas Fresno
PACIFIC OCEAN
AZ
N W E S
Solvang
Los Angeles Anaheim

0 75 150 Miles
0 75 150 Kilometers

MAP WORK

Immigrants settled in rural and urban communities alike.

Name a city where Armenian immigrants settled.

FORMING COMMUNITIES

Immigrants from the same country formed dozens of communities throughout the state. The map above shows some of the places where immigrants settled.

Swedish immigrants, for example, founded a community near Turlock in Stanislaus County in 1901. They became successful farmers, raising melons and other crops. The town of Solvang in Santa Barbara County was founded in 1911 by immigrants from Denmark. They built Solvang to look very much like a Danish village. If you were to visit Solvang during the summer, you might see a festival where the residents celebrate the culture of their Danish ancestors. Storytellers, gymnasts, dancers, and musicians put on Danish costumes for the festival.

Between 1900 and 1920, 388,289 people immigrated to California. The immigrant communities helped the newcomers to feel at home in California and get used to life here.

Rural and Urban

Some of the newcomers settled in the rural areas of the state. Many came because they had seen ads for jobs. A 1913 ad from a farmer in Yuba County attracted harvesters from 27 different countries. They included workers born in Germany, Italy, Greece, Syria, and Cuba. Look at the World Map on pages R10–R11 to find these countries.

Rural California was now home to a great many cultures. During the early 1900s, the chicken farms around Petaluma attracted immigrants from Ukraine, Germany, Ireland, Denmark, and Japan. Immigrants from India settled around Yuba City and began growing cling peaches. The parents of Jasswinder Bains, whom you read about in Chapter 1, were among them. Chinese Americans lived in fishing villages around Monterey Bay and in small farming towns in the Sacramento-San Joaquin Delta.

Other immigrants settled in urban areas. Most immigrants in the cities were only offered low-paying jobs. Many Filipinos in Los Angeles, for

Many immigrants formed organizations to strengthen their communities. These mutual aid societies were similar to the *mutualistas* you read about in Chapter 9. They helped immigrants settle in California, find jobs, and get used to life here. The Korean American *Chin'mok-hoe* (Friendship Society) in San Francisco offered support and friendship for its members. Members of *huiguan* (hway GWUN), a Chinese American mutual aid society, met Chinese immigrants as they came off ships. They gave them food and a place to stay. They also lent them money.

Immigrants worked at many different jobs, such as fisherman (above) and clothing maker in factories (right).

instance, worked as servants in homes. Others became busboys in restaurants, carrying huge trays of dishes from the tables to the kitchens. Women from Russia and Poland ran sewing machines in the clothing factories of Los Angeles. They received very little pay for long hours of work.

275

CONTRIBUTING TO CALIFORNIA

Immigrants brought ideas, foods, skills, and customs that were new. All of these—and much more—contributed to the diversity of our state. You can see some of their contributions in the chart below.

Europeans played a leading role in building California's movie companies. One of the leading movie studios in Hollywood is Metro-Goldwyn-Mayer (MGM). It was created by two Jewish immigrants: Samuel Goldwyn, from Poland, and Louis B. Mayer, from Russia.

Successful Immigrants

Some immigrants found California disappointing. Many of them faced discrimination and, despite their hard work, remained poor. Others, however, achieved great things. For example, Gaetano Merola came to California from Italy in 1921. Two years later he started the San Francisco Opera, the second-oldest company in the United States.

Ernest Bloch was a musician from Switzerland. He arrived in the United States in 1916. Nine years later he became director of the San Francisco Conservatory of Music. He wrote many pieces of music, such as *Sacred Service*. These are still played and enjoyed today.

Do you ever think about where some of your toys come from? One of the most popular toys, the yo-yo, was brought to California by an

SOME CONTRIBUTIONS BY CALIFORNIA IMMIGRANTS

CONTRIBUTION	MADE OR INTRODUCED BY	COUNTRY OF ORIGIN	APPROXIMATE DATE
Cable Car	Andrew Hallidie	England	1871
Figs	George and John Seropian	Armenia	1884
Fortune Cookie	Makota Hagiwara	Japan	1894
Griffith Park	Griffith J. Griffith	Wales	1896
Yo-Yo	Pedro Flores	Philippines	1920

CHART WORK

Immigrants have contributed to California in many ways.

1. Who made a contribution to California's agriculture? What was it?
2. Who invented the cable car?

Flores yo-yos, such as this one (right), are the models for many of the ones kids use today.

immigrant. Pedro Flores came to California from the Philippines. He found a job clearing tables and helping waiters in a hotel in Santa Monica. In 1927 he began making and selling yo-yos. Filipino children grew up playing with this toy. Two years later, the Flores Yo-Yo Company was making yo-yos in Los Angeles. A salesman, Donald Duncan, discovered Flores and his toy. He bought the company from Flores and made yo-yos popular all over the United States.

WHY IT MATTERS

The immigrants who came to California early in this century contributed to our state's many different cultures. Much of our everyday life—from the clothes we wear to the foods we eat—has been shaped by the contributions of the immigrants who came at this time.

✔/ Reviewing Facts and Ideas

MAIN IDEAS

- Millions of immigrants entered the United States between 1900 and 1930.

  - Many immigrants formed communities with others from their home countries.

  - Immigrants contributed to life in California in many different ways.

THINK ABOUT IT

1. Why did many immigrants to California in the early 1900s decide to settle in rural areas?

2. How did the mutual aid societies assist newcomers?

3. **FOCUS** How did immigrants contribute to California in the early twentieth century?

4. **THINKING SKILL** Name one *cause* and one *effect* of the Alien Land Law that was passed by the state government of California in 1913.

5. **WRITE** Suppose you moved to another country. What ideas or customs of the United States would you want to contribute to that country's culture?

Jubilee
in Allensworth

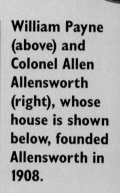

Not all of California's newcomers came from other countries. People came to California from the rest of the United States, too. One of these was Colonel Allen Allensworth, who came from Kentucky.

He and William Payne founded the town of Allensworth in the San Joaquin Valley in 1908. It was the first all–African American town in California.

William Payne (above) and Colonel Allen Allensworth (right), whose house is shown below, founded Allensworth in 1908.

Each spring, Californians celebrate Allensworth—the man and the town. People gather in Allensworth for an Old Time Jubilee. Many are descendants of Allensworth's first settlers. Sounds of jazz, blues, and gospel music fill the air. There is a picnic, and storytellers entertain young people with stories of Colonel Allensworth and his dream.

At the Allensworth Old Time Jubilee, visitors enjoy the storytelling (top). Many people celebrate Allensworth by dressing in the style of the town's early settlers (left and above).

279

THINKINGSKILLS

Identifying Stereotypes

VOCABULARY
stereotype

WHY THE SKILL MATTERS

In Lesson 1 you learned that some Californians became jealous of the success of Japanese American farmers. In Chapter 9 you read about the problems faced by Mexican immigrants and by "Okies." Earlier you learned about discrimination against Chinese immigrants.

In each of these instances, some people held stereotypes (STER ee uh tips) about a group of people. A stereotype is an idea that all the people in a group are the same in some way. Stereotypes often, but not always, express a dislike of that group.

Suppose someone says, "Fourth graders are noisy in class." You have been doing your work quietly! You would probably feel that this stereotype is unfair. It is also untrue.

Some members of a group may act or look the same way. But that does not mean that *all* the members do. This can make it difficult to recognize stereotypes. For example, maybe some fourth graders *are* noisy. But the statement suggests that *all* fourth graders are noisy, and this makes it a stereotype. Identifying stereotypes helps us to think of people as individuals, not just as members of groups. This also helps us to treat people fairly.

USING THE SKILL

You can sometimes recognize a stereotype by words such as *always*, *every*, or *all*. Another way to spot a stereotype is to think of an example that does not fit the statement. Look at the following sentences.

- *All elderly people do not work.*
You can recognize this stereotype because of the word *all*. Do you know an elderly person who works?
- *American kids love peanut butter.*
This statement suggests that all American kids love peanut butter. Some kids love it, but some do not.
- *Some girls like to play softball.*
This is not a stereotype because it is only about *some* girls. It does not say that all girls like to play softball. There are girls who do, but some like other sports. Some do not like any sport at all!

A senior citizen works at his computer.

HELPING Yourself

- A **stereotype** is an idea that all the people in a group are the same in some way.

- To identify a stereotype, look for words that suggest "always," "every," or "all."

- Look for examples that do not agree with what the stereotype is saying.

TRYING THE SKILL

Read the points in the Helping Yourself box, then identify the stereotypes in each of the following sentences. Remember that a stereotype does not have to say bad things. Some stereotypes say good things about people.

- *Some immigrants find it hard to learn English.*

- *Immigrants always take jobs away from other Americans.*

- *Japanese American farmers are all successful.*

- *Immigrants eat strange food.*

Which of these sentences present stereotypes? How can you tell? If a sentence does not contain one of the "clue words," does that mean it is not a stereotype?

REVIEWING THE SKILL

1. What is a stereotype?
2. Why are stereotypes unfair?
3. Do all stereotypes say bad things about people? Explain your answer.
4. Why is it important to identify stereotypes?

1900   1917   1941   1960   1980

CALIFORNIA BOOMS

READ ALOUD

In the 1920s moviegoers around the world began to take note of a small neighborhood in Los Angeles. At the end of the movie they were watching, four short words always seemed to appear. They were: "Made in Hollywood, U.S.A."

Focus Activity

READ TO LEARN
How did California boom during the early twentieth century?

VOCABULARY
industry
derrick

PEOPLE
Cecil B. DeMille
Edward L. Doheny
Joseph B. Strauss

PLACES
Hollywood
Los Angeles
Signal Hill
Bakersfield
Golden Gate

THE BIG PICTURE

From 1900 to 1930 California's economy boomed, or grew very rapidly. For some it seemed as if nothing could stop California's economy. Even disasters seemed, in a strange way, to help.

You read in Chapter 1 about the San Francisco earthquake of 1906. The city was ruined by this disaster. But the building industry boomed as the city was rebuilt. An industry is all the businesses that make one kind of product or provide one kind of service.

The economy of the state was also improved by America's entry into World War I in 1917. California farmers sent food to the men and women serving in the war in Europe. They also grew cotton to make uniforms for the soldiers. This meant jobs for growers and farmworkers. But two other industries grew in California in the early 1900s. They would change life in our state forever.

Stories about the West in the 1800s, known as *Westerns*, were a favorite topic of Hollywood movies.

HOLLYWOOD

Today **Hollywood** is the movie capital of the world. But the first American movie companies were started thousands of miles away in New York and New Jersey. Those companies controlled the rights to use film equipment such as cameras. So other filmmakers began looking for a place where they could avoid this control.

Southern California was about as far away as they could get! It was a good location in other ways, too. Movie cameras in those days did not work well indoors. They needed lots of strong sunlight. Southern California certainly had plenty of sun!

The movie business started in California in 1908. In 1913 **Cecil B. DeMille** made the first full-length movie in Hollywood. It was a success. Others followed DeMille's example. Soon the movie business was an important part of California's economy.

Charlie Chaplin (right) and Laurel and Hardy (above) were early Hollywood stars.

By 1923 more than 20,000 film actors and actresses were working in California. By the 1930s movies were one of California's biggest industries. They continue to be an important industry today. You will learn more about today's movie industry in Chapter 11.

GUSHING OIL

The movies, however, were not California's biggest industry. Another industry had been growing since 1892, when Edward L. Doheny (doh HEE nee) noticed a wagon on a Los Angeles street. The wagon held a dark and sticky soil. Doheny found out where the soil came from and began to dig a deep hole. And there he discovered oil.

Oil! A boom in Los Angeles happened almost overnight. Oil derricks sprang up all over the city to drill for this valuable resource. A derrick is a tower used to support drilling machines. Within five years, 2,300 wells were dug in the city. Some Los Angelenos even had derricks in their backyards.

During the 1920s, huge underground fields of oil were discovered. The largest was at Signal Hill in Long Beach.

Other oil fields were found around Bakersfield. The production of oil became the largest industry in California.

At first oil was used to make lamp fuel. Soon railroad trains and ships had engines that burned this cheap fuel instead of coal. Factories, too, used oil. From oil came the ideal fuel for automobiles —gasoline. Automobiles became more and

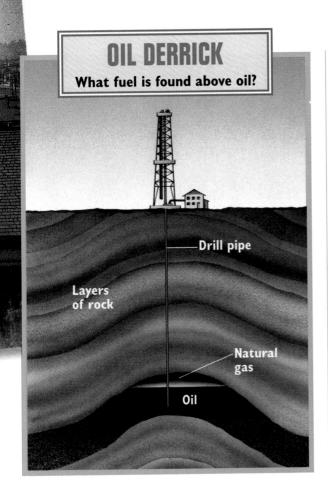

OIL DERRICK

What fuel is found above oil?

Drill pipe

Layers of rock

Natural gas

Oil

more popular around this time. By 1925 the city of Los Angeles had one automobile for every three people. The average for the whole country was only one car for every seven people.

Bridging the Gap

The increase in cars led to a demand for more and better roads. In San Francisco some people began to talk about building a road, or bridge, across the Golden Gate. The Golden Gate is the narrow body of water between Marin County and San Francisco where San Francisco Bay joins the Pacific Ocean.

Oil wells filled backyards in Culver City in the early 1900s (above). The Golden Gate Bridge (left) was built in the 1930s.

Many people thought such a bridge was impossible. But the engineer Joseph B. Strauss believed it could be done. He spent nine years convincing San Francisco voters to pay for the project. In 1930 they voted for it. It took seven more years to build the Golden Gate Bridge.

WHY IT MATTERS

Before 1900 California's economy was mainly agricultural. After oil became the state's biggest industry, more and more Californians owned cars. Hollywood made California seem exciting and glamorous. In the early 1900s California started to look like the place we know today.

✓ Reviewing Facts and Ideas

MAIN IDEAS

- Many film businesses moved to Hollywood in the 1910s.
- Oil was discovered in Los Angeles in 1892.
- Joseph B. Strauss planned the Golden Gate Bridge.

THINK ABOUT IT

1. Why did filmmakers move to California?

2. Name four uses for oil.

3. **FOCUS** What caused a boom in California during the early 1900s?

4. **THINKING SKILL** What *stereotype* might people have about Hollywood actors and actresses? Identify what makes it a stereotype.

5. **GEOGRAPHY** How did California's climate help filmmakers?

WAR AND PEACE IN CALIFORNIA

READ ALOUD

During World War II millions of women worked in factories to help defend our country. A popular song celebrated these women and gave them a nickname.

All the day long, whether rain or shine,
She's part of the assembly line,
She's making history working for victory,
Rosie . . . Rosie the riveter.

THE BIG PICTURE

World War II began in 1939, when German soldiers marched into Poland. Soon it was being fought all over the globe. Germany, Italy, and Japan formed the Axis. They fought against the Allies, led by Great Britain, France, China, and the Soviet Union.

The United States at first tried to stay out of the war. Our country helped by giving supplies to the Allies. But on December 7, 1941, Japanese planes bombed the United States Navy base at Pearl Harbor, Hawaii. They wanted to destroy America's ships in the Pacific Ocean. The attack came without warning. It killed 2,403 people. The next day the United States declared war on Japan. Germany and Italy, in turn, declared war on the United States. Our country was now in the most deadly war ever fought.

Focus Activity

READ TO LEARN
How did World War II affect California?

VOCABULARY
Axis
Allies
internment camp
manufacture
aerospace
Cold War
suburb
freeway

PEOPLE
Jeanne Wakatsuki Houston
Franklin D. Roosevelt
Henry J. Kaiser
Henry Doelger

PLACES
Pearl Harbor, Hawaii
Richmond
Daly City

INTERNMENT

The bombing of Pearl Harbor made people afraid that California might be attacked as well. Some Californians thought that Japanese Americans and Japanese immigrants might help Japan in the war.

Because of these fears, the government sent Japanese Americans to internment camps. An internment camp is a place where people are imprisoned during wartime. Many of these camps were in unsettled areas around the Rocky Mountains.

More than 110,000 people were sent to the camps. Most lost their homes and businesses when they were imprisoned. Yet there was no evidence that these people had helped Japan to harm our country.

One person remembers how terrible the camps were. Jeanne Wakatsuki Houston was born in Los Angeles. She was just seven years old when her family was sent to the Manzanar internment camp in Owens Valley. The camp was surrounded by barbed wire and armed guards. How did Houston feel about living there?

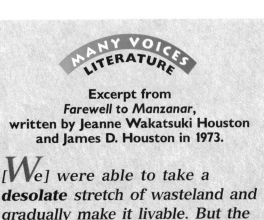

MANY VOICES LITERATURE

Excerpt from
Farewell to Manzanar,
written by Jeanne Wakatsuki Houston and James D. Houston in 1973.

[We] were able to take a desolate stretch of wasteland and gradually make it livable. But the entire situation there, especially in the beginning—the packed sleeping quarters, the communal mess halls, the open toilets—all this was an open insult.

desolate: empty, barren
communal: shared
mess halls: cafeterias

The 442nd Regiment

Many Japanese Americans joined the armed forces, even though their families remained in the camps. The 442nd Regiment, for example, was made up entirely of Japanese Americans. It received 18,143 medals, more than any other unit in the army.

Manzanar internment camp in 1942, photo by Dorothea Lange.

THE UNITED STATES AT WAR

The war was a terrible time for most people. Still it offered new opportunities for some.

Willie Stokes worked on a cotton farm in Mississippi. Early in World War II, he learned that companies on the West Coast were hiring workers to build ships. Stokes left Mississippi and came to Richmond, California. There he got a job in the shipyards as a welder. A welder joins pieces of metal together using heat.

Wartime Shipyards

President Franklin D. Roosevelt (ROH zuh velt) asked the shipbuilding industry to build ships faster than the enemy could sink them. Henry J. Kaiser (KĪ zur), a powerful businessman, accepted the challenge.

Kaiser advertised for workers throughout the country. Many who came were African Americans from the South. The African American population of California was less than 125,000 in 1940. By 1950 it had risen to more than 460,000.

By late 1942 there were five new shipyards in California. They were designed to build cargo ships, known as Liberty ships, as quickly as possible. Every part of a ship was numbered. Thousands of men and women worked around the clock. At night huge lights were turned on. "The speed was unbelievable," remembered Alyce Kramer. "Muscles were strained, hearts were busting with hope and pride." Look at the diagram on the next page to learn more about Liberty ships.

Large rivets (above) were used to build Liberty ships. Factory workers (right) build an airplane.

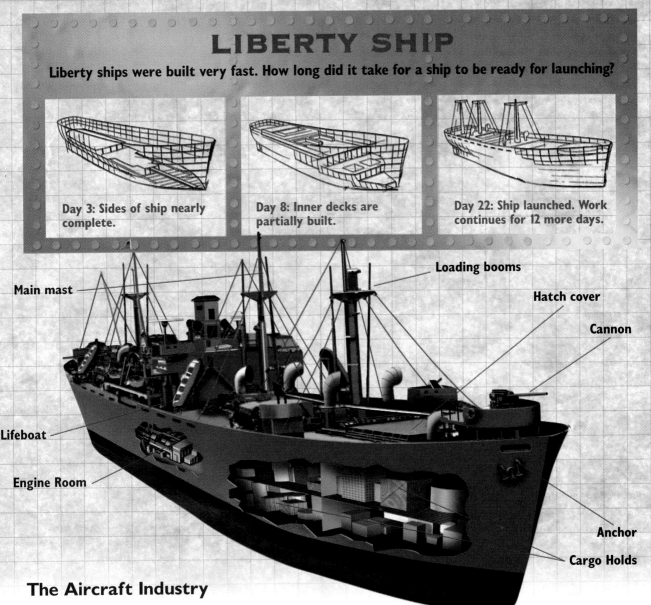

LIBERTY SHIP

Liberty ships were built very fast. How long did it take for a ship to be ready for launching?

Day 3: Sides of ship nearly complete.

Day 8: Inner decks are partially built.

Day 22: Ship launched. Work continues for 12 more days.

Main mast

Loading booms

Hatch cover

Cannon

Lifeboat

Engine Room

Anchor

Cargo Holds

The Aircraft Industry

In addition to ships, airplanes were needed for the war effort. Six large companies in Southern California built factories to manufacture planes. To manufacture is to make large amounts of goods in factories. The mild climate made this region ideal for testing and storing airplanes. By 1943 more than 280,000 Californians were working in the aircraft industry.

With so many men in the armed forces, women were able to get factory jobs they would not have been given before. Nearly half of the aircraft workers in California, for example, were women. Like "Rosie the riveter,"

from the song, they worked hard to help the Allies win the war.

After the war, many women were asked to give up their manufacturing jobs. Yet their experiences had long-lasting effects. Women had shown that they could do the same jobs as men. "I found out I could do a lot of things that I didn't know I could do," recalled aircraft worker Marie Baker.

Also after the war a new industry grew out of the aircraft industry. It was known as aerospace. Californians now began to build machines that traveled to the stars.

Infographic   Aerospace over California

California's aerospace industry began in 1904, when Glenn Martin built an airplane factory in Santa Ana. Since then, California's aerospace industry has grown. What contributions to aerospace transportation has California made?

APOLLO 11
In July 1969 astronauts from the United States became the first people to land on the moon. Most of their spaceship, *Apollo 11*, was built in Palmdale.

X-15
A rocket powers the X-15, making it the fastest airplane ever. During a flight in 1967, its speed was measured at over 4,500 miles an hour.

DOUGLAS DC-3
The Douglas DC-3 was the first successful passenger airplane. First flown in 1935, the DC-3 was built to last. There are still around 3,000 DC-3s flying today.

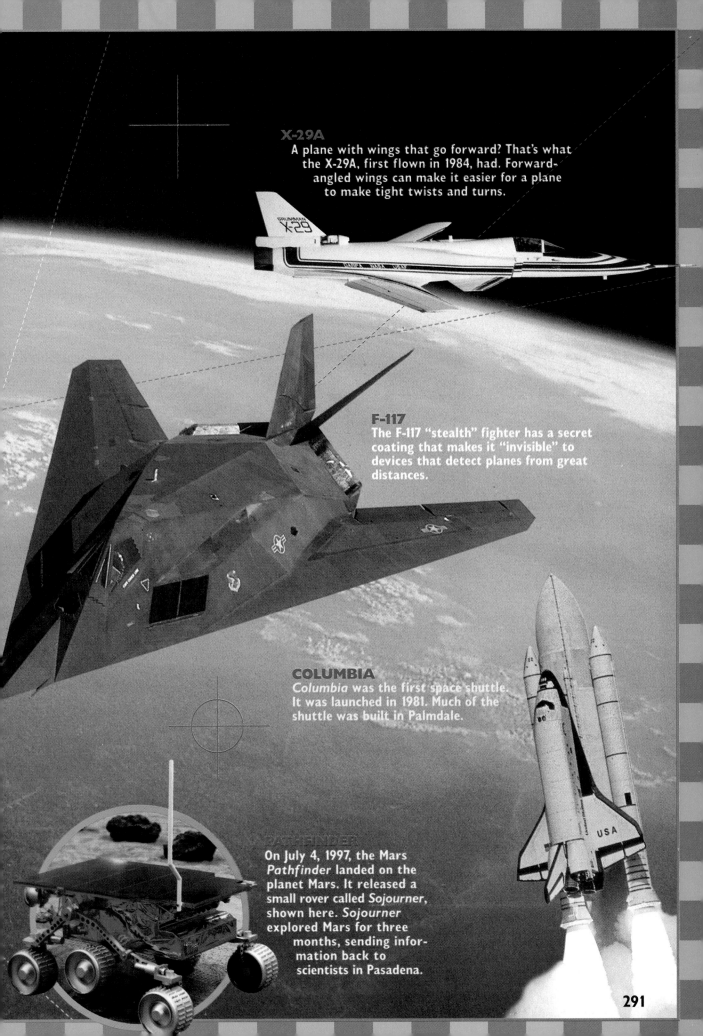

X-29A

A plane with wings that go forward? That's what the X-29A, first flown in 1984, had. Forward-angled wings can make it easier for a plane to make tight twists and turns.

F-117

The F-117 "stealth" fighter has a secret coating that makes it "invisible" to devices that detect planes from great distances.

COLUMBIA

Columbia was the first space shuttle. It was launched in 1981. Much of the shuttle was built in Palmdale.

PATHFINDER

On July 4, 1997, the Mars *Pathfinder* landed on the planet Mars. It released a small rover called *Sojourner*, shown here. *Sojourner* explored Mars for three months, sending information back to scientists in Pasadena.

291

AFTER THE WAR

World War II ended in August 1945. Our country entered a peaceful time. Many Americans wanted to enjoy the good life that they had fought to defend during the war.

A Time of Peace

For California, the end of the war seemed to start a time of almost unending economic growth. Millions of people moved here. Look at the graph below to see how our state's population grew.

Many of the newcomers found jobs building weapons for our country's defense. Why was the government spending so much on weapons? World War II was over. But the United States feared that another war could start with a different enemy—the Soviet Union. This country was made up of Russia and its neighbors, but it broke apart in 1991. This time of unfriendliness between the United States and the Soviet Union from 1945 to 1991, is known as the Cold War.

New Houses

In addition to jobs, the millions of new Californians needed places to live. The United States government tried to help. It lent the men and women who had served in the armed forces money to buy houses.

But new houses were needed— fast! Builders planned whole communities that could be built quickly and cheaply. They located these communities, known as suburbs, a short drive from large cities.

San Franciscan Henry Doelger (DAWL jur) built one such community, called Westlake, in Daly City in 1949. Some people, like the singer Malvina Reynolds, thought his houses looked like "little boxes." Yet Doelger was praised for giving buyers homes that they could afford.

Freeways

To connect the new suburbs and cities, freeways were built. A freeway is a fast road that has no toll. California was one of the first states in the country to start building freeways. But it was hard to keep pace with the need for more roadways. As more people bought cars to travel back and forth to work, the need for new roadways kept rising. At one point the state was spending $1 million a day on new roads!

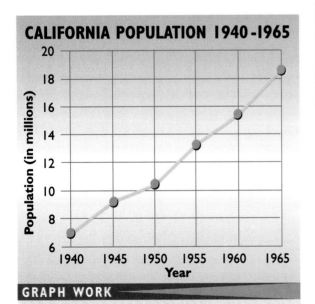

CALIFORNIA POPULATION 1940-1965

Population (in millions) vs *Year*

GRAPH WORK

Our state's population grew by over 11 million people from 1940 to 1965.

When did it pass 10 million people?

WHY IT MATTERS

The 1940s and 1950s brought great changes to our state. Our economy grew. Women and African Americans gained new job opportunities. Whole new industries and towns grew, as our state's population more than doubled. But for Japanese Americans, World War II brought discrimination. Many lost their homes, farms, and businesses.

✓ Reviewing Facts and Ideas

MAIN IDEAS

- After the bombing of Pearl Harbor, Japanese Americans in California were sent to internment camps.
- California's shipbuilding and aerospace industries boomed.
- After the war, suburbs and freeways were built to make room for new Californians.

THINK ABOUT IT

1. Why were Japanese Americans imprisoned in internment camps during World War II?

2. Why were freeways built in California?

3. **FOCUS** How did World War II affect life in California?

4. **THINKING SKILL** Identify one *cause* and one *effect* of the growth in California's population after the war.

5. **WRITE** Imagine you are the first woman to work at a shipyard. Describe your first day at work.

PROTEST IN CALIFORNIA

READ ALOUD

Cesar Chavez was proud of the farmworkers who were fighting for their rights. In 1966 he wrote: "If this spirit grows . . . one day we can . . . help correct a lot of things that are wrong in this society. But that is for the future. Before you can run, you have to learn to walk."

THE BIG PICTURE

The 1960s and 1970s were a time of many protests in California and the rest of the United States. Many people at this time shared Chavez's view that "a lot of things" were "wrong in this society." These people looked at our country's strong economy and were angry that not everyone was sharing in the good times. They thought citizens and government should try to make life better for everyone. Many other Americans disagreed, however. They felt that our country was offering its people enough.

Disagreements grew during the Vietnam War. This was a war between South Vietnam and North Vietnam. It lasted from 1954 to 1975. American armed forces fought on the side of South Vietnam. Americans argued over whether we should be fighting in this faraway war.

Focus Activity

READ TO LEARN
Why did many Californians protest in the 1960s and 1970s?

VOCABULARY
Vietnam War
demonstration
civil rights
segregate
Rumford Act
labor union
boycott
Proposition 13

PEOPLE
Martin Luther King, Jr.
William Byron Rumford
Marian Ashe
Cesar Chavez
Dolores Huerta

PLACES
Berkeley
Alcatraz Island
Delano

Year of the Antiwa
MARCH
WITH GIs
AGAINST THE
WAR APRIL 6
smc

PROTEST

In the early 1960s students at the University of California in Berkeley were angry. Some businesses in Berkeley would not hire African Americans. Students organized demonstrations to demand an end to this practice. A demonstration is a large gathering of people who want to make their feelings known. A number of students were arrested during the demonstrations.

In 1964 the university decided that students could not plan their demonstrations on school grounds. The protesters believed that planning a demonstration was part of their right to free speech. Free speech is the right to express your views. The United States Constitution protects this right.

Students protested the university's decision. They thought the university was trying to control what they believed. A student named Mario Savio gave a fiery speech against the university. He called it a "machine," and told the students, "You've got to make it stop." These demonstrations convinced the university to drop the rule.

Berkeley students also protested the Vietnam War. Sometimes their demonstrations became violent. Police often came to the school to keep order and protect property.

These protesters, demanding changes to the way our country was run, shocked many Americans. Their ideas were different from what people were used to thinking. People all over the country began to think of California as a place where new ideas could be tried out.

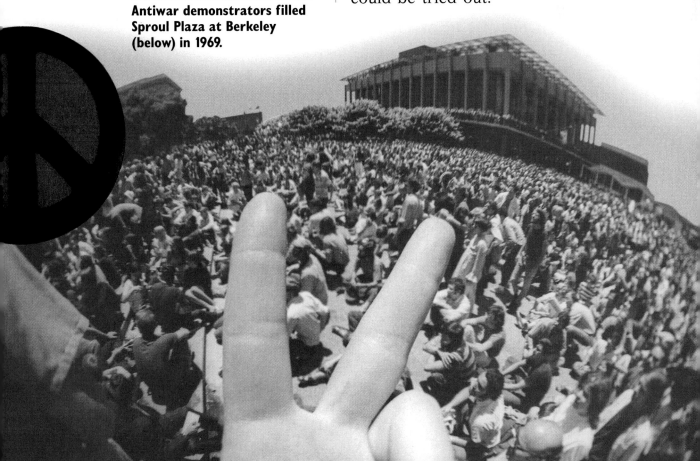

Antiwar demonstrators filled Sproul Plaza at Berkeley (below) in 1969.

RIGHTS FOR CALIFORNIANS

Along with free speech, protesters in the 1960s were very concerned about civil rights. Civil rights are the rights of all people to be treated equally under the law.

Martin Luther King, Jr., from Georgia, was a leader in the movement for civil rights. The protests he led inspired many Californians to fight discrimination.

In California many white landlords would not sell houses or rent apartments to African Americans, or Hispanics. They wanted to keep communities segregated, or separate. So did some homeowners. As a result, African Americans often had to live in run-down or dangerous neighborhoods.

William Byron Rumford, a representative in the state legislature, called for change. He helped make a law called the Rumford Act, which passed in 1963. It said that California property owners could not discriminate because of race.

Native Americans also faced discrimination and other problems. They suffered from poor schooling and healthcare. Many had no jobs. A group called Indians of All Nations wanted to call attention to these problems. So its members took over Alcatraz Island in San Francisco Bay from 1969 to 1971. The group said that Alcatraz belonged to Native Americans

African American Museum and Library at Oakland

Lawmaker William Rumford, from Berkeley, fought against segregated housing in California.

under a treaty. Their action made the country more aware of how Native Americans lived.

California women also worked to improve their lives. Marian Ashe served as the head of a government group concerned with women. She tried to get more places for child care. Working women with young children needed these places. She also argued for better education for women who were already working. That way they could get better-paying jobs.

FARMWORKERS ORGANIZE

Cesar Chavez was a farmworker since he was a child. He knew how farmworkers lived. When he grew up, he became a leader of the drive to improve life for farmworkers.

Chavez believed that farmworkers need a labor union. A labor union is a group of workers who organize to make agreements with their employer. In 1962 Chavez and Dolores Huerta, from Stockton, formed a union. It was called the National Farm Workers Association. They were joined by a Filipino man named Philip Vera Cruz. Chavez and Huerta traveled to farms throughout California urging farmworkers to join. It became part of the United Farm Workers, or UFW.

In 1965 Filipino American and Mexican American grape pickers in Delano went on strike. The Delano workers wanted higher wages and better working conditions. The Delano strike was a success.

Cesar Chavez (left) fought to improve the poor living conditions (right) of farmworkers.

Boycott

Other grape growers, however, still treated workers poorly. Three years later, the UFW called for a boycott of all California grapes. A boycott is a refusal to do business with a company. Many people all over the country supported the farmworkers. They boycotted California grapes.

Because of the boycott, 26 grape growers signed an agreement with the UFW in 1970. The agreement gave workers better pay and working conditions. Workers would get a one-week paid vacation.

Buy only UFWOC AFL-CIO lettuce

297

PROPOSITION 13

Ronald Reagan, a former actor, became governor of our state in 1967. Reagan did not approve of protests. He promised to clean up what he called the "mess at Berkeley." Reagan also promised to fight what he called "big government" and "high taxes." Reagan left office in 1975. In 1980 he was elected President of the United States.

Many Californians shared Reagan's beliefs. They also felt that government was too big and taxes too high. They thought the government was spending too much money trying to fix California's problems.

In June 1978, voters passed Proposition 13. This initiative cut taxes on property by more than half. Cities, counties, and schools now had much less tax money to spend.

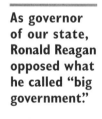

As governor of our state, Ronald Reagan opposed what he called "big government."

WHY IT MATTERS

Californians were leaders in the fight for social change in the 1960s and 1970s. This legacy of citizen action remains with us as we prepare to meet the challenges of the twenty-first century.

✔ Reviewing Facts and Ideas

MAIN IDEAS

- University students in the 1960s fought for the right of free speech.
- The Rumford Act made racial discrimination in housing illegal.
- Farmworkers formed the UFW to win better pay and conditions.
- Voters passed Proposition 13, which lowered taxes on property.

THINK ABOUT IT

1. Name three things Berkeley students protested in the 1960s.

2. Name one effect of the grape boycott.

3. **FOCUS** Why did many people protest in the 1960s and 1970s?

4. **THINKING SKILL** Make a _conclusion_ about California in the 1960s.

5. **WRITE** Suppose you are a homeowner in California in 1978. Write a letter to a newspaper making a case for or against Proposition 13.

CITIZENSHIP
MAKING A DIFFERENCE

A Really Good Problem

DIAMOND BAR—
Fifth graders Jennifer Duncan and Kyle Smith have a problem, but they don't mind. Jennifer and Kyle are conflict managers at Quail Summit Elementary School. Their job is to help other students settle arguments peacefully. "Most fights start because of name calling, teasing, cutting in line, or disagreeing over the rules of a game," says Jennifer.

About nine years ago, teacher Patricia Anderson started the school's Conflict Resolution Program. "Before we had this program, I noticed at recess that lots of students just didn't know how to solve problems, so they screamed or got in fights."

The conflict managers, who are fourth and fifth graders, receive one day of training. "We learned," says Jennifer, "that different people have different ways of expressing themselves when they are upset." If a conflict manager sees students disagreeing or pushing in line, they ask the students if they want help resolving their conflict.

If the students agree, they go to a quiet place. Everyone follows certain rules. The students must tell the truth, work hard to solve the conflict, and may not interrupt one another. "The toughest part of this job," explains Kyle, "is when kids are mad, they keep blaming each other. Sometimes it's hard to get them to stop and listen." Solving the conflict usually takes the whole recess. Mrs. Anderson explains, "It's better not to have a conflict because then you have to spend the whole recess solving it."

Conflict managers also give out small "Caught Being Good" cards when they see someone doing something good, such as taking turns, cooperating in playing games, or including other children in their play. Kyle likes his job. He says the program "keeps the school feeling safe."

" . . . get them to stop and listen."

Jennifer Duncan
Kyle Smith

CHAPTER 10 REVIEW

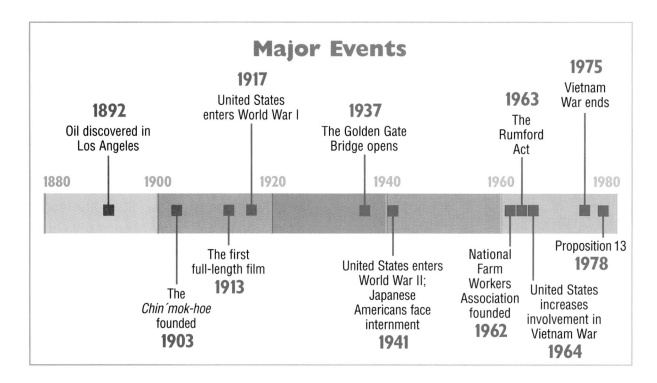

Major Events

1892 Oil discovered in Los Angeles

1917 United States enters World War I

1937 The Golden Gate Bridge opens

1963 The Rumford Act

1975 Vietnam War ends

1880   1900   1920   1940   1960   1980

The first full-length film **1913**

The *Chin´mok-hoe* founded **1903**

United States enters World War II; Japanese Americans face internment **1941**

National Farm Workers Association founded **1962**

United States increases involvement in Vietnam War **1964**

Proposition 13 **1978**

THINKING ABOUT VOCABULARY

Number a sheet of paper from 1 to 10. Next to each number write the word or phrase that best fits the definition.

boycott   manufacture
civil rights   mutual aid society
derrick   segregated
industry   stereotype
internment camps suburbs

1. A refusal to do business with a company

2. A tower used to support drilling machines

3. Communities that are near large cities

4. A group in which the members help one another

5. To make large amounts of goods in factories

6. An idea that all people in a group are the same in some way

7. Places where people are imprisoned during wartime

8. The rights of all people to be treated equally under the law

9. All of the businesses that make one kind of product or provide one kind of service

10. Separate

THINKING ABOUT FACTS

1. How were immigrant communities helpful to newcomers?

2. What became the largest industry in California in the 1920s?

3. Why did so many women work during the war?

4. What was the Rumford Act about? Why was it important?

5. Name three problems or issues people demonstrated about during the period 1900–1965.

THINK AND WRITE

WRITING AN ADVERTISEMENT
Suppose you want new immigrants to join your mutual aid society. Design and write an advertisement that will encourage people to join.

WRITING ABOUT PERSPECTIVES
Describe the fears and concerns that led the government to imprison Japanese Americans in internment camps during World War II. Do you think these were realistic fears? Why or why not?

WRITING A JOURNAL
Suppose you are a woman working to manufacture airplanes. Describe what it is like to work in the factories.

APPLYING THINKING SKILLS

IDENTIFYING STEREOTYPES
1. What is a stereotype?
2. What words can help you recognize a stereotype?
3. Decide if the following is a stereotype: All women hate football.
4. Decide if this statement is a stereotype: Some blue-eyed people need glasses.
5. Why is identifying stereotypes important?

Summing Up the Chapter

Use the horizontal organization chart below to organize information from the chapter. Under each main topic write at least two more words or phrases from the chapter that are related to that topic. When you have completed the chart, use it to answer the question "How did California change from the early 1900s to the 1970s?"

NEWCOMERS BUILD CALIFORNIA	BOOMING INDUSTRIES	WAR AND PEACE IN CALIFORNIA	PROTEST IN CALIFORNIA
immigrants	movies	Pearl Harbor	Vietnam War

UNIT 4 REVIEW

THINKING ABOUT VOCABULARY

Number a sheet of paper from 1 to 10. Next to each number write the word or term from the list that best completes the sentence.

Cold War   immigrant
communication   investors
democratic republic   reformers
drought   reservoir
Great Depression   strike

1. _____ put money into a business in the hopes that they will make money if the business is successful.

2. The _____ was a time of conflict between the United States and the Soviet Union.

3. A _____ is one in which citizens elect representatives to make decisions for them.

4. _____ is the exchange of information between people.

5. An _____ is a person who leaves one country to come and live in another.

6. _____ wanted to improve the way government was run.

7. When workers _____, they refuse to work until employers meet their demands.

8. The _____ was a period when many businesses failed and people lost their jobs, homes, and farms.

9. A long period with little rain is a _____.

10. A natural or human-built lake used to store water is a _____.

THINK AND WRITE

WRITING A REPORT
Do some research in the library and write a report on the New Deal.

WRITING AN INTERVIEW
Suppose you were able to interview Jeanne Wakatsuki Houston. Write three questions you would ask and her possible responses.

WRITING A SUMMARY
Summarize the changes in communication and transportation that took place between the late 1850s and 1870.

BUILDING SKILLS

1. **Elevation maps** How can you tell that a map shows elevation?

2. **Reference sources** How are reference books different from other books?

3. **Reference sources** What resources could you use if you were doing a report on dams?

4. **Identifying stereotypes** What is a stereotype?

5. **Identifying stereotypes** How do stereotypes lead to discrimination?

YESTERDAY, TODAY &
TOMORROW

You have read about some of the changes that took place in California. Many of these changes were related to technology. What kinds of new technology do you predict will become important in your life?

READING ON YOUR OWN

Here are some books you might find at the library to help you learn more.

DRAGON'S GATE
by Laurence Yep
A young Chinese immigrant's story of working to build the transcontinental railroad.

DAMS
by Andrew Dunn
Everything you always wanted to know about dams.

BASEBALL SAVED US
by Ken Mochizuki
A Japanese American boy describes life in a World War II internment camp.

UNIT REVIEW PROJECT

Design a California Economy Map

1. Think about how the economy of California was different before 1900 and after 1900.
2. On two pieces of paper, trace an outline of California.
3. Using different-colored markers or paints, label one map "California's Economy Before 1900" and the other map "California's Economy After 1900."
4. Draw and cut out pictures showing industries represented by the products they manufactured and created. You might include oranges and plums to represent agriculture, planes to represent aerospace, and so on. You can also include technologies that helped the economy.
5. Glue each picture onto the page with the correct map.
6. Share your maps with the class.

California's Economy Before 1900.

Gold   Locomotive

Plums   Oranges

California's Economy After 1900.

Oranges   Oil

Plums   Airplane

GETTY MUSEUM (BELOW)
GRADUATION DAY AT
STANFORD UNIVERSITY

THE GREAT SEAL OF THE STATE OF CALIFORNIA

EUREKA

CALIFORNIA
INSTITUTE OF
TECHNOLOGY
RADIO TELESCOPE

California in the Twenty-First Century

" . . . we have fulfilled our dream."

Ginger Tang
See page 344.

WHY DOES IT MATTER?

Today California has much to celebrate. From movies to computers to garlic bulbs, Californians produce a wide variety of goods enjoyed by people all over the world. We are also lucky to live in a state where a blend of different cultures helps us to better understand the world we live in. In Unit 5 you will read all about California's government and economy and what makes them special. What problems do you think people in California might have in the next century? It is never too early to think about your place in California's future!

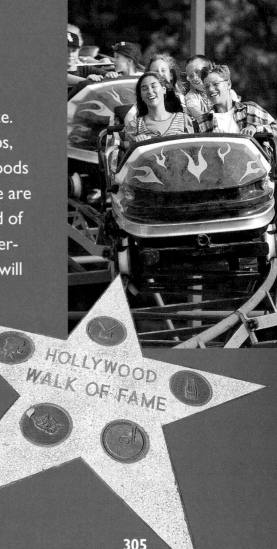

ROLLER COASTER (ABOVE)
STAR ON HOLLYWOOD
SIDEWALK

Adventures with
NATIONAL GEOGRAPHIC

SEMICONDUCTOR DR

Looking to the Future

When it comes to the latest technologies, our state is state of the art. With streets such as Semiconductor Drive, Silicon Valley—in the San Jose area—is the nation's leading computer-manufacturing region. At San Francisco's Exploratorium, schoolchildren explore three-dimensional computer worlds. Wearing a wired glove and goggles, a girl in Novato explores a world existing only in computers. And everyone benefits from the use of computers in medical research, a booming enterprise in San Diego. In California—the future is now.

GEO JOURNAL

What is your favorite cyberexperience, real or imagined?

CHAPTER
11

California and the World

THINKING ABOUT PEOPLE AND CULTURE

California provides many important goods and services to the economy of the United States, and it is a top vacation spot as well. We are lucky to have rich farmland, many bustling cities, and top attractions, such as Disneyland and Yosemite National Park. Read on to find out about California's economy.

CANADA

UNITED STATES

Oakland
Fremont

CALIFORNIA

Palmdale

San Onofre State Beach

PACIFIC OCEAN

MEXICO

Large cranes like these load and unload much of the trade goods flowing through California ports such as Oakland.

■ **Surfboards**
SAN ONOFRE
STATE BEACH

Surf's up! California's beaches, like the one at San Onofre, are just one of the many things that attract visitors to our state.

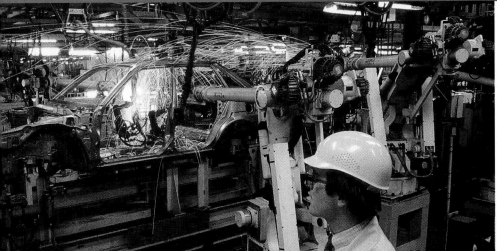

■ **Automobile Factory**
FREMONT

This automobile factory is co-owned by a Japanese auto company and a United States auto company.

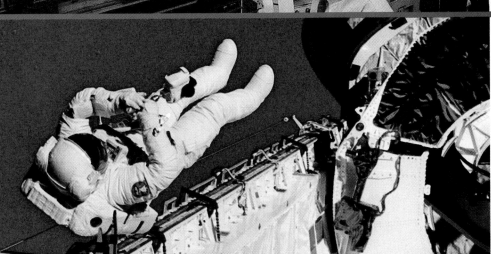

■ **Space Shuttle**
IN EARTH ORBIT

Many of our country's space ships have been built in Palmdale and other Southern California cities.

309

VACATION PARADISE

Focus Activity

READ TO LEARN
Why do people love to visit California?

VOCABULARY
economy
services
tourism
historic site

PEOPLE
James Vail
Julia Morgan
Walt Disney

PLACES
San Luis Obispo
Santa Barbara
Columbia
Anaheim

READ ALOUD

"To all who come to this happy place: Welcome." These words greet the millions of people who visit Disneyland every year. Disneyland is only one of the attractions that bring visitors to California. In 1995, 57 million people visited our state from other places. That is nearly twice the number of people who live here!

THE BIG PICTURE

People visit our state because it has so much to offer. Its many natural attractions are just the start of it. California also has exciting cities full of fun and interesting things to see and do.

The money that visitors spend while they are here helps our economy. As you read in Chapter 2, an economy is the way a place uses or produces natural resources, goods, and services. Services are jobs in which people help others, rather than make things.

To help all these visitors, businesses hire workers known as service workers. Over 650,000 Californians have jobs helping visitors to our state.

Dear Shawn,
   California is so cool, and I do not mean the weather! It is always sunny here.
   After our plane landed, we rode a shuttle to our hotel. The next day we rented a car and drove to the beach. I went swimming in the ocean!
   Tomorrow we're going to tour a movie studio and see how they make movies. I can't wait!

     See you,
     Terry

California Poppy
USA 20¢

Shawn Miller
200 Village Dr.
Dayton, OH 45459

TOURISM AND THE ECONOMY

People who travel on vacations are called tourists. The many different kinds of businesses that sell goods and services to tourists make up the tourism industry. Read Terry's postcard to her cousin Shawn. What goods and services does she describe?

Money for California

Tourism is one of California's largest industries. In 1996 the tourism industry earned more than $58 billion. That money gets spent in every county in our state. In thinly populated Modoc County, tourists still spent over $27 million in 1996.

Tourism provides jobs for service workers, like this hotel employee.

In Los Angeles County tourists spent over $12 billion!

As you read, the tourism industry is also a large employer. The airline pilots, flight attendants, shuttle drivers, hotel workers, rental car clerks, ticket sellers, and movie studio tour guides who helped Terry and her family enjoy their vacation are all employed in the tourism industry.

Dockweiler State Beach

A WEALTH OF ATTRACTIONS

What do the 57 million tourists who visit our state each year come to see and do? California has a wealth of attractions. Just about anything a visitor could want can be found within our borders.

Many tourists are attracted by our state's natural beauty. For example, over 4 million people visit Yosemite National Park each year. Other tourists come to sample the excitement of our fast-paced cities. There they can spend a day at a museum or an amusement park. They can also learn about our history or visit world famous sites like the Golden Gate Bridge. Look at the map on the right to see just some of California's many tourist attractions.

Redwood National Park is home to mighty redwood trees.

The Gold Rush remains alive at Columbia State Historical Park.

CALIFORNIA TOURIST SITES

Redwood National Park

Humbolt Redwoods State Park

Lassen Volcanic National Park

Lake Tahoe

Point Reyes National Park

San Francisco

Columbia State Historic Park

Yosemite National Park

Monterey Bay Aquarium

King's Canyon National Park

Sequoia National Park

Hearst Castle State Historic Park

Mission Santa Barbara

Six Flags Magic Mountain

Universal Studios

Disneyland

Sea World

Hotel del Coronado

San Diego's Hotel del Coronado in an old photograph and today (inset).

TAKING IN THE SIGHTS

How did tourism become such a big part of California's economy? Back in the 1880s the railroad companies began advertising California's scenery and climate all over the country. They wanted people to ride on their trains, and trains were the best way to get here in those days. Once in California, the wealthy tourists relaxed at fancy hotels built by the railroads, such as the Hotel del Coronado in San Diego.

In the 1920s the automobile helped to make it cheaper to visit California. More people could afford a California vacation. In 1925 James Vail opened a new kind of hotel in San Luis Obispo. It was designed for these automobile travelers. Combining the words *motor* and *hotel,* he called it a motel. It was the first motel in the country.

Visitors love a ride on a cable car.

Shamu, Sea World's biggest star.

Our state's colorful past has also attracted visitors. It is preserved at historic sites. Historic sites are buildings, battlefields, or other places where events from our past took place. Perhaps the most popular historic sites in our state are the 21 Spanish missions. Many of them were rebuilt in the 1920s and 1930s. Mission Santa Barbara is the most visited mission. It is called the Queen of the Missions.

Gold Rush historic sites have also proved popular with tourists. In 1945 the entire town of Columbia became a state historic park. A visit there is like stepping back in time. You can even pan for gold!

Historic homes are also popular with visitors. None is more popular than the home of newspaper owner William Randolph Hearst. Architect Julia Morgan designed a "castle" to house Hearst's huge art collection. Visitors today marvel at the beauty of Morgan's creation.

Walt Disney created a new kind of tourist attraction. In 1955 he opened Disneyland in Anaheim. Disneyland combines amusement park rides and movie magic. It is the most popular tourist site in California. Today Disney's company is building a new amusement park, "Disney's California Adventure." Its theme is the ideas people have had about California itself.

Infographic

California's Economy

Suppose California were a country of its own. Its economy would be the seventh largest of all the countries in the world! What goods and services make California's economy strong?

We're Number One

California is the top agricultural state in the nation. Our state's farmers are the top growers of 75 different crops, including garlic.

Out of This World

Manufacturing is the third largest part of California's economy. Satellites are one of the things that California companies make. Satellites orbit, or go around, Earth. One company in El Segundo has made about half the satellites in the world!

At Your Service

Services make up the largest part of California's economy. Tourism, healthcare, and business services are three important service industries.

Construction
584,800

Mining
29,600

Farming
470,900

Services
4,859,900

Manufacturing
1,928,700

Transportation and Utilities
641,600

Trade
3,028,700

Government
2,040,500

Source: California Department of Trade & Commerce

CALIFORNIA EMPLOYMENT, 1997

Computer Kings

California is a leader in computers. An area known as Silicon Valley has more computer manufacturers than any other area its size.

Here to Help

About two million Californians work for the government. They include police officers, firefighters, teachers, soldiers, hospital workers, and lawmakers. Some take care of the roads, which is one government service we couldn't get around without.

Cash Stash

The second biggest part of the California economy has a lot to do with money. This industry includes banking, insurance, and real estate. San Francisco is our state's largest center for these businesses.

WHY IT MATTERS

People from all over the country and the world like to visit California. These visitors make tourism one of the largest parts of the California economy. California has a huge economy—but it is a huge state. California's many goods and services provide the jobs and good wages that help our state stay healthy.

✓ Reviewing Facts and Ideas

MAIN IDEAS

- The economy is the way a place uses or produces natural resources, goods, and services.
- Tourism is one of California's major industries.
- Some of California's popular tourist attractions are amusement parks and historic sites.

THINK ABOUT IT

1. What is the economy?

2. Why is tourism important for California?

3. **FOCUS** What kinds of places do tourists like to visit in California?

4. **THINKING SKILL** What _conclusion_ can you make about California's economy? What facts support your conclusion?

5. **WRITE** Write a paragraph about one fun place in California that you have been to and that visitors might enjoy.

Surfing, U.S.A.

"Surf's up, dude!" When many people think of California, they picture bright sun, big waves, and surfers. Surfing is a popular sport for tourists and a way of life for some Californians.

Surfing was born long ago on an unknown island in the Pacific Ocean. In 1912 a Hawaiian surfer, Duke Kahanamoku, taught a few Californians to ride the waves on long, heavy redwood boards.

After World War II, lighter boards made of new materials made surfing easier. Surfers liked the waves at Huntington Beach and Malibu. In the cold waters of Northern California, they wore wet suits to stay warm.

Today surfers battle pollution in the waters. Members of the Surfrider Foundation hold beach cleanup days. The way to keep this legacy alive is to hit the beach!

Hawaiians have been surfing for a long time (left). Modern surfers use wet suits and short boards (below).

Duke Kahanamoku, riding the waves above, was a champion swimmer as well as a surfer. He won two Olympic gold medals for swimming. Surfers today like to "shoot the curl" (left).

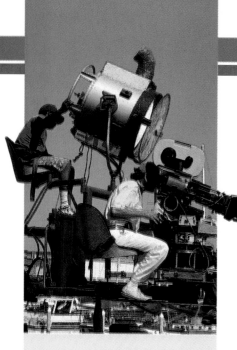

CALIFORNIA COMMUNICATES

Focus Activity

READ TO LEARN
Why are movies one of California's most important industries?

VOCABULARY
filmmaker

PEOPLE
Penelope Spheeris
George Lucas

PLACES
Hollywood
Los Angeles

READ ALOUD

"I like going to the movies because it's fun," explains 13-year-old Michelle Bowman. Her favorites? *"Scary movies, funny movies, and adventures."* She enjoyed taking her two-year-old brother to see his first movie. *"He didn't really understand the funny parts,"* she grins, *"but he laughed when we laughed."*

THE BIG PICTURE

You read in Chapter 8 that communications is the exchange of information between people. Movies are a form of communications. So are television programs. California is a leader in both these forms of communications. In the studios in Hollywood, Californians produce the movies and television programs that entertain millions of people like Michelle Bowman every day. Like tourism, the movie and television industries are a big part of California's economy. The film industry makes about $22 billion a year and employs about 650,000 people.

A FILM DIRECTOR

Sometimes when you are enjoying a movie in a theater or on television, it seems to go by very quickly. You may wish that it were longer! Making a movie, however, takes a long time—and a great deal of work.

Penelope Spheeris (SFIHR us) is a film director. As a director, she is responsible for directing the actors and crew on the movie set. However, her job involves much more.

"At the beginning," she says, "I make sure that the script can be filmed. I help to choose the actors who will appear in the movie. I also work on the budget. A year may pass from the time we get the script to the time the movie is completed."

On the Set

Finally, Spheeris begins to "shoot" the movie. Shooting often takes six to seven weeks.

"That's the fun part," she says. "Of course, it's hard work. I start rehearsing the actors at six in the morning. Three hours later the camera people start shooting. Then, at the end of the day, I go to watch the dailies—

A movie camera (below) records images on film. Penelope Spheeris (above) is with one of her actors.

the film we shot the day before. I may be working for 18 hours straight."

Why does Spheeris make movies? "I think film is a great way to tell the truth—at least the truth as I see it," she says.

Spheeris also says that moviemaking is a team effort. "Part of the reason I do this is because I enjoy working with other people. There are actors, camera operators, lighting crews, editors, writers, and so many others. They all deserve credit for what you see in the theater."

HOW A FILM IS MADE

STAGE 1
Before Filming

SCRIPT:
A writer uses a book, play, or original idea to write a script.

MONEY:
The film company decides how much money to spend.

LOCATION:
Scouts find places to film.

STAGE 2
Filming

CREW:
Crew members create sets, lighting, and costumes.

"ACTION!":
The director supervises filming of scenes.

STAGE 3
After Filming

EFFECTS:
Technicians make special effects.

EDITING:
Editors edit the film to make scenes fit together.

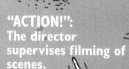

MUSIC:
The composer writes background music, and musicians record it.

STAGE 4
Distribution

THE ADS:
Writers prepare advertising, and publicists prepare press kits and other materials.

HOLLYWOOD IS BIG BUSINESS

California takes movies and television seriously. It was the first state to have a college program to teach students moviemaking.

Two of the best film schools in the country are in **Los Angeles**. They have produced many successful **filmmakers**, or people who make movies. **George Lucas**, who directed the *Star Wars* movies, is one. He went to school at the University of Southern California. Penelope Spheeris went to the University of California at Los Angeles.

Getting the Word Out

You can see from the diagram on the previous page that making a movie is a lot of work. The work does not end when the filming is finished. A publicist like Marcy De Veaux (DUH VOH) helps with a film's distribution. Her job is to publicize, or let people know about, a film or TV show.

"You never, ever get bored," says De Veaux of her job. "I try to convince newspaper reporters to write about shows that are going to come on television," she says. In 1996 De Veaux publicized the show *C-Bear and Jamal*. The "press kit" she sent to reporters described the show's star, ten-year-old Jamal, and his stuffed animal pal, C-Bear.

WHY IT MATTERS

What is your favorite kind of movie? Movies tell stories of adventure, romance, and friendship that teach us about ourselves. They are one of the most important parts of American culture. When people in other countries think about the United States, they often think of the American movies they have seen. When many Americans think of movies, they think of California.

✓ Reviewing Facts and Ideas

MAIN IDEAS

- Many Californians take part in making films and TV programs.
- The film industry is an important part of the California economy.

THINK ABOUT IT

1. What are two jobs in the film industry?
2. What things have to be done before a director begins filming?
3. **FOCUS** How are movies important to California?
4. **THINKING SKILL** Put in *sequence* some of the steps in making a movie.
5. **WRITING** Make a press kit for your favorite movie or television show by writing short descriptions of the show's characters.

Marcy De Veaux (left) is just one of the many people who help make movies.

CITIZENSHIP
VIEWPOINTS

Sometimes it is fun to be scared at the movies. But is it a good thing?

SHOULD PEOPLE WATCH VIOLENT MOVIES?

Hollywood films can make you laugh, cry, or shiver with fear. Some of the most popular films include scenes of violence— bullets fly, cars explode, and too much blood is shown. Characters in these films—often the heroes—punch, kick, and shoot to get what they want.

People disagree about whether watching all this violence is a good thing. Lacey Gooch says that violent movies confuse people about right and wrong. Harris Liu says that movies are a way to forget about real life. He does not think that movies really affect how people behave. Chris Tanja thinks that older people can watch violent movies, but he worries that children might want to imitate the way a violent character acts if that character seems cool.

Read and consider viewpoints on this issue. Then answer the questions that follow.

Three **DIFFERENT** Viewpoints

1 **LACEY GOOCH**
Fresno, CA
Excerpt from interview, 1997

"... people shouldn't watch violent movies."

I think people shouldn't watch violent movies [because these films] affect the way they behave. If they see an actor do something bad, they think, "He did it, maybe I can do the same." A lot of people see movies and they don't think about how it's make-believe. If people are not raised to know right from wrong, they could be influenced [to do bad things] by violent movies.

2 **HARRIS LIU**
West Covina, CA
Excerpt from interview, 1997

"They aren't about real life."

I've grown up watching violent movies and I've never robbed anyone or tried to hurt anyone because of what I've seen. Most people have enough sense to realize that the movies are a place to . . . forget about your problems. They aren't about real life. If you're going to get in trouble, you'll do it whether you see violent movies or not.

3 **CHRIS TANJA**
Bakersfield, CA
Excerpt from interview, 1997

"... only teens and adults should watch . . ."

My opinion is that only teens and adults should watch violent movies. Some people have strong minds and they know that the movies are not really true. Others, especially young children, have wide-open minds, letting any idea come into their heads. A lot of times young children will imitate a character in a movie, so watching violent movies is not a good idea for them.

BUILDING CITIZENSHIP

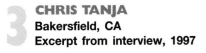

1. What is the viewpoint of each person?
2. In what ways do the viewpoints agree? How do they disagree?
3. What other viewpoints might people have on this issue? How could you find out what opinions people in your community have on this issue?

SHARING VIEWPOINTS

Discuss what you agree with or disagree with about these and other viewpoints. Make sure you give reasons to support your opinion. Then, as a class, write two statements about violent movies that all of you can agree with.

MAKING TOMORROW TODAY

Focus Activity

READ TO LEARN
Why is California a center for high-tech industries?

VOCABULARY
high technology
Silicon Valley
silicon
software

PEOPLE
Steve Wozniak
Steve Jobs

PLACES
Santa Clara
Cupertino
Santa Clara Valley
Palo Alto
San Diego
Sorrento Valley
Napa

READ ALOUD

Play a game that puts you at the controls of a helicopter. Create a newsletter about your favorite hobby. Work on a tricky math problem. Design a tree house. What do all these projects have in common? They are all things you can do on a computer.

THE BIG PICTURE

Ten-year-old Katherine comes home with her mother and brother Edward. She pushes a button on her key chain. The door unlocks and the house lights up. As the three enter, the phone rings. Katherine's father has called from his cellular phone. He will be home soon!

Katherine's mother heads for the computer. She puts the finishing touches on a diagram for a house she is designing. Katherine cannot wait to use the computer. She wants to research an assignment on the Internet. Edward plugs in a video game.

Everyone in this family uses high technology. High technology, or high tech for short, is the use of computers and other electronics to meet new wants and needs. The remote-control key chain, the cellular phone, the computer, and the video game all use high technology. How did Californians help make all this possible?

THE COMPUTER REVOLUTION

Almost one in three American families today has a computer at home. Before the 1970s a computer would hardly fit in your home!

Early computers were huge and very expensive. For example, the UNIVAC computer filled a whole room and cost about $500,000. Only very big businesses or government offices could afford to buy one.

The PC Is Born

How did computers get so much smaller? One important invention helped: the microprocessor, also known as a microchip. About the size of your little finger, a microprocessor is the brain of a computer. The first one was sold in 1971 by a company in Santa Clara.

In 1975 a 26-year-old engineer named Steve Wozniak bought a microprocessor for $20. In a garage in Cupertino, Wozniak and his

21-year-old friend Steve Jobs used the micro-processor to build a small, easy-to-use computer.

The two friends soon started a business building what became known as personal computers, PCs. In a short time, Jobs and Wozniak's company became very successful. A new industry was born.

Personal computers have changed people's lives. Businesses now use computers to keep track of their sales, to design buildings, and even to make books like the one you are reading. At home, people use PCs to write research papers, solve math problems, and even pay their bills.

Steve Jobs (above left) helped make PCs (above right) popular. A UNIVAC computer (below) in 1951.

SILICON VALLEY

SILICON VALLEY

Most of California's computer industry is located in the Santa Clara Valley. San Jose is the largest city in the Santa Clara Valley. Until the 1950s this area was known mostly for its agricultural products. Today it is known as Silicon Valley. Silicon is a material used in making microchips. These tiny electrical parts power today's computers.

The Santa Clara Valley is rich in human resources. That is one reason it became the center of California's computer industry. Stanford University, for example, is in the valley town of Palo Alto. The University of California at Berkeley is also nearby. Students and teachers from these famous universities made many of the discoveries that made the computer revolution possible.

William Hewlett and David Packard were computer pioneers. They graduated from Stanford in 1934. In 1938 they started a company in Packard's garage in Palo Alto. Today their company is a computer industry leader.

Many have followed Packard and Hewlett's example. Each year 3,000 new companies are started in Silicon Valley. Together these companies help make Silicon Valley an engine for California's economy.

Buyers should know what to look for (below) when shopping for a PC (right).

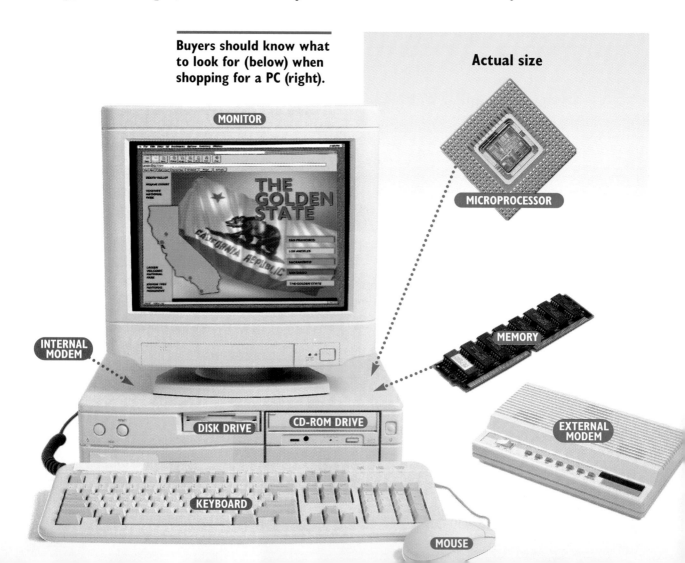

Actual size

MONITOR

THE GOLDEN STATE

CALIFORNIA REPUBLIC

MICROPROCESSOR

MEMORY

INTERNAL MODEM

DISK DRIVE

CD-ROM DRIVE

EXTERNAL MODEM

KEYBOARD

MOUSE

Using Software

You would not be able to do much on your computer without software. Software is a program, or set of instructions, that tells the computer what to do. Software lets you use your computer to write letters or school papers, add numbers, draw pictures, or play games.

There are about 6,500 software companies in California. More than half of them are in Silicon Valley. One type of software is known as multimedia (mul tih mee dee uh). Multimedia software mixes sounds, words, pictures, and movies. You can learn about geography or make up your own movies using multimedia software. In one part of San Francisco, there are so many multimedia software companies that it is nicknamed Multimedia Gulch. (A gulch is a narrow valley.)

Think Digital

Do you know what "01000001" means? To a computer, these numbers stand for the letter *A*. Computers read a code that uses only binary numbers. Binary numbers are made up of two choices: 0 or 1. Each 0 or 1 is one "bit" of information. A string of eight bits—such as 01000001—is called a byte. There are one million bytes in a megabyte. A personal computer may store thousands of megabytes of information.

No matter what we want a computer to remember, the computer stores it as binary numbers. Such computers are "digital" because they use numbers, or digits, to stand for any kind of information.

Going On-line

The Internet is the newest advance in computers. You read in Chapter 9 that the Internet is a computer network. It connects computers all over the world. If you have an Internet connection, you can "talk" on your computer to just about any other computer in the world that also has an Internet connection.

But with all those computers, how do you find your way? In 1994 two young Californians, still in their twenties, invented a tool, or search engine, to make it easier to find your way on the Internet. David Filo and Jerry Yang's invention is used by millions of people each day.

INTO THE FUTURE

Many high-tech inventions have been paid for by the government. The Internet, for example, was first developed by the government. It was a way for the armed forces to get and exchange information.

During the Cold War, California gained greatly from the government spending money on high tech. But since the end of the Cold War in 1991, the government has spent less. This hurt California's economy. Many people lost their jobs. Between 1989 and 1994, for example, California lost almost half its jobs in the aerospace industry.

California's economy has had to change. Businesses needed to find customers besides the government. California aerospace companies, for example, once built rockets for the United States Air Force or NASA. Now they sell rockets to companies that put communications satellites into outer space.

Communications satellites make cellular, or wireless, phones possible. These phones do not have wires to carry information. When you make a cellular phone call, your voice is sent to a satellite. The satellite sends your voice anywhere in the world to the phone number you are calling.

Wireless telephones have given a boost to the economy of San Diego. About 100,000 people in San Diego work in companies that make wireless phones. Most of them are in the Sorrento Valley.

Californians build satellites (above) that keep people in touch and the latest cars (left) that keep people moving.

For many of us, machines are a part of everyday life.

Biotechnology is another high-tech industry. It was invented by California scientists in the 1970s. Biotechnology uses tiny creatures or cells to make health and medical products. Biotechnology has been used to create drugs to treat disease, such as insulin for people with diabetes.

Teaching for the Future

High-tech companies face a challenge. They need to hire people who are good in math and science and know how to use computers. A growing number of schools are teaching students high-tech skills.

The New Technology High School in Napa is one such school. Every student there has a computer. They learn how to create software and how to do research on the Internet.

WHY IT MATTERS

California is a place where people like to try out new ideas. It has been a leader in inventing new technologies, such as the personal computer. Today computers and high tech are a strong part of our state's economy.

High technology has changed the way many people live and work. It can give them more tools to enrich their lives. But for some workers, new technologies have meant hard times. Many jobs once done by people can now be done by machines.

Reviewing Facts and Ideas

MAIN IDEAS

● Personal computers were invented in California.

● Silicon Valley became a center of the computer industry because it is rich in human resources.

● Wireless phones and biotechnology are two new kinds of technology in California.

THINK ABOUT IT

1. What is Silicon Valley?

2. How does a cellular phone differ from a regular phone?

3. **FOCUS** What has made California a center of high technology?

4. **THINKING SKILL** *Compare and contrast* UNIVAC and personal computers.

5. **WRITE** What need do you have that high technology might solve? Describe the technology that would meet your need.

329

THINKING SKILLS

Identifying Fact and Opinion

VOCABULARY

fact
opinion
bias

WHY THE SKILL MATTERS

In the last section, you read about high technology. You learned that there are many computer companies in Silicon Valley. This statement is a fact. A fact is a statement that can be proven true. You can make sure it is true by checking the information in a reference source, such as an encyclopedia.

Suppose, however, that somebody told you that she thinks the computer companies in Texas are better than the ones in Silicon Valley. This statement cannot be proven. Rather, it is an opinion. An opinion is a statement of a person's belief or feeling. Another person might believe that Colorado's computer companies are the best.

Facts and opinions are very different kinds of statements. It is important to be able to tell them apart because the decisions we make should be based on facts. That way you can make up your own mind using correct information.

One way to tell them apart is by looking for bias. Bias is a one-sided presentation of information. Opinions often show bias. Suppose the person who liked Texas's computer companies told you only good things about them and only bad things about California's computer companies. Her opinion would show bias.

USING THE SKILL

Read this passage from a magazine article. Then identify which statements are facts and which are opinions.

The computer companies in Silicon Valley hire thousands of workers to design and make computers. These companies give high pay to workers with high-tech skills. Cities in other parts of California should offer computer companies free rent. I think this would help California's economy by bringing more high-wage jobs to the state.

Fiber-optic cables (below and right) can carry many calls. A wireless phone (far right).

Which statements in the article are facts? Which are opinions? The first two sentences are facts. They can be proven true or untrue. You could check the information in a reference source.

Sometimes you can tell opinions by the use of such word clues as *I think, I believe, the best,* or *should.* These word clues appear in the last two sentences. So these sentences could not be proven true. Opinions do not always have word clues, however.

TRYING THE SKILL

You have just identified facts and opinions in a passage about the computer industry. Now read this next passage about another kind of high technology. When you are done, figure out which of the statements are facts and which

express the author's opinions. Use the Helping Yourself box to guide you in identifying these two kinds of statements.

When you make a phone call on a regular telephone, your voice travels over cables. Miles and miles of these cables have to be buried underground for phones to work. A better choice would be to change all phones into wireless phones. They do not need wires, only satellites orbiting Earth. I believe that it will take only 20 years for wireless phones to replace regular phones in homes and businesses.

Which of these statements could be proven true? Which statements do you think are opinions? What did you do to identify these facts and opinions?

REVIEWING THE SKILL

1. In what ways is a fact different from an opinion?

2. Why does a word clue like *the best* often tell you that the speaker is expressing an opinion?

3. How would the reference section of the library help you to decide if certain statements were facts or opinions?

4. When is it useful to be able to tell a fact from an opinion?

CALIFORNIA AND THE PACIFIC RIM

Focus Activity

READ TO LEARN
Why is international trade important to California's economy?

VOCABULARY
Pacific Rim
international trade
NAFTA
agribusiness

PLACES
South Korea
Fremont
Long Beach
San Pedro
Pusan

READ ALOUD

Giant ships longer than two football fields set sail from the busy port of Pusan, in South Korea. They cross the Pacific Ocean carrying cars, computer parts, and shoes bound for Los Angeles. Meanwhile, ships from Los Angeles carry airplane parts and wireless phones to the South Korean port.

THE BIG PICTURE

South Korea is just one of the countries of the Pacific Rim. The Pacific Rim is made up of the countries that touch the Pacific Ocean. You can see these countries on the map on the next page.

Bordered by the Pacific Ocean, California is in the right place for international trade. International trade is the exchange of goods between countries. In 1997 California's top five trading partners were Japan, Canada, Mexico, South Korea, and Taiwan.

California also has ties with countries closer to our borders. The United States has a trade treaty with Mexico and Canada. It is called the North American Free Trade Agreement, or NAFTA. The three countries promise to cooperate in trading with one another. For example, they do not place taxes on each other's products. They also obey similar rules for how products should be made.

PACIFIC OCEAN

RUSSIA

ALASKA
(U.S.)

CANADA

NORTH
KOREA

UNITED
STATES

CHINA   SOUTH
KOREA   JAPAN

ATLANTIC
OCEAN

HONG
KONG
MACAU

HAWAII
(U.S.)

MEXICO

TAIWAN

NORTHERN
MARIANA IS.
(U.S.)

GUATEMALA   HONDURAS
EL SALVADOR   NICARAGUA

VIETNAM   PHILIPPINES

THAILAND

GUAM
(U.S.)

MARSHALL
ISLANDS

COSTA RICA
PANAMA

CAMBODIA   BRUNEI

COLOMBIA

MALAYSIA

PALAU   FEDERATED STATES
OF MICRONESIA

Equator

ECUADOR

SINGAPORE

INDONESIA

PAPUA
NEW GUINEA

NAURU
TUVALU

KIRIBATI

PERU

SOLOMON
ISLANDS

WESTERN
SAMOA

VANUATU

AMERICAN
SAMOA
(U.S.)

FRENCH
POLYNESIA
(FR.)

CHILE

FIJI

AUSTRALIA

TONGA

PACIFIC OCEAN

INDIAN
OCEAN

NEW
ZEALAND

0   1,000   2,000 Miles

0   1,000   2,000 Kilometers

MAP WORK

Many countries are located on the Pacific Rim.

1. Which South American countries are located on the Pacific Rim?

2. Is Russia a Pacific Rim country?

3. Which island country is due west of California?

TRADING IDEAS

Trade involves more than just the exchange of goods. Trade also involves the exchange of ideas. California is an important force in the trading of ideas. These ideas can lead to cooperation between countries.

One example of cooperation between countries is in the auto industry. Companies from many countries design their cars in Southern California. They employ car designers from California. The companies want to take advantage of the California style.

In Fremont an American auto company and a Japanese company cooperate in the building of cars. The two companies are co-owners of an automobile factory. The factory uses the skills of Japanese and American workers to make cars for both companies.

333

A CENTER FOR TRADE

California is a center for trade. Most of California's trade flows through ports at Oakland, San Diego, Los Angeles, and Long Beach. In 1995 Long Beach was the busiest port in the United States. The Port of Los Angeles in San Pedro was the second busiest port.

Trade flows in two directions. We buy, or import, goods that we need from other countries. We sell, or export, to other countries the goods that they need.

Imports

Californians love cars. In 1997 our state imported 225,000 cars. Most of the cars came from Japan and Germany. Some of the petroleum to power those cars also came from other countries. As California's petroleum supplies begin to run out, our state will probably need to import more petroleum.

California also imports many high-tech goods. In 1993, for example, more than twice the number of microchips and computers were imported to California than were exported. These goods can be made more cheaply in other countries.

Superfreighters, such as this one at Long Beach, carry trade goods between countries.

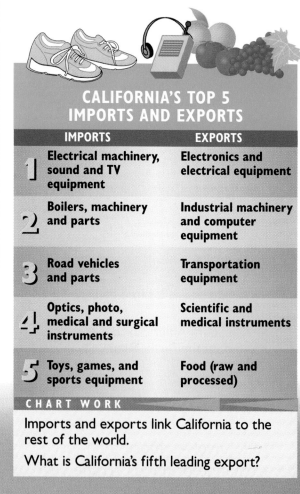

CALIFORNIA'S TOP 5 IMPORTS AND EXPORTS

	IMPORTS	EXPORTS
1	Electrical machinery, sound and TV equipment	Electronics and electrical equipment
2	Boilers, machinery and parts	Industrial machinery and computer equipment
3	Road vehicles and parts	Transportation equipment
4	Optics, photo, medical and surgical instruments	Scientific and medical instruments
5	Toys, games, and sports equipment	Food (raw and processed)

CHART WORK

Imports and exports link California to the rest of the world.

What is California's fifth leading export?

Exports

You read in Lesson 2 that people around the world enjoy the films and television shows made in California. Did you know that makes them exports? It does. Films and television shows are an important California export. In 1997 Hollywood movies made almost 6 billion dollars in other countries.

It is not as easy to sell goods and services in another country as it is to sell them here. Our country's government helps companies do business in other countries. Sometimes our government has to convince a country to allow imports from America. China, for example, did not allow California growers to ship grapes to China until 1997.

Our state government also helps businesses. Ann Veneman works for our state's agricultural office. She helps California growers take part in trade shows in other countries. At trade shows, companies in the same industry set up tables to display their products. "Californians can make contact with foreign buyers through trade shows," she explains.

Sister Cities

A company needs to know the rules of business in a country where it wants to sell its good. Sookyung Chang is a Korean American who lives in Los Angeles. She is a psychologist, or a person who studies human behavior. Chang advises American business people on how to get to know business people in South Korea. She explains that South Koreans "don't do business unless they know people at a personal level."

Chang is also a leader of Los Angeles's Sister City program with Pusan, South Korea. The Sister City program matches a United States city with a city in another country. People in Pusan and Los Angeles can learn about the other city's culture.

The Sister City program is run by citizens acting on their own. "What we can't accomplish through our governments," says Chang, "we can do privately [ourselves]."

Movies are a big California export. They are shipped in cans such as these.

335

AGRICULTURE AND TRADE

International trade is very important to California farmers. In 1995 they exported almost $12 billion worth of farm products. More than half went to countries in the Pacific Rim.

In the 1800s, when California was part of Mexico, rancheros exported hides and tallow. Today ranches still produce California's biggest farm export: beef. Japan buys more California beef than any other country. Cotton is the second biggest farm export. The third largest export is grapes.

Tonya Pavich (bottom left) and her family are just some of the California farmers who export their crops.

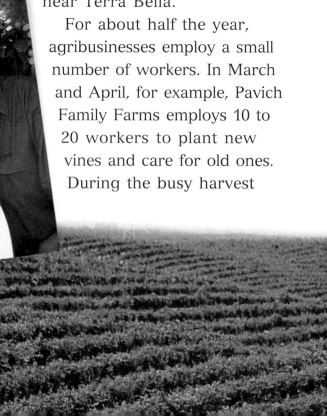

An Agribusiness

As you read in Chapter 2, the Central Valley grows much of our state's cotton, grapes, and other farm goods.

Some of the Central Valley's largest producers are agribusinesses, like Pavich Family Farms. An agribusiness is a large farm owned by a company. A small farm in California might have less than one square mile of land. Pavich Family Farms owns over six square miles in different places. Some of its land is in Arizona. The company grows grapes, melons, and vegetables.

Pavich Family Farms is a big grower of organic grapes. Organic grapes are grown without any chemical fertilizers or bug sprays. Most of Pavich's grapes are grown near Terra Bella.

For about half the year, agribusinesses employ a small number of workers. In March and April, for example, Pavich Family Farms employs 10 to 20 workers to plant new vines and care for old ones. During the busy harvest

season, however, the farm hires more than 1,000 workers to pick grapes by hand. The harvest runs from May until October.

Agribusinesses sell their own crops directly to grocery stores and other markets. At Pavich Family Farms that job falls to Tonya Pavich. She is in charge of advertising and working with grocery stores.

Pavich also works to export the farm's grapes overseas. "We ship 1 to 2 percent of our total crop, approximately 26,000 to 50,000 cases," she explains. The farm's grapes are taken by truck to a Los Angeles airport. There they are put in special containers. Most of the grapes are flown to Europe. The farm is just starting to export to Japan and Taiwan.

WHY IT MATTERS

International trade plays a key role in our state's economy. If California were a country, it would be the largest trading country in the world.

✓ Reviewing Facts and Ideas

MAIN IDEAS

- California's location on the Pacific Rim and next to Mexico makes it a good place for international trade.
- California's most important exports are high-tech goods.
- California farmers and ranchers export many agricultural products, including beef, cotton, and grapes.

THINK ABOUT IT

1. What is NAFTA?

2. What are the top three farm products that California exports?

3. **FOCUS** In what way is international trade important to California's economy?

4. **THINKING SKILL** Is this statement a *fact* or an *opinion*: "The Sister City program is a good thing for Los Angeles."

5. **GEOGRAPHY** Does your town have a Sister City? What would you like to tell someone in your Sister City about your part of California?

CHAPTER 11 REVIEW

THINKING ABOUT VOCABULARY

Number a sheet of paper from 1 to 10. Next to each number write the word or phrase from the list that best fits the definition.

agribusiness
filmmaker
high technology
historic site
international trade

NAFTA
silicon
Silicon Valley
software
tourism

1. A material used in making microchips
2. The exchange of goods between countries
3. The industry that sells goods and services to people on vacations
4. The trade treaty between the United States, Canada, and Mexico
5. A person who makes movies
6. The use of computers and other electronics to meet new wants and needs
7. A large farm owned by a company
8. A building, battlefield, or other place where events from our past took place
9. A program or set of instructions that tells a computer what to do
10. An area in California that is an important center of the country's computer industry

THINKING ABOUT FACTS

1. Why is the tourism industry important to California?
2. Name three industries in California other than tourism.
3. About how many people in California work in the movie industry? What are some of the jobs they have?
4. What does a publicist do?
5. How did the microprocessor help in the creation of personal computers?
6. How did PCs change people's lives?
7. What does multimedia software contain?
8. Why is biotechnology important?
9. How do agribusinesses sell their crops?
10. What is the Pacific Rim? Name the key Pacific Rim trading partners.

THINK AND WRITE

WRITING A TRAVEL PAMPHLET
You have read about the many tourist activities that make California special. Write and illustrate a travel guide to the state.

WRITING AN ADVERTISEMENT
Suppose you are a publicist for a movie about California. Write an advertisement that tells people about the movie.

WRITING A LIST
Write a list of goods California imports and a list of goods it exports.

APPLYING STUDY SKILLS

IDENTIFYING FACT AND OPINION

1. What is the difference between a fact and an opinion? Identify items 2, 3, and 4 below as either fact or opinion. Explain your answers.

2. "More movies are made in California than anywhere else in the world."

3. "Everyone needs to learn how to use a computer."

4. "International trade is important to California's economy."

5. Why is it important to know the difference between a fact and an opinion?

OPINION

Everyone loves visiting California.

FACT

Tourism is a big industry in California.

Summing Up the Chapter

Use the following cause-and-effect chart to organize information in the chapter. Fill in the blank spaces on the chart. Then use the information to write a paragraph that answers the question "How have industries in California changed American culture?"

CAUSE	EFFECT
California has many sights to attract tourists.	
More movies are made in California than any other place in the world.	
The microprocessor is invented.	
	California trades with the countries of the Pacific Rim.

CHAPTER 12

The People of California

THINKING ABOUT PEOPLE AND CITIZENSHIP

Have you ever thought about the kind of role citizens play in our government? Maybe you've thought about ways you would like to help our state or your local community. Read on to learn how our local, state, and national governments work and how you can play an important part!

CANADA

UNITED STATES

CALIFORNIA

PACIFIC OCEAN

MEXICO

TODAY'S CALIFORNIANS

Focus Activity

READ TO LEARN
Who are California's people today?

VOCABULARY
ethnic group
refugee

READ ALOUD

"I was surprised when I arrived [in America] to see so many kinds of people," said one young immigrant from Mexico. "I found people from Korea and Cambodia and Mexico. In California I found not just America, I found the world."

THE BIG PICTURE

Almost one out of every eight people in the United States lives in California. That makes California the most populous of the United States. Californians come from just about every place on Earth. In 1993 people came to California from over 90 different countries. More people from more ethnic groups live in California than in any other state. An ethnic group is a group of people who share a common cultural heritage or whose ancestors lived in the same country or area.

This rich mix of people from different cultures makes California special. On the streets of the cities in our state, you will find people from Italy, Nigeria, Japan, Mexico, Ireland, China, to name just a few countries. You will also find Native Americans and people from each of the 50 United States. Together they make California the great place it is.

The Agua Cahuilla Festival, Cinco de Mayo, and Danish Days in Solvang (left to right) are just some events celebrated in our state.

342

A DIVERSE STATE

To get an idea of our state's rich ethnic diversity, go to one of the many festivals that take place throughout the year. At these festivals, or celebrations, people preserve their ethnic customs and share them with others.

A World of Festivals

Every July the Lotus Festival brings together many of the Asian and Pacific Islander cultures of Los Angeles. The lotus is a beautiful water flower important to many Asian cultures. The sounds of Japanese, Mandarin and Cantonese Chinese, and Tagalog fill the air. Hawaiian hula dancers and brightly costumed dancers from India entertain the crowd.

At Oakland's *Juneteenth* celebration crowds enjoy jazz and gospel music performers. Juneteenth celebrates June 19, 1865, the day when African Americans in Texas learned that they had been freed from slavery.

Danish Days in Solvang mean it is time for *aebleskiver* (AY bul skee vur). Immigrants from Denmark brought this yummy pastry with them.

A walk down Olvera Street in Los Angeles is a trip into California's Mexican past. On May 5 things really get exciting. That is Cinco de Mayo, which honors an important day in Mexico's history. On that day in 1862, Mexican soldiers defeated an invading French army. Today mariachi bands play. People enjoy Mexican food. Everyone gathers to celebrate Mexico's history and heritage.

343

IMMIGRANTS TODAY

California has long drawn people from around the world. After 1968 a new wave of immigrants started to come to California. Most came from Mexico, the Philippines, Central America, South America, East Asia, and Southeast Asia.

A New Wave of Immigrants

What caused this change in immigration? One reason was that in 1968 a new law made it easier for people from many Asian countries to come to the United States to live. Until then, immigration laws had discriminated against people from Asian countries.

Wars and other problems have driven people in many countries to seek safety in California. Many immigrants from Vietnam, Laos, and Cambodia, for example, came as refugees after the Vietnam War. A refugee is someone who leaves unsafe conditions in his or her homeland. Other refugees came from Central America and South America.

The new immigrants are a lot like the old immigrants. They have come to California seeking opportunity and freedom. Ginger Tang, for example, left Taiwan for California in 1973. She hoped that her children would have a better chance to go to a good university here. "It was very hard at times," she explains, "but we have fulfilled our dream." Another immigrant, from Vietnam, stressed the freedom in the United States. "What I like most [about the United States]," he said, "is *freedom*, to move, to do business."

Some of the immigrants in California are illegal immigrants. That is, they came without getting permission to enter the country. Some Californians believe that illegal immigrants hurt our state. They think that illegal immigrants cost the state government money. Other Californians believe that these immigrants help our state's economy. They point out that illegal immigrants buy goods, pay taxes, and, in some cases, do jobs that others do not want to do.

In 1994 voters passed a law known as Proposition 187. Under this law, illegal immigrants would have lost many public benefits. Opponents of the law challenged it in court. In 1998 a federal judge ruled that most of Proposition 187 was not allowed by the United States Constitution. Governor Gray Davis chose not to appeal the decision.

Immigrants becoming citizens at a ceremony in San Francisco (above).

Infographic

The People of California

California has people from all over the world. As you can see from the graphs on this page, most of today's immigrants come from different countries than the immigrants of 1900. People from Mexico make up the biggest group of these immigrants.

IMMIGRANTS TO CALIFORNIA, 1900

Immigrants (in thousands)

80
60
40
20
0

Canada | Germany | Great Britain* | Ireland | Italy

Country

*Does not include Ireland
Source: United States Census Bureau

IMMIGRANTS TO CALIFORNIA, 1995

Immigrants (in thousands)

40
30
20
10
0

China | India | Mexico | Philippines | Vietnam

Country

Source: Immigration and Naturalization Service

MAJOR CALIFORNIA ETHNIC GROUPS, 1995

- European American
- African American
- Native American
- Hispanic*
- Asian American/ Pacific Islander

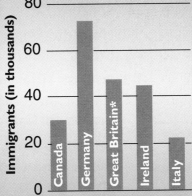

17,178,200
9,102,000
3,338,900
2,250,800
192,700

*Includes Spanish-surnamed people of all ethnic or national origins
Source: Demographic Research Unit, State of California

WHAT WE SHARE

Most Californians are proud of their ethnic heritage. They enjoy keeping that heritage alive and sharing it with others.

Whatever our different backgrounds, however, Californians share many things. For example, we love our state, and we are proud of it.

We also share important ideas. We obey the same laws. We believe in our form of government. We respect the freedom of other people. Respect for others is part of our common heritage.

DID YOU KNOW?

How do immigrants become citizens?

To become a United States citizen, an immigrant must live in the United States for five years. He or she must also be at least 18 years old.

Immigrants who apply for citizenship have to prove that they can read, write, and speak English. They also take a test on United States history and government.

If they meet these requirements, they must then say a special Oath of Allegiance, or loyalty, to the United States. They swear to "support and defend the Constitution and laws of the United States of America against all enemies."

As citizens, they have nearly all the rights and responsibilities of Americans born in the United States. They can vote, join the military, and run for most government offices.

WHY IT MATTERS

California's diverse population is a source of great strength for the state. People with valuable skills and rich customs add to California's economy and culture.

✓✓ Reviewing Facts and Ideas

MAIN IDEAS

- California has the largest population of any state in the United States.
- California's population includes people from many different ethnic groups.
- Today's immigrants come mainly from Mexico and countries in Asia, Central America, and South America.

THINK ABOUT IT

1. Name some things that Californians share.

2. How did immigration to the United States change after 1968? Why?

3. **FOCUS** How are immigrants to California today similar to immigrants to California in the past?

4. **THINKING SKILL** Why, do you think, might someone from another country or state _decide_ to move to California?

5. **WRITE** Write about one custom of an ethnic group to which you belong or which is a part of your heritage. Share what you wrote with your classmates.

CITIZENSHIP
MAKING A DIFFERENCE

Helping Young Immigrants

FOUNTAIN VALLEY—
Kim-Oanh Ngyuyen-Lam (KIHM WAN WIHN LAM) knows how hard it is being an immigrant. Kim was only 15 years old when she and her family left Vietnam at the end of a horrible war.

Once she got to the United States, Kim-Oanh's greatest challenge was being unable to communicate with others. School was especially difficult at first. She was the only Vietnamese student. "All around me people were talking, laughing, exchanging stories. But for me, it was just pure noise. I did not know how to ask for directions. I hardly ever spoke in class. I felt awful. It was a long time before I understood that not being able to speak English did not mean I had no knowledge. But I felt ashamed of what I knew and who I was instead of proud."

Kim-Oanh's experiences made her want to help other young newcomers learn English. She went to college and became a teacher. "I tried to help [my non-English-speaking students] see that they will not always have to struggle with English. I also want them to know that their culture and customs give them something very valuable to share with their classmates."

Kim-Oanh also worked with the parents of her students. "I tell parents not to be afraid to take part in school activities like open houses and parent conferences. They don't have to stay away just because of their language. I also tell them to talk to their children about their cultural heritage."

Today Kim-Oanh trains future teachers. She shares stories of her own life with them. She wants teachers to understand that although immigrant students may not be able to express themselves well using English, they have a lot to share with the class. "My goal," she says, "is to make sure students who are new to this country do not have to go through what I did."

"... culture and customs give them something very valuable ..."

Kim-Oanh Ngyuyen-Lam

GOVERNING CALIFORNIA

Focus Activity

READ TO LEARN
What role do citizens play in our government?

VOCABULARY
city council
mayor
city manager
legislative branch
governor
executive branch
judicial branch
State Supreme Court
resolution
President
Congress

PEOPLE
Pete Wilson
Anthony Kennedy
Earl Warren

PLACES
Monterey Park
Sacramento
Washington, D.C.

READ ALOUD

Lanie Wheeler is part of Palo Alto's city government. She believes that citizens and government need to work together to make things better. "No level of government can . . . fix [what] is broken," she explains. "Leaders of government . . . must ask citizens to join them in [building] a brighter future."

THE BIG PICTURE

Citizens often act together to solve problems. In Chapter 2, for example, you read about how citizens have tried to conserve the state's resources. Sometimes, however, problems are too big for citizens alone to solve. Those are the kinds of problems governments help to solve.

The United States has a form of government called a democratic republic (dem uh KRAT ihk rih PUB lihk). In a democratic republic the people pick representatives to run the government for them. That means that the government's power to make laws comes from the people.

The California constitution is the guide for running our state's government. It explains that the government is divided into three branches, or sections. The constitution describes the responsibilities of each branch.

City workers in Monterey Park maintain parks (left) and provide "911" emergency services (below).

GOVERNMENT CLOSE TO HOME

The town or city where you live has a local government. Local governments try to solve the problems that affect us every day. They build and fix roads. They decide where houses and businesses can be located. They run parks and libraries. They provide police and fire protection to citizens. Helping people is what government is about.

Calling 911

Like most cities, Monterey Park has a city council and a mayor. The city council is a group of representatives that makes the city's laws and decides how it should spend its money. The mayor is the head of the city government. Monterey Park also has a city manager. A city manager runs a city's daily business.

In 1991 the citizens of Monterey Park near Los Angeles faced a serious safety problem. Most of the people who lived in Monterey Park

were Chinese Americans or Hispanic Americans. That meant that many of the "911" emergency calls in the city came from people who spoke Chinese or Spanish.

Yet there were no "911" operators who spoke Chinese. Only two spoke Spanish. That made it hard for people calling for help to be understood.

Monterey Park's city council looked into hiring new "911" operators who spoke English as well as Chinese or Spanish. Residents came to the meeting to express their views. The city manager supported the plan. At the end of the meeting, the city council voted to hire the new "911" operators.

STATE GOVERNMENT

California's state government is located in Sacramento, our state's capital. As you can see from the chart below, there are three branches of state government. Each branch has different duties and responsibilities.

The legislative (LEJ ihs lay tihv) branch of state government makes the laws. It has two parts. One part is the State Senate. There are 40 state senators, who can be elected for only two 4-year terms. The other part is the State Assembly. It has 80 State Assembly members, who can be elected for three 2-year terms. Each senator and Assembly person is elected by the voters of a certain district, or area, of the state.

The governor is the head of the executive (eg ZEK yuh tihv) branch of state government. In California the governor can be elected for only two 4-year terms.

The judicial (joo DIHSH ul) branch of state government makes sure people follow our state's laws. This branch of government is made up of the courts. All citizens can work in the courts. For example, they may sit on a jury, a group of citizens who decide if someone is guilty of a crime.

The highest court in California is the State Supreme Court. This court has seven judges. The governor selects the judges.

THREE BRANCHES OF STATE GOVERNMENT

EXECUTIVE Governor	LEGISLATIVE Legislature (80 Assembly Members, 40 Senators)	JUDICIAL Supreme Court (7 Judges)
• Signs or vetoes bills • Carries out laws • Nominates justices to the State Supreme Court	• Makes laws for our state • Decides how much money to spend	• Makes sure our laws follow the state constitution

CHART WORK

Our state government is located in Sacramento. It has three branches.

1. How many Assembly members are there? How many senators?
2. Who heads the executive branch?
3. What are the duties of the State Supreme Court?
4. Which branch makes laws?

Voters then decide whether to elect them to terms of 12 years.

Government Takes Action

From 1987 to 1992 the worst drought since the 1930s hit California. People had to cut back on how much water they used every day. Still there was not enough water for everyone. The state government had to take action to meet the challenge.

Pete Wilson became governor of California in 1991. Governor Wilson formed a Drought Action Team to come up with a plan to make sure that cities and farms did not run out of water. Following the team's advice, Wilson set up a Drought Water Bank. The bank bought water from places in the state that had extra water. It then sold the extra water to places that needed it.

The state legislature also took action during the drought. In 1991 members of the State Assembly and Senate introduced a Water Recycling Bill. The bill, or idea for a law, called for the state to recycle about 326,000 gallons a year by the year 2000. That is enough water for a city the size of Los Angeles. A second bill required the state to write a new water plan every five years. This State Water Plan would explain how the state will protect, conserve, and use its water resources.

Assembly members and senators voted to pass the bills. After the governor signed them, the bills became laws. In this way the legislature made sure the state would be ready to deal with future droughts.

The Assembly (right) and Senate make laws. The State Supreme Court (below) has seven judges.

HOW A BILL BECOMES A LAW

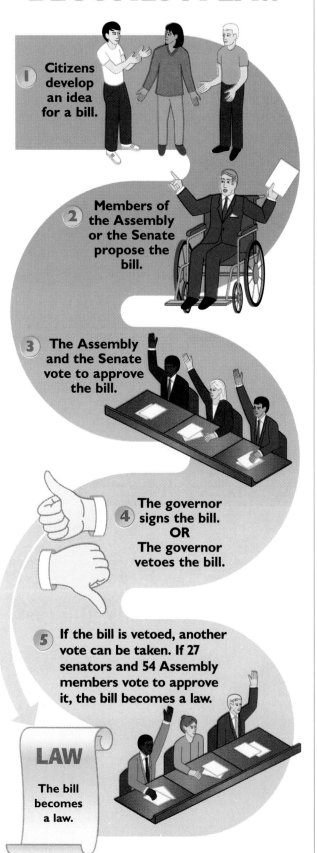

1. Citizens develop an idea for a bill.

2. Members of the Assembly or the Senate propose the bill.

3. The Assembly and the Senate vote to approve the bill.

4. The governor signs the bill. **OR** The governor vetoes the bill.

5. If the bill is vetoed, another vote can be taken. If 27 senators and 54 Assembly members vote to approve it, the bill becomes a law.

LAW The bill becomes a law.

A LAW IN CALIFORNIA

Did you know that you could help make a new law in California? A group of young people did just that.

The California Youth Connection is made up of young people in foster care. Foster children are raised by adults who act as parents for them because their parents have died or can no longer take care of them.

Most kids can drive at 16 years old as long as a parent signs their driver's license form. But foster parents were not allowed to sign the form for their foster kids. Foster youths had to wait until they were 18 years old to get a driver's license.

Youth Connection took action. They talked to people in the legislature. They explained that they wanted to be able to drive in order to get to their jobs and earn money.

Assembly member Rusty Areias of Salinas agreed to introduce a bill to change the law. It passed in 1992. Now a foster youth can get a driver's license at 16, like other teenagers. Follow the arrows in the chart to see how the bill became a law.

Passing a Resolution

Another way to make a law is by a resolution. A resolution is a statement of a decision made by a legislature. The legislature must vote to pass a resolution. In 1951 both the Senate and the Assembly voted to make "I Love You, California," the official state song. You can sing along with it on the next page.

I Love You, California

MANY VOICES MUSIC

Words by
F. B. SILVERWOOD

Music by
A. F. FRANKENSTEIN

OUR NATIONAL GOVERNMENT

As you have seen, local and state governments handle many problems in California. The national, or federal, government is responsible for all of the United States. It handles issues faced by the whole country, such as dealing with other countries.

The home of our country's government is in Washington, D.C. It is organized much like California's state government. It has executive, legislative, and judicial branches.

The President

The President of the United States heads the country's executive branch. Every four years American voters elect a President. The President carries out the laws of the United States and meets with leaders of foreign countries. The President also leads the nation's military.

Several Presidents have come from California. President Herbert Hoover (1929–1933) went to college here. President Richard Nixon (1969–1974) was born and raised in the state. President Ronald Reagan (1981–1989) moved to California as a young man.

Congress

The legislative branch of our country's government is known as Congress. Congress makes the laws of our country. Like California's legislature, Congress is made up of two parts. They are called the Senate and the House of Representatives.

Voters of each state elect two senators. In 1992 California became the first state to elect two women, Dianne Feinstein and Barbara Boxer, as senators.

Voters also pick representatives for the House of Representatives. The number of representatives each state has varies. States with bigger populations have more representatives. California has 52 representatives in the House of Representatives. In contrast, North Dakota has only one representative.

Congress **works in the Capitol building (below). Ronald Reagan (right) and Earl Warren (far right) served our country's government.**

The Supreme Court

The United States Supreme Court, is the highest court in our country. Its nine judges make sure all laws follow the United States Constitution. Anthony Kennedy, from Sacramento, is one of the nine judges on the Supreme Court today.

The Supreme Court is led by the Chief Justice. One of the most important Chief Justices, Earl Warren, came from Kern City, near Bakersfield. He served as Chief Justice from 1953 to 1968.

WHY IT MATTERS

Governments help solve many problems, large and small. Since we live in a democratic republic, it is citizens who decide how they want our government to be run.

Reviewing Facts and Ideas

MAIN IDEAS

- The mayor, city council, and city manager are officials of local governments.
- California's state government is made up of a governor, a Senate, an Assembly, and a supreme court.
- A bill becomes law if it is approved by the legislature and the governor.
- The national government makes laws that affect all Americans.

THINK ABOUT IT

1. What does the governor of California do?

2. What is the State Supreme Court's main job?

3. **FOCUS** What role do citizens play in our local, state, and federal governments?

4. **THINKING SKILL** Why is _making a decision_ an important skill for members of the state legislature?

5. **WRITE** Write a letter to your Assembly member explaining your idea for a bill. Ask him or her how to propose it in the State Assembly.

Reading Newspapers

VOCABULARY

current event   editorial   byline
news article   headline   dateline
feature article

WHY THE SKILL MATTERS

In the last section you read about citizens taking part in government. Are you interested in learning more about your government? One good way to get information about government is by reading the newspaper.

Newspapers report on current events, or the things that happen every day. Some newspapers print just stories about the events that go on in a city or town. Others write about events all over the country and around the world.

USING A NEWSPAPER

Newspapers have different parts. The front part of a paper contains mostly news articles. These are stories based on facts about events that happened. Inside are feature articles. A feature article has many details about a person, subject, or event.

Newspapers also have parts that give you information about sports, movies, and television. An editorial might make you think harder about an issue. Editors—the people who run the paper—usually write editorials. They express their ideas, or opinions, about an issue.

USING A NEWS ARTICLE

Look at a newspaper. What is the thing that first catches your attention? You may notice the words printed in large letters at the top of each article. They form the headline of the article. It sums up the main idea of the story.

Now look at the news article on the next page. As you can see, the headline is "Citizens Debate New Law."

One thing you might not notice at first is an article's byline. The byline tells the reader who wrote the story. The author of that story is Andrew Garcia.

Another useful part of an article is its dateline. The dateline tells you when and where the story was written. As you can see, the dateline in the story tells that it was written in San Francisco on July 17.

A news article that gives you all the facts should answer five questions. They are: (1) *Who* was involved in the story? (2) *What* took place? (3) *When* did the event happen?

(4) *Where* did it happen?

(5) *Why* did it happen?

Use the Helping Yourself box to guide you in reading the article on the next page. Does the article answer the five questions? The answer to the first question, for example, might be "the citizens of San Francisco." Can you sum up the article in your own words?

D.C. The headline for an article in the newspaper reads, "President Signs Immigration Bill." What kind of article do you think this is? Why do you think so? Another article is called "Immigration Law Is a Step in the Right Direction." What kind of article do you think this is? Why do you think so?

TRYING THE SKILL

You just read a news article about San Francisco's citizens debating a controversial issue. Why, do you think, is a newspaper a good way to learn about such an event? What other sources might give you information about the event?

Now suppose you wanted to find out about a new law passed in Washington,

REVIEWING THE SKILL

1. Name three different kinds of articles that appear in newspapers.

2. How can you tell that the article below is a news article instead of an editorial?

3. Why is it important for some news articles to have a dateline?

4. How would a newspaper help you learn about California?

CITIZENS DEBATE NEW LAW

By Andrew Garcia

SAN FRANCISCO, July 17—Hundreds of citizens jammed yesterday's meeting of the Presidio Trust. The Presidio Trust is the organization that runs the Presidio.

The Presidio used to be a military base. Now it is an 800-acre national park next to the Golden Gate Bridge.

The members of the Presidio Trust plan to tear down some of the old military buildings.

Citizens were given a chance to air their views. "Those buildings should not be torn down," argued Diana Rogers. "They should be used to house homeless people."

Others disagreed. "The buildings are old and run-down. They should be torn down because they're not safe," John Marucci answered.

EDUCATION AND THE ARTS IN CALIFORNIA

Focus Activity

READ TO LEARN
In what ways is California a leader in education and the arts?

VOCABULARY
public

PEOPLE
Phoebe Apperson Hearst
Sue Grafton
Walter Mosley
Maxine Hong Kingston
Wayne Thiebaud
Masami Teraoka
Beatrice Wood

PLACES
Watts

READ ALOUD

In 1997 President Bill Clinton spoke to graduates of the University of California at San Diego. He told them, "You have [made this university a] shining example of excellence. This is a great university for the twenty-first century."

THE BIG PICTURE

Since its founding in 1868, the University of California has grown to nine campuses and over 150,000 students. Phoebe Apperson Hearst gave large sums of money to support the University's early growth. Today most of the money for the University and for the other public colleges and universities in our state comes from taxes paid by citizens.

Some of our state's colleges and universities are privately funded. Religious organizations have been responsible for founding many of our state's private schools. In fact, California's earliest college was founded by the Roman Catholic Church in 1851. Together our state's nearly 2,000 colleges and universities, both public and private, help prepare over 2,000,000 students each year to meet the challenges of the future.

Schools help students, like these college graduates, prepare for life.

AN EDUCATION LEADER

California has over 140 public colleges and universities. Most are two-year community colleges. Some, like the University of California at Berkeley and the University of California at Los Angeles, are four-year schools, famous around the world for academic excellence.

Making Dreams Come True

Dr. Selmira Sanchez was born in Los Angeles. She got a job right after high school. But friends made her realize that education could open more doors for her.

Sanchez enrolled at East Los Angeles College. She worked hard and made good grades. Later she went to medical school at the University of California at San Diego.

Today Sanchez is a children's doctor. Her patients are glad to have a doctor to whom they can speak Spanish. Sanchez is happy that she can help her community.

"I look back at my education, and it was very challenging," she remembers. "Sometimes I felt I couldn't do it. But help from teachers made it possible."

California's system of public education has come under pressure in recent years. The number of students has grown more rapidly than the money to pay for more schools. California will have to work hard to stay a leader in education.

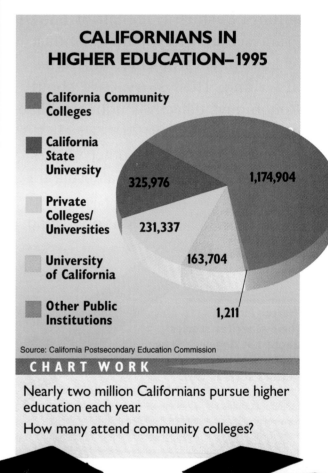

CALIFORNIANS IN HIGHER EDUCATION–1995

- California Community Colleges
- California State University
- Private Colleges/ Universities
- University of California
- Other Public Institutions

325,976
1,174,904
231,337
163,704
1,211

Source: California Postsecondary Education Commission

CHART WORK

Nearly two million Californians pursue higher education each year.

How many attend community colleges?

THE ARTS IN CALIFORNIA

California is also a leader in the arts. The songs, movies, books, paintings, and other works created here are popular around the world.

Writing About California

Have you ever read a "hard-boiled" detective story? California authors Dashiell Hammett of San Francisco and Raymond Chandler of Los Angeles invented this type of writing. Their stories are about "tough-guy" detectives fighting crime in big cities. Today Sue Grafton, Walter Mosley, and other writers carry on this California tradition. Mosley's inspiration for writing comes from stories he heard from his parents. His mother's immigrant family told him stories of Jewish life in Russia. His father told him tales of growing up as an African American in the southern United States.

Other writers draw on their immigrant heritage for their stories. Maxine Hong Kingston wrote about her Chinese American heritage in *The Woman Warrior* and *Tripmaster Monkey.*

Walter Mosley (below) writes stories about Los Angeles. Many California musicians use guitars such as this.

Handmade guitar by Danny Ferrington, Santa Monica

360

Beatrice Wood, Bottle, courtesy Garth Clark Gallery

Visual Arts

Painting in California dates back to the rock paintings of the Chumash and other Native Americans. Later arrivals brought their own art forms.

Today artists work in many forms and styles. Wayne Thiebaud, for example, is a painter. He is inspired by California's landscapes. He uses colorful and realistic city scenes for his subjects. In his playful paintings, curving freeways snake around palm trees and factories. Masami Teraoka is also a painter. He blends Japanese art forms and American customs in his paintings. He explains that his paintings come from "the humor and seriousness of two cultures—East and West—clashing."

Until her death in 1998, Beatrice Wood was one of our state's best-known artists. Her beautiful pottery won her many honors. In 1994 Governor Wilson declared her a California Living Treasure. Italian immigrant Simon Rodia spent 30 years building three towers in the Watts neighborhood of Los Angeles. Rodia sculpted steel, tile, and bits of everyday objects to make the world-famous Watts Towers. When he finished building the towers, he gave them to the city. "I had in my mind to do something big," Rodia once said, "and I did."

The Sounds of California

California is home to just about every kind of music there is. You might hear a Mexican mariachi band or a symphony orchestra one day. You might hear a Filipino band or the latest rock group the next.

Music in California is often driven by a spirit of experiment. The Beach Boys and Dick Dale, for example, changed popular music when they introduced the "surf sound" in the early 1960s.

Classical composer Harry Partch from Oakland created sounds that no one had heard before. He even built all the instruments for his own orchestra, using things like glass bowls and bamboo.

Today Californians continue to create new styles of music. "Rock en español" blends American rock with Spanish words. There are even composers writing music for the Internet. One day you might be able to play in an "Internet Orchestra."

361

SHOWCASES FOR THE ARTS

Not every Californian is an artist. But for millions of people in California, the arts play an important part in their lives. California has some of the best museums, theaters, dance groups, and symphony orchestras in the world.

Homes of the Arts

You can start your tour at California's first art museum. The Crocker Art Museum in Sacramento was built in 1873. It houses some paintings and sculptures from Europe. Mostly, however, it features art made by California artists. The Oakland Museum of California collects art made only by California artists. It offers a complete history of the fine arts in California since the Gold Rush.

For the arts of Asia, stop in at the San Francisco Asian Art Museum. It is one of the best museums of Asian art in the United States.

California's newest major art museum is at the Getty Center in Los Angeles. Its brilliant, white buildings are high in the Santa Monica Mountains. They make up what is almost a whole city of the arts. Works by famous European artists like Van Gogh, Rembrandt, and Rubens are just part of the story. The Getty Center also leads the world in finding ways to preserve art works from things like earthquakes. That is pretty important in California!

California also has some of our country's best performing arts centers. The Orange County Center for

Vincent van Gogh, *Irises*, courtesy The Getty Center

Vincent van Gogh's famous *Irises* (left) hangs in the Getty Center in Los Angeles (below).

the Performing Arts, for example, puts on plays, ballets, symphonies, and operas all in one place. If you want to get in on the action yourself, try the San Jose Children's Musical Theater, shown in the photo below. For over 30 years it has given kids the chance to sing, dance, act, and, who knows, be a star.

These are only a few of the thousands of places where you can find art in California. You could probably design your own California arts tour. You might just start at your neighborhood library. After all, a library is a home for the art of writing.

WHY IT MATTERS

California's strong system of education helped make our state an economic giant. The arts make living in California more fun and enjoyable.

Evelyn Cisneros flies high at the San Francisco Ballet.

✓ Reviewing Facts and Ideas

MAIN IDEAS

- California has a large and diverse public education system, with over 140 public colleges and universities.
- Painters, sculptors, musicians, and writers create California's rich assortment of arts.
- California has a wealth of fine architecture, concert halls, and museums to showcase the arts.

THINK ABOUT IT

1. What does a public education help people achieve?

2. What are some of the subjects that California artists paint?

3. **FOCUS** What has made California a leader in education and the arts?

4. **THINKING SKILL** What *effect* has California's system of public education had on our state's economic growth?

5. **WRITE** Describe a California custom, person, or landscape in a short story.

CALIFORNIA'S CITIES

READ ALOUD

The city of Los Angeles stretches over 465 square miles. Some 3.6 million people live there. Another 6 million people live in the area around Los Angeles. In an average day, commuters drive a total of 85 million miles in Los Angeles County. That is the same as driving more than 3,400 times around the world!

THE BIG PICTURE

Los Angeles and San Francisco are the centers of the largest metropolitan areas in California. *Metropolitan* means "city." A metropolitan area is a large city and the communities that are close to it. One reason many people live in cities is the variety of jobs they offer. You have read about the growth of the manufacturing and service industries in California. Many of these jobs are found in California's large cities. Today urban growth places a strain on many natural resources. Working together, we can solve these problems.

Focus Activity

READ TO LEARN
What challenges do California's cities face?

VOCABULARY
metropolitan area
commute
aquifer
smog
telecommuter

PLACES
Los Angeles
Mono Lake
Danville
San Mateo

EDGE CITIES

Take a drive down Interstate 10 in Los Angeles. Starting in Santa Monica, you will pass downtown Los Angeles and Monterey Park. After going more than 65 miles, you will have passed through about 16 different urban and suburban communities.

It was not always this way. Tom Nielsen grew up in Orange County. He remembers that back in the 1930s and 1940s this area was mostly rural.

It seemed that the three miles from Fullerton [to Anaheim] was a long distance. . . . Well, now you don't know where Fullerton or Anaheim or any place stops.

Where people work has changed as well. In the past most people who lived in the Los Angeles area would commute, or travel to their jobs, in Los Angeles. Since then, many businesses have moved to suburbs and rural areas.

These suburbs, explains writer Joel Garreau, are now cities themselves. He calls them "edge cities" because they grow up on the edge of bigger cities. In the Los Angeles area alone, there are 26 edge cities, including Irvine and Riverside.

San Francisco (opposite page) and Los Angeles (below) are two of California's cities.

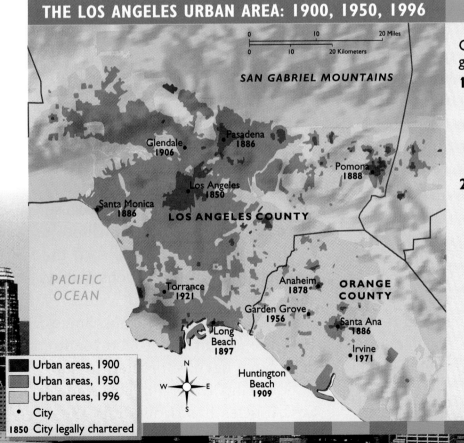

THE LOS ANGELES URBAN AREA: 1900, 1950, 1996

0   10   20 Miles
0   10   20 Kilometers

SAN GABRIEL MOUNTAINS

Glendale 1906
Pasadena 1886
Pomona 1888
Los Angeles 1850
Santa Monica 1886
LOS ANGELES COUNTY
PACIFIC OCEAN
Torrance 1921
Anaheim 1878
ORANGE COUNTY
Garden Grove 1956
Santa Ana 1886
Long Beach 1897
Irvine 1971
Huntington Beach 1909

N W E S

■ Urban areas, 1900
■ Urban areas, 1950
□ Urban areas, 1996
• City
1850 City legally chartered

MAP WORK

California's cities have grown a lot in the 1900s.

1. In 1950 would you have passed through any rural areas when driving between Glendale and Anaheim? What about today?

2. When did Irvine become a city?

365

Mono Lake (right) has started to recover from the low water levels of the past (below).

WATER AND AIR

The growth of California's cities has involved important trade-offs. For example, more people, more jobs, more factories, and more offices also mean more cars, more air pollution, less open space, and a greater demand for scarce natural resources, like water. Californians today are struggling to find a balance: how to allow for growth and change while making sure California remains a great place to live.

Thirsty Cities

California's cities use a lot of water. As you read in Chapter 9, cities like San Francisco and Los Angeles built long aqueducts to carry water. The state and federal governments built important water projects, too.

These water projects helped California grow. But they also damaged the environment. Pumping fresh water from the Sacramento Delta, for example, allowed salty water from the ocean to come in. The salty water killed birds and fish there.

Pumping from aquifers can be a source of water for thirsty cities like San Bernardino and Riverside. An aquifer is a layer of rock or gravel that traps water underground. But aquifers do not have enough water, and they take a long time to refill. Also, once the water is pumped out, the ground often sinks because there is no water to hold it up.

The story of Mono Lake, at the northern end of the Owens Valley, shows how complicated water issues can be in California. Since 1941 the streams that feed Mono Lake have been redirected to supply drinking water for Los Angeles. Los Angeles has grown into the second largest city in the country.

HOW AN AQUIFER WORKS

Aquifers supply water for California's cities and farms. How does water get from underground to the surface?

PUMP

GROUND

ROCK AND SOIL

UNDERGROUND STREAM

But Mono Lake has lost half its water, making it dangerous for fish and birds. A 1983 court case led to some improvements. Today the state government pays Los Angeles not to pump as much water. Mono Lake has begun to recover.

Conserving water is something you can do, and it is not that hard. A 1991 state law, for example, requires new toilets to use no more than 1.6 gallons of water in each flush.

Clean Air

Growing cities create another problem: dirty air. Highways are crowded with cars and trucks that pollute the air. Power plants that make electricity for homes also burn fuels. Burning fuel adds to smog. Smog is a mixture of smoke and fog.

Eight of the country's ten smoggiest cities are in California. Every year more than 28 million Californians breathe polluted air. This can lead to itchy eyes, sore throats, and breathing problems.

People created smog. Now we want to reduce it. What can we do? One thing is to change our cars. Since 1994 a new kind of catalytic converter—a special car part—has reduced the pollution our cars give out as they burn gas. A new kind of gasoline sold in California burns more cleanly, too. Some vehicles have different engines that do not run on gasoline. They have electric batteries or burn natural gas. These kinds of power do not contribute as much to smog.

The area around Los Angeles still has the most polluted air in the country. But the air is getting cleaner. Today there are about half as many smoggy days in Los Angeles as there were in 1980.

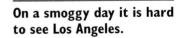

On a smoggy day it is hard to see Los Angeles.

CITIES GROWING

Commuters who work in cities face a challenge just getting to work. As metropolitan areas grow, some workers must travel greater distances to their jobs.

Cities have tried to create alternate forms of transportation. In the San Francisco Bay Area and in Los Angeles, large rapid-transit rail systems speed commuters past backed-up traffic. In the 1980s cities like Sacramento, San Diego, and San Jose built light-rail lines from outlying areas to their downtown business districts. These systems, however, can be very expensive to build and run. They cannot meet the transportation challenge alone.

New Approaches

One way people avoid the commuting problem is by working at home. Many people have home offices. They use their computers, telephones, and fax machines to communicate with their bosses and other workers. People who work at home are called telecommuters.

Kathie Blankenship is a telecommuter. She lives in the small town of Danville, east of Oakland. Blankenship is one of about 300,000 people who telecommute in the San Francisco Bay Area.

Blankenship's office in San Mateo is almost 40 miles away from her home. "On a good day, it takes an hour of commute time to get to work," she says. So, two days a week, she works at home. "It's a break for me," Blankenship explains. "I don't have to get in the car for two hours. It's a little easier to accept the other days that I do have to commute."

Blankenship feels that she gets more work done at home. "It gives me uninterrupted time," she explains. When she works at home, she can get up, turn on her computer, and be working almost right away.

She sees only one drawback to telecommuting. "Sometimes," she notes, "I wonder what's going on at the office. Every now and then, I have to pick up the phone and find out."

WHY IT MATTERS

Traffic. Pollution. Smog. Water shortages. Earthquakes. A changing economy. A growing population. You have read about many challenges California citizens face as they look to the future. You have also read about some of the things Californians are doing to try to meet some of these challenges.

Difficulties do not go away overnight. Our biggest problems take years of work to solve. Some never get solved. But people come up with ways to deal with them. By learning about California, you have taken the first step toward shaping its future.

✔️ **Reviewing Facts and Ideas**

MAIN IDEAS

- A metropolitan area is a city and the surrounding communities.
- Suburbs with their own business areas are called "edge cities."
- Air pollution, water scarcity, and long commutes are some of the problems California's cities face.

THINK ABOUT IT

1. What is a metropolitan area?

2. What is telecommuting?

3. **FOCUS** What are two big problems that California's cities face?

4. **THINKING SKILL** What *effect* does burning fuels have on the environment?

5. **GEOGRAPHY** Look at the map on page 365. In what years has Orange County grown the most?

Puddle Jumpers **by sculptor Glenna Goodacre is in San Francisco's Redwood Park.**

GEOGRAPHY SKILLS

Reading Road Maps

VOCABULARY

road map
interstate highway

WHY THE SKILL MATTERS

In the last lesson you read about commuting in California's cities. Some Californians take trains or trolleys to work. Others use buses. In San Francisco people can even ride a cable car. But most people continue to get to work by driving. In California that usually means taking the freeway. A freeway is a large road where cars can travel fast and people do not pay a toll.

How do all these people find out how to get where they are going? Many travelers use a road map. A road map is a map that shows people which roads to use to get from one place to another.

USING THE SKILL

Look at the road map of the San Diego area below. It shows some of the important places to visit in the San Diego area and the roads that connect these places.

The map shows several different kinds of roads. Look at the map key. As you can see, a green line tells you that the road is an interstate highway. An interstate highway connects two or more states. Usually these roads have at least two lanes in each direction, with traffic flowing both ways.

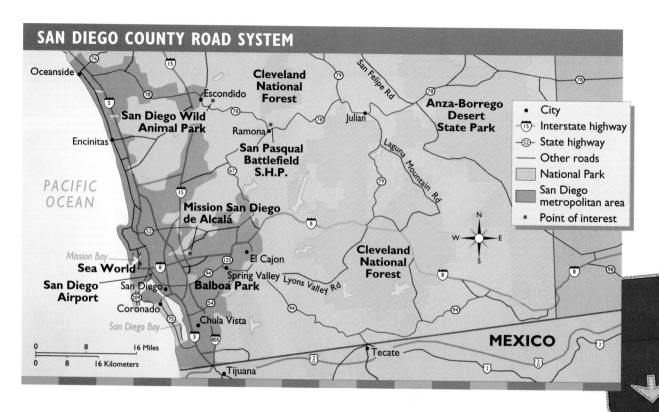

SAN DIEGO COUNTY ROAD SYSTEM

Oceanside
Escondido
Cleveland National Forest
San Felipe Rd
Anza-Borrego Desert State Park
San Diego Wild Animal Park
Ramona
Julian
Encinitas
San Pasqual Battlefield S.H.P.
PACIFIC OCEAN
Laguna Mountain Rd
Mission San Diego de Alcalá
Mission Bay
Sea World
El Cajon
Cleveland National Forest
San Diego Airport
San Diego
Spring Valley
Balboa Park
Lyons Valley Rd
Coronado
San Diego Bay
Chula Vista
MEXICO
Tecate
Tijuana

Key:
- City
- 15 Interstate highway
- 52 State highway
- Other roads
- National Park
- San Diego metropolitan area
- Point of interest

0   8   16 Miles
0   8   16 Kilometers

370

Look back at the map key. What kind of road does a red line stand for? A dotted black line?

You probably noticed that most roads on the map have numbers. The number of the road appears inside a special symbol. What is the number of the road that connects downtown San Diego to the Cleveland National Forest?

If you follow some roads with your finger, you will see that they have more than one number. That is because more than one road may share a certain route.

You may have noticed something else, too. Most even-numbered roads tend to run east and west. Odd-numbered roads usually run north and south. This fact can help drivers to know which way they are going.

HELPING Yourself

- **A road map** helps to guide travelers from one place to another.
- **Road maps show highways and other information needed by road travelers.**
- **Study the map key to identify the symbols and colors used on the map.**

TRYING THE SKILL

Suppose you lived in Julian and worked at Sea World. Which route would you take to get to work? What kinds of roads are on the route? How can you tell?

Suppose you lived in Chula Vista and were planning a trip to the San Diego Wild Animal Park near Escondido. Which route would be the most direct? What kinds of roads are on this route?

The road map on this page also shows parks, historic sites, and other features of interest in the San Diego area. How can you find a national park on this map?

REVIEWING THE SKILL

1. What does a road map show?
2. According to the map, which interstate highway runs east to west? What did you do to find the answer? Look at the road map again. What route would you take to visit Ramona if you started from Balboa Park in San Diego?
3. What kind of road is highway 5?
4. Why is it important to be able to read a road map?

CHAPTER 12 REVIEW

THINKING ABOUT VOCABULARY

Number a sheet of paper from 1 to 10. Beside each number write **C** if the underlined term is used correctly. If it is not, write the term that would correctly complete the sentence.

1. The <u>legislative branch</u> of government makes the laws.

2. An <u>edge city</u> is a large city and the communities close to it.

3. An <u>immigrant</u> is someone who flees unsafe conditions in his or her homeland.

4. <u>Public</u> colleges are partly supported by money from taxes paid by citizens.

5. A <u>resolution</u> is a statement about a decision made by an assembly.

6. A <u>service</u> job is one in which people help others instead of making things.

7. Someone who works at home and talks to fellow workers by phone is a <u>commuter</u>.

8. <u>Congress</u> is the legislative branch of our country's government.

9. <u>Smog</u> is a mixture of smoke and fog.

10. The <u>governor</u> is the head of city government.

THINKING ABOUT FACTS

1. Why are festivals important?

2. Name three reasons why immigrants come to California.

3. What does local government do?

4. When was the State Water Plan established? Why was it necessary?

5. What are the two parts of the state legislative branch? What do they do?

6. How many years is a term for the President of the United States?

7. How many branches of national government are there? Name them.

8. Name two visual artists from California.

9. What are some problems caused by the growth of California's cities?

10. How can smog be reduced?

THINK AND WRITE ◄▬▬▬▶

WRITING A PARAGRAPH

Write a paragraph about the ways in which immigrants help strengthen California.

WRITING A SUMMARY

Write a summary of the way California's state government works.

WRITING AN EXPLANATION

Explain what causes smog and what some of the things are that can be done to reduce it.

APPLYING STUDY SKILLS

READING NEWSPAPERS

1. What do newspapers provide?

2. What five questions should every news article answer?

3. In which section would you find an article about Congress passing a new law? Would it be in the front or back of the newspaper?

4. If an article is presenting an opinion about why this new law is a good idea, what type of article is it?

5. Why are newspapers important?

APPLYING GEOGRAPHY SKILLS

READING ROAD MAPS

Use the map at right to answer the following questions.

1. What does a road map show?

2. How does the map show which roads are interstate highways?

3. On which interstate highway can you travel from north to south?

4. Which roads would you take from Milpitas to the San Jose Arena?

5. Why is it important to be able to read road maps?

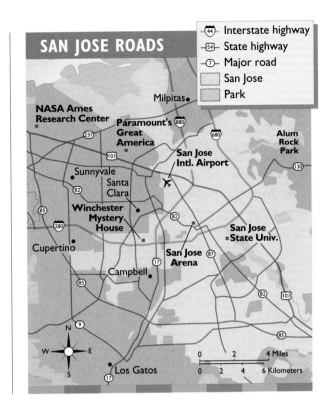

SAN JOSE ROADS

Interstate highway
State highway
Major road
San Jose
Park

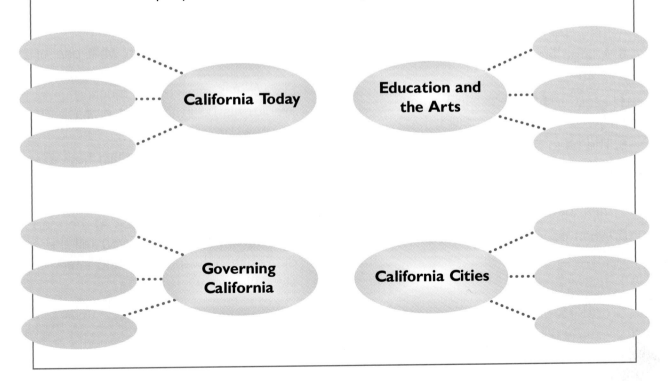

Summing Up the Chapter

Use the following spider map to organize information from the chapter. Write at least one piece of information in each blank circle. When you have filled in the map, use it to write a paragraph that answers the question "How do people make California the special place that it is?"

California Today

Education and the Arts

Governing California

California Cities

UNIT 5 REVIEW

THINKING ABOUT VOCABULARY

Number a sheet of paper from 1 to 10. Next to each number write the word or term from the list that best completes the sentence.

agribusiness   Pacific Rim
commute   refugee
Congress   resolution
economy   software
governor   Supreme Court

1. The set of instructions that tells a computer what to do is _____.

2. A _____ is a statement of a decision made by a legislature.

3. A _____ is someone who flees unsafe conditions in his or her homeland.

4. The _____ is the way a country or other place uses or produces natural resources, goods, and services.

5. The highest court in our country is the _____.

6. A large farm owned by a company is an _____.

7. _____ is the legislative branch of our country's government.

8. The head of the executive branch of state government is the _____.

9. The _____ is made up of the countries that touch the Pacific Ocean.

10. When people travel to jobs, they _____.

THINK AND WRITE

WRITING A PARAGRAPH
Write a paragraph explaining the ways in which citizens can be involved in government in a democratic republic.

WRITING A DESCRIPTION
Write a paragraph describing how the computer industry is important to California.

WRITING A SUMMARY
Write a summary of California's international trade with Pacific Rim countries. Describe why this trade is important to California and the rest of the United States.

BUILDING SKILLS

1. **Fact and opinion** Find one fact and one opinion in Unit 5.

2. **Fact and opinion** What are some word clues that tell you a writer is expressing an opinion?

3. **Reading newspapers** In what part of the newspaper would you find an article about a city council meeting? Would this be in the front or back of the newspaper?

4. **Reading road maps** Explain how a road map is different from an elevation map.

5. **Reading road maps** Look at the map on page 370. How can you tell the difference between state and interstate highways?

YESTERDAY, TODAY &
TOMORROW

In this unit you have read about the birth of computers. Today computers are everywhere. People at home, at school, and in business use them. How do you think computers might be used in the future?

READING ON YOUR OWN

Here are some books you might find at the library to help you learn more.

THE CITY BY THE BAY—A MAGICAL JOURNEY AROUND SAN FRANCISCO
by Tricia Brown
A fun guide to the history and famous sites of San Francisco.

STEVE WOZNIAK, INVENTOR OF THE APPLE COMPUTER
by Martha E. Kendall
The story of Steve Wozniak, the engineer who created the Apple PC.

HOANG ANH: A VIETNAMESE AMERICAN BOY
by Diane Hoyt-Goldsmith
The daily life of a young immigrant to California.

UNIT REVIEW PROJECT

Making a California Scrapbook

1. Work with a partner and brainstorm all of the ways California is a special place, from its people to industries, trade, government, and fun activities to do. List these on a sheet of paper.
2. Then work together to create a scrapbook about California using this information. Think about how you might show each item. You might cut out pictures from a magazine or newspaper or make pictures using markers, crayons, or colored pencils. You might also include a description of each item.

3. Write a heading for each of your illustrations, such as "California's People," "California's Trade," or "Fun Activities to Do in California."
4. Make a cover and create a title for your scrapbook. Then compile all of your pages and staple them into a book.
5. Share your scrapbook with classmates.

REFERENCE SECTION

The Reference Section has many parts,
each with a different type of information.
Use this section to look up people,
places, and events as you study.

CALIFORNIA HISTORY

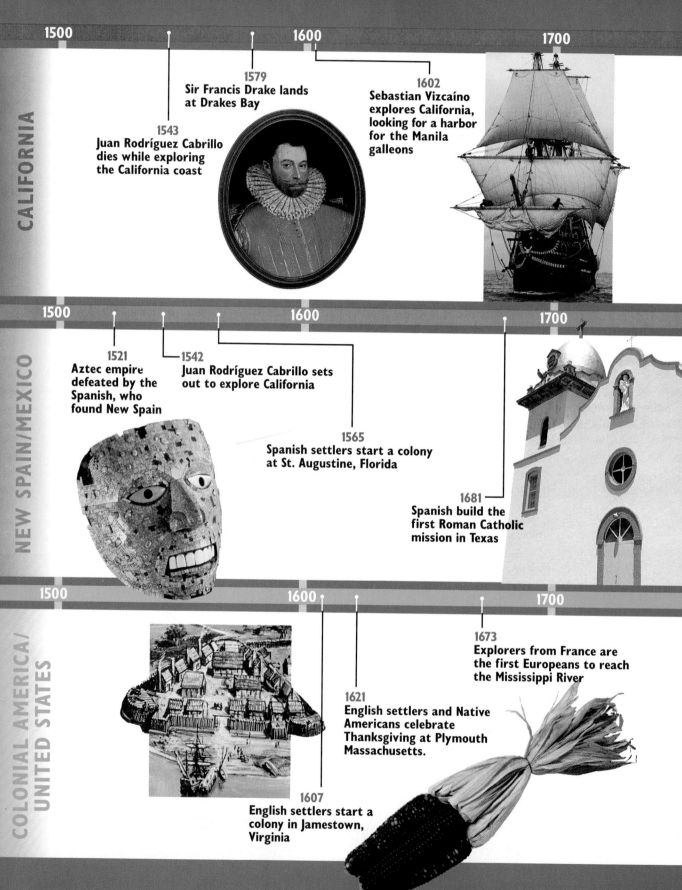

CALIFORNIA

1500   1600   1700

1579
Sir Francis Drake lands at Drakes Bay

1543
Juan Rodríguez Cabrillo dies while exploring the California coast

1602
Sebastian Vizcaíno explores California, looking for a harbor for the Manila galleons

NEW SPAIN/MEXICO

1500   1600   1700

1521
Aztec empire defeated by the Spanish, who found New Spain

1542
Juan Rodríguez Cabrillo sets out to explore California

1565
Spanish settlers start a colony at St. Augustine, Florida

1681
Spanish build the first Roman Catholic mission in Texas

COLONIAL AMERICA/ UNITED STATES

1500   1600   1700

1673
Explorers from France are the first Europeans to reach the Mississippi River

1621
English settlers and Native Americans celebrate Thanksgiving at Plymouth Massachusetts.

1607
English settlers start a colony in Jamestown, Virginia

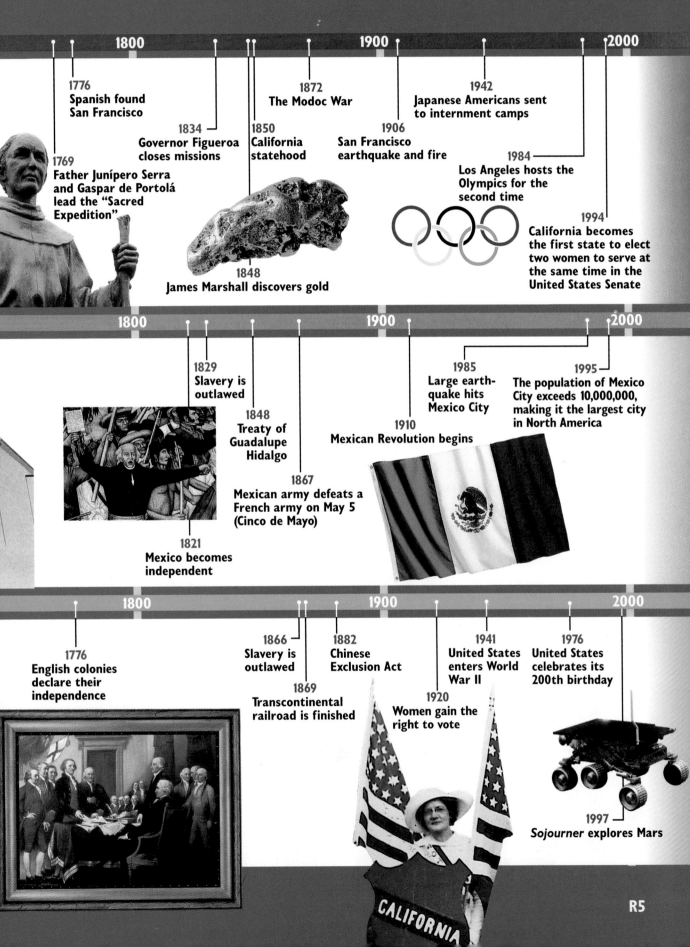

TIME LINE 1500 TO 2000

1800 | **1900** | **2000**

1776
Spanish found
San Francisco

1769
Father Junípero Serra
and Gaspar de Portolá
lead the "Sacred
Expedition"

1834
Governor Figueroa
closes missions

1850
California
statehood

1872
The Modoc War

1848
James Marshall discovers gold

1906
San Francisco
earthquake and fire

1942
Japanese Americans sent
to internment camps

1984
Los Angeles hosts the
Olympics for the
second time

1994
California becomes
the first state to elect
two women to serve at
the same time in the
United States Senate

1800 | **1900** | **2000**

1829
Slavery is
outlawed

1848
Treaty of
Guadalupe
Hidalgo

1867
Mexican army defeats a
French army on May 5
(Cinco de Mayo)

1821
Mexico becomes
independent

1910
Mexican Revolution begins

1985
Large earth-
quake hits
Mexico City

1995
The population of Mexico
City exceeds 10,000,000,
making it the largest city
in North America

1800 | **1900** | **2000**

1776
English colonies
declare their
independence

1866
Slavery is
outlawed

1869
Transcontinental
railroad is finished

1882
Chinese
Exclusion Act

1920
Women gain the
right to vote

1941
United States
enters World
War II

1976
United States
celebrates its
200th birthday

1997
Sojourner explores Mars

OUR FIFTY STATES

ALABAMA
★
Montgomery

DATE OF STATEHOOD 1819

NICKNAME Heart of Dixie

POPULATION 4,273,084

AREA 52,423 sq mi;
135,776 sq km

REGION Southeast

CONNECTICUT
★ Hartford

DATE OF STATEHOOD 1788

NICKNAME Constitution State

POPULATION 3,274,238

AREA 5,544 sq mi;
14,359 sq km

REGION Northeast

ALASKA

Juneau ★

DATE OF STATEHOOD 1959

NICKNAME The Last Frontier

POPULATION 607,007

AREA 656,424 sq mi;
1,700,138 sq km

REGION West

★
Dover

DELAWARE

DATE OF STATEHOOD 1787

NICKNAME First State

POPULATION 724,842

AREA 2,489 sq mi;
6,447 sq km

REGION Northeast

ARIZONA
★
Phoenix

DATE OF STATEHOOD 1912

NICKNAME Grand Canyon State

POPULATION 4,428,088

AREA 114,006 sq mi;
295,276 sq km

REGION Southwest

★
Tallahassee

FLORIDA

DATE OF STATEHOOD 1845

NICKNAME Sunshine State

POPULATION 14,399,985

AREA 65,758 sq mi;
170,313 sq km

REGION Southeast

ARKANSAS
★
Little Rock

DATE OF STATEHOOD 1836

NICKNAME Land of Opportunity

POPULATION 2,509,793

AREA 53,182 sq mi;
137,741 sq km

REGION Southeast

★
Atlanta

GEORGIA

DATE OF STATEHOOD 1788

NICKNAME Peach State

POPULATION 7,353,225

AREA 59,441 sq mi;
153,952 sq km

REGION Southeast

CALIFORNIA
★
Sacramento

DATE OF STATEHOOD 1850

NICKNAME Golden State

POPULATION 31,878,234

AREA 163,707 sq mi;
424,001 sq km

REGION West

CALIFORNIA REPUBLIC

HAWAII

★
Honolulu

DATE OF STATEHOOD 1959

NICKNAME The Aloha State

POPULATION 1,183,723

AREA 10,932 sq mi;
28,314 sq km

REGION West

Denver ★

COLORADO

DATE OF STATEHOOD 1876

NICKNAME Centennial State

POPULATION 3,822,676

AREA 104,100 sq mi;
269,619 sq km

REGION West

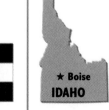
★ Boise
IDAHO

DATE OF STATEHOOD 1890

NICKNAME Gem State

POPULATION 1,189,251

AREA 83,574 sq mi;
216,457 sq km

REGION West

ILLINOIS
★
Springfield

DATE OF STATEHOOD 1818

NICKNAME **The Prairie State**

POPULATION **11,846,544**

AREA **57,918 sq mi;
150,008 sq km**

REGION **Middle West**

MAINE
Augusta
★

DATE OF STATEHOOD 1820

NICKNAME **Pine Tree State**

POPULATION **1,243,316**

AREA **35,387 sq mi;
91,652 sq km**

REGION **Northeast**

INDIANA
★
Indianapolis

DATE OF STATEHOOD 1816

NICKNAME **Hoosier State**

POPULATION **5,840,528**

AREA **36,420 sq mi;
94,328 sq km**

REGION **Middle West**

MARYLAND
Annapolis ★

DATE OF STATEHOOD 1788

NICKNAME **Free State**

POPULATION **5,071,604**

AREA **12,407 sq mi;
32,134 sq km**

REGION **Northeast**

IOWA
★
Des Moines

DATE OF STATEHOOD 1846

NICKNAME **Hawkeye State**

POPULATION **2,851,792**

AREA **56,276 sq mi;
145,755 sq km**

REGION **Middle West**

Boston ★

MASSACHUSETTS

DATE OF STATEHOOD 1788

NICKNAME **Bay State**

POPULATION **6,092,352**

AREA **10,555 sq mi;
27,337 sq km**

REGION **Northeast**

Topeka ★

KANSAS

DATE OF STATEHOOD 1861

NICKNAME **Sunflower State**

POPULATION **2,572,150**

AREA **82,282 sq mi;
213,110 sq km**

REGION **Middle West**

MICHIGAN

★
Lansing

DATE OF STATEHOOD 1837

NICKNAME **Wolverine State**

POPULATION **9,594,350**

AREA **96,810 sq mi;
250,738 sq km**

REGION **Middle West**

KENTUCKY
★
Frankfort

DATE OF STATEHOOD 1792

NICKNAME **Bluegrass State**

POPULATION **3,883,723**

AREA **40,411 sq mi;
104,664 sq km**

REGION **Southeast**

MINNESOTA

St. Paul ★

DATE OF STATEHOOD 1858

NICKNAME **North Star State**

POPULATION **4,657,758**

AREA **86,943 sq mi;
225,182 sq km**

REGION **Middle West**

LOUISIANA

Baton Rouge ★

DATE OF STATEHOOD 1812

NICKNAME **Pelican State**

POPULATION **4,350,579**

AREA **51,843 sq mi;
134,273 sq km**

REGION **Southeast**

MISSISSIPPI

★
Jackson

DATE OF STATEHOOD 1817

NICKNAME **Magnolia State**

POPULATION **2,716,115**

AREA **48,434 sq mi;
125,444 sq km**

REGION **Southeast**

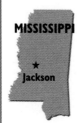

OUR FIFTY STATES

★ Jefferson City
MISSOURI

DATE OF STATEHOOD 1821

NICKNAME Show Me State

POPULATION 5,358,692

AREA 69,709 sq mi;
180,546 sq km

REGION Middle West

MONTANA
★ Helena

DATE OF STATEHOOD 1889

NICKNAME Treasure State

POPULATION 879,372

AREA 147,046 sq mi;
380,849 sq km

REGION West

NEBRASKA

Lincoln ★

DATE OF STATEHOOD 1867

NICKNAME Cornhusker State

POPULATION 1,652,093

AREA 77,358 sq mi;
200,357 sq km

REGION Middle West

NEVADA

★ Carson City

DATE OF STATEHOOD 1864

NICKNAME Silver State

POPULATION 1,603,163

AREA 110,567 sq mi;
286,369 sq km

REGION West

NEW HAMPSHIRE

Concord
★

DATE OF STATEHOOD 1788

NICKNAME Granite State

POPULATION 1,162,481

AREA 9,351 sq mi;
24,219 sq km

REGION Northeast

NEW JERSEY

★
Trenton

DATE OF STATEHOOD 1787

NICKNAME Garden State

POPULATION 7,987,933

AREA 8,722 sq mi;
22,590 sq km

REGION Northeast

★
Santa Fe

NEW MEXICO

DATE OF STATEHOOD 1912

NICKNAME Land of Enchantment

POPULATION 1,713,407

AREA 121,598 sq mi;
314,939 sq km

REGION Southwest

NEW YORK
Albany ★

DATE OF STATEHOOD 1788

NICKNAME Empire State

POPULATION 18,184,774

AREA 54,475 sq mi;
141,090 sq km

REGION Northeast

NORTH CAROLINA

Raleigh ★

DATE OF STATEHOOD 1789

NICKNAME Tar Heel State

POPULATION 7,322,870

AREA 53,821 sq mi;
139,396 sq km

REGION Southeast

NORTH DAKOTA

Bismarck
★

DATE OF STATEHOOD 1889

NICKNAME Peace Garden State

POPULATION 643,539

AREA 70,704 sq mi;
183,123 sq km

REGION Middle West

OHIO
★
Columbus

DATE OF STATEHOOD 1803

NICKNAME Buckeye State

POPULATION 11,172,782

AREA 44,828 sq mi;
116,105 sq km

REGION Middle West

OKLAHOMA

★
Oklahoma City

DATE OF STATEHOOD 1907

NICKNAME Sooner State

POPULATION 3,300,902

AREA 69,903 sq mi;
181,049 sq km

REGION Southwest

★ Salem

OREGON

DATE OF STATEHOOD 1859

NICKNAME Beaver State

POPULATION 3,203,735

AREA 98,386 sq mi;
254,820 sq km

REGION West

PENNSYLVANIA
Harrisburg ★

DATE OF STATEHOOD 1787

NICKNAME Keystone State

POPULATION 12,056,112

AREA 46,058 sq mi; 119,290 sq km

REGION Northeast

RHODE ISLAND
Providence ★

DATE OF STATEHOOD 1790

NICKNAME Ocean State

POPULATION 990,225

AREA 1,545 sq mi; 4,002 sq km

REGION Northeast

SOUTH CAROLINA
★ Columbia

DATE OF STATEHOOD 1788

NICKNAME Palmetto State

POPULATION 3,698,746

AREA 32,007 sq mi; 82,898 sq km

REGION Southeast

SOUTH DAKOTA
Pierre ★

DATE OF STATEHOOD 1889

NICKNAME Mount Rushmore State

POPULATION 732,405

AREA 77,121 sq mi; 199,743 sq km

REGION Middle West

TENNESSEE
★Nashville

DATE OF STATEHOOD 1796

NICKNAME Volunteer State

POPULATION 5,319,654

AREA 42,146 sq mi; 109,158 sq km

REGION Southeast

TEXAS
Austin ★

DATE OF STATEHOOD 1845

NICKNAME Lone Star State

POPULATION 19,128,261

AREA 268,601 sq mi; 695,677 sq km

REGION Southwest

UTAH
Salt Lake City ★

DATE OF STATEHOOD 1896

NICKNAME Beehive State

POPULATION 2,000,494

AREA 84,904 sq mi; 219,901 sq km

REGION West

VERMONT
★ Montpelier

DATE OF STATEHOOD 1791

NICKNAME Green Mountain State

POPULATION 588,654

AREA 9,615 sq mi; 24,903 sq km

REGION Northeast

VIRGINIA
Richmond ★

DATE OF STATEHOOD 1788

NICKNAME Old Dominion

POPULATION 6,675,451

AREA 42,769 sq mi; 110,772 sq km

REGION Southeast

WASHINGTON
★ Olympia

DATE OF STATEHOOD 1889

NICKNAME Evergreen State

POPULATION 5,532,939

AREA 71,303 sq mi; 184,675 sq km

REGION West

WEST VIRGINIA
★ Charleston

DATE OF STATEHOOD 1863

NICKNAME Mountain State

POPULATION 1,825,754

AREA 24,231 sq mi; 62,758 sq km

REGION Southeast

WISCONSIN
Madison ★

DATE OF STATEHOOD 1848

NICKNAME Badger State

POPULATION 5,159,795

AREA 65,503 sq mi; 169,653 sq km

REGION Middle West

WYOMING
Cheyenne ★

DATE OF STATEHOOD 1890

NICKNAME Equality State

POPULATION 481,400

AREA 97,818 sq mi; 253,349 sq km

REGION West

Sources: population—U.S. Bureau of Census; area—U.S. Bureau of Census, 1991; capital—*World Almanac*, 1995.

Central America and West Indies

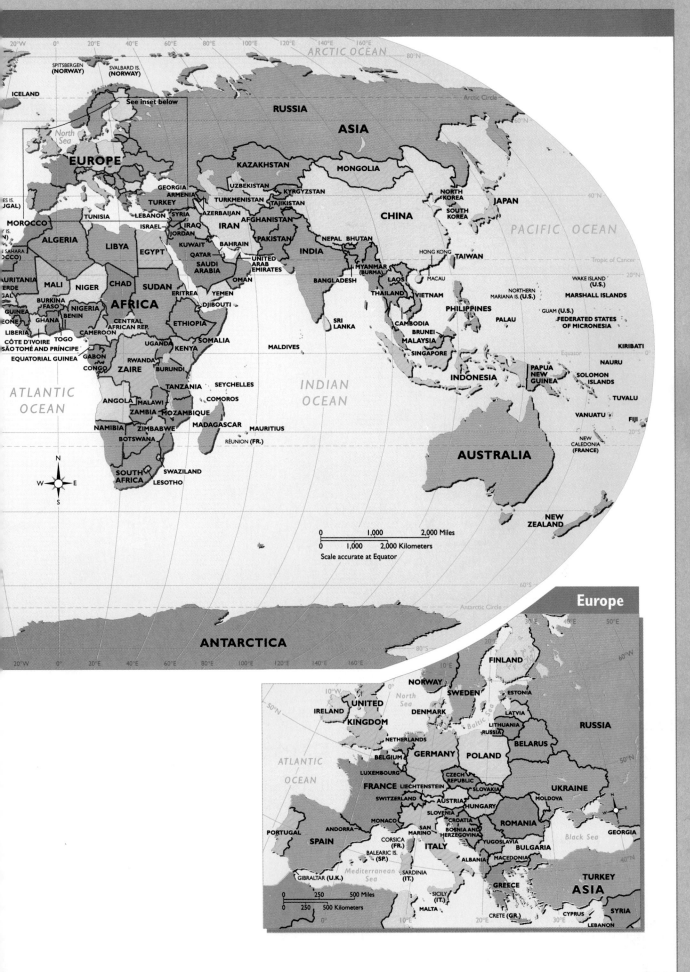

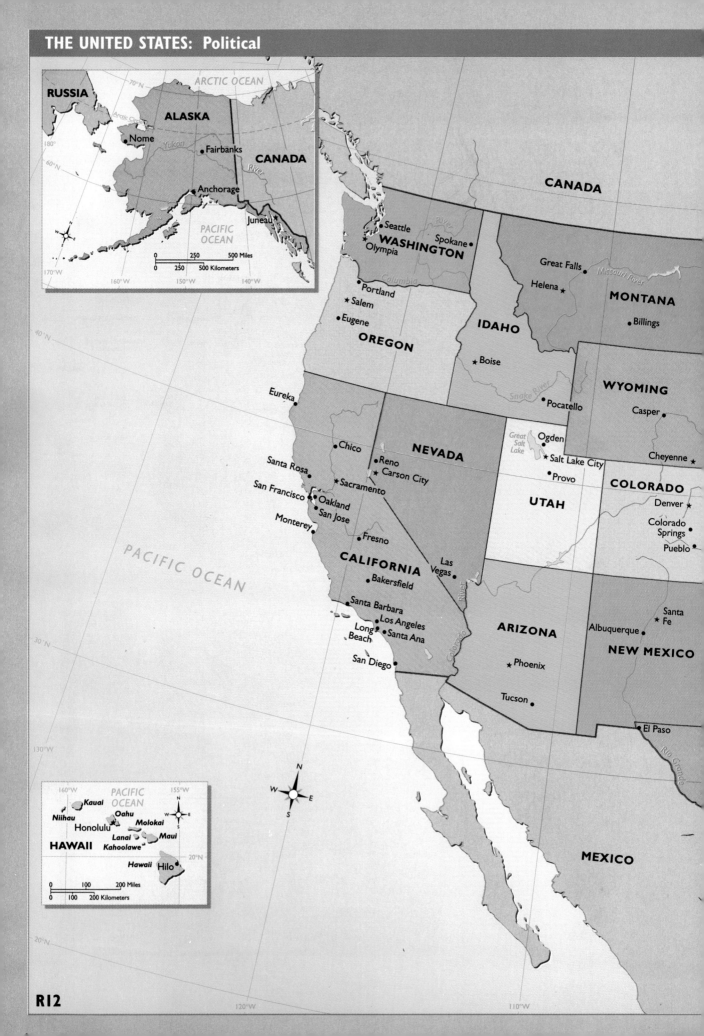

ARCTIC OCEAN

RUSSIA

ALASKA

Nome

Fairbanks

CANADA

Yukon

River

Anchorage

Juneau

PACIFIC
OCEAN

0   250   500 Miles
0   250   500 Kilometers

CANADA

Seattle

WASHINGTON   Spokane

Olympia

Great Falls   Missouri River

Helena

MONTANA

Billings

Portland

Columbia

Salem

Eugene

OREGON

IDAHO

Boise

Snake River

Pocatello

WYOMING

Casper

Eureka

Chico

NEVADA

Great
Salt
Lake

Ogden

Salt Lake City

Cheyenne

Santa Rosa

Reno

Carson City

Provo

COLORADO

San Francisco

Sacramento

Oakland

San Jose

UTAH

Denver

Colorado
Springs

Monterey

Fresno

Pueblo

PACIFIC OCEAN

CALIFORNIA

Las
Vegas

Bakersfield

River

Santa Barbara

Los Angeles

Long   Santa Ana

Beach

ARIZONA

Colorado

Santa
Fe

Albuquerque

NEW MEXICO

San Diego

Phoenix

Tucson

El Paso

Rio Grande

PACIFIC
OCEAN

Kauai

Niihau

Oahu   Molokai

Honolulu

Lanai   Maui

Kahoolawe

HAWAII

Hawaii   Hilo

0   100   200 Miles
0   100   200 Kilometers

MEXICO

N

W   E

S

CANADA

NORTH DAKOTA
• Grand Forks
★ Bismarck Fargo

SOUTH DAKOTA
★ Pierre
• Sioux Falls

NEBRASKA
• Lincoln

MINNESOTA
• Duluth
• Minneapolis ★ St. Paul

Lake Superior

WISCONSIN
• Green Bay
★ Madison • Milwaukee

MICHIGAN
Lake Michigan
• Grand Rapids ★ Lansing
• Detroit

Lake Huron

Lake Ontario

NEW YORK
• Buffalo ★ Albany

MAINE
★ Augusta

• Burlington **VERMONT** • Montpelier **NEW HAMPSHIRE** • Portland
★ Concord

MASSACHUSETTS ★ Boston
Hartford ★ • Providence
CONNECTICUT **RHODE ISLAND**

IOWA
• Cedar Rapids • Rockford
• Davenport ★ Des Moines
• Omaha

ILLINOIS
• Chicago • Gary
• Peoria
★ Springfield

INDIANA
• Fort Wayne
★ Indianapolis
• Evansville

OHIO
• Toledo • Cleveland
★ Columbus
• Cincinnati

• Wheeling

PENNSYLVANIA
• Pittsburgh ★ Harrisburg
Newark • • New York
NEW JERSEY
★ Trenton
• Philadelphia
★ Dover
• Baltimore **DELAWARE**
★ Annapolis
MARYLAND
Washington, D.C.

MISSOURI
Kansas City •
★ Jefferson City
• St. Louis

KANSAS
Kansas City •
★ Topeka
• Wichita

Missouri River
Platte River

KENTUCKY
• Louisville
★ Frankfort

WEST VIRGINIA
★ Charleston

VIRGINIA
★ Richmond
• Norfolk

70°N

Ohio

TENNESSEE
★ Nashville • Knoxville
• Memphis

NORTH CAROLINA
★ Raleigh
• Charlotte

ARKANSAS
• Fort Smith
★ Little Rock

OKLAHOMA
• Tulsa
★ Oklahoma City

Arkansas River
Red River

SOUTH CAROLINA
★ Columbia
• Charleston

ATLANTIC OCEAN

MISSISSIPPI
• Birmingham
★ Jackson

ALABAMA
★ Montgomery

GEORGIA
★ Atlanta
• Columbus
• Savannah

TEXAS
• Fort Worth • Dallas
★ Austin
• Houston
• San Antonio
• Laredo • Corpus Christi

LOUISIANA
• Shreveport
★ Baton Rouge
• New Orleans

• Biloxi • Mobile

★ Tallahassee • Jacksonville

FLORIDA
• Tampa
• Miami

Gulf of Mexico

30°N

THE BAHAMAS

CUBA

⊛ National capital   ★ State capital   • Other city

0   150   300 Miles
0   150   300 Kilometers

100°W   90°W   80°W   **R13**

RUSSIA

ARCTIC OCEAN

70°N

BROOKS RANGE
ALASKA
60°N
ALASKA RANGE
▲ Mt. McKinley
20,320 ft.
(6,194 m)

Bering
Sea

CANADA

Yukon River

170°W
160°W
150°W
140°W

0   250   500 Miles
0   250   500 Kilometers

CANADA

Missouri River

Puget Sound

Mt. Rainier
14,410 ft.
(4,391 m)
▲ Mt. St. Helens
8,366 ft.
(2,550 m)

CASCADE RANGE

COAST RANGES

Columbia River

▲ Mt. Hood
11,235 ft.
(3,424 m)

COLUMBIA PLATEAU

Snake River

ROCKY MOUNTAINS

Yellowstone River

▲ Granite Peak
12,799 ft.
(3,900 m)

BLACK HILLS

TETON RANGE

40°N
130°W

Cape Mendocino

▲ Mt. Shasta
14,162 ft.
(4,316 m)

GREAT BASIN

Great Salt Lake

GREAT SALT LAKE DESERT

WASATCH RANGE

▲ Kings Peak
13,528 ft.
(4,123 m)

GREAT
PLAI

COAST RANGES

Sacramento River

SIERRA NEVADA

CENTRAL VALLEY

Lake Tahoe

San Francisco Bay

Monterey Bay

San Joaquin River

▲ Mt. Whitney
14,491 ft.
(4,418 m)

DEATH VALLEY

MOJAVE DESERT

PACIFIC OCEAN

Lake Mead

Colorado River

River

▲ Mt. Elbert
14,433 ft.
(4,398 m)

Pikes Peak
▲ 14,107 ft.
(4,301 m)

COLORADO PLATEAU

Wheeler Peak
13,065 ft.
(3,982 m)

▲ Humphreys Peak
12,633 ft.
(3,850 m)

Channel Islands

Solton Sea

SONORA DESERT

Gila River

30°N

Pecos River

Guadalupe Peak
8,751 ft.
(2,667 m)

Rio Grande

EDWAR
PLATE

PACIFIC OCEAN

160°W

Kauai

Oahu

155°W

Maui

HAWAII

Hawaii
▲ Mauna Kea
13,796 ft.
(4,205 m)

20°N

0   100   200 Miles
0   100   200 Kilometers

120°W

110°W

Gulf of California

MEXICO

CANADA

Lake of
the Woods

Lake Superior

GREAT

LAKES

MESABI RANGE

St. Lawrence River

WHITE MTS.

GREEN MTS.

▲ Mt. Washington
6,288 ft.
(1,917 m)

ADIRONDACK
MTS.

Lake Ontario

Hudson River

Cape Cod

Long Island

Lake Huron

Lake Michigan

CENTRAL PLAINS

River

Mississippi

Lake Erie

ALLEGHENY
PLATEAU

APPALACHIAN MOUNTAINS

Susquehanna
River

40° N

Delaware Bay

70° W

Platte River

Missouri

River

River

Wabash
River

Ohio

River

ALLEGHENY MOUNTAINS

Potomac
River

Chesapeake Bay

ATLANTIC COASTAL PLAIN

Cape Hatteras

Arkansas

River

INTERIOR

PLAINS

OZARK
PLATEAU

River

Tennessee

▲ Mt. Mitchell
6,684 ft.
(2,037 m)

PIEDMONT

OUACHITA
MOUNTAINS

Red

River

Mississippi
River

River

Savannah River

ATLANTIC OCEAN

Brazos

River

Alabama

River

Chattahoochee

River

30° N

Colorado River

GULF COASTAL PLAIN

Mobile Bay

Mississippi Delta

Galveston Bay

Gulf of Mexico

Lake
Okeechobee

Bahama Islands

N
W   E
S

150   300 Miles

150   300 Kilometers

Florida Keys

Straits of Florida

80° W

90° W

CUBA

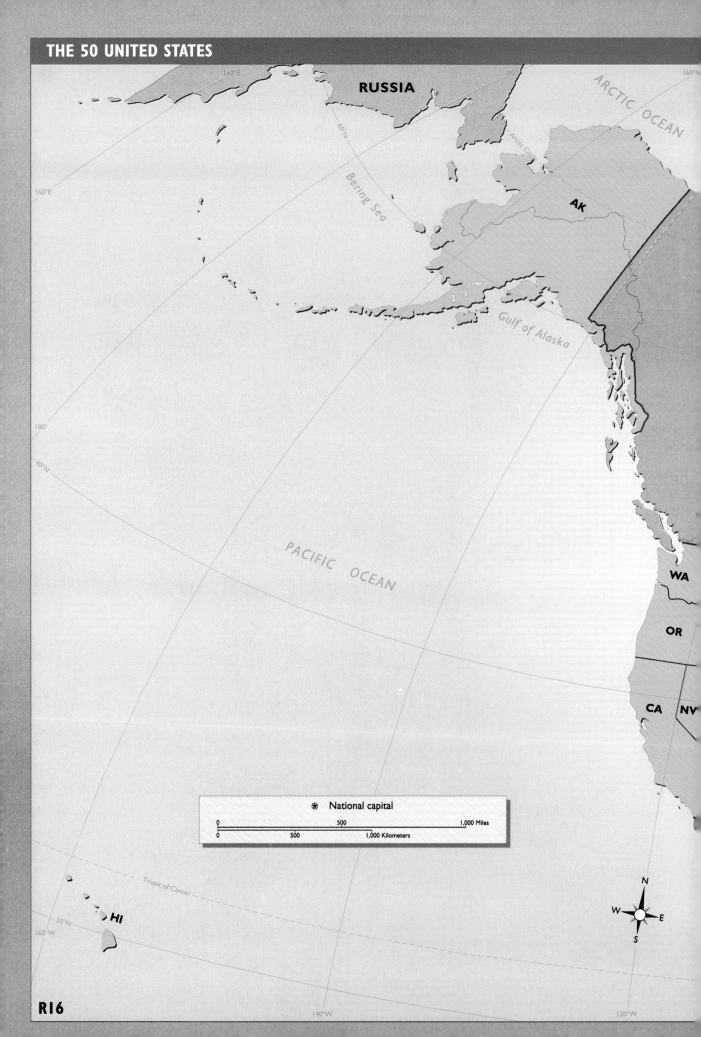

RUSSIA

ARCTIC OCEAN

AK

Bering Sea

Gulf of Alaska

PACIFIC OCEAN

WA

OR

CA   NV

⊛   National capital

| 0 | 500 | 1,000 Miles |
| 0 | 500 | 1,000 Kilometers |

Tropic of Cancer

HI

N
W   E
S

Greenland
(DENMARK)

CANADA

Hudson Bay

Great Lakes

MT
ND
MN
MI
ID
WI
MI
ME
SD
VT
WY
NY
NH
NE
IA
MA
CT
PA
RI
UT
IL
OH
NJ
CO
KS
IN
Washington, D.C.
MO
WV
MD — DE
AZ
NM
KY
VA
OK
AR
TN
NC
MS
AL
GA
SC
LA
TX
FL

UT

ATLANTIC OCEAN

Gulf of Mexico

MEXICO

CUBA

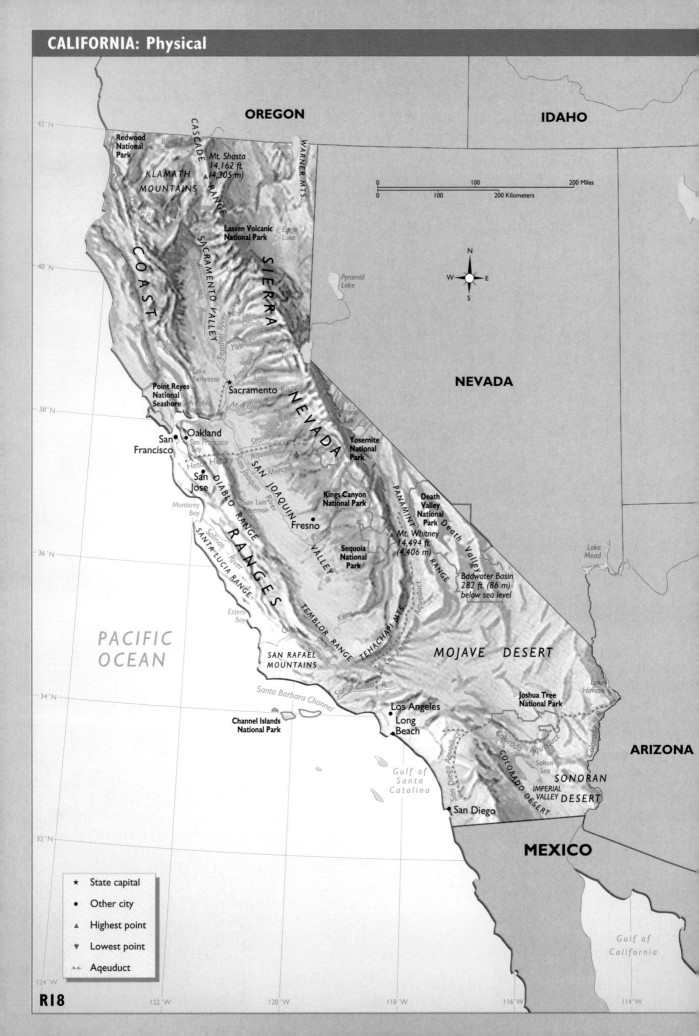

CALIFORNIA: Physical

OREGON

IDAHO

NEVADA

ARIZONA

MEXICO

PACIFIC OCEAN

Redwood National Park

KLAMATH MOUNTAINS

CASCADE RANGE

Mt. Shasta 14,162 ft. (4,305 m)

WARNER MTS.

Goose Lake

Lassen Volcanic National Park

Eagle Lake

Pyramid Lake

COAST

SACRAMENTO VALLEY

SIERRA

Feather River

Yuba River

American River

Lake Oroville

Lake Tahoe

Sacramento River

Lake Berryessa

Point Reyes National Seashore

Mokelumne

Mono Lake

★ Sacramento

San Pablo Bay

● Oakland

San Francisco

San Francisco Bay

Hetch Hetchy

Stanislaus R.

Yosemite National Park

NEVADA

● San Jose

DIABLO RANGE

San Joaquin River

Aqueduct

Merced

San Joaquin

Kings Canyon National Park

PANAMINT RANGE

Death Valley National Park

Death Valley

Monterey Bay

San Luis Reservoir

● Fresno

Kings

VALLEY

Sequoia National Park

Mt. Whitney 14,494 ft. (4,406 m)

Badwater Basin 282 ft (86 m) below sea level

Lake Mead

SANTA LUCIA RANGE

Salinas River

SAN JOAQUIN

Kern

Aqueduct

Estero Bay

TEMBLOR RANGE

Cuyama River

Kern

TEHACHAPI MTS.

Los Angeles

MOJAVE DESERT

Lake Havasu

San Rafael Mountains

Santa Barbara Channel

Santa Clara R.

Joshua Tree National Park

Colorado Aqueduct

Colorado R.

Channel Islands National Park

● Los Angeles

● Long Beach

Los Angeles Aqueduct

San Diego Aqueduct

Colorado Aqueduct

Salton Sea

SONORAN DESERT

Gulf of Santa Catalina

COLORADO DESERT

IMPERIAL VALLEY

● San Diego

Gulf of California

Legend:

- ★ State capital
- ● Other city
- ▲ Highest point
- ▼ Lowest point
- ⋯ Aqueduct

Scale:
0 — 100 — 200 Miles
0 — 100 — 200 Kilometers

42°N
40°N
38°N
36°N
34°N
32°N

124°W 122°W 120°W 118°W 116°W 114°W

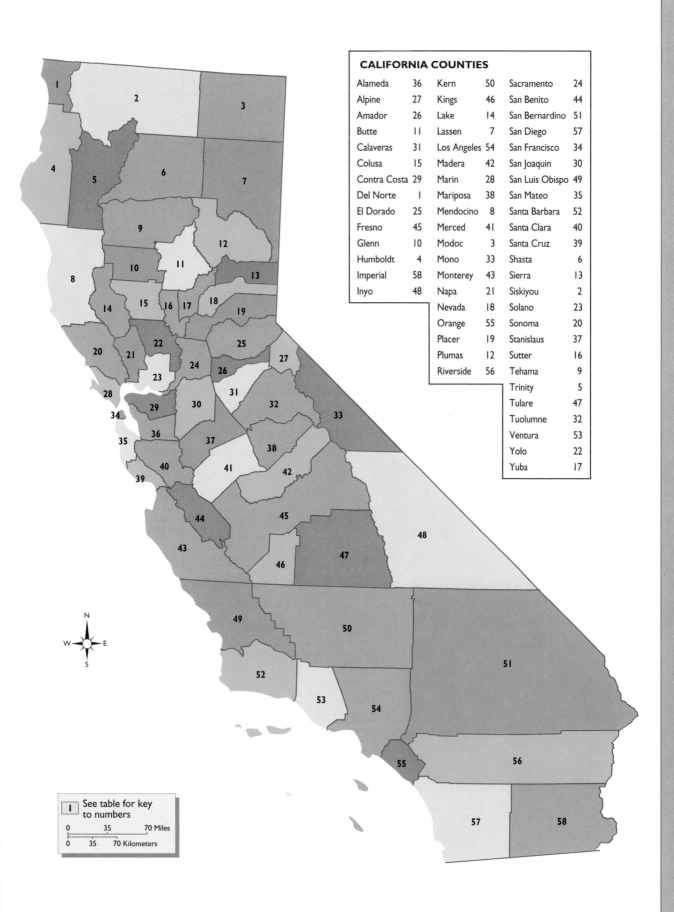

CALIFORNIA COUNTIES

Alameda	36	Kern	50	Sacramento	24
Alpine	27	Kings	46	San Benito	44
Amador	26	Lake	14	San Bernardino	51
Butte	11	Lassen	7	San Diego	57
Calaveras	31	Los Angeles	54	San Francisco	34
Colusa	15	Madera	42	San Joaquin	30
Contra Costa	29	Marin	28	San Luis Obispo	49
Del Norte	1	Mariposa	38	San Mateo	35
El Dorado	25	Mendocino	8	Santa Barbara	52
Fresno	45	Merced	41	Santa Clara	40
Glenn	10	Modoc	3	Santa Cruz	39
Humboldt	4	Mono	33	Shasta	6
Imperial	58	Monterey	43	Sierra	13
Inyo	48	Napa	21	Siskiyou	2
		Nevada	18	Solano	23
		Orange	55	Sonoma	20
		Placer	19	Stanislaus	37
		Plumas	12	Sutter	16
		Riverside	56	Tehama	9
				Trinity	5
				Tulare	47
				Tuolumne	32
				Ventura	53
				Yolo	22
				Yuba	17

N
W E
S

1 See table for key to numbers

0   35   70 Miles

0   35   70 Kilometers

Map Builder

CALIFORNIA: LAND USE

The map on the facing page is a special kind of map. Each transparent overlay shows a particular use of land in our state. You can build a map that gives you a larger picture of land use in California. Start by lifting all the transparent overlays to see the base map. The base map shows the land and water of our state. Now cover the base map with the first overlay and see where in California the land is covered mostly with forests. Bring the second overlay down to see where the land is covered mostly with grazing land and cropland. When you bring the third overlay down to cover the rest, you will see major urban areas in our state. Compare the locations and amounts of land used for growing crops and for urban development. Which kind of land use is shown for the area where you live?

OREGON

IDAHO

Goose Lake

KLAMATH

MODOC PLATEAU

MTS.

CASCADE RANGE

Klamath R.

Pit River

Shasta Lake

COAST

Sacramento River

SIERRA

SACRAMENTO

RANGES

VALLEY

Russian River

Honey Lake

NEVADA

San Francisco Bay

SAN

JOAQUIN

San Luis Reservoir

San Joaquin River

Mono Lake

Owens River

SAN

ANDREAS

VALLEY

Monterey Bay

Salinas River

COAST

CALIFORNIA

Mt. Whitney
14,494 ft.
(4418 m)

DEATH VALLEY

Owens Lake

SANTA

LUCIA

RANGES

Badwater
282 ft. (86 m)
below sea level

RANG

FAULT

TEHACHAPI MTS

MOJAVE DESERT

PACIFIC OCEAN

SAN GABRIEL MTS

SAN BERNARDINO MTS.

anta Barbara Channel

Channel

Salton Sea

Islands

IMPERIAL VALLEY

ARIZONA

UTAH

N
W E
S

0   50   100 Miles

0   50   100 Kilometers

MEXICO

GOVERNORS *of* CALIFORNIA

SPANISH GOVERNORS	TERM
Gaspar de Portolá	1769–1770
Pedro Fages	1770–1773
Fernando Rivera y Moncada	1773–1775
Felipe de Neve	1775–1782
Pedro Fages	1782–1791
José Antonio Roméu	1791–1792
José Joaquin de Arrillaga	1792–1794
Diego de Borica	1794–1800
José Joaquin de Arrillaga	1800–1814
José Argüello	1814–1815
Pablo Vicente de Solá	1815–1822

MEXICAN GOVERNORS	TERM
Luis Argüello	1822–1825
José María Echeandía	1825–1831
Manuel Victoria	1831–1832
Pío Pico	1832
José Maria Echeandía (South)	1833
Agustin V. Zamorano (North)	1833
José Figueroa	1833–1835
José Castro	1835–1836
Nicholás Gutiérrez	1836
Mariano Chico	1836
Juan Bautista Alvarado	1837–1842
Manuel Micheltorena	1842–1845
Pío Pico	1845–1846
José María Flores	1846

MILITARY GOVERNORS	TERM
John D. Sloat	1846
Robert F. Stockton	1846–1847
John C. Frémont	1847
Stephen W. Kearny	1847
Richard B. Mason	1847–1849
Persifor F. Smith	1849
Bennett Riley	1849

INTERIM GOVERNOR	TERM
Peter H. Burnett	1849–1851

STATE GOVERNORS	TERM
John McDougal	1851–1852
John Bigler	1852–1856
J. Neely Johnson	1856–1858
John B. Weller	1858–1860
Milton S. Latham	1860
John G. Downey	1860–1862
Leland Stanford	1862–1863
Frederick F. Low	1863–1867
Henry H. Haight	1867–1871
Newton Booth	1871–1875
Romualdo Pacheco	1875–1876
William Irwin	1876–1880
George C. Perkins	1880–1883
George Stoneman	1883–1887
Washington Bartlett	1887–1888
Robert W. Waterman	1888–1891
Henry H. Marknam	1891–1895
James H. Budd	1895–1899
Henry T. Gage	1899–1903
George C. Pardee	1903–1907
James N. Gillett	1907–1911
Hiram W. Johnson	1911–1917
William D. Stephens	1917–1923
Friend W. Richardson	1923–1927
Clement C. Young	1927–1931
James Rolph, Jr.	1931–1934
Frank F. Merriam	1934–1939
Culbert L. Olson	1939–1943
Earl Warren	1943–1953
Goodwin J. Knight	1953–1959
Edmund G. Brown	1959–1967
Ronald Reagan	1967–1975
Edmund G. Brown, Jr.	1975–1983
George Deukmejian	1983–1991
Pete Wilson	1991–1999

Source: *California—An Interpretive History*, Rawls & Bean

FAMOUS CALIFORNIANS

Steven Spielberg
Born in Cincinnati, Ohio, in 1946; now lives in the Los Angeles area; film director; known for films such as *E.T.*, *Jurassic Park*, and *Amistad*; won Academy Award for *Schindler's List* in 1993.

Litefoot
Born in California; lives in Oklahoma; actor and Native American rap artist; known for role in the film *The Indian in the Cupboard*.

Diane E. Watson
Born in 1933 in Los Angeles; the first African American woman to be elected to the California State Senate; served from 1978 to 1998.

Cruz Bustamante
Born in Dinuba in 1953; elected Lieutenant Governor in 1998, the first Hispanic to hold statewide office in over 120 years.

Winona Ryder
Born in Winona, Minnesota, in 1971; moved to Elk, California, at seven; film actress; won a Golden Globe award for *The Age of Innocence*.

Michele Kwan
Born in Torrance in 1980; now lives in Lake Arrowhead; won world and national figure skating titles and a silver medal at the 1998 Winter Olympics.

Frank Gehry

Born in Toronto, Canada, in 1929; moved to Los Angeles in 1947; architect; designed major buildings in Japan, Europe, and America.

Jonny Moseley

Born in Puerto Rico in 1975; lives in Tiburon; won the gold medal for moguls freestyle skiing in 1998 Winter Olympic Games.

Jackie Joyner-Kersee

Born in East St. Louis, Illinois, in 1962; now lives in Los Angeles; track-and-field athlete; winner of three Olympic gold medals.

John Singleton

Born in Los Angeles in 1970; film writer and director; known for the films *Boyz N the Hood* and *Rosewood*; nominated for an Academy Award for film direction.

Ellen Ochoa

Born in Los Angeles in 1958; lives in La Mesa; NASA astronaut; in 1993 became the first hispanic woman to fly into outer space, aboard the space shuttle *Discovery*.

Chang-Lin Tien

Born in Wuhan, China, in 1935; came to United States in 1956; lives in Berkeley; chancellor of the University of California, Berkeley, from 1990–1997.

Tiger Woods
Born in 1975 in Cypress; won many professional golf tournaments, including the Masters in 1997.

Alice Walker
Born in Eatonton, Georgia, in 1944; now lives in San Francisco; writer; known for *The Color Purple*, which won the Pulitzer Prize in 1983.

Luis Valdez
Born in Delano in 1940; playwright and film director; founded the award-winning theater group El Teatro Campesino; known for his films *Zoot Suit* and *La Bamba*.

Ralf Hotchkiss
Born in Illinois in 1947; lives in Oakland; professor at San Francisco State University; codesigned the lightweight Wheelchair Whirlwind.

Monica Lozano
Born in Los Angeles in 1956; lives in Los Angeles; associate publisher of *La Opinión*, the largest Spanish-language newspaper in the United States.

Amy Tan
Born in Oakland in 1952; now lives in San Francisco; author of *The Joy Luck Club*; winner of the National Book Award.

ANIMALS AND PLANTS OF CALIFORNIA

1 California Condor
2 Gull
3 Great White Shark
4 Sea Lion
5 Brown Bear
6 Weasel
7 Badger
8 Redwood
9 Red-Tailed Hawk
10 Opossum
11 Giant Sequoia
12 Deer
13 Chinook Salmon (E)
14 Lamprey
15 Sacramento Splittail
16 Slough Thistle
17 Raccoon
18 California Valley Quail
19 Porcupine
20 Sidewinder
21 Oak
22 Bighorn Sheep
23 Bobcat
24 California Golden Poppy
25 Golden Trout
26 Antelope Squirrel
27 Cottontail Rabbit
28 Roadrunner
29 Tricolored Blackbird
30 Tule
31 Great Blue Heron
32 Morning Glory
33 Gecko
34 Burrowing Owl
35 Horned Lizard
36 Rubber Rabbitbrush
37 Rattlesnake
38 Sage Grouse
39 Coyote
40 San Joaquin Kit Fox (E)
41 Mojave Popcorn Flower
42 Joshua Tree
43 Mountain Lion
44 Desert Tortoise (T)
45 Creosote Bush
46 Drummond's Anemone

(E) Endangered
(T) Threatened

Dictionary of GEOGRAPHIC TERMS

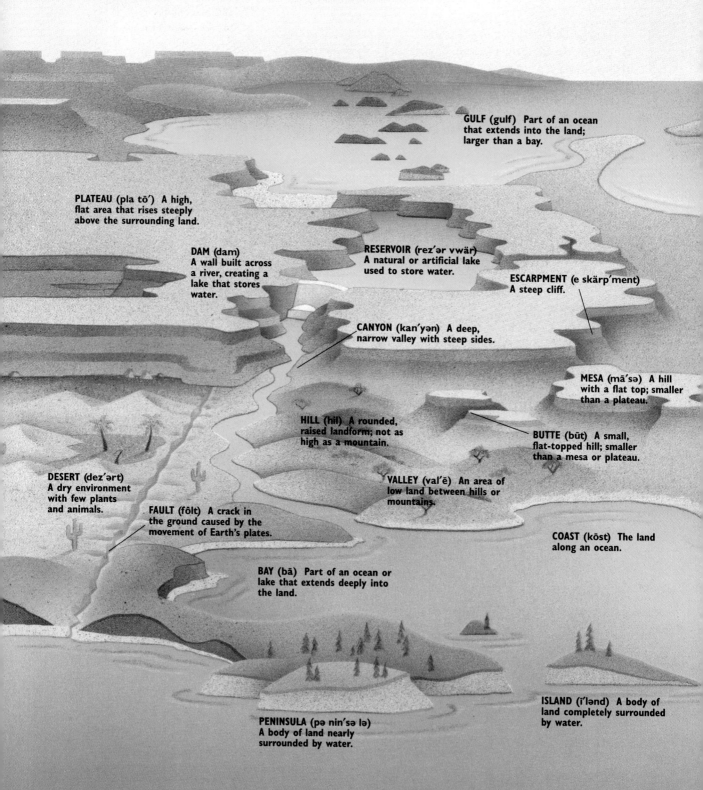

GULF (gulf) Part of an ocean that extends into the land; larger than a bay.

PLATEAU (pla tō′) A high, flat area that rises steeply above the surrounding land.

DAM (dam) A wall built across a river, creating a lake that stores water.

RESERVOIR (rez′ər vwär) A natural or artificial lake used to store water.

ESCARPMENT (e skärp′ment) A steep cliff.

CANYON (kan′yən) A deep, narrow valley with steep sides.

MESA (mā′sə) A hill with a flat top; smaller than a plateau.

HILL (hil) A rounded, raised landform; not as high as a mountain.

BUTTE (būt) A small, flat-topped hill; smaller than a mesa or plateau.

DESERT (dez′ərt) A dry environment with few plants and animals.

VALLEY (val′ē) An area of low land between hills or mountains.

FAULT (fôlt) A crack in the ground caused by the movement of Earth's plates.

COAST (kōst) The land along an ocean.

BAY (bā) Part of an ocean or lake that extends deeply into the land.

PENINSULA (pə nin′sə lə) A body of land nearly surrounded by water.

ISLAND (ī′lənd) A body of land completely surrounded by water.

VOLCANO (vol kā′nō) An opening in Earth's surface through which hot rock and ash are forced out.

MOUNTAIN (moun′tən) A high landform with steep sides; higher than a hill.

PEAK (pēk) The top of a mountain.

HARBOR (här′bər) A sheltered place along a coast where boats dock safely.

GLACIER (glā′shər) A huge sheet of ice that moves slowly across the land.

CANAL (kə nal′) A channel built to carry water for irrigation or transportation.

LAKE (lāk) A body of water completely surrounded by land.

PORT (pôrt) A place where ships load and unload their goods.

TRIBUTARY (trib′yə ter ē) A smaller river that flows into a larger river.

SOURCE (sôrs) The starting point of a river.

TIMBERLINE (tim′bər līn) A line beyond which trees do not grow.

RIVER BASIN (riv′ər bā′sin) All the land that is drained by a river and its tributaries.

WATERFALL (wô′tər fôl) A flow of water falling vertically.

MOUNTAIN RANGE (moun′tən rānj) A row or chain of mountains.

PLAIN (plān) A large area of nearly flat land.

RIVER (riv′ər) A stream of water that flows across the land and empties into another body of water.

BASIN (bā′sin) A bowl-shaped landform surrounded by higher land.

DELTA (del′tə) Land made of soil left behind as a river drains into a larger body of water.

MOUTH (mouth) The place where a river empties into a larger body of water.

BARRIER ISLAND (bar′ē ər ī′lənd) A narrow island between the mainland and the ocean.

OCEAN (ō′shən) A large body of salt water; oceans cover much of Earth's surface.

R29

Gazetteer

Gazetteer

This Gazetteer is a geographical dictionary that will help you to pronounce and locate the places discussed in this book. Latitude and longitude are given for cities and some other places. The page numbers tell you where each place first appears on a map or in the text.

A

Acapulco (äk ə pül′kō) A city on the west coast of what was once New Spain and is now Mexico. (t. 92)

Africa (af′ri kə) A continent south of Europe, between the Atlantic and Indian oceans. (m. G5, t. G4)

Alcatraz Island (al′kə traz ī′lənd) An island in San Francisco Bay. (t. 296)

Alta California (äl′tə kal ə fôr′nya) The Spanish name for present-day California. (p. 146)

American River (ə mer′i kən riv′ər) A river in Northern California near Coloma. (m. R18, t. 170)

Anaheim (an′ə hīm) A city in Orange County, in Southern California, where Disneyland is located; 34°N, 118°W. (m. G8, t. 313)

Angel Island (an′jəl ī′lənd) An island in San Francisco Bay where Chinese immigrants waited to find out whether they would be allowed into the United States. (t. 273)

Antarctica (ant ärk′ti kə) A continent located in the Southern Hemisphere. (m. G5, t. G4)

Appalachian Mountains (ap ə lā′chē ən moun′tənz) A chain of mountains with rounded peaks that runs through the eastern United States. (m. G10)

Arctic Ocean (ärk′tik ō′shən) An ocean that surrounds the North Pole. (m. G5, t. G4)

Asia (ā′zhə) The largest continent, located in the Eastern and Northern hemispheres. (m. G5, t. G4)

Atlantic Ocean (at lan′tik ō′shən) An ocean that borders North and South America, western Europe, and Africa. (m. G4, t. G4)

Australia (os trāl′yə) A continent and country located in the Eastern and Southern hemispheres. (m. G5, t. G4)

B

Baja California (bä′hə kal ə fôr′nyə) A long, narrow peninsula south of California and part of Mexico. (m. 103, t. 104)

Bakersfield (bā′kərz fēld) A city in the San Joaquin Valley of California; 35°N, 119°W. (m. G6, t. 265)

Beckwourth Pass (bek′wərth pas) A Sierra Nevada pass discovered in 1851 by James Beckwourth; it was used by some of the gold seekers known as the Forty-Niners. (m. 154, t. 173)

Berkeley (bûr′klē) A city in Northern California where student protests were held in the 1960s; 38°N, 122°W. (m. R21, t. 295)

Boca (bō′kə) A town in the Sierra Nevada in California; 39°N, 120°W. (m. 33, t. 33)

C

Cahuenga Pass (kä hweng′gə pas) The site where Californios led by Andrés Pico surrendered to United States forces led by John C. Frémont; connects the San Fernando Valley with the rest of Los Angeles; 34°N, 118°W. (m. 161, t. 162)

California (kal ə fôr′nyə) One of the Pacific states of the West region. (m. G6, t. G6)

pronunciation key

a	at	ī	ice	u	up	th	thin	
ā	ape	îr	pierce	ū	use	th	this	
ä	far	o	hot	ü	rule	zh	measure	
âr	care	ō	old	ù	pull	ə	about, taken,
e	end	ô	fork	ûr	turn		pencil, lemon,
ē	me	oi	oil	hw	white		circus
i	it	ou	out	ng	song		

Cascade Range (kas kād′ rānj) A mountain range extending from Northern California through Oregon and Washington. (m. G8)

Central Valley region (sen′trəl val′ē rē′jən) One of four regions of California. (m. 9, t. 16)

Channel Islands (chan′əl i′ləndz) A chain of eight islands in the Pacific Ocean off the coast of Southern California. (m. G8, t. 88)

China (chī′nə) A country in eastern Asia. (m. R11, t. 172)

Chinatown (chī′nə toun) A neighborhood in San Francisco that is home to large numbers of Chinese Americans. (t. 226)

Clear Lake (klir lāk) A lake in the Coast Ranges of Northern California; 39°N, 122°W. (m. 59, t. 61)

Coast Ranges (kōst rān′jəs) A mountain range in western California, Oregon, and Washington, on the Pacific Coast. (m. G11, t. 11)

Colorado Desert (kol ə rad′ō dez′ərt) A desert in California once farmed by the Yuma. (m. 11, t. 73)

Columbia (kə lum′bē ə) A town in the Sierra Nevada that was once an important Gold Rush center and is now a state historic park; 38°N, 120°W. (m. 312, t. 313)

Continental Divide (kon tə nen′təl di vīd′) An imaginary line running along the peaks of the Rocky Mountains that divides rivers that flow east from rivers that flow west.

Cupertino (kü pər tē′nō) A town in Santa Clara County where Steve Jobs and Steve Wozniak started a business selling personal computers; 37°N, 122°W. (m. 373, t. 325)

D

Daly City (dā′lē cit′ē) A suburb of San Francisco, largely developed by Henry Doelger; 37°N, 122°W. (t. 292)

Danville (dan′vil) A small town east of Oakland; 38°N, 122°W. (t. 368)

Davis (dā′vis) A city in Northern California, and one location of the University of California; 38°N, 121°W. (t. 246)

Death Valley (deth val′ē) A desert in California; the driest place in the United States. (m. 33, t. 32)

Delano (de′lə nō) A small farming town in the San Joaquin Valley; headquarters of the United Farm Workers union; 36°N, 119°W. (m. 271, t. 297)

Desert region (dez′ərt rē′jən) One of four regions of California. (m. 9, t. 16)

Dominguez Rancho (dō ming′gez rän′chō) A rancho near present-day Los Angeles where Californios defeated United States forces on October 8, 1846; 34°N, 118°W. (m. 161, t. 160)

Donner Lake (don′ər lāk) A lake in the Sierra Nevada named after the Donner party; 39°N, 120°W. (t. 155)

Donner Pass (don′ər pas) A pass in the Sierra Nevada where the Donner party became stranded; 39°N, 120°W. (m. 154, t. 216)

Drakes Bay (drāks bā) A bay on the Point Reyes Peninsula where Francis Drake landed in 1579; 38°N, 122°W. (m. 82, t. 91)

Dutch Flat (duch flat) A town in the California Sierra Nevada in Placer County; 39°N, 120°W. (m. 220, t. 218)

E

Eastern Hemisphere (ēs′tərn hem′is fîr) The half of Earth east of the prime meridian. (m. G5, t. G5)

Ebbets Pass (e′bits pas) A mountain pass in the Sierra Nevada. (t. 152)

El Camino Real (el kä mē′nō rä äl′) A walking trail that connected Spanish missions in California; it means "The King's Highway." (m. 113, t. 113)

El Segundo (el sā gün′dō) A town in Southern California where the Tree Musketeers opened a recycling center; 34°N, 118°W. (t. 46)

England (ing′lənd) An island country in Europe that sent settlers and explorers, like Francis Drake, to North America. (m. R11, t. 90)

Europe (yür′əp) A continent located in the Eastern and Northern hemispheres. (m. G5, t. G4)

F

Folsom (fŭl′səm) A town just east of Sacramento in central California; 38°N, 120°W. (t. 215)

Fort Ross (fôrt ros) A Russian settlement in Sonoma County, north of San Francisco, from 1812–1840; a state historic park today; 38°N, 123°W. (t. 140)

Fremont (frē'mont) A city in Alameda County, between Oakland and San Jose; location of an automobile factory jointly owned by an American company and a Japanese company; 38°N, 122°W. (t. 333)

Fresno (frez'nō) The city with the sixth-largest population in California, located in the San Joaquin Valley; 36°N, 119°W. (m. G6, t. 14)

G

Golden Gate (gōl'dən gāt) The name given to the narrow body of water between Marin County and San Francisco; crossed by the famous Golden Gate Bridge; 37°N, 122°W. (t. 285)

Great Plains (grāt plānz) High, fairly dry plain; the western part of the Interior Plains. (m. G10)

Gulf of California (gulf uv kal ə fôr'nya) An arm of the Pacific Ocean, between Baja California and the mainland of Mexico. (m. G11)

H

Hetch Hetchy Valley (hech hech'ē val'ē) A beautiful valley inside Yosemite National Park flooded by the Hetch Hetchy reservoir; San Francisco's drinking water supply; 38°N, 120°W. (m. 239, t. 253)

Hollywood (hol'ē wŭd) An area within the city of Los Angeles, California, that is a major center of the film industry; 34°N, 118°W. (m. 271, t. 283)

Huntington Beach (hun'ting tən bēch) A city in Orange County known for its great surfing beaches; 33°N, 118°W. (m. 365, t. 316)

I

Imperial Valley (im pir'ē əl val'ē) A farming area in the Colorado Desert known for its lettuce, cantaloupe, and other crops. (m. G6, t. 251)

India (in'dē ə) A country in southern Asia. (m. R11, t. 243)

Indian Ocean (in'dē ən ō'shən) An ocean between Africa, southern Asia, and Australia. (m. G5, t. G4)

Isthmus of Panama (is'məs əv pan'ə mä) A narrow stretch of land in Central America. (m. 172, t. 172)

J

Japan (jə pan') A country of eastern Asia made up of many islands in the Pacific Ocean; one of California's leading trading partners. (m. R11, t. 28)

Joshua Tree National Park (josh'ū ə trē nash'ə nəl pärk) A national park in the Mojave Desert of California, known for its Joshua, or yucca, trees. (m. R18, t. 20)

K

Klamath River (kla'məth riv'ər) A river in northwestern California that begins in the Klamath Mountains and flows into the Pacific Ocean. (m. R18)

L

Lake Erie (lāk îr'ē) The most southern of the five Great Lakes; it is located on the border between the United States and Canada. (m. G9)

Lake Huron (lāk hyùr'ən) The second-largest of the five Great Lakes; it is located on the border between the United States and Canada. (m. G9)

Lake Michigan (lāk mish'i gən) The third-largest of the five Great Lakes; it lies between the states of Michigan and Wisconsin. (m. G9)

Lake Ontario (lāk on târ'ē ō) The smallest of the five Great Lakes; it is located on the border between the United States and Canada. (m. G9)

Lake Superior (lāk sə pîr'ē ər) The largest of the five Great Lakes; it is located on the border between the United States and Canada. (m. G9)

Lake Tahoe (lāk tä'hō) A mountain lake in the Sierra Nevada known for its deep, blue water; 39°N, 120°W. (m. G8, t. 12)

Lava Beds National Monument (lä'və bedz nash'ə nəl mon'yə mənt) A rough land in eastern Siskiyou County, California. (m. 169, t. 169)

Locke (lok) A town in the Sacramento Delta founded by Chinese in 1915; 38°N, 120°W. (t. 226)

Long Beach (long bēch) A city in Los Angeles County known for its large port; 34°N, 118°W. (m. G7, t. 284)

Los Angeles (lôs an'jə ləs) Founded as a pueblo in 1781, it is today California's largest city; 34°N, 118°W. (m. G6, t. 11)

M

Manila (mə nil′ə) The capital city of the Philippines. (m. 82, t. 92)

Mexico (mek′si kō) A country in North America, south of and bordering the southwestern United States. (m. G9, t. 137)

Mexico City (mek′si kō sit′ē) A city built on the site of the Aztec city Tenochitlán; now the capital of Mexico; 19°N, 99°W. (t. R5)

Mission San Gabriel (mi′shən san gä′brē el) A mission founded by Spanish priests in 1771 in what is now Los Angeles County. (m. 113, t. 118)

Mississippi River (mis ə sip′ē riv′ər) One of the longest rivers in North America; it flows south from northern Minnesota into the Gulf of Mexico. (m. G10)

Missouri (mi sür′ē) One of the Plains states of the Middle West region. (m. G9, t. 212)

Mojave Desert (mō hä′vē dez′ərt) A desert in southeastern California. (m. 11, t. 61)

Mono Lake (mō′nō lāk) A lake at the northern end of Owens Valley that supplies drinking water for Los Angeles. (m. G8, t. 366)

Monterey (mon tə rā′) A city along the central California coast; it was at one time the capital of California; 37°N, 122°W. (m. G6, t. 136)

Monterey Bay (mon tə rā′ bā) An inlet of the Pacific Ocean named by Sebastian Vizcaíno. (m. 94, t. 93)

Monterey Park (mon tə rā′ pärk) A city in California, near Los Angeles; 34°N, 118°W. (t. 349)

Mountain region (moun′tən rē′jən) One of four regions of California. (m. 9, t. 12)

Mount Shasta (mount shas′tə) The second-highest mountain in California; 41°N, 122°W. (m. R18, t. 27)

Mount Whitney (mount wit′nē) The highest mountain in the United States outside of Alaska; elevation 14,494 feet; located in southeastern California, in the Sierra Nevada range; 36°N, 118°W. (m. G11, t. 12)

N

Napa (nap′ə) A city in Northern California; 38°N, 122°W. (t. 329)

New Helvetia (nü hel vā′shə) One of the largest settlements in the Sacramento Valley, built by Johann Sutter from Switzerland. (t. 153)

New Spain (nü spān) The Spanish colony in North America, made up of all or parts of the lands now called Mexico, Central America, and the United States. (m. 85, t. 85)

North America (nôrth ə mer′i kə) A continent in the Northern and Western hemispheres. (m. G4, t. G4)

Northern Hemisphere (nôr′thərn hem′i sfîr) The half of Earth north of the equator. (m. G5, t. G5)

O

Oakland (ōk′lənd) A city on the east side of San Francisco Bay; a major West Coast shipping port and railroad terminus; 37°N, 122°W. (m. G7, t. 343)

Oregon Trail (or′i gən trāl) A wagon trail the Donner party followed west from Missouri. (m. 154, t. 154)

Owens Valley (ō′ənz val′ē) A high mountain valley, 200 miles northeast of Los Angeles. (m. 256, t. 252)

P

Pacific Coast region (pə sif′ik kōst rē′jən) One of four regions of California. (m. 9, t. 10)

Pacific Ocean (pə sif′ik ō′shən) An ocean that borders western North and South America and eastern Asia. (m. G4, t. G4)

Palm Springs (päm springz) A city in the Desert region of California; 34°N, 117°W. (m. R21, t. 20)

Palo Alto (pal′ō al′tō) A town in Santa Clara County, near San Jose, where Stanford University is located; 37°N, 122°W. (t. 326)

pronunciation key

a at; ā ape; ä far; âr care; e end; ē me; i it; ī ice; îr pierce; o hot; ō old; ô fork; oi oil; ou out; u up; ū use; ü rule, ù pull; ûr turn; hw white; ng song; th thin; th this; zh measure; ə about, taken, pencil, lemon, circus

Pearl Harbor, Hawaii (pûrl här′bər hə wī′ē) The location of a United States Navy base that was bombed by Japanese planes on December 7, 1941. (t. 286)

Point Mugu (point mü gü′) The current name of a place once called Muwu by the Chumash people of California. (m. 94, t. 87)

Promontory, Utah (prom′ən tôr ē ū′tô) The place where the Pacific Railroad was completed. (m. 220, t. 221)

Pusan, South Korea (pü′sän south kə rē′ə) The chief port of South Korea and the Sister City of Los Angeles, California; 35°N, 129°E. (t. 335)

Q

Quincy (kwin′sē) A town in the Sierra Nevada in Northern California where citizens made a plan to save jobs and trees; 40°N, 121°W. (t. 45)

R

Redwood National Park (red′wŭd nash′ə nəl pärk) A national park in the Coast Ranges of California. (m. G8, t. 23)

Richmond (rich′mənd) A city in Northern California where many Liberty ships were built in World War II; 38°N, 122°W. (m. G7, t. 288)

Riverside (riv′ər sīd) A large city in Southern California once known for its many orange groves; 34°N, 117°W. (m. G6, t. 242)

Rocky Mountains (rok′ē moun′tənz) A high mountain range that stretches from Canada through the western United States into Mexico. (m. G10, t. 216)

S

Sacramento (sak′rə men′tō) The capital of California, in the central part of the state; 38°N, 121°W. (m. G6, t. 153)

Sacramento River (sak′rə men′tō riv′ər) A river that flows 382 miles from the Cascades through Northern California into San Francisco By. (m. G6, t. 17)

St. Joseph, Missouri (sānt jō′səf mi sûr′ē) A city in the Plains states of the Middle West region; the starting point of the Pony Express; 39°N, 94°W. (t. 212)

San Andreas Fault (san an drā′əs fält) Where two of Earth's plates meet in California; movement of these plates can cause an earthquake. (m. 26, t. 24)

San Diego (san dē ā′gō) A port city in Southern California; it is the second-largest city in California; 33°N, 117°W. (m. G6, t. 328)

San Diego Bay (san dē ā′gō bā) An inlet of the Pacific Ocean on the California coastline. (m. 83, t. 106)

San Francisco (san frən sis′kō) A port city in central California, on the Pacific Ocean; 38°N, 122°W. (m. G11, t. 179)

San Francisco Bay (san frən sis′kō bā) A bay off the Pacific Ocean on the California coastline at the city of San Francisco. (m. G11, t. 17)

San Joaquin River (san wä kēn′ riv′ər) A river that flows 350 miles from the Sierra Nevada through central California into San Francisco Bay. (m. G6, t. 17)

San Jose (san hō zā′) First founded as a pueblo in 1777, it is now the largest city in Northern California; 37°N, 122°W. (m. G6, t. 114)

San Luis Obispo (san lü′əs ə bis′pō) A city in California where the first motel was opened, in 1925; 35°N, 121°W. (m. R21, t. 88)

San Mateo (san mä tā′ō) A city west of San Francisco Bay; 37°N, 122°W. (t. 368)

San Pablo Bay (san pä′blō bā) A northern extension of San Francisco Bay. (t. 144)

San Pascual (san päs kwäl) The site of a battle in 1846 between United States forces and the Californios during the Mexican War; east of present-day Escondido; also spelled *San Pasqual*. (m. 161, t. 160)

San Pedro (san pā′drō) A part of the city of Los Angeles where the port of Los Angeles is located. (m. 209, t. 231)

Santa Barbara (san′tə bär′bər ə) A city in Southern California; 34°N, 120°W. (m. G8, t. 41)

Santa Barbara Channel (san′tə bär′bər ə chan′əl) A body of water that lies between the Pacific Coast and the Channel Islands. (R18, t. 66)

Santa Clara (san′tə kler′ə) A city in the Santa Clara Valley; 37°N, 122°W. (t. 325)

Santa Clara Valley (san'tə klerʹə valʹē) A valley in California with several cities that make up a key center of the country's computer industry. (t. 326)

Santa Rosa (san'tə rōʹzə) A Northern California city known for its rich soil and pleasant climate; 38°N, 122°W. (m. 243, t. 246)

Sierra Nevada (sē erʹə nə vadʹə) A mountain range in eastern California. (m. G8, t. 12)

Signal Hill (sigʹnəl hil) An area in Long Beach where oil was discovered in the 1920s. (t. 284)

Solvang (solʹvəng) A town in Santa Barbara County founded by immigrants from Denmark; 34°N, 120°W. (m. 274, t. 274)

Sonoma (sə nōʹmä) A city north of San Francisco where the Bear Flag Revolt took place; 38°N, 122°W. (m. 161, t. 159)

Sorrento Valley (sə renʹtō valʹē) A valley in California where many cities have businesses that make wireless telephones; 32°N, 117°W. (t. 328)

South America (south ə merʹi kə) A continent in the Southern and Western hemispheres. (m. G4, t. G4)

Southern Hemisphere (suthʹərn hemʹi sfîr) The half of Earth south of the equator. (m. G5, t. G5)

South Korea (south kə rēʹə) A country occupying the southern part of the Korean peninsula. (m. R11, t. 335)

Spain (spān) A country in southwestern Europe that began establishing colonies in North and South America in the 1500s. (m. R11, t. 84)

Stockton (stokʹtən) A town that served miners' needs during the Gold Rush of 1849; 38°N, 121°W. (m. G7, t. 180)

Sutter's Mill (sutʹərz mil) John Sutter's mill, built along the south fork of the American River in 1847; 38°N, 121°W. (t. 170)

T

Tenochtitlán (te nōch tē tlänʹ) The ancient Aztec capital city once located in what we now call Mexico. (m. 83, t. 85)

Trinity River (trinʹə tē rivʹər) A river in Northern California. (m. R18, t. 68)

W

Washington, D.C. (wôʹshing tən dē cē) The home of our country's government; 39°N, 77°W. (m. G9, t. 354)

Watts (wäts) A neighborhood in Los Angeles. (t. 361)

Western Hemisphere (wesʹtərn hemʹi sfîr) The half of Earth west of the prime meridian. (m. G5, t. G5)

Y

Yamato Colony (yä mäʹtō kolʹə nē) An agricultural community founded in the San Joaquin Valley in 1906. (m. 274, t. 273)

Yosemite National Park (yō semʹi tē nashʹə nəl pärk) A part of the Sierra Nevada range in California that became a park in 1890. (m. G8, t. 12)

Biographical Dictionary

The Biographical Dictionary tells you about the people you have learned about in this book. The Pronunciation Key tells you how to say their names. The page numbers tell you where each person first appears in the text.

A

Ashe, Marian (ash), 1924– California woman who served as the head of a government group concerned with the improvement of women's lives. (p. 296)

Austin, Mary (os'tən), 1868–1934 Author of the 1903 book *The Land of Little Rain*, in which Owens Valley is described as it existed before the building of the aqueduct to Los Angeles. (p. 252)

B

Bartolomea (bär tō lō mä'ə), 1800s Tongva girl who told of missionaries forcing the people of her town to be baptized and live in a Roman Catholic mission. (p. 119)

Beasley, Delilah (bēz'lē), 1866?–1934 Woman who studied and wrote about the lives of African Americans. Starting in 1923, her newspaper column in the *Oakland Tribune* discussed laws and customs that were unfair to black people. (p. 235)

Beckwourth, James (bek'wərth), 1798–1867? African American who was born in slavery and became a famous "mountain man." He discovered a safer pass in the Sierra Nevada, making travel easier. (p. 173)

Bidwell, John (bid'wel), 1819–1900 Leader of the first wagon train of settlers to arrive in California, in 1841. (p. 153)

Bloch, Ernest (blok), 1880–1959 Swiss immigrant to California in 1916. He wrote many pieces of music and became the director of the San Francisco Conservatory of Music. (p. 276)

Bright, Josefina Fierro de (brīt), 1900s Defender of immigrant rights and first president of the Congress of Spanish Speaking People. (p. 262)

Burbank, Luther (bûr'bank), 1849–1926 Farmer who used science to develop about 800 new kinds of plants while living in Santa Rosa in the late 1800s. (p. 246)

Burnett, Peter (bûr net'), 1807–1895 Chosen in 1849 to be the first governor of the state of California. (p. 190)

C

Cabrillo, Juan Rodríguez (kə brē'yō), ?–1543 Conquistador who led the first European expedition along the coast of California, in 1542. (p. 86)

Carrillo, José Antonio (kə rē'yō), 1796–1862 Led Californio soldiers to victory in a battle with Americans at Dominguez Rancho in 1846. One of eight Californio delegates present at the convention to write the California constitution. (p. 189)

Castro, José (kas'trō), 1810–1860 Mexican colonel who ordered John C. Frémont and his men out of California in 1845. This action led to the Bear Flag Revolt. (p. 159)

Cermeño, Sebastián Rodríguez (sər men'yō), late 1500s–early 1600s Ship captain who in 1595 sailed from New Spain to Manila and back to California, exploring Monterey Bay and other points along the California coast. (p. 92)

pronunciation key

a	at	ī	ice	u	up	th	thin
ā	ape	îr	pierce	ū	use	th	this
ä	far	o	hot	ü	rule	zh	measure
âr	care	ō	old	ủ	pull	ə	about, taken,
e	end	ô	fork	ûr	turn		pencil, lemon,
ē	me	oi	oil	hw	white		circus
i	it	ou	out	ng	song		

Chaffey, George (chaf′ē), 1848–1932 Engineer who built a 70-mile canal in 1900 that brought water from the Colorado River to the Imperial Valley. His canal turned the desert into rich farmland. (p. 251)

Chavez, Cesar (chä′vez, sā′zär), 1927–1993 A leader in the drive to improve lives of farmworkers. In 1962, with Dolores Huerta, he formed a union called the National Farm Workers Association. (p. 297)

Clay, Henry (klā), 1777–1852 Senator from Kentucky who helped work out the Compromise of 1850, enabling California to become a state. (p. 190)

Columbus, Christopher (kə lum′bəs), 1451–1506 Italian sea captain who reached the islands of the Caribbean Sea in 1492. (p. 84)

Cortés, Hernan (kôr tās′), 1485–1547 Spanish conquistador who landed in Mexico in 1519. He and his armies conquered parts of Mexico and Central America and named the land New Spain. (p. 85)

Crespí, Juan (kres pē′), 1721–1782 Aide to Junípero Serra who traveled with the "Sacred Expedition" party and kept a journal describing what he saw. (p. 108)

D

Dame Shirley (dām shûr′lē), 1819–1906 The pen name of Louise Amelia Knapp Smith Clappe, who traveled to California with her husband during the Gold Rush. Her letters to her sister describing life in a mining camp were published in 1854. (p. 182)

De Los Angeles, Maria Juana (wän′ə), 1800s One of only a few Native Americans to receive a land grant after California missions closed in 1834. Her husband had been a leader of the Luiseño people. (p. 139)

DeMille, Cecil B. (də mil′), 1881–1959 Director of the first full-length movie in the United States, in 1913. (p. 283)

Disney, Walt (diz′nē), 1901–1966 Famous moviemaker and creator of Disneyland. (p. 313)

Doelger, Henry (däl′jər), 1906–1978 Planned a community of affordable houses called Westlake in Daly City in 1949. Communities like this were in much demand to house increasing populations after World War II. (p. 292)

Doheny, Edward L. (dō′nē), 1856–1935 Discovered oil in Los Angeles in 1892, leading to a huge oil boom. (p. 284)

Donner, George (don′ər), 1784–1847 Leader of a group of about 90 settlers from Missouri known as the Donner party. In the winter of 1846–1847, the Donner party became stranded in heavy snow. About 40 members of the party died. (p. 154)

Donner, Tamsen (don′ər), 1803–1847 Wife of George Donner, leader of the ill-fated Donner party, which left Missouri in 1846 for California. She died with her husband after being stranded in the Sierra Nevada. (p. 154)

Drake, Francis (drāk), 1543?–1596 English explorer sent by the queen of England to find the Northwest Passage. Historians believe that on his journey he landed at Point Reyes, claiming California for England. (p. 90)

E

Echeandía, José (e chē ən dē′ə), ?–1855 Governor of Mexican California during the time the first settlers from the United States arrived overland in California, in 1826. (p. 152)

Edson, Katherine Philips (ed′sən), 1870–1933 California reformer whose remarkable efforts led to women's suffrage and a minimum wage law for women and children. (p. 234)

Estanislao (e stän ē slō′), early 1800s Yokuts Indian who led a revolt of Native Americans against Mission San José in 1828. Battles like this prevented Mexicans from settling in the San Joaquin Valley at that time. (p. 137)

pronunciation key

a **at**; ā **ape**; ä **far**; âr **care**; e **end**; ē **me**; i **it**; ī **ice**; îr **pierce**; o **hot**; ō **old**; ô **fork**; oi **oil**; ou **out**; u **up**; ū **use**; ü **rule**, u̇ **pull**; ûr **turn**; hw **white**; ng **song**; th **thin**; th **this**; zh measure; ə **about**, taken, pencil, lemon, circus

F

Ferrelo, Bartolomé (fər el′ō), 1500s Spanish ship pilot of the first European expedition along the California coast. He was named commander of the expedition when Juan Rodríguez Cabrillo died in 1543. (p. 89)

Figueroa, José (fē gä rō′ə), 1792–1845 Governor who closed the missions in California in 1834, attempting to divide the land between Native Americans and Mexican settlers. (p. 137)

Flores, Pedro (flôr′es), 1900s Philippine immigrant who began a successful yo-yo company in Los Angeles in 1929. (p. 277)

Frémont, Jessie (frē′mont), 1824–1902 Wife of John C. Frémont. She and her husband wrote many exciting books about their travels in the American West. (p. 159)

Frémont, John C. (frē′mont), 1813–1890 United States Army captain who led a band of armed men into California in 1845, declaring California independent from Mexico and starting the Bear Flag Revolt. (p. 159)

G

Gálvez, José de (gäl′väs), 1729–1787 A special official to the king of Spain. He planned the "Sacred Expedition" to set up the first European settlements in California, in 1768. (p. 104)

Grafton, Sue (graf′tən), 1940– Modern writer carrying on the California crime-writing tradition. (p. 360)

H

Hearst, Phoebe Apperson (hûrst, fē′bē ap′ər sən), 1842–1919 Wealthy supporter of the University of California, she served on its governing board from 1897 to 1919. The mother of newspaper owner William Randolph Hearst, she also helped found what became the Parent-Teacher Association. (p. 358)

Hidalgo, Miguel (ē dal′gō, mē gel′), 1753–1811 Roman Catholic priest who convinced many Mexican people to go to war for independence from Spain in 1810. (p. 136)

Higuera, Prudencia (ē gwâr′ə), 1828–? Woman who wrote about her life on Rancho El Pinole in California in the mid-1800s. (p. 143)

Holt, Benjamin (hōlt), 1849–1920 Stockton, California, inventor of the "caterpillar track" tractor in 1904. (p. 241)

Houston, Jeanne Wakatsuki (hū′stən), 1935– Japanese American who wrote about her experiences in the Manzanar internment camp in the Owens Valley during World War II. (p. 287)

Huerta, Dolores (wer′tä), 1929– Formed a union for farmworkers with Cesar Chavez in 1962 called the National Farm Workers Association. (p. 297)

J

Jackson, Helen Hunt (jak′sən), 1830–1885 Wrote *A Century of Dishonor* in 1881. This book criticized how the government treated Native Americans. (p. 195)

Jobs, Steve (jobz), 1955– Built the first small, easy-to-use computer in 1975, with his engineer friend Steve Wozniak. Together they started the Apple computer business. (p. 325)

Johnson, Hiram (jon′sən), 1866–1945 Governor of California from 1911 to 1919, he was a strong leader of the movement to reform California's government. (p. 232)

José, Nicolas (ho sä′), late 1700s Native American who helped organize an unsuccessful revolt at Mission San Gabriel in 1785. (p. 122)

Judah, Theodore (jü′də), 1826–1863 Engineer responsible for the building of the first transcontinental railroad. (p. 215)

K

Kaiser, Henry J. (kī′zər), 1882–1967 California businessman known for building thousands of Liberty ships during World War II. (p. 288)

Kearney, Denis (kär′nē), 1847–1907 Irish immigrant who became a San Francisco labor leader and politician. He campaigned for laws that discriminated against Chinese Americans. (p. 226)

Kearny, Stephen Watts (kär′nē), 1794–1848 United States general in the Mexican War who was defeated by Andrés Pico's army of Californios in the Battle of San Pascual. (p. 160)

Kennedy, Anthony (ken′i dē), 1936– Supreme Court justice, from Sacramento. (p. 355)

King, Martin Luther, Jr. (king), 1929–1968 Major civil rights leader from Alabama during the 1960s. He inspired many Californians to fight discrimination. (p. 296)

Kingston, Maxine Hong (kings′tən), 1940– Writer who wrote about her Chinese American heritage in her books *The Woman Warrior* and *Tripmaster Monkey*. (p. 360)

Kintpuash (kint′pü ash), 1837–1873 Leader of the Modoc in the Modoc War. (p. 195)

Kuskov, Ivan (küs′kov), 1765–1823 Russian fur hunter who built Fort Ross north of Bodega Bay, California, in 1812. (p. 140)

Kyutaro, Abiko (kyü tä rō), 1865–? Japanese immigrant to California in 1885. He became a successful businessman, published a Japanese American newspaper, and started an agricultural community called Yamato Colony. (p. 273)

L

Lasuén, Fermín (fər mēn′ läs wen), 1736–1803 Priest who doubled the number of Spanish missions in California after the death of Father Serra in 1784. (p. 113)

Lucas, George (lü′kəs), 1944– Movie director who made *Star Wars* in 1977 and later started his own special-effects company, Industrial Light and Magic, in San Rafael, California. (p. 321)

M

Marshall, James (mär′shəl), 1810–1885 California settler who discovered gold in the earth while building Sutter's Mill in 1848. This discovery launched the Gold Rush. (p. 170)

Mason, Biddy (mā′sən), 1818–1891 Enslaved woman brought to California from Georgia by her owner, Robert Smith. Her refusal to go with Smith to Texas led to the freedom of all enslaved persons in California. (p. 191)

Moctezuma II (mäk tə zü′mə), 1480?–1520 Aztec emperor defeated by Hernan Cortés in 1520. (p. 85)

Morgan, Julia (mor′gən), 1872–1957 The first woman to practice as an architect in California, she became best known for creating Hearst Castle. (p. 313)

Morse, Samuel F. B. (môrs), 1791–1872 Painter and inventor of the telegraph. His invention enabled people to communicate quickly over long distances. (p. 214)

Mosley, Walter (mōz′lē), 1952– African American writer carrying on the California crime-writing tradition. His inspiration comes from his parents' stories of their heritages. (p. 360)

Muir, John (myùr), 1838–1914 California settler who explored and wrote about the Sierra Nevada and founded the Sierra Club. He also helped create Yosemite National Park. (p. 12)

Mulholland, William (mul hol′ənd), 1855–1935 Chief engineer for Los Angeles who convinced the city's leaders and voters in 1905 to build an aqueduct that would bring water from Owens River, over 200 miles away. (p. 252)

N

Neve, Felipe de (nev′āy), 1728–1784 Governor who offered cash, supplies, and animals to settlers willing to start farming towns in California, in exchange for food. He hoped this would help feed soldiers living in early presidios. (p. 114)

---

pronunciation key

a at; ā ape; ä far; âr care; e end; ē me; i it; ī ice; îr pierce; o hot; ō old; ô fork; oi oil; ou out; u up; ū use; ü rule, ù pull; ûr turn; hw white; ng song; th thin; th this; zh measure; ə about, taken, pencil, lemon, circus

O

Ortega, José (or tä′gə), 1734–1798 One of Portolá's soldiers on the "Sacred Expedition." He was the first to spot San Francisco Bay, from the top of a hill near the present-day city of Pacifica. (p. 109)

P

Parkhurst, Charlotte (pärk′hûrst), ?–1879 First woman stagecoach driver, who got her job with Wells, Fargo and Company by dressing as a man and applying for the job as "Charlie Parkhurst." (p. 211)

Pérez, Eulalia (per′ez), ?–1878 The "keeper of the keys," or *llavera*, at Mission San Gabriel. She was in charge of locking all the mission's buildings at night. (p. 120)

Pico, Andrés (pē′kō), 1810–1876 Californio leader who won the Battle of San Pascual in 1846. (p. 160)

Polk, James K. (pōk), 1795–1849 President of the United States from 1845 to 1849, during the Mexican War. (p. 158)

Portolá, Gaspar de (por toh lah′) late 1700s Spanish army captain who, along with Junípero Serra, led the "Sacred Expedition." (p. 106)

R

Reyes, Francisco (rā′əs), 1700s First alcalde of Los Angeles, he was of African and Spanish heritage. (p. 115)

Riley, Bennett (rī′lē), 1787–1853 Last military governor in California. He was responsible for holding a convention in 1849 where Californians took the first steps toward statehood. (p. 188)

Roosevelt, Franklin Delano (rō′zə velt), 1882–1945 The 32nd President of the United States, from 1933 to 1945. He created the New Deal programs to fight the Great Depression and led the country during World War II. (p. 264)

Ruef, Abraham (rüf), 1864–1936 Political "boss" who used money from big businesses to bribe city officials. His misuse of power and money led the citizens of San Francisco to reform the way government was run. (p. 232)

Ruiz, Bernarda (rü ēs′), 1800s California woman who set up a meeting between Frémont and Pico at Cahuenga Pass in 1847. At this meeting the Californios surrendered, and the fighting in California ended. (p. 162)

Rumford, William Byron (rum′fərd), 1908–1986 Representative in the California legislature who helped make a law called the Rumford Act, in 1963, that said California property owners could not discriminate because of race. (p. 296)

S

Serra, Junípero (ser′ə, hū nē′pe rō), 1713–1784 Missionary from New Spain who worked with José Gálvez to found and lead the first missions in what is now called California. (p. 105)

Sloat, John Drake (slōt), 1713–1784 United States Navy officer during the Mexican War. The war spread to California when he led ships to Monterey in 1846, claiming California as part of the United States. (p. 160)

Smith, Jedediah Strong (smith), 1799–1831 Mountain man who organized a group of fur trappers to travel overland from the Great Salt Lake to California in 1826. His party was the first white American group to make this dangerous journey. (p. 151)

Spheeris, Penelope (sfîr′əs), 1946– Modern movie director. (p. 319)

Stanford, Leland (stan′fərd), 1824–1893 One of the "Big Four" investors in the Central Pacific Railroad. The money he invested made it possible to build the transcontinental railroad. (p. 219)

Steinbeck, John (stīn′bek), 1902–1968 Author of *The Grapes of Wrath*. This book tells of people's journey from Oklahoma to California after a severe drought in the 1930s left their farmland a "Dust Bowl." (p. 265)

Strauss, Joseph B. (strous), 1870–1938 Engineer who, in 1930, convinced San Francisco voters to pay for the building of the Golden Gate Bridge. (p. 285)

Strauss, Levi (strous), 1829–1902 San Francisco shopkeeper who became successful buying Eastern goods and selling them to businesses in the West. With Jacob Davis he made the world's first blue jeans, in 1872. (p. 179)

Sutter, Johann (su'tər), 1802–1880 Swiss immigrant who arrived in Mexican California in 1834. He founded New Helvetia, near present-day Sacramento, and became very important in helping new arrivals settle in the area. (p. 153)

T

Tac, Pablo (toc), 1800s Native American who lived in Mission San Luis Rey from birth and thought of the mission as home. He appreciated the European subjects he learned there. (p. 122)

Tape, Mary (tāp), late 1800s–early 1900s Chinese woman who won her court case against San Francisco schools. Her eight-year-old daughter had not been allowed to go to school because she was Chinese. (p. 227)

Teraoka, Masami (târ ä ō'kə), 1936– California artist who blends Japanese art forms and American customs in his paintings. (p. 361)

Thiebaud, Wayne (tē'bo), 1920– California landscape artist who uses city scenes for his subject matter. (p. 361)

Tibbets, Eliza (tib'əts), ?–1898 Wife of Luther Tibbets. She made sure the orange trees grew strong and healthy. (p. 243)

Tibbets, Luther (tib'əts), 1820–1902 Farmer near Riverside who helped make orange growing a big business in California by introducing navel oranges from South America. (p. 243)

Toypurina (toy pûr ē' nə), 1761–1799 Tongva woman who helped organize an unsuccessful revolt at Mission San Gabriel in 1785. (p. 122)

V

Vail, James (vāl), late 1800s–early 1900s Opened the nation's first motel in San Luis Obispo, to meet the needs of increasing numbers of people traveling to California by car. (p. 313)

Vallejo, Mariano Guadalupe (vä yä'hō), 1808–1890 Mexican colonel captured and held prisoner during a revolt led by John C. Frémont in 1846. (p. 159)

Vizcaíno, Sebastián (vēs kä ē'nō), 1550?–1616? Explorer who led an expedition from New Spain in search of a safe harbor along the coast of California in 1602. He incorrectly described Monterey Bay as a " fine harbor sheltered from all winds." (p. 95)

W

Warren, Earl (wôr'ən), 1891–1974 From Kern City, he served as Chief Justice of the United States Supreme Court from 1953 to 1968. (p. 355)

Wood, Beatrice (web), 1894–1998 A well-known ceramicist, or maker of pottery, who lived in Ojai, she was declared a California Living Treasure in 1994. (p. 361)

Wilson, Pete (wil'sən), 1933– Governor of California from 1991 to 1999. He also served as mayor of San Diego and as United States senator from California. (p. 351)

Wozniak, Steve (woz'nē ak), 1950– Engineer who built the first small, easy-to-use computer in 1975, with his friend Steve Jobs. Together they started the Apple computer business. (p. 325)

(continued from page ii)
Acknowledgments

©1981 by J.S. Holliday. From *They Saw the Elephant* by JoAnn Levy ©1990 by JoAnn Levy. From *Songs of the Gold Rush* by Richard A. Dwyer & Richard E. Lingenfelter ©1964 by the Regents of the University of California. From *Off At Sunrise* by Charles Glass Gray ©1976 by the Henry E. Huntington Library. From *A Short History of California* by Tom Cole ©1981 by Tom Cole. From *The Shirley Letters* by Louise Clappe ©1970 by Peregrine Press. From *The History of California* by Hubert Howe Bancroft ©1888 by the History Company Publishers. From *The Other Californians* by Robert Heizer & Alan Almquist ©1971 by the Regents of the University of California. From *A Century of Dishonor* by Helen Jackson ©1972 Reprinted by Scholarly Press, Inc. From *California Classics* by Lawrence Powell ©1971 by Lawrence Powell. *Conquests and Historical Identities in California 1769-1936* by Lisbeth Haas ©1995 by the Regents of the University of California. From *Western America* by LeRoy Hafen, Eugene Hollon, Carl Rister ©1970 by Prentice-Hall, Inc. From *Dr. History's Sampler* by Jim Rawls ©1994 by James Rawls & Leonard Nelson. From *Roughing It* by Mark Twain ©1993 by the Regents of the University of California. From *The Big Four* by Oscar Lewis ©1996 by

Alfred A. Knopf, Inc. From *Why and How: Why the Chinese Emigrate and The Means They Adopt* ©1871 by Lee, Shepard, & Dillingham. From *Up and Down California* by Francis Farquhar ©1966 by the Regents of the University of California. From *The Yosemite* by John Muir ©1912. From *The Chemehuevis* by Carobeth Laird ©1976 by the Malki Museum. From *Mojave* by Diane Siebert ©1988 by Diane Siebert. From *The Way We Lived* by Malcolm Margolin ©1993 by Malcolm Margolin. From *Californian Indian Nights* compiled by Edward Gifford & Gwendoline Block ©1958 by the Arthur H. Clark Company. From *Missions of the Los Angeles Area* by Dianne MacMillan ©1996 by Lerner Publications Company. From *Chief Red Fox is Dead* by James J. Rawls ©1996 by Harcourt Brace & Company. From "Spanish Voyages to the Northwest Coast of America" by Henry R. Wagnar ©1929 by California Historical Society. From *Juan Rodriguez Cabrillo* by Harry Kelsey ©1986 by The Huntington Library. From "Eastern Coastal Chumash" by Campbell Grant from *California* ©1978 by The Smithsonian Institution. From *Crossing the Schoolhouse Border* by Laurie Olsen ©1988 by A California Tomorrow Policy.
(continued on page R54)

pronunciation key

a **at**; ā **ape**; ä **far**; âr **care**; e **end**; ē **me**; i **it**; ī **ice**; îr **pierce**; o **hot**; ō **old**; ô **fork**; oi **oil**; ou **out**; u **up**; ū **use**; ü **rule**; ů **pull**; ûr **turn**; hw **white**; ng **song**; th **thin**; th **this**; zh **measure**; ə **about**, **taken**, **pencil**, **lemon**, **circus**

Glossary

This Glossary will help you to pronounce and understand the meanings of the vocabulary in this book. The page number at the end of the definition tells where the word first appears.

A

adobe (ə dō′bē) Brick made from clay and straw that is dried in the sun. (p. 120)

aerospace (âr′ō spās) The industry that builds planes and space vehicles. See **industry**. (p. 289)

agribusiness (ag′rə biz nis) A large farm owned by a company. (p. 336)

agriculture (ag′ri kul chər) The business of growing crops and raising animals. (p. 18)

alcalde (äl cäl′dā) A person who served as both mayor and judge. (p. 115)

Allies (al′īz) Great Britain, France, China, and the Soviet Union—nations that fought against the Axis in World War II. See **Axis**. (p. 286)

ancestor (an′ses tər) A person in your family, starting with your parents, who was born long before you. (p. 61)

aqueduct (ak′wə dukt) A canal or pipe for bringing water from a faraway source. (p. 252)

aquifer (ak′wə fər) A layer of rock or gravel that traps water underground. (p. 366)

archaeology (är kē ol′ə jē) The study of old tools, old houses, and other things people leave behind. (p. 60)

artifacts (är′tə fakts) The things people leave behind. (p. 60)

asphalt (as′fôlt) A thick tar that can seep to Earth's surface. (p. 65)

Axis (ak′sis) Germany, Italy, and Japan—nations that fought against the Allies in World War II. See **Allies**. (p. 286)

B

barrio (bär′ē ō) A neighborhood where Mexican Americans live. (p. 262)

bay (bā) A part of an ocean or lake that cuts deeply into the land. (p. 10)

Bear Flag Revolt (bâr flag ri vōlt′) The first battle fought by Californians to be free from Mexico. (p. 159)

bias (bī′əs) A one-sided presentation of information. (p. 330)

Big Four (big fôr) Four California men—Leland Stanford, Charles Crocker, Collis Huntington, and Mark Hopkins—who became investors in the Central Pacific Railroad. See **investor**. (p. 219)

border (bôr′dər) A line that people agree on to separate two places. (p. 8)

boycott (boi′kot) A refusal to do business with a company. (p. 297)

brand (brand) A mark on a cow's hip made with a hot iron, which identifies the ranch to which the cow belongs. (p. 143)

bribe (brīb) Money paid to an official to do something. (p. 231)

byline (bī′līn) A line at the beginning of a newspaper or magazine article that names the writer. (p. 356)

C

Californio (kal ə fôr′nē ō) A person who lived in California. (p. 146)

canal (kə nal′) An inland waterway built by people for transportation or irrigation. (p. 251)

capital (kap′i təl) A city where a government meets. (p. 190)

cardinal direction (kär′də nəl di rek′shən) One of the main directions of the globe; north, south, east, and west. (p. G6)

Central Pacific Railroad (sen′trəl pə sif′ik rāl′rōd) A railroad owned by the Big Four, which became the Southern Pacific Railroad. See **Big Four**. (p. 219)

Chinese Exclusion Act (chī nēz′ ek sklü′zhən akt) A law that kept out Chinese immigrants. See **immigrant**. (p. 226)

circle graph (sûr′kəl graf) A graph that shows how the parts of something make up or fit into the whole. See **graph**. (p. 177)

citizen (sit′ə zən) A person who is born in a country or who has earned the right to become a member of that country by law. (p. 45)

pronunciation key

a	at	ī	ice	u	up	th	thin
ā	ape	îr	pierce	ū	use	th	this
ä	far	o	hot	ü	rule	zh	measure
âr	care	ō	old	ù	pull	ə	about, taken,
e	end	ô	fork	ûr	turn		pencil, lemon,
ē	me	oi	oil	hw	white		circus
i	it	ou	out	ng	song		

city council (sit′ē koun′sil) A group of representatives that makes a city's laws and decides how it should spend its money. (p. 349)

city manager (sit′ē man′əj ər) A person who runs a city's daily business. (p. 349)

civil rights (siv′əl rīts) The rights of all people to be treated equally under the law. (p. 296)

climate (klī′mit) The pattern of weather of a certain place over many years. (p. 32)

coast (kōst) The land next to an ocean. (p. 10)

Cold War (kōld wôr) The belief that the United States would be in a war against the Soviet Union. (p. 292)

colony (kol′ə nē) A place that is ruled by another country. (p. 85)

communication (kə mū ni kā′shən) The exchange of information between people. (p. 214)

commute (kə mūt′) To travel to a job. (p. 365)

compass rose (kum′pəs rōz) A small drawing on a map that shows directions. (p. G6)

Compromise of 1850 (kom′prə mīz) An agreement that California would join the United States as a free (nonslave) state, but California police would help capture slaves who had escaped from the South. (p. 190)

conclusion (kən klü′zhən) A statement that tells how facts are connected. (p. 198)

Congress (kong′gris) The legislative branch of the United States government, which makes national laws. See **legislative branch**. (p. 354)

conquistador (kon kēs′tə dôr) The Spanish word for the soldiers who conquered the Americas in the 1500s. (p. 84)

conservation (kon sər vā′shən) The careful use of a natural resource. (p. 46)

constitution (kon sti tü′shən) A plan of government. (p. 189)

continent (kon′tə nənt) One of Earth's seven large bodies of land—Africa, Antarctica, Asia, Australia, Europe, North America, and South America. (p. G4)

convention (kən ven′shən) A formal meeting for a special purpose. (p. 189)

convert (kən vûrt′) To change a person's religious beliefs. (p. 105)

culture (kul′chər) A way of life that includes work, play, and family life. (p. 19)

current events (kur′ənt i vents′) The things that happen every day. (p. 356)

D

dam (dam) A wall built across a river to create a reservoir. See **reservoir**. (p. 253)

dateline (dāt′lin) A line that tells when and where a newspaper story was written. (p. 356)

decision (di si′zhən) A choice that helps you reach a goal. (p. 48)

degree (di grē′) A unit for measuring distance on Earth's surface; also a unit for measuring temperature. Represented by the symbol °. (p. 96)

delta (del′tə) Land formed by soil and sand left behind by one or more rivers. (p. 17)

democratic republic (dem ə krat′ik ri pub′lik) A government in which citizens elect representatives to make decisions for them. (p. 230)

demonstration (dem ən strā′shən) A large gathering of people who want to make their feelings and beliefs known. (p. 295)

deport (dē pôrt′) An action of the government of a country that forces people to leave that country. (p. 262)

derrick (der′ik) A tower used to support drilling machines. (p. 284)

desert (dez′ərt) An area that gets less than 10 inches of rain in an average year. (p. 20)

diputación (dē pü ta syōn′) A group of wealthy and important people who were elected by California settlers and who advised the governor. (p. 140)

discrimination (di skrim ə nā′shən) An unfair difference in the way people are treated. (p. 226)

diseño (dē se′nyō) A map showing a rancho's borders. See **rancho**. (p. 139)

diversity (di vûr′si tē) Many different kinds. (p. 62)

drought (drout) A long period with very little rain. (p. 241)

Dust Bowl (dust bōl) A seven-year drought in an area in the Great Plains of the United States that turned the land into dust. See **drought**. (p. 264)

E

earthquake (ûrth′kwāk) A shaking of the earth. (p. 24)

economy (i kon′ə mē) The way a country or other place uses or produces natural resources, goods, and services. (p. 39)

editorial (ed i tôr′ē əl) A newspaper article that gives opinions rather than facts. (p. 356)

elevation (el ə vā′shən) The height of land above sea level. (p. 216)

empire (em′pīr) A large area with different groups of people ruled by a single country or ruler. (p. 85)

engineer (en jə nîr′) Someone who is skilled in designing and building things. (p. 215)

environment (en vī′rən mənt) The surroundings in which people, plants, or animals live. (p. 36)

equator (i kwā′tər) An imaginary line that lies halfway between the North Pole and the South Pole, at 0° latitude. (p. G5)

ethnic group (eth′nik grüp) A group of people whose ancestors come from the same country or area and/or who share a common cultural heritage. (p. 342)

executive branch (eg zek′yə tiv branch) The branch of government that carries out laws. (p. 350)

expedition (ek spi dish′ən) A journey of exploration. (p. 86)

export (ek′spôrt) Something sold or traded to another country. (p. 145)

F

fact (fakt) A statement that can be checked and proven true. (p. 330)

fault (fôlt) A crack in the ground caused by moving plates. See **plate tectonics**. (p. 24)

fertile (fûr′təl) Soil that is good for growing crops. (p. 18)

fertilizer (fûr′tə lī zər) Chemicals and natural products added to soil to make it more fertile. See **fertile**. (p. 39)

fiesta (fē es′tə) The Spanish word for celebration. (p. 147)

filmmaker (film′mā kər) A person who makes movies. (p. 321)

Forty-Niner (fôr tē nī′nər) A person who went to California in 1849 to find gold. (p. 172)

freeway (frē′wā) A fast road that has no toll. (p. 292)

frontier (frun tîr′) The edge of a settled area. (p. 114)

fuel (fū′əl) Something that is burned to make energy. (p. 40)

G

galleon (gal′ē ən) A big, heavy ship with many decks for carrying cargo or goods. (p. 92)

geography (jē og′rə fē) The study of Earth and the way people, plants, and animals live on and use it. (p. 8)

global grid (glō′bəl grid) The crisscrossing lines of latitude and longitude on a map or globe. (p. 98)

Gold Rush (gōld rush) A rapid movement of people in search of gold. (p. 171)

government (guv′ərn mənt) The laws and people that run a country, state, city, or town. (p. 27)

governor (guv′ər nər) The head of the executive branch of state government, elected by all the people in the state for no more than two 4-year terms. See **executive branch**. (p. 350)

granary (grā′nə rē) A building used for storing food. (p. 74)

graph (graf) A special diagram that shows information in a clear way. See **line graph**. (p. 176)

Great Depression (grāt di presh′ən) A time of hardship in many countries. (p. 264)

H

harbor (här′bər) A sheltered place along a coast where boats can be docked. (p. 10)

harvest (här′vist) A gathering of a crop or resource. (p. 68)

headline (hed′līn) A title printed in large letters at the beginning of a newspaper article. (p. 356)

hemisphere (hem′i sfîr) Half a sphere; one of the four hemispheres of Earth—Northern, Southern, Eastern, and Western hemispheres. (p. G5)

high technology (hī tek nol′ə jē) The use of computers and other electronics to meet new wants and needs. (p. 324)

historic site (hi stôr′ik sīt) A building, battlefield, or other place where an event or events took place. (p. 313)

historical map (hi stôr′i kəl map) A map that shows information about past events and where they occurred. (p. G11)

human resource (hū′mən rē′sôrs) The knowledge, skills, and energy of people. (p. 42)

hydraulic mining (hī dro′lik mī′ning) A process in which miners used hoses to shoot water at hillsides thought to have gold. See **placer**. (p. 185)

hydroelectric power (hī drō i lek′trik pou′ər) Electricity made from flowing water in rivers. (p. 255)

I

immigrant (im′i grənt) A person who comes to a new country to live. (p. 222)

import (im′pôrt) Something brought in from another country for sale or use. (p. 144)

industry (in′də strē) All the businesses that make one kind of product or provide one kind of service. (p. 282)

initiative (i nish′ə tiv) The right of citizens to suggest laws and then vote on them. (p. 232)

intermediate direction (in tər mē′dē it di rek′shən) Any direction in between two cardinal directions— northeast, southeast, southwest, northwest. (p. G6)

international trade (in tər nash′ə nəl trād) The exchange of goods between countries. (p. 332)

internment camp (in tûrn′mənt kamp) A place where people are imprisoned during wartime. (p. 287)

interstate highway (in′tər stāt hī′wā) A road with at least two lanes of traffic in each direction that connects two or more states. (p. 370)

investor (in vest′ər) Someone who puts money into a business and expects a share of the profit. (p. 219)

irrigation (ir i gā′shən) The use of ditches or pipes to bring water to fields. (p. 73)

isthmus (is′məs) A narrow stretch of land with water on both sides. (p. 172)

J

judicial branch (jü dish′əl branch) The branch of government that makes sure people follow our laws. (p. 350)

L

labor union (lā′bər ūn′yən) A group of workers who organize to make agreements with their employer. (p. 297)

landform (land′fôrm) Any of the shapes that make up Earth's surface. (p. 8)

landform map (land′fôrm map) A map that shows the landforms of an area. (p. G10)

land grant (land grant) Free land the Mexican government gave to Mexicans who settled in California. (p. 139)

latitude (lat′i tüd) A measure of distance north or south of the equator on Earth. See **parallel**. (p. 96)

legislative branch (lej′is lā tiv branch) The branch of government that makes laws. See **Congress**. (p. 350)

legislature (lej′is lā chər) A group of representatives who make laws. (p. 190)

line graph (līn graf) A graph that shows how something has changed over time. See **graph**. (p. 176)

llavera (yä vä′rä) The "keeper of the keys" at a Spanish Mission. (p. 120)

locator (lō′kāt ər) A small map or globe set onto another map that shows where the main map is located. (p. G8)

longitude (lon′ji tüd) A measure of distance east or west of the prime meridian on Earth. See **meridian, prime meridian**. (p. 97)

M

Manifest Destiny (man′ə fest des′tə nē) The belief that the United States had the right to take over other countries' lands in America. (p. 158)

manufacture (man yə fak′chər) To make large amounts of goods in factories. (p. 289)

map key (map kē) An explanation of what the symbols on a map represent. (p. G7)

market (mär′kit) A place where goods are bought and sold. (p. 240)

mayor (mā′ər) The head of the city government. See **alcalde**. (p. 349)

meridian (mə rid′ē ən) A line of longitude. See **longitude**. (p. 97)

mestizo (mes tē′zō) A person who is part Spanish and part Indian. (p. 146)

metropolitan area (met rə pol′i tən âr′ē ə) A large city and its suburbs. See **suburb**. (p. 364)

Mexican War (mek′si kən wôr) A war between Mexico and the United States for possession of Texas that spread to California. (p. 160)

migrant labor (mī′grənt lā′bər) People who move from place to place to harvest different crops as they ripen. (p. 261)

mineral (min′ər əl) A nonrenewable natural resource, such as silver ore and iron ore, that is found in the earth. (p. 40)

minimum wage (min′ə məm wāj) The lowest amount of money a business can pay its workers. (p. 235)

mission (mish′ən) A Spanish settlement in the Americas where priests taught Native Americans the Christian religion. (p. 104)

missionary (mish′ə ner ē) A person who teaches religious beliefs to others who have different beliefs. (p. 105)

Modoc War (mō′dok wôr) A war between the United States and the Modoc, which lasted from 1872 to 1873. (p. 195)

mother lode (muth′ər lōd) A gold-rich area in the central Sierra Nevada foothills. (p. 175)

mutual aid society (mū′chü əl ād sə sī′i tē) A group in which the members help each other. (p. 275)

mutualista (mū chü ə lē′stə) A group of people who organize to help others. (p. 262)

N

NAFTA (naf′tə) North American Free Trade Agreement—a trade treaty in which the United States, Canada, and Mexico promise to cooperate in trading with one another. (p. 332)

natural resource (nach′ər əl rē′sôrs) Something found in the environment that people can use. (p. 38)

New Deal (nü dēl) A series of programs that put people to work during the Great Depression. See **Great Depression**. (p. 264)

news article (nüz är′ti kəl) A story based on facts about an event or events that happened. (p. 356)

nonrenewable resource (non ri nü′ə bəl rē′sôrs) A natural resource that is limited in supply and cannot be replaced, such as a fuel or mineral. (p. 40)

Northwest Passage (nôrth′west′ pas′ij) A route to Asia through North America. See **Strait of Anián**. (p. 90)

pronunciation key

a at; ā ape; ä far; âr care; e end; ē me; i it; ī ice; îr pierce; o hot; ō old; ô fork; oi oil; ou out; u up; ū use; ü rule; ủ pull; ûr turn; hw white; ng song; th thin; th this; zh measure; ə about, taken, pencil, lemon, circus

ocean (ō′shən) One of Earth's four largest bodies of water—the Arctic, Atlantic, Indian, and Pacific oceans. (p. G4)

opinion (ə pin′yən) A personal belief or feeling. (p. 330)

outline (out′līn) A plan for organizing written information about a subject. (p. 78)

Pacific Rim (pə sif′ik rim) All the countries that touch the Pacific Ocean. (p. 332)

panning (pa′ning) A process in which a miner scooped dirt into a shallow pan, filled the pan with water, and spilled out the water and dirt. Any heavy gold in the dirt would stay in the pan. (p. 180)

parallel (par′ə lel) Another name for a line of latitude. *See* **latitude**. (p. 96)

pass (pas) A narrow gap between mountains. (p. 173)

pelt (pelt) The skin of an animal. (p. 151)

petroleum (pə trō′lē əm) A fuel, commonly called oil, that formed underground from dead plants. (p. 40)

physical map (fiz′i kəl map) A map that shows natural features of Earth. (p. G10)

placer (plas′ər) A Spanish word that means "a sandy stream bank." (p. 180)

plain (plān) A large area of nearly flat land. (p. 11)

plate tectonics (plāt tek ton′iks) The theory that Earth's surface is made up of plates that are constantly moving. *See* **earthquake**. (p. 24)

plaza (plä′zə) A square park. (p. 115)

political map (pə lit′i kəl map) A map that shows information such as cities, capitals, states, and countries. (p. G9)

political party (pə lit′i kəl pär′tē) A group of people who share similar ideas about government. (p. 233)

pollution (pə lü′shən) Anything that makes air, water, or soil dirty or unsafe to use. (p. 44)

population (pop yə lā′shən) The number of people who live in a place or area. (p. 42)

precipitation (pri sip i tā′shən) The moisture that falls to the ground as rain, snow, sleet, or hail. (p. 34)

President (prez′i dənt) The person who is head of the executive branch of the United States government. *See* **executive branch**. (p. 354)

presidio (pri sid′ē ō) A fort where Spanish soldiers lived. (p. 114)

prime meridian (prīm mə rid′ē ən) The line of longitude, marked 0°, from which other meridians are numbered. (p. 97)

Proposition 13 (prop ə zish′ən) A law that cut taxes on property in California by more than half. (p. 298)

public (pub′lik) Anything that is partly supported by taxes. (p. 358)

pueblo (pweb′lō) A farming town. (p. 114)

rain shadow (rān shad′ō) The side of a mountain that is usually dry because precipitation falls on the other side. (p. 35)

rancho (ran′chō) A ranch where cattle, horses, and other animals were raised. (p. 139)

recycle (rē sī′kəl) To use something again instead of throwing it away. (p. 46)

reformer (ri fôrm′ər) A person who wants to improve the way government is run. (p. 232)

refrigeration (ri frij′ə rā shən) The process of keeping food cool to preserve it. (p. 242)

refugee (ref′yü jē) Someone who flees unsafe conditions in his or her homeland. (p. 344)

region (rē′jən) An area with common features that set it apart from other areas. (p. 9)

religion (ri lij′ən) A way of worshiping the God or gods a group's members believe in. (p. 60)

renewable resource (rē nü′ə bəl rē′sôrs) A natural resource that can be replaced for later use, such as a forest. (p. 39)

representative (rep ri zen′tə tiv) A person who speaks for one or more people. (p. 188)

republic (ri pub′lik) A government in which people choose leaders to represent them. (p. 159)

reservation (rez ər vā′shən) Land set aside by the United States government for Native Americans to live on. (p. 195)

reservoir (rez′ər vwär) A natural or human-built lake used to store water. *See* **dam**. (p. 253)

resolution (rez ə lü′shən) A statement of a decision made by a legislature. (p. 352)

revolt (ri vōlt′) To resist with violence. (p. 122)

Richter scale (rik′tər skāl) A scale for measuring how strong an earthquake is. (p. 26)

road map (rōd map) A map that shows roads. (p. 370)

Rumford Act (rum′fərd akt) A law passed in California in 1963 that said California property owners could not discriminate because of race. (p. 296)

rural (rur′əl) A country way of life. (p. 19)

scale (skāl) The measurement a map uses to indicate the real size of a place on Earth. (p. G8)

segregate (seg′ri gāt) Separate. (p. 296)

services (sûr′vis əz) Jobs in which people's work is helping others, rather than making things. (p. 310)

shaman (shā′mən) A religious leader and healer. (p. 76)

silicon (sil′i kon) A material used in making microchips. *See* **Silicon Valley**. (p. 326)

Silicon Valley (sil′i kon val′ē) A key center of the country's computer industry, located in the Santa Clara Valley, named for silicon. *See* **silicon**. (p. 326)

slavery (slā′və rē) The practice of making one person the property of another. (p. 86)

smog (smog) A kind of air pollution; a combination of smoke and fog. (p. 44)

software (sôft′wâr) A program or set of instructions that tells a computer what to do. (p. 327)

source (sôrs) The place where a river begins. (p. 12)

squatter (skwot′ər) A person who settles on land without permission from the owner of the land. (p. 196)

State Supreme Court (stāt sə prēm′ kôrt) The highest court in the state. (p.350)

stereotype (ster′ē ə tīp) An idea that all the people in a group are the same in some way. (p. 280)

Strait of Anián (strāt uv ä nē än′) An imaginary waterway to Asia through North America; a narrow body of water. *See* **Northwest Passage**. (p. 86)

strike (strīk) An action in which workers refuse to work until employers meet their demands. (p. 261)

suburb (sub′ûrb) A community near a large city. (p. 292)

suffrage (suf′rij) The right to vote. (p. 234)

Supreme Court (sə prēm′ kôrt) The highest court of the United States. (p. 355)

sweat house (swet hous) A building where men and boys sat around an open fire until they sweated. (p. 68)

symbol (sim′bəl) Anything that stands for something else. (p. G7)

T

tax (taks) Money people pay to the government so it can perform public services. (p. 140)

technology (tek nol′ə jē) The use of skills, ideas, and tools to meet people's needs. (p. 213)

telecommuters (tel ə kə mūt′ərz) People who work at home, using telephones, fax machines, and computer modems to communicate with their bosses and other workers. (p. 368)

telegraph (tel′ə graf) A way of sending messages by sending an electrical code through a wire. (p. 214)

temperature (tem′pər ə chər) A measurement of how hot or cold something is—often the air. (p. 33)

time line (tīm līn) A diagram that shows when events took place. (p. 156)

tomol (tō′mäl) A kind of light canoe. (p. 65)

tourism (tùr′iz əm) The many different kinds of businesses that sell goods and services to people who travel on vacations. (p. 311)

tractor (trak′tər) A small, powerful vehicle for pulling farm machinery. (p. 241)

transcontinental (trans kon tə nen′təl) Crossing an entire continent. (p. 215)

transportation (trans pər tā′shən) The movement of people and goods from one place to another. (p. 210)

transportation map (trans pər tā′shən map) A map that shows how to travel from one place to another. (p. G10)

trapper (trap′ər) Someone who traps, or catches, animals, such as beavers, for their fur. (p. 151)

treaty (trē′tē) An agreement to make peace. (p. 162)

Treaty of Guadalupe Hidalgo (trē′tē uv gwäd′əl üp ā ē dal′gō) The agreement that ended the war between Mexico and the United States. *See* **treaty**. (p. 162)

tributary (trib′yə ter ē) A small river that flows into a larger river. (p. 17)

tule (tü′lē) A kind of reed that people used to build houses and boats. (p. 72)

U

urban (ûr′bən) Of a city. (p. 11)

V

valley (val′ē) Flat, V-shaped, or U-shaped area between mountain ranges. (p. 17)

vaquero (vä kâr′ō) A cowhand. (p. 142)

viceroy (vīs′roi) A ruler picked by a king. (p. 86)

Vietnam War (vē et näm′ wôr) A war (1954–1975) in which the United States fought on the side of South Vietnam in its fight against North Vietnam. (p. 294)

vigilante (vij ə lan′tē) A citizen who takes the law into his or her own hands. (p. 194)

W

wetland (wet′land) Land that is wet much of the time, such as a swamp or a marsh. (p. 17)

---

pronunciation key

a **at**; ā **ape**; ä **far**; âr **care**; e **end**; ē **me**; i **it**; ī **ice**; îr **pierce**; o **hot**; ō **old**; ô **fork**; oi **oil**; ou **out**; u **up**; ū **use**; ü **rule**; ù **pull**; ûr **turn**; hw **white**; ng **song**; th **thin**; <u>th</u> **this**; zh **measure**; ə **about, taken, pencil, lemon, circus**

index

This Index lists many topics that appear in the book, along with the pages on which they are found. Page numbers after an *m* refer you to a map. Page numbers after a *p* indicate photographs, artwork, or charts.

Cover: MSD

Maps: Geosystems

Chapter Opener Globes: Greg Wakabayashi

Illustrations: Bernard Adnet: p 41; Hal Brooks: p 245; Chris Duke: p 181; Joe Forte: pp 58-59, 82-83, 102-103,134-135, 208-209, 238-239; Jim Griffin: p 219; Nick Harris: pp 224-225; Henry Hill: pp 26, 34-35, 285, 367; Joe LeMonnier: p 256; Shane Marsh: pp 92-93; Michael Maydak: pp R26-R27; Karen Minot: pp R28-R29; Tony Randazzo: p 289; Victoria Raymond: p 263; Dennis Schofield: pp 168-169, 270-271; Stephen Schudlich: pp 314-315; Tony Silvia: p 61; Terry Sirrell: p 320; Nina Wallace: p 352; David Wenzel: pp121, 254; all other illustrations by the McGraw-Hill School Division

Photography Credits: All photographs are by the McGraw-Hill School Division except as noted below.

iii: t. Dan Guravich/Photo Researchers; b.l. Robert Finken/Picture Cube; b.r. Superstock. iv: t.l. Gordon Graham/National Geographic Image Collection; b.l. T.J. Florian/Photo Network; b.r. Jerry Jacka/The Heard Museum. v: l. Oakland Museum of California; m. Tom Myers; r. Bancroft Library. vi: t. The Granger Collection; b.l. Michael Sewell/Visuals Unlimited; b.r. John F. Mason/The Stock Market. vii: Jim Corwin/Photo Researchers; b.m. Mickey Pfleger/Photo 20-20; b.l., b.r. Chuck O'Rear/Westlight. viii: Ken Chernus/FPG. ix: l. California State Parks; r. The Granger Collection. x: t. Richard Hutchings/Photo Researchers; b. History Collections, Los Angeles County Museum of Natural History. G2: l. John Lamb, Tony Stone Images; r. Galen Rowell. G3: t. Uniphoto, Inc.; m. Bruce Dale; b. Raymond Gehman. 2-3: PhotoDisc. 2: t. C.Vergara/Photo Researchers; m. D.Young-Wolff/PhotoEdit; b. Kevin Schafer. 3: b.r. Joseph Dovala/PhotoNetwork; t.r. Robert Finken/The Picture Cube. 4: t. Jeff Foott; b. David Muench, Tony Stone Images. 4-5: Bruce Forster, Tony Stone Images. 5: t. The Granger Collection, New York; b. © Jim Russi and Adventure Photo & Film. 7: b. Robert Holmes; b.m. Kunio Owaki/The Stock Market; t. Ted Streshinsky/Photo 20-20; t.m. Neil Gilchrist/Photo 20-20. **Chapter 1** 8: John Henley/The Stock Market.

9: Galen Rowell/Mountain Light. 10: r. Mark E. Gibson; l. Phil Crews. 12-13: David Muench Photography. 13: r. Steve Raymer/National Geographic Image Collection. 16: t.l. Mark E. Gibson. 16-17: David Weintraub/Photo Researchers. 17: Dan Guravich/Photo Researchers. 18: t.l. Lawrence Migdale. 19: r. Mark Gibson. 20: Carr Clifton/Minden Pictures. 21: t.l. Robert Siebert; b.r. Rod Planck/Photo Researchers. 22. Pete Saloutas/The Stock Market; 23: r. David Muench; m. Tom Wurl/Stock Boston; b.l. Mark E. Gibson; b.r. Mark Newman/Photo Network. 24: t.l. L. Burr/Liaison International; b. Tom Myers. 25: Tom Myers. 26: Mark Downey/Liaison. **Chapter 2** 31: t. Dave Brown/The Stock Market; t.m. Karen Kasmauski/Woodfin Camp; b.m. Bill Ross/Westlight; b. Joel Sartore/National Geographic Image Collection. 32: t.l. courtesy of KPIX Television, CBS Inc. 32-33:b. PhotoDisc. 36: b.r. Daniel J. Cox/Tony Stone Images; b.l. Raymond G. Barnes/Tony Stone Worldwide; m.b. Ralph H. Wetmore II/Tony Stone Images. 37: b. Robert Finken/The Picture Cube. 38: t. Bob Thomason/Tony Stone Images. 39: b. Kim Robbie/The Stock Market; t. Superstock, Inc. 40: b. Ruth Dixon/Stock Boston; b.l. Superstock, Inc. 42: b.l. Lawrence Migdale. 43: r. Fairsite School. 44: t.l. Lori Adamski Peek/Tone Stone Images. 45: t.r. Tom Myers; b. Jane Braxton Little. 46: b. Jim Corwin/Tony Stone Images. 47: t.l. Photo courtesy of the Tree Musketeers. 48: b.l. inset Stephen Frisch/Stock Boston; b. Kathleen Campbell/Liaison International. 49: t.r. Mark E. Gibson; m.r. Tom Myers. 54:t.l. San Diego Historical Society; t.r. Brooks-Brown/Photo Researchers; m.r. The Granger Collection; b. David Olsen/Tony Stone Images. 55: t. Deborah Davis/PhotoEdit; b. James Randklev/Tony Stone Images. 56: t. The Granger Collection, New York; b. Mort Kunstler. 56-57: Giraudon/Art Resource. 57: t. The Granger Collection, New York; b. Jean-Leon Huens. **Chapter 3** 60: t. The Bancroft Library; b. William B. Dewey/Santa Barbara Museum of Natural History. 62-63: t. The Oakland Museum of California. 63: b. Jerry Jacka. 64: t. Edward S. Curtis/National Geographic Image Collection. 65: l., r. Santa Barbara Museum of Natural History. 66: t.l. San Diego Historical Society; t.r. Santa Barbara Museum of Natural History; b. James Randklev/Tony Stone Images. 67: Santa Barbara Museum of Natural History. 68: r. Jim Corwin/Photo Researchers; b. Tom McHugh/Photo Researchers. 69: r. The Bancroft Library; l. Denver Art Museum. 70: t. Jerry Jacka; m. Jell B. Sandved/Visuals Unlimited; b. Dugan Aguilar. 71: r. San Diego Historical Society; m. The Heard Museum; b. Jerry Jacka. 72: San Diego Historical Society. 72-73: b. M. Segal/Panoramic Stock Images. 73: l. Robert Holmes/Holmes Photography. 73: r. The Huntington Library. 74: r. San Diego Historical Society; l.NAA, Smithsonian Institution #41886-0; 74-75: Henry Wolf/The Image Bank; 75: l. Field Museum, Chicago #A-10563; m. San Diego Museum of Man; r. Field Museum, Chicago #A-9518. 76: Courtesy of the National Museum of the American Indian, Smithsonian Institution #24371. 77: Lawrence Migdale. 79: Courtesy of the National Museum of the American Indian, Smithsonian Institution #N36078 **Chapter 4** 84: t.l. Photo Network. 85: b. The Granger Collection; r. The British Museum. 86: The Granger Collection. 87: b.r. Mark E. Gibson. 88: t. Stephen Kraseman/Tony Stone Images. 89: b.l. The Oakland Museum of California; m. Seaver Center; History Collections, Los Angeles County Museum of Natural History. 90: t.l. Gordon Graham/National Geographic Society; 90-91: b. Gary Moon/Tony Stone Images. 91: t.l. National Portrait Gallery, London/Superstock, Inc.; t.r. Susan Middleton/California Academy of Science. 94: inset l. PhotoNetwork; inset m.l. Superstock, Inc.; inset r. Seaver Center, History Collections, Los Angeles County Museum of Natural History. 95: Don Landwherle/The Image Bank. **Chapter 5** 104: t. The Bancroft Library. 105: b.l. Tony Freeman/PhotoEdit, b.r. The Granger Collection. 106: t. The Bancroft Library. 107: b. Mark Sexton/Peabody Essex Museum; t.r. Gaspar de Portola en su Cuidad Natal en Balaguer-Lleida. 108-109: Christies Images/Superstock. 110: b. North Wind Pictures. 111: b.r. Henry Groskinsky. 112: b. British Museum; t.l. Michael Sewell/Visual Pursuit. 114: b.l. Seaver Center, History Collections, Los Angeles County Museum of Natural History. 115: t. Chuck Place. 116-117: T.J. Florian/Photo Network. 117: t.r. Ahmad M. Abdalla/Photo Network; m.r. Chuck Place; b.r. Pete Saloutos/The Stock Market. 118: Tony Freeman/PhotoEdit. 119: b. Lawrence Migdale/Stock Boston; t. Tony Freeman/PhotoEdit. 120: USC/Department of Special Collections; b.l. Santa Barbara Mission Archive-Library. 122: New York Public Library Picture Collection. 123: Loren Bommelyn. 125: The Granger Collection. 127: Michael Evans/Sygma. 130: t., b. Oakland Museum of California; m.l. George Grall/National Geographic Images Collection; m.r. Bancroft Library. 131: t. Bancroft Library; b. Don Mason/The Stock Market. 132: t. Myrleen Ferguson, PhotoEdit; b. California State Library. 132-133: Geoffrey C. Clifford, The Stock Market. 133: t. Museum of New Mexico; b. Bancroft Library. **Chapter 6** 136: t.r., t.l. North Wind Pictures. 137: b. Michael Newman/PhotoEdit; t. California History Section, California State Library. 138: Seaver Center for Western History Research, Natural History Museum of Los Angeles County. 139: m. Bancroft Library, University of California, Berkeley; t. Bancroft Library, University of California, Berkeley. 140: b. Pat & Tom Leeson/Photo Researchers, Inc.; t. The Granger Collection. 141: b. Myrleen Ferguson/PhotoEdit. 142: t. Seaver Center for Western History Research, Natural History Museum of Los Angeles County. 143: b.r. Tom Myers; l. The Bancroft Library, University of California, Berkeley. 144: b.r. Seaver Center for Western History Research, Natural History Museum of Los Angeles County. 145: t.r. The Granger Collection. 146: t. Mark E. Gibson; b. courtesy Shirley Jolliff/Alta California Dance Co. 147: b. Shirley Jolliff/Alta California Dance Co. 148: b.r. inset Clarence Towers; b.l. Bruce Hands/The Image Works; m. Superstock, Inc.; t. Bob Daemmrich/The Image Works. 148-149: b. Superstock, Inc. 149: b. Tom Myers Photography. 149: t.r. John Elk III. 150: t.l. James Amos/Corbis. 151: t. The Granger Collection; b. Ron Spomer/Visuals Unlimited. 152: t. Peter Newark's Western Americana. 152-153: b. North Wind Picture Archives. 153: m., t. Tom Myers Photography. 155: b. Baron Wolman/Tony Stone Images; m.r. James Amos/Corbis. 158: t. Cindy Charles/PhotoEdit. 159: t.l. National Portrait Gallery, Smithsonian Institution/Art Resource, NY; t.r. The Granger Collection; b. Corbis-Bettmann. 160: Seaver Center for Western History Research, Natural History Museum of Los Angeles County. 161: t.r. Brown Brothers; b.l. Cindy Charles/PhotoEdit; b.r. Peter Newark's American Pictures; t.m. Bancroft Library, University of California, Berkeley; m., b.m. Seaver Center for Western History Research, Natural History Museum of Los Angeles County. 164: l. Seaver Center for Western History Research, Natural History Museum of Los Angeles County. 165: b. The Granger Collection; m. California Department of Parks and Recreation Photographic Archives/Tom Meyers; t. Seaver Center for Western Research, Natural History Museum of Los Angeles County. **Chapter 7** 170: t.l. Superstock; b.r. The Granger Collection. 171: r. Corbis-Bettmann; b.l. California Historical Society FN-12015. 173: l. Oakland Museum of California; b.r. The Granger Collection; t.r. California Historical Society FN-25814. 174: b. Superstock, Inc. 175: m. Oakland Museum of California. 177: b.r. Superstock, Inc. 178: The Granger Collection. 178-179: b. San Francisco Maritime Museum. 182: t. inset Underwood Photo Archives, SF.; b. inset California State Library/Tom Myers. 182-183: b. California State Library/Tom Meyers. 184-185: t. California State Library/Tom Myers. 185: b. Tom Myers. 186: m., b. Levi Strauss & Co. Archives. 186-187: Daniel R. Westergren/National Geographic Society. 187: b.r. Peter Newark's Western America. 188: t.l. Tom Myers Photography. 188-189: b. Superstock. 189: b.r. California State Archives. 191: t. The Granger Collection; b. Library of Congress 714086 USZ62-763. 192: The Granger Collection. 193: b.r. Analisa Castaneda. 194: t.l. Society of California Pioneers. 195: b.r. The Granger Collection; b.m. California Historical Society FN-30839. 196: Seaver Center, History Collections, LA County Museum of Natural History. 197: b. California State Library/Tom Myers. 198: t. The Bancroft Library; b. California Historical Society FN-30840. 199: Huntington Library/Superstock. 204: b. W. A. Todd, Jr./The Picture Cube; m.l., m.r., The Granger Collection; t. Corbis-Bettman. 205: Collection of the New York Historical Society; b. Tom Myers. 206: t. Jonathan Selig, m. David Young-Woolf, b. Andy Sacks, all Tony Stone Images. 206-207: Uniphoto, Inc. 207: t. Chad Slattery, b. George Lepp, both Tony Stone Images. **Chapter 8** 210-211: b. Peter Newark's American Pictures. 210: t.l. Los Angeles County Museum of Natural History, Seaver Center For Western History Research. 211: m. The Granger Collection. 212: t.l. Superstock, Inc.; t.r. Peter Newark's Western America. 213: b.l. Sam Abell/National Geographic Image Collection. 214: t. California State Railroad Museum; b.r. The Granger Collection. 215: b. California State Railroad Museum. 216-217: PhotoDisc. 218: t.l. John Cunningham/Visuals Unlimited. 219: t. Corbis-Bettmann. 220: t. The Granger Collection. 220-221: b. Oakland Museum History Department. 222-223: San Diego Chinese Historical Museum. 222: t.l. California State Railroad Museum. 225: t. MMSD (Southern Pacific Photos). 226: b.r. Michael Sewell/Visuals Unlimited; b.l. Frank Pedrick/The Image Works. 227: b. Art Department/San Francisco State University; t. The Granger Collection. 228: Underwood Photo Archives. 229: t.l. George Tiedemann/Sports Illustrated, Time Inc.; t.r. Joe Sohm/Unicorn Stock Photos; b. David Madison/Bruce Colmean, Inc. 230: t.l. California Historical Society. 231: Tom Myers. 232: b.l. The Granger Collection; b.r. Culver Pictures; t. California Historical Society. 234: t. California History Section/California State Library/Tom Myers. 234-235: b. Corbis-Bettmann. 235: t. Library of Congress. **Chapter 9** 240: Oakland Museum of California. 241: t.r. John and Diane Harper/New England Stock Photo; m. Culver Pictures, Inc.; b. Arthur C. Smith III/Grant Heilman. 242: Department of Special Collections, U.S.C. Library; t.r. Sunkist Growers. 244-245: PhotoDisc. 244: t. Tom Myers; b.l. Kenneth Garrett/Woodfin Camp; b.r. John F. Mason/The Stock Market. 245: t. Superstock; m. Tom Myers; b.l. Rick H. Browne/Stock Boston; b.r. Rosenfeld Images/Photo Researchers. 246: b.r. U.C. Davis; b.l. Archive Stock Photos; b.m. Corbis-Bettmann. 250: Alexander Lowry/Photo Researchers. 251: t. Robert Holmes; b., m. California State Railroad Museum. 252: b., t. L.A. Department of Water Power. 253: r. Mark E. Gibson; l. Corbis-Bettmann. 255: Peter Menzel/Stock Boston. 256: b.r. Jim Richardson/Westlight. 256-257: Ron Chapple/FPG International. 257: t. California Department of Water Resources; m. Peter Menzel/Stock Boston; b. Tom Campbell/Tony Stone Images. 258: Jim Cummins/FPG International. 259: t. Myriam Cardenas; m. Robert Duncan; b. Glenda Huniston. 260: Robert Holmes. 260-261: J.O. Tucker/National Geographic Image Collection. 262: Special Collections Dept., U.S.C. Library. 264: b. Corbis-Bettmann; t.l. Archive Photos. 265: Corbis-Bettmann. 266: t.r. Diego Rivera, "The Making of a Fresco Showing the Building of a City", 1931, 22'7" x 29'9", San Francisco Art Institute; b.l. Photodisc. 267: t. Tai Dang; t.r. Photodisc; b. Nancy Hoyt Belcher/Photo Network. **Chapter 10** 272: t.l. California State Parks/Tom Myers. 273: t.r. California Historical Society, San Francisco. FN-18240; b. California State Parks/Tom Meyers. 275: m.r., t.l. Underwood Photo Archives; b. Robin L. Sachs/PhotoEdit. 277: t.l. Lawrence Migdale/Stock Boston, Inc.; m. courtesy of the Donald F. Duncan Family Collection/The National Yo-Yo Museum, Chico, California, photo by Lynne & Mike Dustan. 278: m.r. California State Parks/Tom Myers; t.r. California Dept. of Parks and Recreation Photographic Archives/Tom Myers; b. Leonard Penhale/California State Parks. 279: m.r. courtesy California State Parks; l., t.r. California State Parks. 280: b. Todd Powell/Tony Stone Images. 281: l. Roberto Soncin Gerometta/Photo 20-20; t.r. Lawrence Migdale. 282: t. Underwood Photo Archives. 283: t.l. The Granger Collection; b. FPG International; t.r. Superstock, Inc. 284: b. Superstock, Inc.; t. Culver Pictures, Inc. 286: t. UPI/Corbis/Bettmann. 287: b. Archive Photos; t. Dorothea Lange/Superstock, Inc. 288: b. Archive Photo/Lambert; t.l. courtesy SS Jeremiah O'Brien. 290-291: bkgnd. Superstock, Inc. 290: b. Mark Greenberg/Envision; m. NASA/The Image Works; t.r., t.l. Photri. 291: t.r. Photri; m.l. Ross Harrison Koty/Tony Stone Images; b.r. Hank Morgan/Science Source/Photo Researchers, Inc.; b.l. JPL/NASA. 293: l. Alon Reininger/Contact Press Images/The Stock Market; t.r. Bill Ross/Tony Stone Images. 294: t. Ted Streshinsky/Photo 20-20; b.r. Tom Myers. 295: b. Bill Brant/Black Star; t.l. inset Tom Myers. 296: t. Courtesy The African American Museum and Library at Oakland. 297: m.b. Tom Myers/The Cesar E. Chavez Foundation; b.l. UPI/Corbis-Bettmann/The Cesar E. Chavez Foudnation; b.r. Wolfgang Spunbarg/PhotoEdit. 298: b. McLaughlin Historical File 1/FPG. 299: b. courtesy Patricia Anderson. 304: t.l. Tom Bonner/courtesy J. Paul Getty Museum; t.m. Tom Myers; t.r. David Ryan/Photo 20-20; b. Chris Cheadle/Tony Stone Images. 305: t. Bob Randall for MMSD; b. Superstock. 306: t.l. Karen Kasmauski; b.l., b.r. Pixar. 306-307: K. Harriger, Westlight. 307: t. Charles O'Rear; m. Exploratorium; b. Peter Menzel. **Chapter 11** 309: b.m. Lawrence Migdale; t. Tom Paiva/FPG; t.m. Terry Barner/Unicorn Stock Photos; b. PhotoDisc. 310: b.l. Eric Sander/Liaison International; t.l. Tom Myers. 310-311: b. John Post/Panoramic Images. 311: t. Michael Newman/PhotoEdit. 312: t. Bill Ross/Westlight; m. Tom Myers; b.l. inset Superstock, Inc.; b. California History Section California State Library/Tom Meyers. 313: b.l. Thomas J. Edwards/The Picture Cube; t.l. Tom Myers; m. Bill Aron/Photo Researchers, Inc. 316: t. North Wind Picture Archives; m. inset Lewis Portnoy/Uniphoto Picture Agency. 316-317: r. & l. Marvy!- Original/The Stock Market. 317: t.r. inset Underwood Photo Archives; Aaron Chang/The Stock Market. 318: t. Landau/Westlight; b. Superstock, Inc. 319: t.r. Penelope Spheeris/Gersa; b. Joe Sohm/Uniphoto. 321: b. Craig T. Mathew/Mathew Photographic Services. 322: t. Ken Chernus/FPG International. 323: t. courtesy of Lacey Gooch; m. courtesy Harris Liu; b. courtesy Christian Tanja. 324: t. Allan H. Shoemake/Viesti Associates. 325: b. Underwood Photo Archives; m. Gary Parker/Apple Computer, Inc. 326: t.r. Chuck O'Rear/Westlight. 327: b. Don Mason/The Stock Market. 328: m.l. Mug Shots/The Stock Market. 328: b. Volkswagen USA; t. Loral Space & Communications. 329: t. Mark Scott/FPG International. 330: b. Tom Myers. 331: b.l. Chuck Savage/The Stock Market; r. inset Jose Pelaez/The Stock Market. 332: t. Nathan Benn/Stock Boston. 334: b. Gary Conner/PhotoEdit. 335: b. Superstock, Inc. m.l. courtesy Pavich Family Farms. 336-337: t., b. Tom Myers. 339: t. Dave Mager for MMSD. **Chapter 12** 340: b. Bob Daemmrich/The Image Works; m. R. Lord/The Image Works; t. J. Greenberg/The Image Works. 341: t.r. Dion Ogust/The Image Works; b.r. Lawrence Migdale/Stock Boston; m.r. David Young-Wolff/PhotoEdit; m.l. Bob Daemmrich/Stock Boston; b.l. Superstock; t.l. Michael Newman/PhotoEdit. 342: t. Chuck Savage/The Stock Market. 343: b.r. Lawrence Migdale; b.l. Robert Holmes; t.r. Ted Streshinsky/Photo 20-20. 344: L. Dematteis/The Image Works. 345: Richard Hutchings/Photo Researchers. 347: b. Kim Oanh-Lan. 348: Jim Corwin/Photo Researchers. 349: t.r. Michael Newman/PhotoEdit; t.l. Tony Freeman/PhotoEdit. 350: Soncin Gerometta/Photo 20-20. 351: b. courtesy, California State Supreme Court; t. Tom Myers. 353: Dede Gilman/Photo Network. 354-355: Greg Pease/Panoramic Images. 355: r. Collection, The Supreme Court of The United States, courtesy The Supreme Court Historical Society; l. Diana Walker/Gamma Liaison. 357: John Elk III. 358: courtesy University of California/San Diego. 359: Superstock. 360: b.l. Peter Serling, courtesy W.W. Norton; b.r. Thomas Wedell; t.r. Superstock. 361: r. R. Scheltema/Liaison; l. Bottle, 1987, 12.5" height, Beatrice Wood, photo by John White, courtesy Garth Clark Gallery. 362: t. Vincent Van Gogh, "Irises" © J. Paul Getty Trust; b. John Stephens, courtesy the Getty Center. 363: t. Pat Kirk, San Jose Musical Theater; b. Mickey Pfleger/Photo 20-20. 364-365: Tomas Barbudo/Panoramic Images. 364: t. Stephen Simpson/FPG International. 366: l. Robert Holmes; r. Kaz Chiba/Liaison International. 367: A. Ramey/PhotoEdit. 368: l. Index Stock Photography, Inc.; r. Superstock, Inc. 369: b. Tom Myers. 371: Richard Adams. R3: t. Evan Agostini/Liaison International; b. Steve Rayner/National Geographic Image Collection. R4: t.l. National Portrait Gallery, London/Superstock; t.r. Gordon Graham/National Geographic Image Collection; m.l. Boltin Picture Library; m.r. Bob Daemmrich; b.l. Sidney King/U.S. Dept. of the Interior; b.r. PhotoDisc. R5: t.l. Tony Freeman/PhotoEdit; t.m. Don Mason/The Stock Market; m.l. Robert Frerck/Odyssey; b.l. Superstock; b.m. Corbis-Bettman; b.r. JPL/NASA. R23: b.l. Sirlin Photographers; t.r. A. Berliner/Liaison International; t.m. Spike Nannarello/Shooting Star; b.r. Karin Coper/Liaison International; b.m. Frank Trapper/Sygma; t.l. Jonathan Levine/Liaison International. R24: m.l. Andy Uzzle/Sygma; m.r. Michael Gouverneur/Liaison International; t.l. William Waldron/Liaison International; b.l. John Blaustein/courtesy UC Berkeley; t.r. Nathan Bilow/Allsport; b.r. courtesy, NASA. R25: b.l. Aaron Lauer/San Francisco State University; b.r. James D. Wilson/Liaison International; t.r. George Rose/Liaison International; t.m. Evan Agostini/Liaison International; b.m. courtesy, La Opinion; t.l. David Cannon/Allsport.

(continued from page R41)

Acknowledgments

From *Hearts of Sorrow* by James M. Freeman ©1989 by the Board of Trustees of the Leland Stanford Junior University. "I Love You California" (song) by F.B. Silverwood ©1933 by F.B. Silverwood. From *The Watts Towers* by Leon Whiteson ©1989 by Leon Whiteson. From *Edge City* by Joel Garreau ©1991 by Joel Garreau. From *San Francisco Chronicle* ©1997 by the San Francisco Chronicle. From *Los Angeles Times* ©1997 by the Los Angeles Times. From *Chinese Women of America* by Judy Yung ©1986 by University of Washington Press. From *The Land of Little Rain* by Mary Austin ©1974 by University of New Mexico Press. From *The Man Behind the Magic* by Katherine Barrett and Richard Greene ©1991 by Viking Press. From *Life in a California Mission, Monterey in 1786, The Journals of Jean François De La Pérouse* by Malcolm Margolin and Linda Gonslaves Yamane ©1989 by Heyday Books, Berkley. From *Environmental Profiles* by Linda Katz, Sarah Orrick, & Robert Honig ©1993 by Linda Katz, Sarah Orrick, & Robert Honig.

The Princeton Review
Handbook of
Test-Taking Strategies

READ QUESTIONS CAREFULLY

The most common mistake students make when they take a test is to answer the questions too quickly. Rushing through a test causes careless mistakes. Don't rush. Read each question carefully. Make sure you understand the question BEFORE you try to answer it.

Use the map to answer questions 1 through 3.

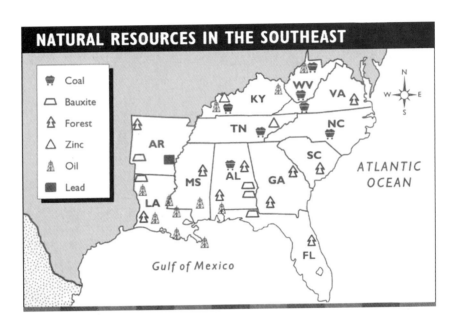

NATURAL RESOURCES IN THE SOUTHEAST

1   In which state is oil an important natural resource?

   A   Georgia   **C**   Louisiana

   B   North Carolina   **D**   Tennessee

2   South Carolina's natural resources include

   F   bauxite   **H**   coal

   G   zinc   **J**   forest

3   In which state would a lead miner be most likely to find a job?

   A   Arkansas   **C**   Florida

   B   West Virginia   **D**   Alabama

Remember: Do not write in your textbook.

TIME LINES

Historical information is sometimes presented in the form of a time line. A time line shows events in the order in which they happened. Time lines are usually read from left to right, like a sentence. If the time line is drawn vertically, it is usually read from top to bottom.

If you read carefully, you should do very well on time line questions.

Look at the time line below. Then answer questions 1 and 2.

Groups Arrive in Hawaii, 500–1900

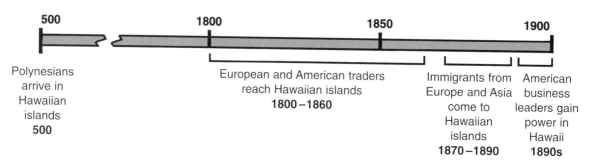

1 Which group was the first to reach the Hawaiian islands?

A   Europeans   C   Asians

B   Americans   D   Polynesians

2 Which of the following most likely occurred in 1845?

F   Traders from Europe and America came to the Hawaiian islands.

G   The first Polynesians arrived in the Hawaiian islands.

H   American business leaders gained power in Hawaii.

J   Asian immigrants came to the Hawaiian islands.

Remember: Do not write in your textbook.

LOOK AT THE DETAILS BEFORE YOU START

Some test questions contain lots of details. These questions may use:

- charts
- graphs
- flow charts
- time lines
- word webs
- maps

Before you try to answer questions like these, take a few moments to study the information that the charts, graphs, maps, or other visuals contain. The questions will be much easier to answer, because you will know exactly where to look for information!

Study the bar graph. Then do questions 1 and 2.

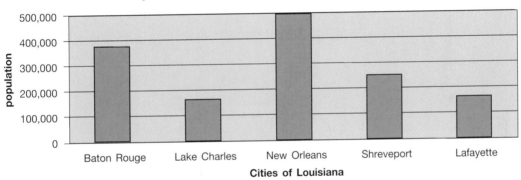

Population of Major Louisiana Cities, 1990

1 In 1990, which Louisiana city had a population of about 380,000?

A Lake Charles
B New Orleans
C Shreveport
D Baton Rouge

2 In 1990, which two Louisiana cities had approximately the same population?

F Baton Rouge and New Orleans
G Lake Charles and Lafayette
H Shreveport and Baton Rouge
J New Orleans and Lake Charles

Remember: Do not write in your textbook.

DIFFERENT TYPES OF GRAPHS

Different types of graphs are used to present numerical information. A **line graph** shows how something changes over time. A line graph might be used to show how the population of the United States has grown over the years. A **bar graph** compares amounts. A bar graph might show the population of different United States cities. A **circle graph** shows how a whole is divided into smaller parts. For example, a circle graph might show how the government divides its budget to pay for roads, education, and other services.

Sometimes you will see a set of questions accompanied by more than one graph. Each question will contain clues to tell you which graph you should read to find the answer. Take the extra time to make sure you are looking at the correct graph. This will help you avoid careless mistakes.

Use the graphs below to answer questions 1 and 2.

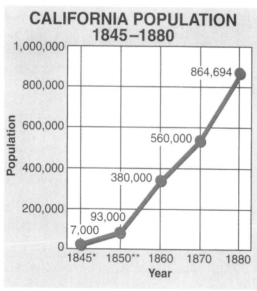

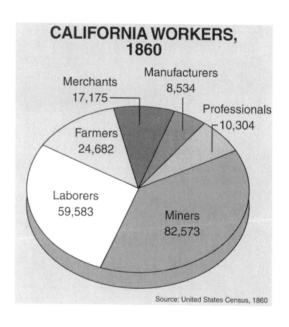

Source: U.S. Bureau of the Census

1 In what year did the population of California reach 380,000?

- **A** 1840
- **B** 1850
- **C** 1860
- **D** 1870

2 How many people were working as professionals in California in 1860?

- **F** 10,304
- **G** 17,175
- **H** 59,583
- **J** 82,573

Remember: Do not write in your textbook.

PROCESS OF ELIMINATION

Sometimes when you read a test question, you will not know the answer right away. If you don't know the answer, don't give up. You may be able to find the correct answer another way.

On a multiple-choice test, you can look at the answer choices. One of the answers will be the best answer. The others will be wrong, or not as good. Look at the choices and see if there are any that you know are definitely wrong. If there are, you can ELIMINATE, or ignore, those answers.

Sometimes you will be able to eliminate all of the answers except one. When that happens, it means that you have found the best answer by the PROCESS OF ELIMINATION.

Try using the process of elimination to answer this question:

1 The largest city in South Dakota is

    A   Los Angeles
    B   Dallas
    C   Sioux Falls
    D   Mexico City

Were you able to eliminate any *wrong* answers? How many?

Now try using the process of elimination to answer this question:

2 The section of the United States Constitution that protects the freedom of Americans is called the

    F   Declaration of Independence
    G   Bill of Rights
    H   Civil War
    J   Star Spangled Banner

Remember: Do not write in your textbook.

OUTSIDE KNOWLEDGE

Many questions on multiple-choice tests ask you to look at a map, a chart, a graph, or a drawing. Then you are asked to choose the correct answer based on what you see. On these questions, the information you need to answer the question will be in the map, chart, graph, or drawing.

Sometimes, however, multiple-choice tests will ask you to remember a fact that you learned in social studies class. You won't be able to find the correct answer on a map, chart, graph, or drawing; the correct answer will be in your memory. We call these OUTSIDE KNOWLEDGE questions.

If you are sure you know the answer to an OUTSIDE KNOWLEDGE question, choose the correct answer. It's that simple! When you're NOT sure what the correct answer is, use the PROCESS OF ELIMINATION to answer the question.

1 Which of these books would probably provide the most information about the life of Martin Luther King, Jr.?

    A an atlas

    B an encyclopedia

    C a novel about the South during the Civil War

    D a collection of poetry

2 Which of the following statements about the southern portion of the United States is true?

    F The South does not have many farms.

    G The South is home to the largest cities in the United States.

    H The South is the most mountainous region in the United States.

    J The South has a warmer climate than the northern United States.

                                     Remember: Do not write in your textbook.

FLOW CHARTS

A flow chart shows the sequence of steps used to complete an activity. It shows the steps in the order they happen. A flow chart usually uses arrows to show which step happens next.

The first thing to do when you look at a flow chart is to see if it has a title. The title will tell you what the flow chart is about. The next thing you should do is find the arrows. The arrows tell you the order in which to read the chart.

Read flow charts carefully. Don't just look at the illustrations. Make sure to read any text beneath the illustrations.

Study the flow chart. Then do questions 1 and 2.

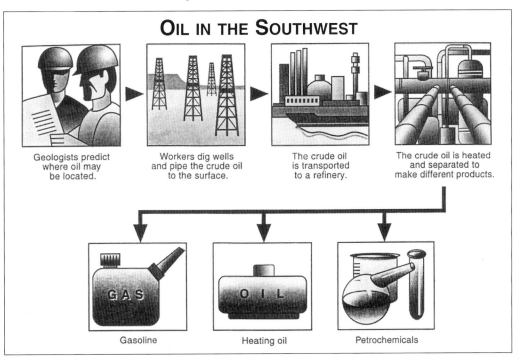

OIL IN THE SOUTHWEST

Geologists predict where oil may be located.

Workers dig wells and pipe the crude oil to the surface.

The crude oil is transported to a refinery.

The crude oil is heated and separated to make different products.

Gasoline

Heating oil

Petrochemicals

1 Which of these questions is answered by the flow chart?

   A What are some of the products that can be made from crude oil?

   B How much does it cost to produce heating oil?

   C Where in the United States is the most crude oil found?

   D How many automobiles are there in the United States?

2 The crude oil is probably transported to the oil refinery in

   F automobiles

   G large ships

   H helicopters

   J tractors

Remember: Do not write in your textbook.

MAPS

The ability to read and understand maps is an important skill in social studies. Many of the multiple-choice tests you take will require you to read a map.

Look carefully at all the parts of a map. Maps contain a lot of information. Whenever you see a map, you should ask yourself questions like these:

- What does the title of the map tell you?
- Where is the map key?
- What symbols are on the map key? What do they stand for?
- Where is the compass rose?
- What does the compass rose tell you?
- Is there a map scale?

Use the map of Pennsylvania to answer questions 1 and 2.

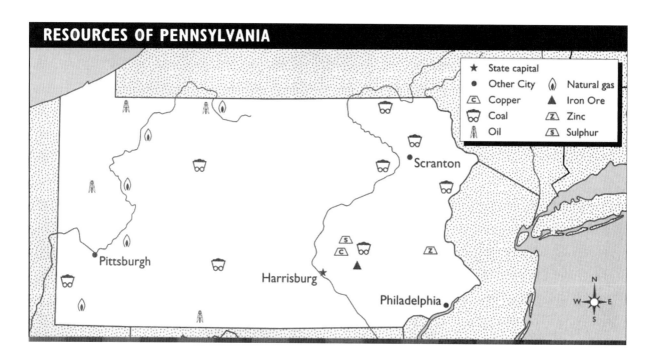

RESOURCES OF PENNSYLVANIA

★	State capital		
●	Other City	◊	Natural gas
C	Copper	▲	Iron Ore
Coal		Z	Zinc
Oil		S	Sulphur

1 Which natural resource is found only in the western part of Pennsylvania?

- **A** zinc
- **B** natural gas
- **C** coal
- **D** iron ore

2 Which of these people would be most likely to find a job near Scranton?

- **F** a driller of oil wells
- **G** a coal miner
- **H** a miner of iron ore
- **J** a zinc miner

Remember: Do not write in your textbook.